Encountering the Book of Psalms

A Literary and Theological Introduction

C. Hassell Bullock

Baker Academic
Grand Rapids, Michigan

© 2001 by C. Hassell Bullock

Published by Baker Academic
a division of Baker Publishing Group
P.O. Box 6287, Grand Rapids, MI 49516-6287
www.bakeracademic.com

Paperback edition published in 2004
ISBN 978-0-8010-2795-6

Fourth printing, February 2009

Printed in the United States of America

　　　　The Library of Congress has cataloged the hardcover edition as follows:
Bullock, C. Hassell.
　　　Encountering the book of Psalms / C. Hassell Bullock.
　　　　　p.　　　cm. — (Encountering biblical studies)
　　　Includes bibliographical references and index.
　　　ISBN 10: 0-8010-2245-2
　　　1. Bible. O.T. Psalms—Criticism, interpretation, etc. I. Title. II. Series.
　　BS1430.2 .B85　　2001
　　223'.206—dc21　　　　　　　　　　　　　　　　　　　　　　　　　　　2001035974

Unless otherwise noted, all Scripture quotations are taken from the HOLY BIBLE, NEW INTERNATIONAL VERSION®. NIV®. Copyright © 1973, 1978, 1984 by International Bible Society. Used by permission of Zondervan. All rights reserved.

Scripture quotations marked RSV are taken from the Revised Standard Version of the Bible, copyright 1952 [2nd edition, 1971] by the Division of Christian Education of the National Council of the Churches of Christ in the United States of America. Used by permission. All rights reserved.

Scripture quotations marked NRSV are taken from the New Revised Standard Version of the Bible, copyright 1989, Division of Christian Education of the National Council of the Churches of Christ in the United States of America. Used by permission. All rights reserved.

Ilustration credits:

The illustration on page 31 (top) is taken from Klaus Seybold, *Introducing the Psalms,* trans. R. Graeme Dunphy (Edinburgh: T. & T. Clark), 1990. Used by permission.

The illustrations on pages 31 (bottom), 32, 33, 40, 51, 70, 128, 138, 152, 153, 157, 168, 180, 184, 191, 193, 211, and 228 are taken from Othmar Keel, *The Symboli.sm of the Biblical World: Ancient Near Eastern Iconography and the Book of Psalms,* trans. Timothy J. Hallett (New York: Seabury, 1978). Used by permission.

The photographs on pages 89, 91, 108, 110, 113, 172, 192, 216, 219, and 234 were taken by Chris Miller.

To the memory of
Rev. Britts E. and Mrs. Lucinda R. Nichols,
my father-in-law and mother-in-law,
who lived in the spirit of the Psalms.

"Blessed in the sight of the LORD
is the death of his saints."
Psalm 116:15

Contents in Brief

Contents

9

Editor's Preface

The strength of the church and the vitality of the individual Christian's life are directly related to the role Scripture plays in them. Early believers knew the importance of this and spent their time in fellowship, prayer, and the study of God's Word. The passing of two thousand years has not changed the need, but it has changed the accessibility of many of the Bible's ideas. Time has distanced us from those days, and we often need guidance back into the world of the Old and New Testaments.

To that end Baker Book House is producing an innovative series of biblical textbooks. The design of this series is to put us back into the world of the biblical text, so that we may understand it as those early believers did and at the same time see it from and for our own day, thus facilitating the application of its truths to our contemporary situation.

Encountering Biblical Studies consists of undergraduate-level texts, and two surveys treating the Old and New Testaments provide the foundation for this series. Accompanying these survey texts are two collateral volumes of readings, which illuminate the world surrounding the biblical text. Built on these basic survey texts are upper-level college texts covering the books of the Bible that are most frequently offered in the curriculum of Christian colleges.

Complementing the series is a set of standard reference books that may be consulted for answers to specific questions or more in-depth study of biblical ideas. These reference books include *Baker Commentary on the Bible, Baker Topical Guide to the Bible, Baker Encyclopedia of the Bible, Baker Theological Dictionary of the Bible,* and *Evangelical Dictionary of Theology.*

The Encountering Biblical Studies series is written from an evangelical point of view, in the firm conviction that the Scripture is absolutely true and never misleads us. It is the sure foundation on which our faith and life may be built because it unerringly leads willing readers to Jesus Christ.

Walter A. Elwell
General Editor

Publisher's Preface

Bible courses must be considered the heart of the curriculum for Christian colleges and evangelical seminaries. For Christians the Bible constitutes the basis for both our spiritual and our intellectual lives—indeed for *all* of life. If these courses are fundamental to Christian education, then the textbooks used for these courses could not be more crucial.

Baker Book House is launching a series of volumes for college-level Bible courses. In this series, Baker will publish texts that are clearly college-level. The textbooks for the basic college survey courses and for the more advanced college courses on individual Bible books will not be written for laypeople or pastors and seminarians, nor will they be primarily reference books. Rather, they will be pedagogically oriented textbooks written with collegians in mind.

Encountering the Book of Psalms attempts to build on the basic survey text, *Encountering the Old Testament: A Christian Survey* (Bill T. Arnold and Bryan E. Beyer). While the survey text is written for college freshmen, this Psalms volume is intended for upper-level collegians.

Rather than providing a sustained exegetical analysis of each verse in the Book of Psalms, this volume surveys the entire book with an emphasis on drawing out its theological message and its practical significance for collegians. It consists of appropriate introduction and survey material with the necessary critical, historical, literary, hermeneutical, and background concerns woven within the exposition of the biblical text.

Guiding Principles

As part of the developing of this volume, the series editors, author, and publisher established the following principles:

1. It must reflect the finest in evangelical scholarship of our day.
2. It must be written at a level that most of today's upper-level collegians can understand.
3. It must be pedagogically sound. This extends not only to traditional concerns like study and review questions, chapter objectives and summaries for each chapter, but also the manner in which the material is presented.
4. It must include appropriate illustrative material such as photographs, maps, charts, graphs, figures, and sidebars.
5. It must seek to winsomely draw in the student by focusing on biblical teaching concerning crucial doctrinal and ethical matters.

Goals

The goals for *Encountering the Book of Psalms* fall into two categories: intellectual and attitudinal. The intellectual goals are to (1) present the factual content of the Book of Psalms, (2) introduce historical, geographical, and cultural background, (3) outline primary hermeneutical principles, (4) touch on critical issues (e.g., why some people read the Bible differently), and (5) substantiate the Christian faith.

The attitudinal goals are also fivefold: (1) to make the Bible a part of students' lives, (2) to instill in students a love for the Scriptures, (3) to make them better people, (4) to enhance their piety, and (5) to stimulate their love for God. In short, if this text builds a foundation for a lifetime of Bible study, the author and publisher will be amply rewarded.

Overarching Themes

Controlling the writing of *Encountering the Book of Psalms* have been three essential theological themes: God, people, and the gospel as it relates to individuals. The notion that God is a person—one and three—and a transcendent and immanent Being has been woven throughout the text. Moreover, this God has created people in his image who are fallen but still the objects of his redemptive love. The gospel is the means, the active personal power that God uses to rescue people from darkness and death. But the gospel does more than rescue—it restores. It confers on otherwise hopeless sinners the resolve and strength to live lives that please God, because they walk in the love that comes from God.

Features

The publisher's aim has been to provide an exceptionally unique resource on the one hand but not to be merely trendy on the other. Some of the distinguishing features we hope will prove helpful to the professor and inspiring to the student include the following:

- liberal use of illustrations—photographs, figures, tables, charts
- sidebars and excursuses exploring exegetical, ethical, and theological issues of interest and concern to modern-day collegians
- chapter outline and objectives presented at the opening of each chapter
- study questions at the end of each chapter
- a helpful glossary
- a bibliography to guide further study

To the Student

Encountering the Book of Psalms in a systematic way for the first time is an exciting experience. It can also be overwhelming because there is so much to learn. You need to learn not only the content of this book of songs but also important background information about the world in which the songwriters lived.

The purpose of this textbook is to make that encounter a little less daunting. To accomplish this a number of learning aids have been incorporated into the text. We suggest you familiarize yourself with this textbook by reading the following introductory material, which explains what learning aids have been provided.

Sidebars

Sidebars isolate contemporary issues of concern and show how the Book of Psalms speaks to these pressing ethical and theological issues.

Chapter Outlines

At the beginning of each chapter is a brief outline of the chapter's contents. *Study Suggestion:* Before reading the chapter, take a few minutes to read the outline. Think of it as a road map, and remember that it is easier to reach your destination if you know where you are going.

Chapter Objectives

A brief list of objectives is placed at the outset of each chapter. These present the tasks you should be able to perform after reading the chapter. *Study Suggestions:* Read the objectives carefully before beginning to read the text. As you read the text, keep these objectives in mind and take notes to help you remember what you have read. After reading the chapter, return to the objectives and see if you can perform the tasks.

Key Terms and Glossary

Key terms have been identified throughout the text by the use of **boldface** type. This will alert you to important words or phrases you may not be familiar with. A definition of these words will be found at the end of the book in an alphabetical glossary. *Study Suggestion:* When you encounter a key term in the text, stop and read the definition before continuing through the chapter.

Study Questions

A few discussion questions have been provided at the end of each chapter, and these can be used to review for examinations. *Study Suggestion:* Write suitable answers to the study questions in preparation for tests.

Further Reading

A helpful bibliography for supplementary reading is presented at the end of the book. *Study Suggestion:* Use this list to explore areas of special interest.

Visual Aids

A host of illustrations have been included in this textbook. Each illustration has been carefully selected, and each is intended not only to make the text more aesthetically pleasing but also more easily mastered.

May your encounter of the Book of Psalms be an exciting adventure!

Author's Preface

No collection of poems has ever exercised as much influence on the Western world as the Book of Psalms. Even though Christianity has accepted the entire Old Testament as the authentic Word of God, none of its books has functioned so ecumenically as the Psalms. The Christian hermeneutic differs from the Jewish, admittedly, particularly in the Christian emphasis upon the messianic nature of the Psalms, but if Christian and Jew can meet and stand on level ground at all, they come closer to that stance when they approach the Psalms than with any other book of the Old Testament. If we Christians have, to our shame, imposed an inferiority complex on certain books of the Hebrew Bible, the Psalms have gratefully escaped this misfortune. The mystery of this phenomenon is in part the human element that pervades these spiritual poems. They are replete with evidences of the human situation with all its complexities. Wherever we are on the spectrum of human achievement or failure, we can find ourselves somewhere in this book. Wherever we are on the spectrum of human life, be it youth or full maturity or declining health or the throes of death, there is a niche in this book that provides reflection upon our condition.

There is another side to this mystery that lies in the pale of divine providence, beyond the domain of human reason. There God has empowered us for living and embellished our lives with a grace that exceeds our understanding. We draw upon this grace *by* grace, and by it are refurbished in life and reminded that, in the words of the Heidelberg Catechism, "I belong—body and soul, in life and in death—not to myself but to my faithful Savior, Jesus Christ." The Psalms infuse us with strength beyond our human powers because the God of the psalmists—and of us—hovers over them in love and mercy. They are his dwelling place, and there we meet him.

The Psalms are as difficult to interpret as any book of the Old Testament, perhaps even the New. Because there are so many human paths down which we may walk as we read the Psalms, the temptation is to assume that we can make our own paths and thus require the Psalms to authorize our ways. But the Psalms cannot mean all things to all people, despite their assorted thoughts and emotions. The historical element remains the control that draws a circle around the interpreter and restricts him or her within a method that does not permit a mere reader-response hermeneutic. Yet the Psalms will speak on levels of meaning that may be more a tributary than the mainstream of the text. "Even though I walk through the valley of the shadow of death, I will fear no evil" (Ps 23:4a) is probably a good illustration of this. Who would deny that this text has comforted millions in the hour of death, and who would deny its comfort yet to millions more! Historically speaking, it probably had a reference to some place and time in David's life before he faced the ultimate moment, when it seemed that an untimely death was approaching; but spiritually speaking, it says far more than that. Indeed, we can put our ultimate moment of life in light of this historical experience, whatever shape it took for David, and sense the Spirit hiding us under the Almighty's protecting wings.

If any book of the Bible requires every resource we have and can acquire to interpret it properly, the Psalms require no less and possibly more. We must have *lived* in the hamlets of human existence before the

Psalms can speak to us in all their power. If we could combine resplendent words, profound emotions, and heavenly music into a single language, then we could begin to hear the Psalms in their richness and perhaps begin to expound them with some degree of adequacy. That will always be our aim.

To take my cue from the Psalms and express my gratitude to all of those who have contributed to the various dimensions of this book, I say:

> I am under vows to you, O God;
> I will present my thank offerings to you. (Ps 56:12)

So as I present them to God, I do it as a public offering of gratitude. They are not in order of ascending or descending gratefulness, for genuine gratitude is a virtue of equal quality wherever it is found, even though its quantity may range up and down the scale. My "thank offerings" go to the board of trustees of Wheaton College, who gave me a sabbatical to work on this manuscript at Tyndale House in Cambridge, England, in the fall of 1999; to the staff of Tyndale House, who made my work there one of the great study pleasures of my life; to my wife Rhonda, who shared the experience with me, and who loves the Psalms as I do; to the Parkview Presbyterian Church of Oak Park, which gave me time away from my pastoral duties to concentrate on my sabbatical project; to the Rev. Loy Mershimer, who responsibly and capably assumed those duties on my behalf and just as capably prepared the key terms and study questions for the book; to the Aldeen Fund of Wheaton College, which underwrote some of the bibliographical work of this writing project; to the Franklin S. Dyrness Chair at Wheaton College, in which I sit with honor and gratitude, and to the memory of the revered servant of Christ for whom it is named; to my friend and faithful bibliographer, Don Patrick, who did all of the bibliographical footwork for this book, and did it with enthusiasm and passion; to the Rev. James Scott, friend and former student, who read several chapters of the manuscript and offered his perceptive insights and suggestions; to Daniel Balint, my former teacher's assistant, called into service again, who read the manuscript with more than an editor's eye and assisted in constructing the sidebars; to my daughter, Becky, who prepared the bibliography for me; to Professor Eugene Merrill, the Old Testament editor of this series, who encouraged me in both the preliminary and the developing stages; to my colleague and the New Testament editor of this series, Professor Walter Elwell, whose encouragement has always been waiting for me down the hallway from my faculty office; to Baker Book House and former editor James Weaver, who makes his writers feel that writer and publisher are one and the same in purpose—to all of these I fulfill my vows before the gracious God of the Psalms and present to him my thank offering in the form of this manuscript. As John Calvin said of his own commentary on the Psalms, I would like also to say of this work:

> If the reading of these my Commentaries confer as much benefit on the Church of God as I myself have reaped advantage from the composition of them, I shall have no reason to regret that I have undertaken this work.[1]

And now I humbly dedicate this book to the memory of my father- and mother-in-law, Rev. Britts E. and Mrs. Lucinda R. Nichols, who lived their lives and served the church in the faith of the psalmists, trusting the God of this book until their triumphant transfer to glory. My father-in-law made his transfer on Palm Sunday of 1992 while we, in our church in Oak Park, Illinois, were acclaiming his Lord and ours with David's words, hundreds of miles away from his hospital room:

> "Hosanna to the Son of David!"
> "Blessed is he who comes in the name of the Lord!"

"Hosanna in the highest!" (Mt 21:9/Ps 118:26)

Surely his praise and ours united as he made his triumphal entry into the heavenly Jerusalem. My mother-in-law made hers in October of 1999 as Rhonda and I recited Psalms 23 and 121 at her bedside. Their lives have touched mine in ways that have made the Psalms all the more meaningful. So in the words of the Jewish benediction, "May the memory of the righteous be for a blessing."

Abbreviations

Old Testament

Genesis	Gn
Exodus	Ex
Leviticus	Lv
Numbers	Nm
Deuteronomy	Dt
Joshua	Jos
Judges	Jgs
Ruth	Ru
1 Samuel	1 Sm
2 Samuel	2 Sm
1 Kings	1 Kgs
2 Kings	2 Kgs
1 Chronicles	1 Chr
2 Chronicles	2 Chr
Ezra	Ezr
Nehemiah	Neh
Esther	Est
Job	Jb
Psalms	Ps(s)
Proverbs	Prv
Ecclesiastes	Eccl
Song of Songs	Sg (Song)
Isaiah	Is
Jeremiah	Jer
Lamentations	Lam
Ezekiel	Ez
Daniel	Dn
Hosea	Hos
Joel	Jl
Amos	Am
Obadiah	Ob
Jonah	Jon
Micah	Mi
Nahum	Na
Habakkuk	Hb
Zephaniah	Zep
Haggai	Hg
Zechariah	Zec
Malachi	Mal

New Testament

Matthew	Mt
Mark	Mk
Luke	Lk
John	Jn
Acts of the Apostles	Acts
Romans	Rom
1 Corinthians	1 Cor
2 Corinthians	2 Cor
Galatians	Gal
Ephesians	Eph
Philippians	Phil
Colossians	Col
1 Thessalonians	1 Thes
2 Thessalonians	2 Thes
1 Timothy	1 Tm
2 Timothy	2 Tm
Titus	Ti
Philemon	Phlm
Hebrews	Heb
James	Jas
1 Peter	1 Pt
2 Peter	2 Pt
1 John	1 Jn
2 John	2 Jn
3 John	3 Jn
Jude	Jude
Revelation	Rv

Part

1

Encountering the Literary and Hermeneutical Dimensions of the Psalms

1

"Begin the Music"

Introducing the Psalms

Outline

- **Names of the Book**
- **Nature of the Book**
- **Place of the Book in the Canon**
- **David's Place in the Book**
- **Titles of the Psalms and Special Terms**
  - Author Titles
  - Historical Titles
  - Titles of Literary or Musical Genre
  - Titles with Musical Terms
  - Titles with Musical Tunes
- **Musical Instruments**
- **Singing**

Objectives

After reading this chapter, you should be able to

1. Give the names of the Book of Psalms.
2. Discuss the nature of the book.
3. Summarize the place of the book in the Canon.
4. Assess David's role in the composition of the Psalms.
5. Discuss the titles of the Psalms and other special terms.

Tehillim

mizmor

On some religious festival the congregation of Israel waited expectantly in the sanctuary to begin their worship, summoned perhaps by the musician or a priest to "sing" and "begin the music":

> Sing for joy to God our strength;
>> shout aloud to the God of Jacob!
> Begin the music, strike the
>> tambourine,
>> play the melodious harp and
>> lyre.
> Sound the ram's horn at the New
>> Moon,
>> and when the moon is full, on
>> the day of our Feast;
> this is a decree for Israel,
>> an ordinance of the God of Jacob. (Ps 81:1–4)

It is rare in the Bible to have such a vivid picture of worship with its musical accompaniments as we have here in Psalm 81. The musical setting sets the stage for the awesome sermon that follows in verses 6–16. It is a succinct summary of Israel's history. In fact, one could cut this page out of Israel's national journal and have a synopsis of God's action that brought Israel into being (vv. 6–10), along with Israel's unfortunate response (vv. 11–16).

The Book of Psalms is a record of God's call and of his people's response, enacted a thousand times in history. The Psalms are a photograph album of ancient Israel in its relationship to God and a mirror of our own relationship and reaction to God who summons his people and promises his presence and secures the future. Any time we try to interpret the Psalms, a journal of Israel's life—so filled with joys and sorrows, inscribed with aspirations and failures—we will find ourselves experiencing a catharsis of the soul.

But before we imbibe deeply of the spiritual riches of the Psalms, we need to deal with some pedestrian matters that will orient us to our study.

Names of the Book

The Hebrew title of this book is appropriately *Tehillim* ("praises"), for praise is a central feature of the poems that comprise this collection. Yet interestingly, although this word in its singular form (*tehillah* "praise") occurs many times in the psalms themselves, it only occurs once as a title to an individual psalm (Ps 145, "Praise of David").

The major Greek versions rendered another Hebrew word, *mizmor* ("song"), found often in the titles of individual psalms, as *psalmos*, and they gave the book the title *Psalmoi* ("Psalms"). This was the title by which the New Testament writers knew the book (Lk 20:42; Acts 1:20). The common English title, of course, is "The Psalms," and we readily see its derivation from the Greek versions.

Another popular English title, "Psalter," comes from Alexandrinus, a fifth-century A.D. copy of the Greek translation known as the Septuagint, which called the book *Psalterion*, meaning "stringed instrument."[1] The word actually occurs several times in the Greek text of the Psalms where it generally translates the Hebrew word *kinnor* ("lyre"), and sometimes *nevel* ("lyre"). Alexandrinus elevates this word to the title of the book.

Nature of the Book

The Book of Psalms is a diversified collection of sacred poems. Many of them are in fact prayers. While we shall not attempt a description of these poems at this point, the book is an anthology of prayers, worship songs, and poems sung and spoken in public and private worship. The psalmists spoke on their own behalf as well as Israel's. All of the Psalms may not have been sung in the temple. While some were written for that purpose, others were written for private use and were subsequently adapted for public worship. The Book of Psalms then was not comparable to hymnbooks in our modern churches. Although it contained many of Israel's temple hymns, they were not likely collected with that purpose in mind. Rather the book, whose composition spans several centuries, was a repository of public and private faith. It was more like the *Book of Common Prayer* than a hymnbook, even though it diverges sharply from both genres.

In the history of Israel and the Christian church the Psalms have had extensive use in both public and private worship,[2] which is very much a reflection of the original purpose of these sacred poems. John Calvin, one of the great commentators on the book, found the Psalms to be a guide for life. He remarked that "in considering the whole course of the life of David, it seemed to me that by his own footsteps he showed me the way, and from this I have experienced no small consolation."[3] Even when David took the wrong turn in the road, he showed us the way we ought not go and then the way to return to the main path (e.g., Ps 51). There is no book of the Bible that affords such spiritual catharsis as the Book of Psalms. Calvin acknowledges this when he calls the book "an anatomy of all parts of the soul."[4]

Place of the Book in the Canon

The Book of Psalms is contained in the third division of the Hebrew Bible, the **Writings,** known in Greek as the Hagiographa. By their varied nature the Psalms belong in this section of the Hebrew Bible, since, in the strictest sense of the terms, they are neither Torah nor prophecy. They have, of course, elements of both of them. It is rather interesting that some commentators have seen a strong prophetic character in the Psalms. Perhaps that is because the psalmists are interpreters of Israel's

spiritual life. A prophetic strain runs through them. Calvin referred to the psalmists as prophets,[5] and Brevard Childs, commenting on Psalms 89 and 132, recognized the prophetic model that came to characterize much of the Psalter: "To be sure, the psalmist has developed this tradition along different lines from the prophet, but increasingly the prophetic model poured its content into the idiom of the psalmist."[6]

In fact, Childs recognized that the major thrust of the collection was prophetic in that the Psalms announced the Kingdom of God: "The Psalter in its canonical form, far from being different in kind from the prophetic message, joins with the prophets in announcing God's coming kingship."[7] We might say that the Psalter was the repository of the prophetic spirit and the archive of the prophetic hope.

David's Place in the Book

Modern scholarship has raised serious questions about David's role in writing the Psalms. Some insist that he wrote all of the seventy-three psalms attributed to him, while others doubt that he wrote many, if any. Those who fall somewhere in between acknowledge that he could have written some of them, perhaps a significant number.

The Talmud attributes all of the Psalms to David.[8] While only seventy-three psalms actually carry the notation that David was the poet, they do so in the larger setting of the poetic reputation that the Books of Samuel and Chronicles lay out for us. The writer of Samuel paints a portrait of David the musician, first as one who plays the lyre (*kinnor*) (1 Sm 16:14–23), and then as one who composes psalms. The writer of Samuel records David's lament over Saul and Jonathan (2 Sm 1:17–27), a poem that has much in common with the laments of the Psalms. However, it is person specific, mentioning both Saul and Jonathan by name, whereas the psalmic laments are not so specific. This lament, according to the superscription, was written in the Book of Jashar, evidently an ancient collection of poetry. The one other reference to that book is the notation that Joshua's famous words upon his defeat of the Amorites (these are also poetry) were also included in it (Jos 10:12–13). The literary link between David's poetry outside the Psalms and the poetry within, however, is best represented by his song of praise "when the LORD delivered him from the hand of all his enemies and from the hand of Saul" (2 Sm 22), which is essentially a duplicate of Psalm 18. The other poetic composition attributed to David in Samuel is the Last Words of David recorded in 2 Samuel 23:1–7. Thus the psalmic associations with David are well attested in the Books of Samuel.

Written after the Judean kingdom had passed into history, the Books of Chronicles also take this information very seriously. Still in that late time, or, perhaps we should say, especially in that late period, David's musical legacy was lodged in the national memory. Thus David took his place alongside the priests as founder of the musical tradition of the temple. He assigned musical duties to the Levites (2 Chr 23:18; see Ezr 3:10), directed the manufacture of musical instruments for the temple (1 Chr 23:5; 2 Chr 7:6; 29:26), and designated the times when the Levites were to perform certain musical duties.

One might argue against Samuel and Chronicles about David's musical role in the temple and contend that it was the result of layers of tradition mounting up in David's column. Yet, his reputation was obviously an enormous one, and his portrait, painted with such careful and personal details in the Books of Samuel, was not likely an invention of Israel's imagination. Therefore, the general setting of David's life and long reign as laid out in Samuel and followed by the Chronicler gives a generous touch of realism to the

strong association of David with the Book of Psalms.

Titles of the Psalms and Special Terms

In this section we will consider the special terms that occur in the Psalms, so that we may understand, as best our current knowledge will allow, the fuller dimensions of the book.

With the rise of form criticism, the study of the Psalms titles became a secondary matter, and the form critics generally assumed they were late and could be ignored as having any meaning in the interpretation of the Psalms. However, a more intentional effort has been made in recent years to understand the role of the titles in the study of the Psalms. Just when were the titles added to the Psalms? Were any of them original? What did the composer who prefixed the titles intend by them? Or how was the editor who added them trying to enhance the Psalms? These are difficult questions. While some of the titles, perhaps most, may have been added long after the composition of the Psalms, they nevertheless must not be viewed as a haphazard exercise.

But even though a logical connection has to be assumed between a given title and the psalm, it is often difficult for us to see. This is particularly noticeable in the historical titles. While pieces of the historical situation may be discernible, and certain verses may qualify as assessments or reflections of that experience, the connection may still not be obvious. As the centuries have passed and life has changed, the meaning of these titles has been lost. Even by the time of the Greek translation, the translators were often stumped by them and could only make a guess at their meaning. As research continues and the Psalms titles continue to be the object of serious study, perhaps we will eventually know much more about their meaning. Yet, unfortunately, the meaning of some of the terms may remain forever obscure.

Author Titles

The authorship question is a difficult one because we cannot be absolutely sure how to read some of the superscriptions in which individuals are mentioned, nor can we be sure that the titles were original to the psalm itself. One term is the simple preposition "to," "by," or "of" (Hebrew *le*). Archaeologists have identified this term on many jar handles found in Israel, where it designates the owner of the jar, "belonging to. . . ." This is not quite the same as finding a poem with the same designation. In this latter context, it could mean "to," in the sense of dedication to that individual, or "by," carrying the nuance of authorship. Based upon the information of the Books of Samuel and Chronicles, I suggest that we understand the term in the authorial sense unless there are indications to the contrary, whether in the superscription or the content of the poem itself. This is the view of Calvin.[9] This preposition is prefixed to the names of David, Solomon, Moses, Asaph, the sons of Korah, and the two Ezrahites. It is a bit difficult to ignore all of these associations and deny that any of them are authorial. At the same time, to put David in a category by himself and deny his compositional role, while allowing others, is hardly a defensible view either,[10] even though we may admit that the titles of the Psalms are in many instances later than the original composition of the psalm.

Some scholars have resorted to a literary explanation of the term, asserting that "to/by/of David" is merely literary convention, designating a particular quality of poetry.[11] However, it is not easy to define precisely what that quality is. So this must remain a rather arbitrary theory.

As table 1.1 shows, many of the psalms have no names attached to them at all. The highest concentration of these (twenty-eight) are in Book 5 (Ps 107–50); but we should also note that Book 5 also contains fifteen Davidic psalms, which counterbalance the heavily Davidic Book 1 (Pss 1–41) with the final collection. Perhaps this concentration of anonymous psalms suggests that the activity of psalm writing had become quite broad and a practice of the common people. The names that appear in the headings are noteworthy individuals or groups in ancient Israel. We may assume that if the writer of a psalm had a recognizable name, he or the compiler might be more likely to attach it to his composition. Or if the public knew of the association of such a name with a particular psalm, it is more likely that it would have stuck to the psalm in the transmission process.

Historical Titles

Thirteen psalms have superscriptions that contain historical information: Psalms 3, 7, 18, 34, 51, 52, 54, 56, 57, 59, 60, 63, and 142. A look at table 1.2 will show that all of these psalms are Davidic and refer to some instance in or information about his life. But we might ask why other historical persons outside of the Davidic era are not mentioned in the Psalm titles.

While some interpreters of the Psalms handily dispose of these historical titles with a dismissive word, the Davidic association has a legitimizing effect on the psalms in which such a title appears. While acknowledging the paucity of information, Leslie McFall suggests that a superscription was put on a psalm as soon as it was composed. He points to Hezekiah's psalm in Isaiah 38 and Habakkuk's psalm in Habakkuk 3. Moreover, we have superscriptive notes for six compositions in the Book of Proverbs, which seem to be integral to those compositions (Prv 1:1; 10:1; 24:23; 25:1; 30:1; 31:1).[12]

Just how close in time to David's life the historical titles were added to the psalms is not possible to tell, but they represent an effort to clothe the psalms in historical garb, that is, to add a touch of realism to them. That does not mean that they were con-

Table 1.1

Author Titles in the Psalms

	Bk 1 (1–41)	Bk 2 (42–72)	Bk 3 (73–89)	Bk 4 (90–106)	Bk 5 (107–50)
Moses				Ps 90	
David	Pss 3–32 (taking 9 and 10 as a single psalm), 34–41	Pss 51–65, 68–71 (taking 70 and 71 as a single psalm)	Ps 86	Pss 101, 103	Pss 108–10, 122, 124, 131, 133, 138–45
Solomon		Ps 72			Ps 127
Asaph		Ps 50	Pss 73–83		
Sons of Korah		Pss 42–49 (taking 42 and 43 as a single psalm)	Pss 84–85, 87–88 (both "sons of Korah" and "Heman" are noted in Ps 88)		
Heman			Ps 88 (both "sons of Korah" and "Heman" are noted)		
Ethan			Ps 89		
Anonymous	Pss 1–2, 33	Pss 66–67		Pss 91–100, 102, 104–6	Pss 107, 111–21, 123, 125–26, 128–30, 132, 134–37, 146–50

shir

trived. In fact, the historical association may come from a personal connection between the poem and the author. In regard to the broad-ranging nature of these poems, Derek Kidner comments that "the nucleus of the psalm—some germinal phrase or sequence—which came to David in the crisis itself," may be the idea he developed at a later time as he reflected upon the event or era.[13]

Titles of Literary or Musical Genre

Other titles fall into the literary or musical category and suggest some literary form or a musical notation. Unfortunately, certainty about the meaning of some of these terms can no longer be achieved, but we will discuss the more generally accepted understanding of them.

1. *Song (shir).* In the Book of Psalms, as would be expected, this term occurs in reference to songs rendered in the temple. However, it also had a secular usage (Prv 25:20; Eccl 7:5). It seems to suggest a vocal rather than an instrumental rendering. This word occurs in conjunction with other words. One such connection is with the Hebrew word *mizmor* (psalm). The difference between these two words may

Table 1.2

The Historical Titles of the Psalms and Their Historical Texts

Ps 3	Ps 7	Ps 18	Ps 34	Ps 51	Ps 52
A psalm of David. When he fled from his son Absalom. 2 Sm 15:13–31	A *shiggaion* of David, which he sang to the LORD concerning Cush, a Benjamite. 2 Sm 16 (Nothing is known of Cush, but David had enemies among the Benjamites. See 2 Sm 16:5–9; 20:1.)	For the director of music. Of David the servant of the LORD. He sang to the LORD the words of this song when the LORD delivered him from the hand of all his enemies and from the hand of Saul. He said: 2 Sm 22:1–51 (duplicate)	Of David. When he pretended to be insane before Abimelech, who drove him away, and he left. 1 Sm 21:10–14	For the director of music. A psalm of David. When the prophet Nathan came to him after David had committed adultery with Bathsheba. 2 Sm 11–12	For the director of music. A *maskil* of David. When Doeg the Edomite had gone to Saul and told him: "David has gone to the house of Ahimelech." 1 Sm 22:6–23

Ps 54	Ps 56	Ps 57	Ps 59	Ps 60	Ps 63	Ps 142
For the director of music. With stringed instruments. A *maskil* of David. When the Ziphites had gone to Saul and said, "Is not David hiding among us?" 1 Sm 23:19; 26:1	For the director of music. To the tune of "A Dove on Distant Oaks." Of David. A *miktam*. When the Philistines had seized him in Gath. 1 Sm 21:11–16	For the director of music. To the tune of "Do Not Destroy." Of David. A *miktam*. When he had fled from Saul into the cave. 1 Sm 22:1	For the director of music. To the tune of "Do Not Destroy." Of David. A *miktam*. When Saul had sent men to watch David's house in order to kill him. 1 Sm 19:11–17	For the director of music. To the tune of "The Lily of the Covenant." A *miktam* of David. For teaching. When he fought Aram Naharaim and Aram Zobah, and when Joab returned and struck down twelve thousand Edomites in the Valley of Salt. 2 Sm 8:13–14	A psalm of David. When he was in the Desert of Judah. 1 Sm 23:14; 24:1	A *maskil* of David. When he was in the cave. A prayer. 1 Sm 22:1; 24:1–7

be that "song" (*shir*) is vocal and "psalm" (*mizmor*) is accompanied by a musical instrument.[14] When used together they would suggest accompanied singing. Another connection occurs as the headings for Psalms 120–34, and the phrase is usually translated "songs of ascents" (*shir hamma'aloth*). It is generally believed that these psalms were sung on special pilgrimages to Jerusalem. This may be suggested by the use of the verb "to go up" in Ezra 2:1 and a noun derived from the verb in Ezra 7:9, *miktam*

maskil

both describing the "going up" from the Babylonian exile. Later the term applied to the fifteen temple steps leading up to the temple proper, where the temple singers sang these psalms, one on each step. Some would, in fact, translate this phrase as "songs of the steps."

2. *Psalm (mizmor)*. As already stated, this word, used fifty-seven times as a technical term in the Psalter,[15] suggests a musical form. As a verb it means to play a musical instrument. In fact, in four of its occurrences in the Psalms the musical instrument is specified (Pss 33:2; 98:5; 144:9; 147:7). Thus, the meaning of the noun is a poetic form intended for musical accompaniment. In the Septuagint (LXX) this word is normally rendered as *psalmos*, from which we get our word "psalm."

3. *Miktam*. There is no consensus on the meaning of this term, so the translations usually render it in transliterated form as we have done here. It occurs in the titles of Psalms 16, 56, 57, 58, 59, and 60, which are all Davidic psalms. Some scholars have suggested that it is related to the Hebrew noun *ketem* ("gold"), and they would render its meaning as "a golden psalm." But this view is not widely accepted. Sigmund Mowinckel connects it to the Akkadian verb *katamu* ("to cover"), associates it with atonement, and translates it "atonement psalm."[16] Hans-Joachim Kraus connects the LXX translation "pillar inscription" (*stelographia*) with the only occurrence of the verb *ktm* in Jeremiah 2:22, for which he suggests the meaning "to be indelible." He hypothetically suggests that "stelographic publication" might make sense, especially in view of the LXX translation of the word *miktam*.[17] B. D. Eerdmans offers an even more attractive interpretation, even though it too is hypothetical. He proposes that, in view of the perilous situation the titles of these psalms suggest, the word suggests the covering of the lips in secrecy. So "a silent prayer" might be the best translation, for David could not have prayed a prayer out loud in any of these situations.[18]

4. *Maskil*. This term too is generally transliterated because the opinions on its meaning vary widely. It occurs in the titles of thirteen psalms: Psalms 32, 42, 44, 45, 52, 53, 54, 55, 74, 78, 88, 89, and 142. The word also occurs in the text of Psalm 47:7. Commentators have rendered it "artistic song" or "didactic song" because it comes from the verb "to be wise or skilled." If we are thinking in terms of the "didactic" poem, most of these psalms, with the exception of Psalms 32 and 78, do not fit into that category well. Kraus points to 2 Chronicles 30:22, which describes levitical activity with the participle of this root (*skl*) and submits that "presenting songs and poems in a skilled, intelligent, and artistic way has something to do with the explanation of" *maskil*.[19] The Levites were evidently singing well-crafted songs. Perhaps that comes as close to the meaning of this term as we can get with our present knowledge of ancient Israelite poetry.

5. *Shiggaion*. This term occurs only once in the Psalms, in the heading of Psalm 7, but the plural form also occurs in the poem of Habakkuk (Hb 3:1). It comes from a verb which means "to err" or "wander," but neither Psalm 7 nor Habakkuk 3 is a penitential psalm or strictly a lament. A. F. Kirkpatrick suggested that it has something to do with the ecstatic, passionate character of the poetry.[20] Kraus connects it to the Akkadian word *segu* ("lamentation") and suggests "agitated lament."[21] We simply will have to wait for further information before we can speak confidently.

6. *Tehillah* (*"song of praise"*). Interestingly, this noun, which in its plural form came to be the Hebrew designation of the entire book of Psalms, occurs as a genre of psalm in Psalm 145, but elsewhere in the body of the Psalms it is used in the sense of "praise" (22:25; 33:1; 34:1; 40:3; 48:10; 65:1; 71:8; 100:4; 106:12, 47; 119:171; 147:1; 148:14; 149:1). In Nehemiah 12:46 this noun occurs in conjunction with "song" ("song of praise"=*shir tehillah*). In view of so many obscure terms, we can be grateful that the meaning of this one is so clear.

7. *Tefillah* (*"prayer"*). This noun appears in the titles of five psalms: Psalms 17, 86, 90, 102, and 142. It also occurs in Habakkuk 3:1 in the phrase "a prayer of Habakkuk the prophet." It is the general term for prayer in the Psalms as well as in the Old Testament. As a term for genre, Kraus proposes that it applies to a prayer of lament or a bidding prayer.[22]

Titles with Musical Terms

We can only wish we knew more about the music of ancient Israel than we do. The information we do have is rather laconic, but it is sufficient to inform us that music played a large role in ancient Israel and in the temple. The following musical terms occur in the Psalms.

1. *Lamenatstseakh* (*"to the choirmaster"*). This expression occurs in the title of fifty-five psalms and in Habakkuk 3:19. The verb from which this noun derives (*natsakh*) means "to lead," "to excel," or "to be at the head," and is so used in Ezra 3:8; 1 Chronicles 23:4; and 2 Chronicles 2:2.[23] The verb occurs in a different Hebrew verbal stem (piel) in 1 Chronicles 15:21 in the sense of "to play the lyre." John Alexander Lamb, basing his view on the Akkadian ritual texts, proposes that this term means "to be recited by the official in charge."[24] Others have

suggested that it was a special title for David, meaning "him who excels."[25] The idea of the choirmaster, in the sense of the one who leads, is still a possibility and is just about as attractive as any of the other proposals.

2. *Binginoth and 'al-neginoth.* The first of these terms, *binginoth*, is made of the preposition "with" (*b*) and the noun *neginoth*, which may mean "stringed instruments" or "stringed accompaniment," the latter indicating the manner of performance. The phrase occurs in the titles of Psalms 4, 6, 54, 55, 67, and 76, with the variant *'al-neginath* ("on stringed instruments") in Psalm 61. The verb from which it derives (*ngn*) means "to run over the strings."[26] We can be pretty certain then that these psalms were to be recited or sung to the strains of stringed instruments.

3. *'al-hashminith* (*"according to the eighth"*). This particular phrase, according to some, suggests that the instruments are tuned for the bass singers ("according to the eighth"). Kraus suggests that it refers not to the voice but to the instrument, "on the eight-stringed (instrument)."[27] It occurs in the titles of Psalms 6 and 12. The phrase also occurs in 1 Chronicles 15:21, where it is joined with the verb "to play a stringed instrument," and the instrument is identified as the lyre. Therefore, it seems that the term is not the instrument itself but the range of voice.

4. *'al-muth,'almuth labben, and 'al-ala-moth.* These three phrases are considered by some to be variants upon one meaning. They may be the counterpart to the preceding phrase, referring to the female range rather than the male.[28] The term *'al-alamoth* occurs in the title of Psalm 46 and in 1 Chronicles 15:20, where it may mean "according to maidens." A. S. Gordon proposes that these are the instruments tuned for the maid-

ens, that is, in a soprano key.[29] The longer term *'almuth labben* occurs in Psalm 9, and the shorter term *'almuth* is found at the end of Psalm 48 (v. 14).

Titles with Musical Tunes

At this point we begin discussing a series of terms that are often interpreted as tune names.

1. *'al-gittith* ("upon gittith"). Psalms 8, 81, and 84 carry this term in their titles. The Targum supposes this to be a musical instrument that originated in Gath. But *gath* also means *winepress*, and in the LXX the title is "according to the winepress" (*hyper tōn lēnōn*), suggesting a vintage song.[30]
2. *'al-tashkheth* ("Do not destroy"). This clause occurs in the titles of Psalms 57, 58, 59, and 75, where it immediately follows the opening phrase, "to the choirmaster." Some scholars have referenced Isaiah 65:8 where this expression occurs and seems to refer to a vintage song, and thus have seen it in the Psalms as an expression of a song tune.
3. *'al-'ayyeleth ha-shachar* ("on the hind of the dawn"). This phrase occurs only in the title of Psalm 22. If we are to understand it as a tune, then we should understand it in the sense of "set to the hind of the morning."[31]
4. *'al-shoshannim* and *'al-shushan eduth* ("on the lilies" and "according to the lily of testimony"). Both are likely hymn tunes, the first occurring in Psalms 45 and 69, and the second in Psalm 60 ("according to the lily of the testimony") and 80 ("to the lilies, a testimony"). The LXX interpreted the word *shoshannim* as "those who change." L. Delekat basically agrees with this translation and refers these psalms to "those whose situation changes for the worse."[32] The word *'eduth* ("testimony") in the second phrase is as problematic as the first noun of the phrase. Perhaps it could refer to the oracle of

Psalm 60:6–8, but there is no such oracle in Psalm 80.[33] The best we can do is leave the matter on the idea that it is a hymn tune and not try to figure out the details, especially since we no longer have the tune and have no idea what kind of musical setting it provided for these psalms.

5. *'al-yonath 'elem rekhoqim* ("set to the dove of the far-off terebinths").[34] This expression occurs only in the title of Psalm 56, and our understanding is insufficient to inform us why this tune was applied to the psalm.

Musical Instruments

Ancient Near Eastern literature gives us quite a bit of information about the various musical instruments used during the Old Testament period. This is especially true of ancient art. Although we do not have any art forms from Israelite society, most likely because of the Old Testament's opposition to images, this is not true of Israel's neighbors, and musical instruments figure prominently among the cultural artifacts represented in this art. The Psalms mention a number of musical instruments, which we can classify in three groups: (1) percussions, (2) winds, and (3) strings.

Two percussion instruments are mentioned in the Psalms: the hand-drum or tambourine (Pss 81:2; 149:3; 150:4)[35] and cymbals (Ps 150:5; 1 Chr 13:8; 15:16–17). The tambourine (*toph*) was used in processions, especially at victory celebrations.[36] Psalm 68:24–25 describes a procession in the temple:

> Your procession has come into view, O God,
> the procession of my God and King into the sanctuary.
> In front are the singers, after them the musicians;

The clay figure of a woman with a hand-drum or tambourine.

with them are the maidens
playing tambourines.

Cymbals (*tsiltselim*)[37] were also used in Israelite worship. Archaeological discoveries from the Late Bronze and Early Iron Ages in Canaan give the impression that this instrument was used widely during that time.[38] Psalm 150 lists cymbals in the orchestra of praise: "Praise him with the clash of cymbals, / praise him with resounding cymbals" (v. 5). One cannot be certain about the difference between the "clash of cymbals" and the "resounding cymbals," but perhaps the difference was in the method of performance rather than the instrument.

The second category of instruments is the wind instruments. Those mentioned in the Psalms are the horn (*shofar*; 47:5; 81:3; 98:6; 150:3), the trumpet (*khatsotserah*), and the flute ('*ugav*; Ps 150:4). The horn was likely the ram's horn, which was used to an-

nounce important occasions (Ex 20:18; 2 Sm 15:10; 1 Kgs 1:34, 39, 41–42; 2 Kgs 9:13) and to sound alarms (Ps 81:3). By the nature of the instrument, however, it was not helpful for accompaniment.

The trumpet seems to have been the favorite instrument of the Chronicler. He uses the noun nineteen times and the verb six times. It was probably of Egyptian origin and is attested in the art and literature of the middle of the third millennium B.C. onwards.[39] This instrument replaced the horn at the coronation of Solomon (971–931 B.C., 1 Kgs 1:34, 39, 41). It appears only once in the Psalms (98:6), where the people acclaim Yahweh as King with an orchestra and singing.

The third wind instrument mentioned in the Psalms, and mentioned only once, is the flute. Flutes made of bone are attested in Egypt as early as the fourth millennium B.C.[40] The double flute (*halil*), which had a brighter sound, is attested in Israel. The figure of the man playing the double flute indicates that it was rather short and as a result would have had higher tones than a longer instrument of its diameter and material. In the Old Testament this instrument was used by prophetic bands (1 Sm 10:5), played at festivals (Is 5:12), and played on joyful and festal occasions (1 Kgs 1:40; Is 30:29).[41]

The third group of instruments was the strings. They seem to have been a favorite accompaniment for singing. The Hebrew word *kinnor* occurs thirteen times in the Psalms, and *nevel* occurs eight, each probably representing a different type of lyre. Keel distinguishes between two kinds of lyres. One has a sounding-box shaped like a jar and a curved yoke, while the other has a rounded bottom with a simple sounding-board, and the yoke-arms are only curved slightly.[42] Since the word *nevel* is also used of a large storage jar (Lam 4:2; Is 30:14), the suggestion is that the *nevel* designates the type of lyre with the jar sounding-box.[43] It would appear that the *kinnor* was more commonly used in ancient Israel (Ps 137:2).

The horn was used in the temple and was the only musical instrument that came to be used in the synagogue.

Musicians playing the tambourine (left), two types of lyres, and the cymbals.

An Egyptian scene with a flautist accompanying the singer on the right, as the vocalist covers his ear to sense the resonance of his voice so that he might have better vocal control.

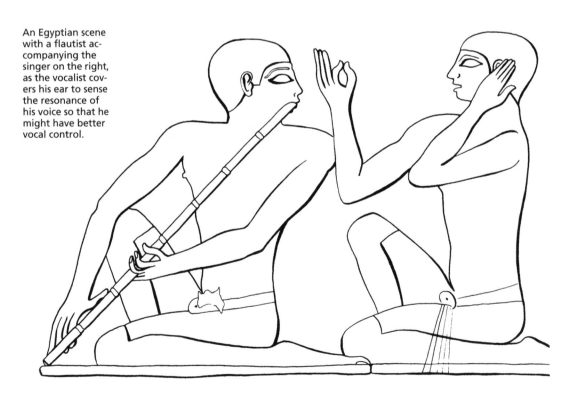

A lyre (*nevel*) with its sounding-box in the shape of a jar on a coin of the First Jewish Revolt (A.D. 66–70).

A lyre (*kinnor*) with a rounded sounding-box on a coin of the First Jewish Revolt (A.D. 66–70).

A large lyre (*nevel*) with a sounding-box in the shape of a jar.

These men, evidently captives, are playing the lyre (*kinnor* or *nevel*), an instrument known in Egypt as early as the second millennium B.C.—perhaps imported from Canaan.

From the pictures of the lyre in ancient art, the number of strings varied, but some lyres had as many as ten strings (Ps 144:9).

As the Psalms show, at times these instruments were played in concert together to accompany singing (2 Chr 5:12–13), while on other occasions the orchestra played to the chanting of praise to God (Ps 150).

Singing

The nature of singing in the tabernacle and temple is another difficult topic. In fact, it is probably not possible to speak generally because practices changed through the centuries of worship. There is evidence, however, that antiphonal singing was in vogue

in early times. After David's slaying of Goliath, the women offered their popular support as they danced and "answered one another" (NIV has simply "sang"): "Saul has slain his thousands, / and David his tens of thousands" (1 Sm 18:7). The double subject would lend itself nicely to antiphonal singing. The refrain of Psalms 118:1–4 and 136 definitely anticipates an antiphonal style of recitation or singing, and Psalm 129 calls for a response as well (v. 1, "let Israel say").

The Psalter attests to the existence of singers in the temple (Pss 68:25; 87:7). Moreover, the witness of the Books of Chronicles to the musical activity in the temple, and particularly to singers, is not likely the Chronicler's

invention. Obviously he knew personally about this great tradition, and he traces it back to the time of David (1 Chr 15:16; 2 Chr 35:15).

The Psalms inform us that the lyre and other instruments accompanied hymns of thanksgiving (Pss 57:8–9; 71:22; 98:5–6). To what extent the congregation joined in the singing activity of the choir we cannot say, but it is quite likely that congregational participation grew with the development of the temple liturgy.

Key Terms

Tehillim
mizmor
Writings
shir
miktam
maskil
tefillah
lamenatstseakh

Study Questions

1. Calvin referred to the psalmists as prophets. Although the book of Psalms is not included in the Hebrew division of the Prophets, how is his assessment accurate?

2. Comment on the literary links between David's poetry outside the Psalms and the poetry within. How does this speak to the issue of David's authorship?

3. Even by the time of the LXX, the logical connection between the titles and content of many psalms had become obscure. What might this suggest about the antiquity of the titles? And content?

4. Read the thirteen historical titles of the psalms along with their historical texts in 1 and 2 Samuel. Comment on the realism this adds to the traditional association of David with the psalms.

5. Familiarize yourself with the musical terms and names of the musical tunes and then read the content of those psalms. What does this awareness of titles add to a reading of the text?

6. What are the three general classes of instruments mentioned in the Psalms, and what are the individual instruments in each class?

2 Listening to the Symphony of Praise

Interpreting the Psalms

Objectives

After reading this chapter, you should be able to
  1. Explain the basis of Hebrew poetry.
  2. Discuss the basic methods of interpreting the Psalms.
  3. Build a foundation for applying the Psalms to life.

parallelism

unit

stich or colon

Scanning the Orchestra: Hebrew Poetry

Parallelism

Although one can appreciate the orchestral concert without being able to identify the various instruments, it is much more enriching when one can sort out the instruments as they come in and go out, and as they join together to produce the beautiful music the composer intended. This metaphor is not strange to the Book of Psalms, for the book closes with a summons to praise the Lord with musical instruments (Ps 150). Using this metaphor to analyze Hebrew poetry, as the heart of the orchestra is the strings, so the heart of Hebrew poetry is a device called *parallelism.* It is a literary pattern that states an idea in one line and focuses more closely on the same idea in the following line, either repeating the thought in different terms or focusing on the thought more specifically.

Dietrich Bonhoeffer speaks theologically about this feature of Hebrew poetry, insisting that a thought is sustained in Hebrew poetry, like a note of music is sustained by the human voice, giving more time to contemplate the ideas.[1]

This form is not simply accidental. It encourages us not to allow the prayer to be cut off prematurely, and it invites us to pray together with one another. That which seems to be unnecessary repetition to us, who are inclined to pray too hurriedly, is actually proper immersion and concentration in prayer.[2]

Synonymous Parallelism

Just as there are violins, violas, cellos, and bass violins in the orchestra, parallelism is also broken down into its constituent instruments. The traditional terms for the subtypes of parallelism are *synonymous* and *antithetic*. Synonymous parallelism simply means that the thought pattern in one line conforms to the pattern in the successive line. That does not mean, of course, that the thought in the successive line will be absolutely parallel. There are often nuances in the second line that enhance or alter the terms of the first line, but they will not contradict it. Robert Alter observes that language tends to shun strict synonymity. Thus he speaks of *focusing*, which means the poet introduces a term in one line and in the following line *focuses* upon the term more specifically, just as we will see in the relationship between terms B and B′ in the example below.[3] The movement is normally from the general to the specific, or from the less specific to the more specific.

Psalm 27:1 provides an illustration of synonymous parallelism:

> The LORD is my light and my salvation—
> whom shall I fear?
> The LORD is the stronghold of my life—
> of whom shall I be afraid?

We call the basic terms of the lines *units*, which are words or phrases that make up the larger thought segment. The larger thought constitutes a *line*. The Greek word for line, *stich*, and the Latin, *colon*, are commonly used to designate this unit. The lines themselves combine to form compound lines, which are named by the Greek or Latin prefixes; for example, a two-line compound thought is called a *distich* or *bicolon*, while a three-line compound thought constitutes a *tristich* or *tricolon*, and so forth.

The reader will keep in mind that a single verse in the Psalms is not necessarily equivalent to a distich or a tristich. As the example from Psalm 27:1 will show, this single verse is composed of *two* distichs.

Stich 1	Stich 2	Stich 3	Stich 4
The LORD (unit 1)		The LORD (unit 1)	

is my light (unit 2)		is the strong-hold (unit 2)	
and my salvation (unit 3)		of my life (unit 3)	
	whom (unit 1)		of whom (unit 1)
	shall I fear? (unit 2)		shall I be afraid? (unit 2)

The first stich (line) above is composed of three basic units, while the second stich is made up of two units. These two lines belong together as a compound thought unit and compose a distich. Stichs three and four also form a distich. This pattern is commonly represented by the number of basic units in a line. Thus each of these distichs exhibits a 3:2 pattern.

Stich 1	A	B	C		
Stich 2				D	E	3:2 distich
Stich 3	A′	B′	C′		
Stich 4				D′	E′	3:2 distich

In the first line "The LORD" is the subject (A), "my light and my salvation" are the complement (B), followed by the two terms (D and E) of the second stich, which is a rhetorical question, "whom shall I fear?" The thought pattern in the second distich follows closely that of the first, even though the parallelism, as is usually the case, is not absolutely synonymous. Describing the Lord in the first line as "my light and my salvation"

involves the two metaphors of "light" and "salvation." At first, they may seem categorically different, but in a military setting *light* and *salvation* ("victory") were closely associated. For obvious reasons, not many victories were won at night.

The second distich describes the Lord as "the stronghold of my life" (B′), again a military figure of speech, suggesting that the psalmist finds a place of "refuge" in the Lord or finds him a "defensive tower," that is, a place that, by its fortified and impregnable nature, contributes to his victory. In fact, units B′ and C′ in the second distich focus the meaning of the corresponding units in the first line (B and C) so that the reader better understands what the psalmist means by "my light and my salvation."

By this time, it is quite obvious that the sense of the first distich is the same as that of the second, but not strictly so. The only two strictly parallel terms in the example are "the LORD" plus the rhetorical question at the end of each distich. The affirmation of both distichs is that the Lord is David's source of security, and therefore he has no need to fear.

The chart that follows shows Psalm 27 separated into units, stichs, distichs, and tristichs.[4] We should be aware that, while the English translation can sometimes be scanned with a degree of accuracy, the Hebrew text is ultimately the basis for scanning. I have separated the individual units in each line in an attempt to illustrate how they are broken down. But it should be understood that the English syntax does not always match up with the Hebrew syntax. Therefore, scanning Hebrew poetry in English translation can be a rather artificial exercise. Nevertheless, it should help to illustrate the process.

[1]The LORD / is my light / and my salvation—

whom / shall I fear?   3:2 distich

The LORD / is the stronghold / of my life—

of whom / shall I be afraid?	3:2 distich
[2]When evil men / advance / against me	
to devour / my flesh,	3:2 distich
when my enemies / and my foes / attack me,	
they will stumble / and fall.	3:2 distich
[3]Though an army / besiege / me,	
my heart / will not fear;	3:2 distich
though war / break out / against me,	
even then / will I be confident.	3:2 distich
[4]One thing / I ask / of the Lord,	
that is / what I seek:	3:2 distich
that I may dwell / in the house / of the Lord	
all / the days of my life,	3:2 distich
to gaze upon / the beauty / of the Lord	
and to seek him / in his temple.	3:2 distich
[5]For in the day / of trouble[5]	
he will keep me / safe / in his dwelling;	2:3 distich
he will hide me / in the shelter / of his tabernacle	
and set me high / upon a rock.	3:2 distich
[6]Then / my head / will be exalted	
above / the enemies / who surround me;	3:3[6] distich
at his tabernacle / will I sacrifice	
with shouts / of joy;	
I will sing / and make music / to the Lord.	2:2:3[7] tristich
[7]Hear / my voice / when I call, O Lord;	
be merciful to me / and answer me.	3:2 distich
[8]My heart / says / of you,	
"Seek / his face!"	
Your face, / Lord, / I will seek.	3:2:3 tristich
[9]Do not hide / your face / from me,	
do not turn / your servant / away in anger;	

you have been / my helper.	3:3:2 tristich
Do not reject me / or forsake me,	
O God / my Savior.	2:2 distich
[10]Though my father / and mother / forsake me,	
the LORD / will receive me.	3:2 distich
[11]Teach me / your way, / O LORD;	
lead me / in a straight path	
because of / my oppressors.	3:2:2 tristich
[12]Do not turn me over / to the desire / of my foes,	
for false witnesses / rise up against me,	
breathing out / violence.	3:2:2 tristich
[13]I am still confident / of this:	
I will see / the goodness / of the LORD	
in the land / of the living.	2:3:2 tristich
[14]Wait / for the LORD;	
be strong / and take / heart	
and wait / for the LORD.	2:3:2 tristich

Antithetic Parallelism

Antithetic parallelism is a method of saying contrasting things in different lines and in different ways. The psalms employ this method, but this thought pattern is never sustained in the Psalms over long stretches of poetry as it is in Proverbs 10:1–15:33. As with synonymous parallelism, the "antithetic" thought is not a perfect antithesis but introduces an idea in the second line that contrasts with the idea in the previous line.

Psalm 1 contains an example of antithetic parallelism. As is the manner of wisdom literature, to which this psalm belongs, the poem draws a contrast between two ways, that of the righteous person and that of the wicked. We should notice that the opening statement introduces unexplained categories of law breaking ("counsel of the wicked," "way of sinners," "seat of mockers"), and then the second statement points in the direction of delighting in the law. The description of the righteous person continues in verse 3 before the psalm brings the life of the wicked into sharp relief to that of the righteous in verses 4 and 5. A concluding contrast between the wicked and the righteous appears in verse 6. The general thought pattern, therefore, is thesis (v. 1) / antithesis (v. 2), thesis (v. 3) / antithesis (vv. 4–5), thesis (v. 6a) / antithesis (v. 6b):

Thesis

Blessed is the man
who does not walk
in the counsel of the wicked
or stand in the way of sinners,
or sit in the seat of mockers.

Antithesis

But his delight
is in the law of the LORD,
and on his law he meditates
day and night.

strophe

Thesis

He is like a tree | planted by streams of water,

| which yields its fruit in season

| and whose leaf does not wither.

Whatever he does prospers.

Antithesis

Not so the wicked! They are like chaff | that the wind blows away

Therefore the wicked | will not stand in the judgment

nor sinners | in the assembly of the righteous.

Thesis

For the LORD watches over the way of the righteous

Antithesis

But the way of the wicked will perish.

Another brief example of antithetic parallelism is found in Psalm 20:7–8.

Thesis	Some trust	in chariots and some in horses,
Antithesis	but we trust	in the name of the LORD our God.
Thesis	They are brought to their knees	and fall,
Antithesis	but we rise	and stand firm.

Strophe

If we want to sustain our metaphor of the orchestra, we should shift now from the instruments to the score of music that musicians must follow. We have already explained the breakdown of the poetry into basic units, which combine to form lines, and the lines combine to form distichs, tristichs, and so on. The next largest thought unit in Hebrew poetry is the **strophe.** Normally multiple stichs compose a strophe. Perhaps this unit belongs more to the categories of Greek and Latin poetry (and thus English) than to Hebrew. Some scholars use the terms strophe and stanza synonymously,[8] while others make a distinction between them, the stanza being a larger unit made up of one or more strophes.[9]

The image of a healthy, fruit-bearing tree describes the life of the righteous (Ps 1:3).

Strophes Set Off by a Refrain

In Psalms 42–43 the first strophe (42:1–5) is a lament describing the psalmist's plight in terms of thirst. This is a powerful metaphor for anyone who has lived through the dry season of the hot, arid climate of the Near East. He laments that he was prevented from going to the temple to worship, and this absence from worship reminded him of a deer craving the fresh streams of water.

Then the psalm picks up a thread from the refrain of 42:5 ("Why are you downcast, O my soul?") and weaves it into strophe 2 (42:6–11), "My soul is downcast within me," focusing his attention on God, "therefore I will remember you. . . ."

In strophe 3 (43:1–5) the poet prays that God may bring him again to the place of worship, and he concludes with the refrain.

Thus we see that the subject matter, the psalmist's longing for God and his inability to attend temple worship, is stretched out through the psalm. The different emphases of each stanza would probably be enough to break the poem into strophes even without the refrain, but the refrain provides a formal division marker.

single strophe. That is, the difference in subject matter from one strophe to another may not be as marked as in Psalm 19. An example is Psalms 42–43, where a refrain sets off one strophe from another, and the subject matter is the psalmist's general trust in God.

Strophe 1	Ps 42:1–5	concludes with the refrain: Why are you downcast, O my soul? Why so disturbed within me? Put your hope in God, for I will yet praise him, my Savior and my God.
Strophe 2	Ps 42:6–11	v. 11 repeats the refrain of v. 5.
Strophe 3	Ps 43:1–5	v. 5 repeats the refrain of 42:5.

My own inclination is to use the term *strophe* as the larger unit above that of the distich or tristich and not use the term *stanza* at all, since the strophic unit is large enough that we generally need not speak about a still larger unit.

A strophe is a logical unit determined by either the subject matter or the structure of the poem. Psalm 19, for example, is composed of two strophes defined by their subject matter. The first six verses contain a hymn of creation and the last eight verses a meditation on the law:

Strophe 1	19:1–6	Hymn of creation
Strophe 2	19:7–14	Meditation on the law

There is no structural marker to distinguish these two parts of the psalm, only the content itself.

Other psalms have literary markers or structural characteristics that define the strophes. In these cases, the subject matter may or may not be self-contained in a

In a few instances the Hebrew alphabet gives a formal structure to the psalm: Psalms 9–10, 25, 34, 37, 111, 112, 119, and 145. These poems, called *alphabet acrostics*, follow the order of the letters of the alphabet, beginning each new strophe or each new line, as the case may be, with a different letter of the Hebrew alphabet. Psalm 119 is perhaps the best known of these psalms. Artistically, it is a masterpiece. The psalm is composed of twenty-two strophes of eight lines each, and all eight lines of each strophe begin with the same letter of the alphabet. It is quite remarkable that the pattern is sustained throughout the psalm. We may compare the Book of Lamentations, which is composed of four acrostic poems. In Poems 1 (Lam 1), 2 (Lam 2), and 4 (Lam 4; chapter 5 is not acrostic although it does have twenty-two verses), each strophe or stanza be-

The Numbering of the Psalms in the Hebrew and Greek Bibles

Twice the Septuagint (LXX) combines two psalms into one: Psalms 9 and 10 in Hebrew appear as Psalm 9 in the LXX, and Psalms 114 and 115 in Hebrew appear as Psalm 113 in the LXX. On two other occasions the Septuagint divides the Hebrew psalm into two separate psalms: Psalm 116 in Hebrew appears as Psalms 114 and 115 in the LXX, and Psalm 147 in Hebrew appears as Psalms 146 and 147 in the LXX. This produces a different numbering for most of the psalms.

Hebrew and Protestant Translations	Greek and Roman Catholic Translations
Pss 1–8	1–8
9 10	9
11–113	10–112
114 115	113
116	114 115
117–146	116–145
147	146 147
148–150	148–50 151

gins with a new letter of the Hebrew alphabet, but the following lines in the same strophe do not conform to the alphabetic pattern. However, in Poem 3 (Lam 3), the middle poem of the book, which is composed of twenty-two strophes of three verses each, every verse of a single strophe begins with the same letter of the alphabet.[10] But in comparison, Psalm 119 sustains the same letter for eight verses in each strophe, which is quite an accomplishment. Obviously, the alphabetic acrostic is quite restrictive, so Psalm 119 strains and stretches the psalmist's vocabulary to its limits, stretched by adherence to the alphabetic structure as well as by his subject, the law.

Chiastic Structure

Another feature of Hebrew poetry is the **chiasm.** This word comes from the Greek word *chiazein*, meaning to place crosswise or in the shape of the Greek letter *chi* (χ).[11] This device may mark the structure of entire psalms or merely parts of psalms. Robert L. Alden, in a study of Psalms 1–50, identifies as many as twenty-one psalms that exhibit this structural characteristic, and he cites Psalm 8 as a model:

A Benediction (v. 1)
  B God's rule (vv. 2–3)
    C Human meanness (v. 4)
    C' Human greatness (v. 5)
  B' Humanity's rule (vv. 6–8)
A' Benediction (v. 9)[12]

The Alphabet Acrostics in the Psalter

Psalms 9–10, evidently a single poem, as it is in the Septuagint (Ps 9), give some evidence of an acrostic, but the sequence of the letters is irregular. Psalm 25 follows the alphabet sequence, but the letter *qof* is missing (the letter *waw* is recessed in v. 5b, that is, it is the second letter rather than the first). Psalm 37 begins every other verse with a different letter of the alphabet, but the letter *'ayin* is also recessed (in v. 28b). Psalms 111 and 112 begin each stich (in this case, each half-verse) with a new letter of the alphabet, and all twenty-two letters are used. The poet of Psalm 119 undertook the massive task of beginning each line of an eight-line strophe (twenty-two strophes in all) with the same Hebrew letter, using the law as the common subject of the poem. Psalm 145 follows the alphabetic sequence verse by verse, but the letter *nun* is missing.[1]

1. Cf. C. Hassell Bullock *An Introduction to the Old Testament Poetic Books*, rev. ed. (Chicago: Moody, 1988), 37–38.

chi with two points. The intention here is to draw a contrast between two ideas:

A Therefore the LORD watches over	B the **way of the righteous**,

B' but the **way of the wicked**	A' will perish.

Thus the psalmist has more than language in his arsenal of literary tools.

Reading the Psalms through the Psalmists' Experience

The synagogue and church have long interpreted the Psalms as having multiple levels of meaning, and anyone who has ever read Psalm 51 and applied it personally has keyed into one or more of those levels of meaning. But, the historical experience of the psalmists is fundamental to understanding their thought. We need to ask the question, "What did the words mean in their historical context?" Since the psalms were written in a specific historical and cultural context, our first obligation to the text is to hear their words in and through that context. Only then can we understand the psalmists' experience.

For example, Psalm 22 begins with the psalmist's lament, "My God, my God, why have you forsaken me?" Christians are likely to hear these words immediately as Jesus' words from the cross. Yet, to be fair to the historical context, we should assume that they were spoken by a real person in ancient Israel, very likely even David himself at some God-forsaken moment of his life. The fact that Jesus cried out these words from the cross does not mean that our interpretation should start there. It is much safer and fairer

If one drew a Greek *chi* (χ) along the letters of this outline, the middle terms (in this case, C and C') would come where the two lines of the *chi* cross. This is a half *chi* with two points, and it is the author's way of drawing attention to certain leading ideas, in this case the contrast between how the psalmist looks at human creatures ("what is man that you are mindful of him, / the son of man that you care for him?"—v. 4) and how the Lord looks at them ("You made him a little lower than the heavenly beings, and crowned him with glory and honor"—v. 5). When we look at the psalm, which follows a verse-by-verse format, the chiastic pattern is easily lost to us. However, chiasm was a literary pattern or a literary way of thinking. In this way the writer could call attention to ideas that were central to his thought merely by the way he structured them.

We have a good example of chiasm in two parallel lines in Psalm 1. In this case the pattern is a full letter *chi*, with all four points, rather than a to the text to begin at the historical/cultural level and hear in them the suffering of an ancient Israelite.

There are two ways in which we may understand Jesus' use of these words, either as *fuller sense* (*sensus plenior*) or **typology.** The interpretive principle of fuller sense assumes that some expressions of human experience in the Old Testament far exceeded the real historical experience of the persons involved. Therefore, being unfulfilled in the historical person's experience, they contain the implicit projection of an experience yet to be and a person yet to live. Franz Delitzsch well illustrates what we mean by fuller sense in his comment on Psalm 22: "David descends, with his complaint, into a depth that lies beyond the depth of his affliction, and rises, with his hopes, to a height that lies far beyond the height of the reward of his affliction."[13]

The fuller meaning can be understood in the *comprehensive sense* as well. That is, the suffering on this occasion was insufficient to qualify for these gigantic terms of the text, so we understand David as summing up the suffering of his entire life. John Calvin illustrates this principle in his comment on this psalm: "From the tenor of the whole composition, it appears that David does not here refer merely to one persecution, but comprehends all the persecutions which he suffered under Saul."[14]

In comparison to the fuller sense, the *typological* interpretation sees Jesus as the *type* of sufferer in Psalm 22, and the psalmist becomes the model. James Mays's interpretation of this psalm belongs in this category, although he prefers to see Jesus as setting himself in its *paradigm*: "He joins the multitudinous company of the afflicted and becomes one with them in their suffering."[15] When the fuller sense method is applied, it recognizes that a future fulfillment is built into the language and meaning of the text, whereas typology looks back to a person or event as representative of a future event or person. It may or may not be a prophetic element built into the text.

This necessary excursus must lead us back to our historical/cultural level of interpretation. As we read further in the psalm, we learn that the psalmist was the object of ridicule by the adversaries of his faith:

All who see me mock me;
    they hurl insults, shaking their
      heads:
"He trusts in the LORD;
    let the LORD rescue him.
Let him deliver him,
    since he delights in him."
(vv. 7–8)

In metaphorical language, he further describes his enemies as "strong bulls of Bashan" and "roaring lions" (Ps 22:12, 13). Bashan was known for its fine cattle (Am 4:1) and the jungle of the Jordan for its lions, and the nature of these beasts obviously contributed a note of fierceness to the psalmist's description of his enemies. Both the fuller sense and the typological meaning are laid on the foundation of the historical/cultural interpretation. We miss something of the magnitude and reality of Jesus' suffering on the cross if we extract Psalm 22 from its historical setting. Further, while apart from the historical/cultural setting of the psalm we can see Jesus suffering *for* us in a vicarious way, when we start with the historical setting of the psalm, we see him suffering *with* us as well. That has been a comfort to countless believers who have passed through the valley of suffering and needed the assurance that Christ was walking with them. The historical/cultural method is necessarily prior to all other interpretive principles.

Reading the Psalms through the Editors' Experience

At this level of interpretation we are dealing with the editor(s) of the Psalm collections and of the final book.[16] The editor(s) had a certain prospectus in mind; that is, he was dealing with certain pressing issues, like the fall of Jerusalem and the end of the Davidic dynasty in Book 3, and he sought to evoke from Israel a particular response of faith. In the case of the Davidic dynasty, he hoped to shift Israel's attention from the human monarchy to the divine King and his reign, and by this to refocus the thought of Israel in order to assuage some of the pain of this traumatic era. It was a way of redirecting Judah's attention to spiritual realities. He consciously and purposely built this motif into Book 3. When he had sewn together the two themes of justice dispensed by the monarchy (Ps 72) and the injustice created by the wicked's prosperity (Ps 73), he had set the stage for dealing with the political disaster of 586 B.C. and its theological corollary: Why had God allowed the destruction of Judah at the hands of the nations (e.g., Pss 79:1, 5–7; 80; 89:50–51), and why had he permitted the fall of the Davidic dynasty (89:39)? Already in Psalm 74:7 the burning of the sanctuary by the Babylonians is in view, and the nation's soul-searching that resulted from this calamity was all but assured by this event. Israel could no longer ignore their sin. The theme is continued in Psalms 79, 80, 83, 85, and 89:39–52. While some of these psalms were evidently written after the disaster of 586 (Pss 74 and 89, for example), that does not consign all of them to that era. Yet they are incorporated into this collection, and the catastrophe of that era cast its shadows over these poems. Thus, when the readers of this disastrous time heard these psalms, the historical overtones of their day framed the terms of the psalms to form a word picture of their own tragic life. The unjust and the wicked, experienced on a personal level by the psalmists (Ps 82:2, for example), easily dissolved into the national enemies who had taken advantage of Judah and given shape to her theological crisis. Whether or not these psalms had originally referenced the national crisis, the editor lent the hues of the crisis to Book 3 by his placement of these psalms within the framework

of a collection that dealt with the crisis and its implications.

Reading the Psalms through the Readers' Experience

The above discussion gives us a precedent for the legitimate application of the psalms to our own personal and corporate situations. At least by the Babylonian exile they were being applied to situations with striking similarities to their original settings. Most scholars have no problem acknowledging that the psalms were written for their first users and hearers.[17] Yet we have ample evidence of their use in the Jewish synagogue and the Christian church and in the personal lives of countless believers through the centuries, where their meaning was appropriated to a situation in different times and different cultures. These interpretations range all the way from *radical reconceptions of the terms of the psalms* to mere *reappropriation of the truth of the psalms to a similar situation*. A single example of the radical reconceptions must suffice. The second-century Christian writing known as the *Epistle of Barnabas* associates the three phrases of Psalm 1:1 with three kinds of meat forbidden by Moses: "the counsel of the wicked" with forbidden seafood, "the way of sinners" with pork, and "the seat of mockers" with forbidden birds.[18] This interpretation was likely a reflection of one of the controversies of the second-century church, and Psalm 1 was used to settle the matter on the basis of Scripture. The method involves reading one's own thoughts into Scripture (eisegesis) rather than drawing out the author's intentions (exegesis).

On the other end of the hermeneutical spectrum is the *reappropriation of the original meaning of the psalms*, and John Calvin is one of the best examples of such an interpreter. In the preface to his commentary on the Psalms, he called the book "An Anatomy of All the Parts of the Soul," and he explains, "for there is not an emotion of which any one can be conscious that is not here represented as in a mirror."[19] We may call this interpretative method *paradigmatic*. That simply means that the original psalmist's experience became a *paradigm* or pattern for measuring and understanding one's own experience. Calvin voices this method when he recognizes his personal experiences in the Psalms,

> in considering the whole course of the life of David, it seemed to me that by his own footsteps he showed me the way, and from this I have experienced no small consolation. As that holy king was harassed by the Philistines and other foreign enemies with continual wars, while he was much more grievously afflicted by the malice and wickedness of some perfidious men amongst his own people, so I can say as to myself, that I have been assailed on all sides, and have scarcely been able to enjoy repose for a single moment, but have always had to sustain some conflict either from enemies without or within the Church.[20]

In his exegesis of the Psalms, Calvin moves easily between the experience of the psalmist and our own. For example, in his comment on Psalm 13:1, "How long, O LORD? Will you forget me forever? How long will you hide your face from me?" Calvin understands the psalm to reflect both David's experiences and ours:

> But here he speaks not so much according to the opinion of others, as according to the feeling of his own mind, when he complains of being neglected by God. Not that the persuasion of the truth of God's promises was extinguished in his heart, or that he did not repose himself on his grace; *but when we are for a long time weighed down by calamities, and when we do not perceive any sign of divine aid, this thought unavoidably forces itself*

upon us, that God has forgotten us.[21] [emphasis added to indicate the change from the historical to the paradigmatic interpretation]

While the historical interpretation (called also the literal or plain sense) is the place where we should begin our interpretation of the Psalms, the paradigmatic method, which has its roots in the Book of Psalms itself as evidenced by the editor's reapplication of the psalms to his historical situation, is also appropriate for the Christian life.

Reading the Psalms through the Apostles' Experience

The Book of Psalms is quoted more often in the New Testament than any other Old Testament book. That is not a coincidence, for the Psalter is filled with imagery and ideas that point directly to Jesus. Its importance for framing our understanding of the Messiah is inestimable. The Savior died on the cross with the wrenching words of Psalm 22:1 and the trusting words of Psalm 31:5 on his lips (Mt 27:46; Lk 23:46); and after his resurrection, he drew upon this book to explain what his death and resurrection meant (Lk 24:44). While the apostles followed this interpretive mode, Jesus did much to provide the grounds on which the early church would see him in the Psalms.

Typology

Typology figures among the methods that the New Testament uses to interpret the Psalms. S. B. Frost defines typology as "a relationship which is inherent between the two matters compared because *there is in fact an objective and historical relationship between them.*"[22]

It finds a person or idea in one era of history and draws attention to the analogous shape or experience of another person or idea. In comparison, *allegory* does not rise out of the historical context but is imposed on the text by the interpreter. The above example of Psalm 1:1 cited from the *Epistle of Barnabas* is an example of allegory, whereas John's application of Psalm 69:9 to Jesus' cleansing of the temple ("Zeal for your house will consume me," Jn 2:17) is an example of typology. That is, the psalmist's zeal for God's house became a model for Jesus' zeal for the temple.

The Old Testament spokesmen themselves introduced this method. Isaiah, for example, used the historical exodus under Moses as a type of the new exodus by which the exiles from Babylonia would be liberated (e.g., Is 43:1–7). Calvin recognized the historical sense of Psalm 45, a royal psalm, perhaps composed in honor of Solomon's marriage to the Egyptian princess, and expounded Solomon as a type of Christ, the psalm setting forth "the holy and divine union of Christ and his Church."[23] Thus, in its literal sense it refers to the Hebrew king, but in its typological sense it refers to Jesus Christ. For Calvin and those who follow him, the underlying justification of this method is that a theological solidarity underlies all of Scripture. This means the exegete has not really done his or her job until the full picture of Scripture has been taken into account.[24] Therefore, it is not only permissible but incumbent upon the interpreter to put the psalm into its larger biblical context. Yet typology can easily get out of hand. Consequently, some interpreters, this writer included, find that the typological interpretation of the Psalms should be handled discreetly, and the New Testament should set its perimeters.

Messianism

Once the reader acknowledges Calvin's principle of exegesis that an underlying unity joins Old Testament Israel and the New Testament church together in a theological connectedness, then interpreting the Psalms messianically springs naturally from this working hermeneutic. Christian readers of the Psalms should exercise caution not to over-messianize this book, but they need not follow the trend of modern scholarship and abandon the category of messianic psalms altogether, so long as their historical meaning is not abandoned. Traditionally a psalm was considered messianic if, having no relationship to its historical context, it *anticipated the Messiah* or *predicted the Messiah.*[25] With the justifiable emphasis of modern scholarship upon the historical meaning of the Psalms, even Psalm 110, interpreted messianically by both Jesus himself (Mt 22:41–46) and the Epistle to the Hebrews (ch. 7), will need to be tested against this historical principle. Tremper Longman provides a helpful rule of thumb for interpreting the Psalms messianically. *First*, since Christians believe Jesus is the Son of God, it is appropriate to apply the Psalms to Christ when they reference God's Son (e.g., Ps 110). *Second*, since the New Testament views Jesus as the Son of David, it is further proper to hear the Messiah King speaking through David the king.[26] I would add a *third* rule: when the New Testament interprets an event messianically, like the messianic overtones of Christ's words on the cross, we can follow the New Testament confidently. As should be obvious, these reasons draw heavily upon the typological method, and they also assume the undergirding theological solidarity that Calvin taught so strongly.

Reading the Psalms through the Literary Critics' Eyes

With the dawn of historical criticism in the modern era, the Psalms became the object of much discussion. The pioneer of the critical study of the Psalms was Hermann Gunkel, who applied the form-critical methodology to the Psalms and attempted to identify the *life situation* (*Sitz im Leben*) out of which the different psalms arose. He hypothesized that the present Psalms were modeled after an older kind of psalm poetry, now mostly lost, which was designed for public worship. However, the Psalms as they have come to us are private poetry, which was adapted for use in the public worship of Israel.[27] At the same time, Gunkel insisted that they had been adapted for Israel's public worship, and thus they fall into categories associated with various cultic functions. He sought to identify the "type" (*Gattung*) as a basic prerequisite for interpreting any single psalm. He proposed seven types: hymns, community laments, songs of the individual, thank offering songs, laments of the individual, entrance liturgies, and royal psalms.[28] Even though their origin was a private hymnody patterned after an almost extinct public hymnody, their use in the temple and synagogue made the public function the primary concern of exegesis. The Psalms, according to this form-critical view, had their origin in the sociological network of ancient Israel. The Psalter as a collection was the product of the religious community, particularly the temple priests and Levites. Even though Gunkel urged that the Psalms were used liturgically in the temple, he did not insist that all of the Psalms were originally written for that purpose. Rather some of them had been personal in their original composition and were subsequently adapted to a liturgical use. To say it another way, the "I" of many of the psalms was the psalmist himself and not a collective "I" for the congregation or nation, even though it later came to be corporate.

Sigmund Mowinckel carried this hypothesis far beyond that point and proposed that virtually all of the psalms were composed for liturgical or cultic purposes.[29] The private poetry that had been part of Gunkel's hypothesis was abandoned by Mowinckel. In his view, it was the non-cultic character of the psalm that had to be proved.[30] In our discussion above we have insisted that an understanding of the historical situation of the psalm is prerequisite to a proper interpretation of the psalm. Even though Gunkel had not entirely made the shift to the public worship function of the Psalms, Mowinckel went all the way and urged that the starting point for interpretation was the function of the Psalms in public worship:

> We must therefore try to understand them historically, on the basis of their own times. But this also means that we must try to find their place and function in the religious life of ancient Israel, or in early Judaism, if a critical historical examination should show that we have both pre-exilic and post-exilic psalms in the Psalter.[31]

Claus Westermann further pioneered the form-critical method of studying the Psalms and simplified the types of psalms to two: psalms of lament and psalms of praise.[32] These are classified according to the speaker, whether it is an individual or the community.[33] Westermann felt compelled to redirect the study of the Psalms from the cultic, as Gunkel and Mowinckel had understood it, to that of worship. He insisted that the "cult" was a theoretical concept invented by form criticism, and that worship was the category in which we must interpret the Psalms.[34]

Westermann subdivided the psalms of lament or petition into lament of the people and lament of the individual, while he broke down the psalms of praise into two basic categories: declarative praise and descriptive praise. Declarative praise is a general way of praising God in that he has acted on behalf of his people, and descriptive praise contains the specifics of what he has done. In descriptive praise, the praise of the people and of the individual are combined. Declarative praise, then, is the only one of the two categories of praise that can be subdivided: declarative psalm of praise of the people, and declarative psalm of praise of the individual.[35]

In comparison to the institutional origin of the Psalms, Erhard Gerstenberger proposed that the Psalms had their origin in the non-institutional circles of ancient Israel, that is, in the family and smaller social settings of life. In view of this, the growth of the Psalter proceeded from religious poems composed in these humble settings to the temple, where the collection became the worship and teaching instrument of the professional priests and temple officials.[36] His categories are the following: dirges and laments, complaints, thanksgiving songs, songs of praise (hymns), royal psalms, and wisdom psalms.[37]

The results of form-critical scholarship provide a fairly extensive, if not standard, list of psalm genres with the elements each includes. Of course, even the staunchest proponents of this view recognize that the writers of the Psalms did not work with inflexible models of these genres, and consequently there are variations within each genre. In our study we shall basically work with Westermann's categories but not restrict ourselves to them.

Reading the Psalms through the Students' Experience

It would be simplistic to try to outline a comprehensive method of interpreting the Psalms that takes into account all of the above methods. Even if we could, some methods would be more appropriate to certain psalms and less appropriate to others. Moreover, the ability of each reader to interpret the Psalms will vary by educational preparation, spiritual temperament, and literary acumen. Interpretation is part science

and part art. It is the "art" where hermeneutical rules break down. Some people simply have a better literary sense than others. They can read a novel and easily follow the plot and read the nuances of all the characters. Others need someone to explain these aspects of the novel to them before they can begin to grasp the meaning of the story. The teacher can lay down rules for interpretation, but their application requires both a bit of literary know-how and artistic inclination. What this book is intended to do for the reader is to provide some information on the literary know-how. The artistic part is basically a divine gift that is developed by instruction and discipline. If one is tone-deaf, no amount of instruction and drill will provide an appreciation for tonal quality. Yet it is true that one can gain a lot of appreciation for music as an art and discipline even if the musical score remains flat. Studying the Psalms is somewhat analogous. The literary science can be acquired, and even a bit of the artistic bent appropriated with effort, but other components that make a reader of the Psalms a good interpreter will come from other sources.

I would include under the "art" rubric the spiritual quality. Regardless of how adept this or any other introductions to the Psalms may be, it cannot equip the reader with the spiritual quality necessary to understand and appreciate the Psalms. That too is the gift of God for which every reader should pray. Unless he or she acquires that quality, no set of interpretive methods, regardless of how erudite it may be, or how well informed on the critical literature, will be adequate. The work of God's Spirit is absolutely necessary for the task that lies ahead of the reader of this book. "The man without the Spirit does not accept the things that come from the Spirit of God, for they are foolishness to him, and he cannot understand them, because they are spiritually discerned" (1 Cor 2:14). This book cannot provide that quality. It can only call attention to the need for it.

There is another factor, aside from the scientific and artistic aspects, that will facilitate the reader's way into a meaningful encounter with the Psalms, the dual factor of experience and age. Experience and age are obviously related but are not synonymous. Some of the experiences of the psalmists will leave readers who have not walked through those places of life unaffected. There is an incarnational requirement that goes along with any study of the Psalms. One has to have "been there" to comprehend fully how that experience has affected the psalmist and how the psalm thus speaks to the reader. My first introduction to the Psalms in an academic setting was in graduate school in a class taught by the revered Professor Samuel Sandmel. I shall never forget the day he looked out over the class and said, "Gentlemen, you are too young to appreciate the Psalms." As my life has moved from experience to experience, as I have proceeded emotionally from valley to mountaintop and into the valley again, the Psalms have become more and more meaningful to me. I cling to them now, or, in a strange sense, they cling to me. I want to fill my memory with their words and phrases so that in the difficult moments of life I can draw upon their strength and wisdom. In my pastoral ministry I have stood by the bedside of the sick and dying and quoted the Psalms to them, or knelt by the body of a person who has just transferred to glory and recited Psalm 23, with their loved one kneeling next to me and repeating those immortal words in unison. The Psalms are for those who walk the joyful paths of life and need a word that will release their tongue and unbind their spirit to praise the God of life. The Psalms are for those who pace the corridors of suffering and sorrow and need a word to unleash their spirit which despair threatens to suffocate. Yet they are not just for the aging and dying. They are for all ages and conditions of life, even though they may not affect young people with the same force and intensity they do those of age and experience.

Having acknowledged that we cannot design a hermeneutical instrument that will satisfy all these requirements, it would nevertheless be irresponsible not to offer a program that each student and teacher may adapt for his or her own use in the interpretation of the Book of Psalms. Therefore, I offer the following practical interpretive program that may be applied in part or in whole when the reader comes to the task of interpreting the individual psalms.

Obviously there has to be some order in a proposal such as this, and I have attempted to ask some of the key questions early in the application of this method. Yet, that does not mean that the order is fixed and should be followed without deviation. The only investigative procedure that should precede all others is to determine, to the extent that is possible, the historical/cultural setting of the psalm.

Principle 1: Determine Who Is Speaking

Generally the psalmist will be speaking on his own behalf or on Israel's or God's. But God also speaks frequently in the Psalms, and the reader should be listening for a change of voice. Psalm 50, for example, begins with the psalmist's announcement that God speaks: "The Mighty One, God, the LORD, / speaks and summons the earth / from the rising of the sun to the place where it sets" (v. 1).

We know immediately that we should be listening for God's voice, and it comes first in verse 5 when he says: "Gather to me my consecrated ones, / who have made a covenant with me by sacrifice." At that point the psalm reverts to the voice of the psalmist: "And the heavens proclaim his righteousness, / for God himself is judge" (v. 6). The next voice we hear is God's again: "Hear, O my people, and I will speak, / O Israel, and I will testify against you: / I am God, your God" (v. 7).

And the divine voice continues through verse 15, when the psalmist briefly interjects with another an-

A vertical net used in Egypt to catch quail.

nouncement that God is about to speak (v. 16a). This final word from God completes the psalm (vv. 16b–23). The Asaph psalms (Pss 50, 73–83) exhibit this characteristic frequently.[38]

Principle 2: Determine if the Psalm Is Personal or Corporate

Readers should ask whether the psalmist is speaking as an individual or on Israel's behalf. This has been a controversial issue in Psalms studies since Hermann Gunkel introduced his view of the psalms as temple songs, speaking with the corporate voice of Israel. An overwhelming number of the Psalms were spoken or prayed by an individual, but there are notable examples where the community or nation speaks. A number of such examples occur in the Songs of Ascents (Pss 120–34). Psalm 124 illustrates this point. Israel celebrates the Lord's miraculous deliverance in times of peril, and this is most evident in the plural pronouns and the summons for Israel to respond:

> If the LORD had not been on our
> side—
> let Israel say—

We have escaped like a bird
> out of the fowler's snare;
> the snare has been broken,
> and we have escaped.
> Our help is in the name of the
> LORD,
> the Maker of heaven and earth.
> (vv. 1, 7–8)

Psalm 126 is another example: "When the LORD brought back the captives to Zion, / we were like men who dreamed" (v. 1). Psalm 132 is another song of the community.

Westermann has broken down his two basic categories of psalms, praise and lament, into individual lament and community lament. In the psalms of praise, he finds evidence for this distinction only in the declarative psalms of praise.

As explained above in "Reading the Psalms through the Editors' Experience," the editor(s) of the book has sometimes positioned individual psalms in a particular place to speak on behalf of Israel. In that case, the community speaks with the words of the individual, or the individual speaks on behalf of the community. So the psalm should be interpreted on both of those levels. Psalm 89, al-

Individual and Corporate Identity

The psalmist could not see himself as an individual apart from Israel. His self-identity was bound up in his participation in the community of faith. Thus, if he was delivered from his troubles and Israel was not, it would be only a partial deliverance. In our Western world, where individualism has become the defining philosophy of personhood, this insight can help us as Christians to find a proper balance between our individual self and the community of faith to which we belong. Our personal identity is only part of who we are—the community of faith in which we live and worship is another vital part, and one is incomplete without the other.

though variously typed, begins with the "I" of the psalmist, and may be called an individual lament:

I will sing of the LORD's great love
forever;
with my mouth I will make your
faithfulness known through all
generations.
I will declare that your love stands
firm forever,
that you established your faithfulness in heaven itself. (vv. 1–2)

Then immediately the poet moves into his long and impassioned consideration of the Lord's covenant with David and its ostensible failure. Obviously the psalmist's concern about the Davidic covenant makes his subject matter a national concern as well. In verse 19 he clearly makes this transition from a personal concern over the matter to a national concern by reference to the Lord's "faithful people":

Once you spoke in a vision,
to your faithful people you said:
"I have bestowed strength on a
warrior;
I have exalted a young man
from among the people.
I have found David my servant;
with my sacred oil I have
anointed him." (vv. 19–20)

If the psalm is an individual lament, as I have suggested, then the psalmist

clearly enlarges his concern to include the community. We can already see the transition in the plural pronoun "our": "our horn" (v. 17), "our shield," "our king" (v. 18).

There are a few instances when the psalmist prays a very personal prayer and then appeals to God on behalf of the community. This is the case with Psalm 25, which is an individual lament, but David closes the psalm with a prayer for Israel, raising the prayer to that of a community intercession: "Redeem Israel, O God, / from all their troubles!" (v. 22). In a similar way, Psalm 131, an individual prayer, closes with a summons to Israel: "O Israel, put your hope in the LORD / both now and forevermore" (v. 3).

Psalm 51, an individual lament, is another example of this balance between the individual and the corporate perspective. After David has confessed his sin against God and pleaded for his forgiveness, he prays that God may build up Jerusalem. It is understandable that David's relationship to Jerusalem was personal—he captured it from the Jebusites and made it his political and religious capital—but this prayer for the welfare of Jerusalem at the end of a very personal psalm comes as a bit of a surprise. One solution is to consider Psalm 51:18–19 as a later addition to the psalm, intended to "correct" the view of sacrifice stated in verses 16 and 17:

You do not delight in sacrifice, or I
would bring it;
you do not take pleasure in
burnt offerings.
The sacrifices of God are a broken
spirit;
a broken and contrite heart,
O God, you will not despise.

But it seems curious that a later would-be psalmist should add such a disparate note to this deeply personal confession:

In your good pleasure make Zion
prosper;
build up the walls of Jerusalem.

Then there will be righteous sacrifices,
whole burnt offerings to delight
you;
then bulls will be offered on your
altar. (vv. 18–19)

If he intended to inject a corrective
word, he did not succeed, because the
last two verses of the psalm involve
the *assumption* that sacrifice is normative in Jerusalem. They are not a defense of the traditional view of sacrifice or a counterstatement to verses
16 and 17. While David's plea is a diversion in one direction, it fits quite
well the view that his individual
identity is tied into the welfare of
Jerusalem, and his personal restoration will be incomplete if Zion does
not prosper.

In summary, the content and
meaning of the Psalms are reapplied
in the Psalter itself, especially from an
individual to a corporate application.
Therefore, our reapplication of them
to our own individual and corporate
circumstances is justified by the interpretive history within the Psalter.

Principle 3: Determine for What Purpose the Psalm Was Written

Occasionally the historical titles
may help us determine the purpose
for which the psalmist wrote. For example, Psalm 51 has the title "A
psalm of David. When the prophet
Nathan came to him after David had
committed adultery with Bath-
sheba." Even though some scholars
do not take this note seriously, it provides a setting in which the meaning
of the psalm is easy to grasp. While I
would not insist that the historical titles necessarily belong to the time of
the psalm's composition, this one
very well could. In that setting, and
against the background of 2 Samuel
11–12, the reader can grasp the meaning of this psalm quite readily.
David's tragic experience gives it
flesh and blood. It incarnates Psalm
51 in a story that illustrates human
sin and divine forgiveness.

The historical setting for most
psalms, however, is not as easy as
this one. The reader is left to deter-

mine the historical/cultural circumstances on the basis of internal information. A good place to start is to ask
the question, What is the problem?
Was it the psalmist's enemies, or
some illness, or a theological issue
that moved him to write the poem?
When the reader has answered this
question, then the next step is to ask
how the psalmist resolved the problem. Did he see his problem as
emerging from the divine plan, to the
extent that his problem was basically
God's problem? That is the dilemma
Samuel found himself in when Israel
demanded a king. The Lord put it in
perspective when he said, "It is not
you they have rejected, but they have
rejected me as their king" (1 Sm 8:7).

In Psalm 69, an imprecatory
psalm, David lays out the abuse his
enemies have perpetrated against
him, and then he puts it in the context
of God's larger plan: "For I endure
scorn *for your sake,* / and shame covers my face" (v. 7; emphasis added).

But David cannot leave the matter
there. Rather he is compelled, rightly
or wrongly, to put the offense in the
context of divine judgment and describe a program of retribution. It
may be his view of what God's punishment would look like when it
came. Or it is possible that David's
heart had turned vindictive toward
his enemies.[39] His two ways of solv-
ing the problem were: (1) recognizing
his suffering to be for God's sake, so
he should not be so much concerned
about vindication, since God will
take care of that; (2) praying that God
will punish them for their ill-treatment of him. These two ways seem
contradictory, unless, of course,
David's description is nothing more
than that and not a prayer that God
will obliterate them. Of course, even
if David was merely turning the matter over to God's sense of judgment
and fairness, it would certainly have
been to his credit if he had prayed for
their salvation. But then we should
not demand that the Old Testament
resolve theological issues in the same
way the New Testament does. While
the Old Testament contains the basic
gospel, we have to admit that pray-

ing for our enemies is not one of its theological principles, although it comes close (see Ex 23:4–5).

Principle 4: Determine the Emotional Orientation of the Psalm

The reader should ascertain whether the author is praising or lamenting. The tone can waver between the two, but often one tone will be dominant. Westermann's division of the Psalms genres into two, praise and lament, set the perimeters for this hermeneutical application.

An illustration of an individual lament is Psalm 27. Nowhere does the psalmist burst forth in praise, but he sustains the lament throughout the poem. Yet the last two verses express his confidence that the Lord has heard him:

> I am still confident of this:
> I will see the goodness of the
> LORD
> in the land of the living.
> Wait for the LORD;
> be strong and take heart
> and wait for the LORD. (vv. 13–
> 14)

Psalm 124 represents a psalm of praise from beginning to end of this short poem. It is the what-if psalm, which reflects upon the horrible thought, "What if the Lord had not delivered us from our enemies!" But it is the "what if" with an exclamation point, not a question mark. Salvation is an accomplished fact, and there is no reason to wonder about the what-ifs of history that never materialized. Rather there is every reason to declare, "Our help is in the name of the LORD, / the Maker of heaven and earth" (v. 8).

An example of a psalm that combines lament and praise is Psalm 13. After a prayer in which David asked the Lord how long he would forget him (vv. 1–2), followed by a petition that God would deliver him out of his crisis, he breaks into a stanza of praise:

> But I trust in your unfailing love;
> my heart rejoices in your salvation.
> I will sing to the LORD,
> for he has been good to me. (vv. 5–6)

The sum of the matter is that, when we interpret the Psalms, it makes a lot of difference whether the mode of the psalmist is lament or praise, or a combination of the two. Even if it is lament alone with a vow to praise or an expression of confidence in the Lord's faithfulness, then that lament has no fixed edges but flows in the direction of praise.

It should not be outside the bounds of Christian piety to ask whether the psalmists were not sometimes angry with God or angry with their enemies. In that case, the reader of the Psalms must allow that perspective to come into the picture. An example of this outside the Psalter is the speeches of Elihu in Job 32–37. The writer of Job clues readers in on how to read the Elihu speeches by informing them three times that Elihu was angry (Jb 32:2, 3, 5). I suggest he intended that the poem be read with that in mind. The interpretive implications are that one need not take some of the things Elihu said entirely seriously because he was angry. One common explanation for the fact that Job does not answer Elihu is that the Elihu speeches were a later addition to the book. However, to defend the integrity of the book, one might also ask if Job did not answer because Elihu was an angry young man and in his better moments would not have spoken quite so bluntly. In view of the Lord's commendation of Job at the end (Jb 42:7), the interpreter of Job can hardly ignore the fact the Lord overlooked a lot of angry words from Job too. The imprecatory psalms (Pss 35, 69, 109) can be read with this perspective, even though this perspective alone is probably not sufficient to explain them.[40]

Principle 5: Determine the Genre of the Psalm if Possible

We have already said a lot about genre but should add here that genre is not the hermeneutical panacea for understanding the Psalms. In fact, paying too much attention to genre may become an obstruction to giving to the individuality of the psalm the kind of attention that it deserves. Having said that, however, genre can be a helpful hermeneutical application. It certainly should not be neglected, even though it ought not to become the item of first importance in interpreting the Psalms. Content is the primary concern of the reader of the Psalter. Everything else is secondary. But then it immediately follows that the interpretation of content depends on many other interpretive factors, one of which is genre.

In our discussion above we have laid out Westermann's two basic categories of praise and lament as foundational to an interpretation of the individual psalms. However, as will become clear in our discussion of the Psalms in part 3, there are other helpful ways of categorizing the psalms. Westermann's approach follows the emphasis of the form-critical school on *form*, but *content* is basic, and we should keep this in mind as we study the Psalms under the rubric of genre.

When we recognize that a psalm is a lament, that will affect the way we approach it. If it is an individual lament, then we should take Westermann's discussion of the form of this psalm into account and look for the constituent parts:

- address, with a cry for help and/or turning to God
- lament, with its three common subjects: God, I (the psalmist), and the enemies
- confession of trust
- petition, that God will be favorable or for God to intervene
- assurance that the psalmist was heard
- vow of praise
- praise of God (when the petition has been answered)[41]

Because the psalmists did not have a list of these items before them, which rather has been constructed on the basis of the psalms, we need not expect to find every single component in every single individual lament. Yet the fact that it is possible to identify common elements in this genre is quite helpful.

Some psalms may exhibit characteristics of more than one genre. We have already made this point above by observing that praise and lament can be combined in a single psalm. This observation may also apply to those psalms which are classified by form *and* content. For example, the imprecatory psalms are generally classified as individual laments, but the additional classification of these psalms as "imprecatory" groups them together under the rubric of content. It cues us into the fact that they share a certain perspective on the world and life, that they have their origin in life's crucible of suffering, and that, for the most part, the psalmist is innocent. The most obvious connotation of the "imprecatory" classification is that the psalmist engages in cursing his enemies or praying that God will curse them, introducing a theological snarl in the interpretation of these psalms.

Principle 6: Determine if There Is a Refrain or Recurring Words and Phrases

Examine the preceding and following psalms to see if the same refrain or words and phrases occur. The recurrence of a refrain is obvious in Psalms 42 and 43:

> Why are you downcast, O my soul?
> Why so disturbed within me?
> Put your hope in God,
> for I will yet praise him,
> my Savior and my God. (42:5, 11; 43:5)

This, of course, is one of the reasons why these two psalms are considered to be a single psalm. This refrain gives a general emotional perspective to the psalm: the psalmist is depressed about something, and the psalm informs us that the problem is that he has been hindered from going to the sanctuary.

Psalm 8 begins and ends with a refrain and puts the psalm into the frame of praise and wonderment: "O

LORD, our Lord, / how majestic is your name in all the earth!"

In our discussion of Psalms 1 and 2, we point to the common words in both of these psalms, suggesting that this was the way the poet of Psalm 1 stitched them together as he put the finishing touches on the Psalter. By this he outlined the contrast between that person who *meditates* on the law of the Lord day and night and that person on the opposite end of the theological spectrum who *conspires* (the two words are the same in Hebrew) against the Lord. If one does not see the contrast, the major impact of these two psalms is lost, at least the impact which the editor intended by putting them together. This means that the message which arises from the juxtaposition of certain psalms is also part of the message of the book and should not be ignored.

This set of interpretive principles is not by any means exhaustive. Rather it is intended as a guide to lead the reader to encounter the Psalms in a systematic way. But as pointed out above, if the Holy Spirit does not supply that edge which no literary or critical method can provide, then the task is woefully incomplete.

Key Terms

parallelism
unit
stich or colon
strophe
chiasm
typology

Study Questions

1. Parallelism is integral to the form of Hebrew poetry. How does this literary device lend itself to sustained thought? Describe the general categories of synonymous and antithetic parallelism and give an example of each.

2. What are the five basic units of Hebrew poetry? Describe them using examples.

3. How did the editor(s) of the final collection of the Psalms deftly apply prior psalms to the national crisis at hand? How does this lend credence to a Christian paradigmatic method of interpreting the Psalms?

4. How does typology differ from allegory? Give three helpful rules for interpreting the Psalms messianically.

5. What are the six practical interpretive principles outlined in this chapter? What is the one element that is crucial to correct understanding?

3 The Seams of the Garment of Praise

The Structure of the Book

Objectives

After reading this chapter, you should be able to
1. Discuss the current thinking on the shaping of the book.
2. Understand the context for interpreting the book as a whole.

The Five Books of the Psalter

The *Midrash on the Psalms*, codified in the ninth century A.D., attests to this fivefold division and draws an analogy to the five books of the Torah. While we cannot be certain when this division was introduced, it was very likely an early editorial feature of the book, since the divisions are quite obvious by the concluding doxologies of each book:

Book 1—Psalms 1–41
    Concluding doxology: 41:13
Book 2—Psalms 42–72
    Concluding doxology: 72:18–19
Book 3—Psalms 73–89
    Concluding doxology: 89:52
Book 4—Psalms 90–106
    Concluding doxology: 106:48
Book 5—Psalms 107–50
    Concluding doxologies: 146–50

There is some disagreement over whether these doxologies were part of the psalms themselves (except, of course, the five psalms that conclude Book 5) or whether the editor added them as an appropriate conclusion to each book. Craigie prefers the latter position,[1] and so does Wilson.[2]

1. Peter C. Craigie, *Psalms 1–50*, Word Biblical Commentary, vol. 19 (Waco: Word, 1983), 30–31.
2. Gerald H. Wilson, *The Editing of the Hebrew Psalter*, SBL Dissertation Series 76 (Chico, Calif.: Scholars, 1985), 157.

Torah psalms

The diverse nature of the Book of Psalms, with its multiple authorship, numerous literary types, assorted content, and long history of compilation, poses a challenge for the interpreter of this book. This list points to a complex history of composition. In view of this, we need to ask the question, Is there evidence of the initial and intermediate stages of the editorial shaping of the book? Further, what can we say about how the book came together in its final form? Some firm data can be put forward to answer both of these questions, but the task of reconstructing a process so complex as this one is formidable indeed. In recent years, scholarship has tended to distinguish the compilation of Books 1–3 from that of Books 4–5. The following discus-

sion presupposes the validity of this approach.

The Fivefold Division of the Psalter

As one does research in the Bible, it is generally a good hermeneutical principle to begin with the obvious, a principle that is too often ignored because we consider the obvious too common to be profound. The path to the profound, however, is sometimes, if not frequently, paved with the obvious. That observation brings us to the fivefold division of the Book of Psalms. While this division is not noted in the Masoretic version of the Hebrew Bible, it is attested in the Jewish literature, and all of the modern translations note this division.[1] Regardless of when this feature was introduced into the book, it is definitely a part of the editorial shaping, and the compilation of the book cannot be understood apart from it.

Further, given the introductory emphasis on the Torah in Psalm 1 (and the other **Torah psalms**, 19 and 119),[2] the fivefold division is quite likely, following the *Midrash on the Psalms*, an intentional allusion to the fivefold division of the Torah or the Law (Pentateuch). When we add to that also the fact that other psalms reinforce the centrality of the law (37:30–31; 40:8; 78:1, 5, 10), then we have a theological statement about the place of the law in Israel's religion written into the structure of the Book of Psalms. This statement ought not be understood, however, as the main thrust of the book, but one among others, such as the kingship of Yahweh, the praise of God, and so on. Thus, the fivefold division is a deliberate editorial feature designed to emphasize the central place of the law (Torah) in Israel's faith. It may very well be true that this design was not initially part of the micro-editorial plan, nor even a conscious part of the first phase of the shaping of the book. Yet, most likely, the editor(s) of the second and final stage of the book (Books 4–5) intentionally imposed a fivefold division in order to emphasize the centrality of the Torah. The potential for this emphasis was already implicit in the collection, and he merely gave it formal recognition.[3] The Torah is thus the encompassing principle of faith in the Psalter or the outline of Hebrew piety. It is the broad theological context within which all of the other emphases can be understood. So we might say, with some exaggeration, of course, but with some justification nevertheless, that all the book contains is embodied in the Torah, much like the rabbinic view that all the prophets preached was found in the Torah. That was quite likely the point of Psalm 119, an acrostic poem on the Torah that exhausts the Hebrew alphabet to enunciate the meaning of the law. All the letters of the alphabet were exploited, one by one, to express the indescribable depth of the law. To survey the entire alphabet was a symbolic way of exhausting human language to say the unutterably deep things of the soul.

The Editorial Seams of the Book: Books 1–3 (Pss 1–89)

When one looks for the stress lines where evidence of the editorial process is visible, it is only natural to look at the beginning and ending of the five books of the Psalter. Speaking generally, Books 1–3 represent the first major edition of the book on the macro-level, and Books 4–5 represent the second and final edition of the macro-shaping of the book as we know it.[4] Obviously, however, the editorial process must be viewed in yet smaller increments.

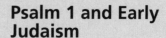

Psalm 1 and Early Judaism

If we give the name "Hebrew faith" to the Old Testament religion of Israel prior to and during the exile, we should assign Psalm 1 to the early age of Judaism, that is, somewhere between the return from exile (about 538 B.C.) and the time of Ben Sirah (about 190 B.C.), when the Torah had clearly come to be recognized as the substance of Israel's theology.

Book 1 (Pss 1–41)

Book 1 (Pss 1–41) is introduced by Psalms 1–2. In fact, Psalm 1 seems to have been put in place as an introduction to the final edition of the book (Pss 1–150), while Psalm 2 was perhaps an introduction to the first macro-edition of the Psalter (Bks. 1–3 or Pss 2–89). Psalm 1 gives evidence of a theology that had settled on the Torah as the spiritual nerve center of the Hebrew faith. Yet, despite the probability that the two psalms were put in place at different times, their literary form and theological emphases are quite compatible.

As to form, we first observe that the use of "blessed" (*'ashre*) in 1:1 and 2:12 forms an *inclusio*, binding these two psalms into a literary unity. Second, the two psalms introduce two different kinds of "meditating." In 1:2 the person who "meditates" (Hebrew *hagah*) on the law is the paragon of faith, while in 2:1 the same word is used of the pagan nations in quite a different sense, that of "conspiring" against the Lord. Third, the contrast of the *way* of the righteous and the *way* of the wicked, which concludes Psalm 1 (v. 6), leads into the warning of 2:11–12 that Israel take heed lest they be destroyed in their *way*,

> Serve the LORD with fear
>   and rejoice with trembling.
> Kiss the Son, lest he be angry
>   and you be destroyed in your way.

This admonition is the mark of both prophetic and wisdom theology. It was written on the doorposts of ancient Israel's spiritual habitat, and this word of judgment characteristically accompanied the word of grace. The verbal escort of the noun *way* in Psalms 1 and 2 is the same word (*'bd*):

- the way of the wicked *will perish* (1:16),
- lest he be angry and you *be destroyed* in your way (2:12).

The contrast set up in Psalm 1 is thus completed with climactic finality in Psalm 2. The correspondences of these two psalms are obviously intentional rather than coincidental. Even though the two psalms may have served a different function—Psalm 2 introducing the first macro-edition of the book (2–89), and Psalm 1 introducing the final edition of the book (1–150)—the editor who installed Psalm 1 was a literary tailor of fine expertise, and he stitched these two psalms together masterfully.

Psalm 2 certainly carries the theme of the exilic and postexilic prophets as they pondered the divine judgment brought upon Israel by Assyria and Babylonia; the ostensible prosperity of these enemy powers made them raise anew the question of when the Lord would bring judgment on Israel's enemies as he had brought it upon Israel.[5] Here is that theme inscribed on the lintel of Israel's sanctuary of praise and lament.

Of course, the central focus on the Torah in Psalm 1 puts the history and life of Israel in focus:

Blessed is the man
who does not walk in the counsel of the wicked
or stand in the way of sinners
or sit in the seat of mockers.
But his delight is in the law of the Lord,
and on his law he meditates day and night. (vv. 1–2)

That is the beginning word of faith, and while a lot more can be said, this statement is a summary of it all. *Meditating* (i.e., reflecting) on the Torah and *meditating* (conspiring) against the Lord and his Anointed One represent the two opposite ways of life that wisdom drew out so clearly. While we do not want to overstate the case, here is an abstract of Hebrew religion as it was represented primarily in the Torah, and as it came to be restated in the Prophets and wisdom literature.

A word should also be said about the messianic nature of Psalms 2 and 89, that is, the opening and closing psalms of this macro-collection. If, as we have suggested, Psalm 2 began the early macro-collection (Bks. 1–3 or Pss 2–89), and Psalm 1 belonged to the final macro-collection (the addition of Books 4–5 to Books 1–3), then we have messianic overtones in the opening and closing psalms of this major edition of the book (2 and 89).[6] While some scholars classify Psalm 2 as a *royal* or a *coronation* psalm,[7] written for the coronation of one of Israel's kings during the monarchy (ca. 1050–586 B.C.), it may very well belong to the exilic era when the monarchy had failed and its future was much in doubt. During that time, the messianic hope assumed renewed vitality. Psalm 2 deals with the rebellion of the nations against the Lord and his anointed king (vv. 1–3), while the Lord knows all along that their power moves are mere child's play because he himself has established Israel's king and decreed that his appointed monarch should rule over the nations (vv. 4–9). Finally, the psalm issues a word of warning to the rebellious kings of the earth (v. 10) and a strong word of admonition that Israel should fear the Lord and take refuge in him (vv. 11–12).[8] This is a precise description of Israel's dilemma after the destruction of Jerusalem in 586 B.C. The question "why?" in verse 1 is the question of the prophets (e.g., Habakkuk) who inquired into the time when Yahweh would punish those nations who perpetrated evil against his people. It seems quite likely, therefore, that Psalm 2 arises out of the time when the editing of Books 1–3 took place, quite likely somewhere between the fall of Jerusalem in 586 and the fall of Babylon in 539 B.C.[9] I am inclined to believe that the messianism of Psalm 2 belongs to the initial composition of the psalm and not to a later period of interpretation. That simply means that the psalmist wrote this poem out of the messianic hope that sustained him.

Even Psalm 72 at the end of Book 2 already points the reader in the direction of the savior-king modeled after the figure of Solomon. He will reign during a time when "the righteous will flourish" (v. 7), and the kings of the earth will pay homage to him:

> The kings of Tarshish and of dis-
> tant shores
> will bring tribute to him;
> the kings of Sheba and Seba
> will present him gifts.
> All kings will bow down to him
> and all nations will serve him.
> (vv. 10–11)

Psalm 2 has laid out the messianic program for this Ruler. In fact, the Lord laughs at those kings who are so presumptuous as to think that they can overpower the Lord's Anointed One (vv. 2–4). The Lord has installed his king on Zion, and the nations are his for the asking:

> "I have installed my King
> on Zion, my holy hill."
> I will proclaim the decree of the
> LORD:
> He said to me, "You are my Son;
> today I have become your
> Father.
> Ask of me,
> and I will make the nations your
> inheritance,
> the ends of the earth your
> possession.
> You will rule them with an iron
> scepter;
> you will dash them to pieces
> like pottery." (vv. 6–9)

The other end of this early macro-collection (Pss 2–89) is marked by Psalm 89, another royal psalm, in which the Lord's covenant with David (2 Sm 7) comes clearly into view. The thrust of this poem is to affirm the Davidic covenant (Ps

---

The Opening Psalm of Book 2

Judging from the form of Psalms 42 and 43, even though they are two separate psalms in the Hebrew text and English translations, the recurring refrain (42:5, 11; 43:5) would suggest they were originally a single psalm. Their form is an alternation between lament and refrain, with a slight variation in Psalm 43:

> 42:2–6 (a) Lament (vv. 2–5)
> (b) *Refrain* (v. 6)
> 42:7–12 (a) Lament (vv. 7–11)
> (b) *Refrain* (vv. 12)
> 43:1–5 (a) Prayer (vv. 1–4)
> (b) *Refrain* (v. 5)[1]

1. Peter C. Craigie, *Psalms 1–50*, Word Biblical Commentary, vol. 19 (Waco: Word, 1983), 325.

89:3–4, 19–37) and ask why the Lord has breached his promises to David (vv. 38–45). Of much interest, as was the case with Psalm 2, is the psalmist's inquiry into how long this intolerable contradiction would last (vv. 46–51). As already observed, this is the question that arose among the prophets of the late preexilic and exilic eras. They believed that, although Yahweh had used the nations as instruments of his wrath against Israel, he would in the course of time punish those nations also. Ezekiel, for example, after having announced the punitive day of the Lord for Judah (chs. 1–24), turned to the nations and announced that their day, too, was coming. In chapters 25–32 he broke the confederation of nations down into its individual members and pronounced judgment upon them one by one. That is the event that Haggai (520 B.C.) also saw in the offing: "'In a little while I will once more shake the heavens and the earth, the sea and the dry land. I will shake all nations, and the desired of all nations will come, and I will fill this house with glory,' says the LORD Almighty" (Hg 2:6b–7).

Korah psalms

Maskil

The term *maskil* occurs in seventeen psalms of the Psalter, thirteen times in the superscription where it designates a type of psalm: 32, 42, 44, 45, 52, 53, 54, 55, 74, 78, 88, 89, 142. It also occurs in that sense in the body of Psalm 47 (v. 7). Three times the participle is used: 14:2/ 53:3 (duplicate psalms) and 41:2. The word comes from the Hebrew verb *skl*, which means "to make wise, instruct, teach," which may suggest a "didactic psalm." Yet this understanding of the word does not always seem appropriate.[1]

1. Peter C. Craigie, *Psalms 1–50*, Word Biblical Commentary, vol. 19 (Waco: Word, 1983), 264.

The Lord's "Anointed" (*mashiakh*) is the focus of both Psalms 2 (v. 2) and 89 (vv. 38, 51). While the primary reference was to Israel's kings, the forward thrust, as Leopold Sabourin calls it, was the messianic hope.[10] We might further say that the terms of this psalm were so outrageously expectant that only the Messiah could fulfill them.[11] Psalm 2 presents the Lord's decree: "You are my Son; / today I have become your Father" (v. 7b). And Psalm 89:26 records the king's response: "You are my Father, / my God, the Rock my Savior."

After having considered the outside seams of the collection (Bks. 1–3), we should take a look at the intermediate seams, those that conclude and begin the three component collections of this macro-psalter (Pss 2–89). We will look particularly at Psalm 41, the last psalm of Book 1, and the opening of Book 2 with the **Korah psalms** (42–49), and conclude this discussion with further considerations of Psalm 72, the final psalm of Book 2, and its relationship to Psalm 73, the first psalm of Book 3.

Just as Psalms 1 and 2 have an interlocking relationship, even though they may not belong to the same editorial stage, Psalm 41, which concludes Book 1, and the opening

psalms of Book 2 (42–43) form a double seam which binds these two books together.

Psalm 41 revisits the scene of Israel's enemies and promises security in the land to that person who regards the weak (v. 2). The life of piety, commended in Psalm 1 and extolled at the end of Psalm 2 (v. 12), is condensed to personal trust in the Lord to deliver the psalmist from his sickness and thus to vindicate him before his enemies' taunting reproach (vv. 2, 5–9). The security concerns that come into focus in Psalm 2 are echoed again in Psalm 41. The psalm concludes with a doxology: "Praise be to the LORD, the God of Israel, / from everlasting to everlasting. / Amen and Amen" (v. 13).

Perhaps even more important is how this concluding psalm interlocks with the opening psalms of Book 2 (42–43). While Psalm 41 is not called a *maskil* as are Psalms 42, 44, and 45, the word nevertheless appears as a participle in 41:1 ("who has regard"). Moreover, David's hope in Psalm 41:12 is that the Lord would "set me in your presence forever," in contrast to the psalmist of 42 and 43, who, restricted from appearing in the temple, asks when that time would come again (42:2). He, too, like David in Psalm 41, is taunted by his enemies, who deride him with the question, "Where is your God?" (42:3). Further, again like David in Psalm 41, he prays that God might vindicate him before his enemies (43:1–4).

Book 2 (Pss 42–72)

A collection of psalms by the "sons of Korah" (42–49) heads up Book 2. The theme of the nations and their ill-treatment of Israel continues in Psalm 44, where the psalmist maintains that Israel had done nothing to deserve the national humiliation it had suffered at the hands of the nations (44:17–22). Further, throughout the Korah psalms are woven the threads of admiration for the monarchy (45), Yahweh's reign over the nations of the world as sovereign King (45:6; 46:8–10; 47), and the security of Jerusalem, where the great King of

Korah and Asaph Psalms

Korah, Asaph, Heman, and Ethan are all associated with the service and music of the sanctuary in David's reign. During Ezra and Nehemiah's time (fifth century B.C.), the temple singers were still called the "sons of Asaph." In view of the long and continued service of these temple servants, we cannot be absolutely sure when these psalms were composed, but whether they were written in the time of David or as late as Ezra, they are still Davidic associates, and that seems to reinforce the Davidic nature of these collections.

	David	Korah	Asaph
Book 1	3–41		
Book 2	51–65; 68–70	42–49	50
Book 3	86	84–85; 87–88	73–83

Other references to Korah, Asaph, Heman, and Ethan are: 1 Chronicles 15:17, 19; 16:5, 7, 37; 25:1, 6; 26:1; 2 Chronicles 5:12; 29:30; 35:15; Ezra 2:41; 3:10; Nehemiah 7:44; 11:22; 12:46.

David and the Psalms

Davidic authorship of the Psalms has been much disputed in the last two centuries of biblical scholarship. The challenge arose partly from the view that Israelite religion developed from the simple to the complex. Thus, the deep religious understanding of the psalms, it was believed, could not have been characteristic of worshipers so early in Israel's history as David's time, that is, 1011–971 B.C. This is not the assumption underlying this study, however. David's deep faith in God is attested both in the Books of Samuel and in the Psalter, and to relegate this quality of faith to a later age is both artificial and contrary to the historical facts.

the universe has chosen to dwell (Pss 46 and 48). These interwoven themes are the template on which the Korah psalms are formed.

J. Clinton McCann has proposed that the Korah psalms (42–49) set the tone in which the rest of Book 2 is to be read.[12] Although the balance of the book (50–72) is composed largely of personal psalms, the national themes that are interwoven with the personal emphases of Psalms 42–49 legitimize a community reading of these psalms in the postexilic period in order to help Israel deal with the exile and dispersion that had devastated the nation and disoriented their faith.[13] The final composition of Book 2 itself, however, may not have been shaped so much by a single national event as by a conglomeration of such events. The compositional prospectus reflects a general national consciousness of Israel's encounter with the nations, particularly as compared with the editorial shape of Book 3 (Pss 73–89), which reveals the histor-

ical lines of the destruction of Jerusalem in 586 B.C. and the end of the Davidic dynasty.

Psalm 72 concludes Book 2 with a doxology (v. 19) and a final note, "This concludes the prayers of David son of Jesse" (v. 20). The finality of this subscription mirrors a stage in the editorial process. It is quite obvious that at some point Psalm 72 concluded a mini-collection of the psalms that may have stood alone (perhaps 42–72). The logical inference is that this collection was added to Book 1 (Pss 2–41) and constituted an early stage of the macro-collection of Books 1–3 (Pss 2–89). I suggest that Books 1 and 2 were edited sometime in the preexilic period and later became the basis of the first macro-edition (Pss 2–89) in the exilic period.

While the colophon (72:20) ascribes these prayers to David, they were not all written by him. The Korah psalms are the most obvious evidence of that. The question we should ask, then, in regard to the authorship of Psalm 72, is whether the superscription should be read "of Solomon," thus attributing to him authorship, or "to Solomon," thus a psalm of David written to his son, or

63

Asaph psalms

Davidic psalms

even "concerning Solomon," which would imply that another author besides David could have written it. Based on the end note, which implies that this too is a psalm of David ("This concludes the prayers of David son of Jesse"), the editor may have considered it to be a psalm of David written to Solomon.[14]

Due to its attention to the kingship, the psalm is generally classified as a royal psalm. Gerald Wilson pays special attention to this fact and points out that at the seams of Books 1–3 are three royal psalms, Psalms 2, 41, and 72.[15] That would imply that the editor of Books 1–3 (Pss 2–89) had an interest in the monarchy and tried to fit his edition of this book with a framework that would highlight this institution and renew interest in its future. Psalm 72 incorporates three petitions on the king's behalf:

- that the king might rule justly (vv. 1–2, 4),
- that his dominion might be secure from his enemies (vv. 8–11),
- that he might live long and be blessed (vv. 5, 15, 17).[16]

It is moving to think that this might be a prayer that David prayed for his son Solomon.

Book 3 (Pss 73–89)

The lead collection in Book 3 (Pss 73–89) is a series of eleven **Asaph psalms** (73–83). The last psalm of Book 2 (72) and the first of Book 3, the first Asaph psalm, form a seam sewn together with two different threads, one idealizing Israel's king (72) and the other reflecting upon the injustice of the world (73). It does not seem to be coincidental that the end of the **Davidic psalms** (72) is a prayer for the monarchy, in the theological vein of Solomon's prayer in 1 Kings 3:6–14 ("Endow the king with your justice, O God," 72:1; compare 1 Kgs 3:11). The other half of the seam, Psalm 73, deals with the prosperity of the wicked much like Psalm 49, the concluding Korah psalm of Book 2. The

combination of the king's justice in Psalm 72 and the injustice of the wicked in Psalm 73 is a perfect blend of theological colors for composing the seam of Books 2 and 3.

Marvin Tate reviews many of the attempts to classify this psalm and suggests it is a "reflective testimony."[17] The problem scholars have with putting a label on Psalm 73 reflects the fact that many of the psalms resist classification. Indeed, if the psalmists had been working with our literary categories, they might have been like the proverbial octopus, wondering which foot to put forward first. There is certainly some validity to the critical categories proposed by modern scholarship, but we should be aware that the psalmists themselves were concerned more with subject matter than form. They were also form-conscious, but not nearly so much as modern scholarship has led us to believe. They could mix genres without any sense of violating genre categories. The problem that Psalm 73 deals with, the prosperity of the wicked, is certainly the object of reflection in the wisdom literature, especially in the Book of Job. Thus a wisdom psalm is as helpful a classification as we can settle upon, although Gunkel identified it both as a wisdom psalm (also Kraus) and an individual psalm of lament (also Westermann).[18]

While the prosperity of the wicked on a personal level was a problem that exercised the wisdom writers, the prophets viewed this problem on an international level. That is the vein in which Habakkuk was thinking when he contemplated the success and prosperity of the Chaldeans in the late seventh century B.C.:

> Therefore he sacrifices to his net
>   and burns incense to his
>   dragnet,
> for by his net he lives in luxury
>   and enjoys the choicest food.
> Is he to keep on emptying his net,
>   destroying nations without
>   mercy? (Hb 1:16–17)

Psalm 73 is another example of how the psalms, though often spoken out of personal grief and misfortune, can be understood on a national scale. While it was written as a personal reflection on the prosperity of the wicked, Psalm 73, with the monarchical focus of Psalm 72, looks in the direction of the national crisis of the Judeans in 586 B.C. and sets that crisis in the context of the divine presence the psalmist had experienced in the sanctuary (73:17). The nationalizing of the problem can be further seen in the fact that the exile comes into focus in the community laments of Psalms 74, 79, 80, 83, 85:1–8, and 89:39–52.[19] Even though the sanctuary was no longer standing as it was when the psalm was originally composed, the truth of the psalm was still powerful and comforting: the mental anguish of the psalmist over the prosperity of the wicked (now the success and wealth of the ungodly Chaldeans) was assuaged in the worship of God.

Summary

When we look at the seams where the first macro-collection (Pss 2–89) was pieced together, we see the tension and hopes of Israel's history written into the collection. On the editorial level, Psalms 2 and 89 ponder the fate of Israel's national enemies, Assyria and Babylonia, who had wrought havoc on God's people. When would he deal with *their* ungodly character? This is the same question that the prophets of the late preexilic and exilic periods posed. We can, therefore, surmise that the compilation of the first macro-collection, Books 1–3, likely took place during the exilic period.

Psalm 41, the concluding psalm of Book 1 (Pss 1–41), reiterates the question of Israel's international insecurity, rounding off the thrust of Psalm 2 and also reinforcing the theme framed by Psalms 2 and 89. The theme of the monarchy accentuates the beginning and ending of Book 1 (Pss 2 and 41) and the end of Book 2 (Ps 72), highlighting its prospects in view of an uncertain future. Kingship was a shaky institution at best, but like the nation at large, its unfaithful-

ness to Yahweh had been thrown into sharp relief by divine forgiveness as Israel reflected on the tragic fall of Jerusalem. The Lord had inscribed his goodwill for the monarchy in the Davidic covenant, and the apparent failure of that covenant, evidenced by the fall of the Davidic dynasty to the Babylonians in 586, invoked both the question of its validity and the anticipation of its renewal, especially in the final psalm of this macro-collection (89). The revival of the nation was hardly conceivable apart from the revival of the monarchy. Yet, while kings did not become a reality again in Israel until 142 B.C., the nation *did* revive with the powerful assistance of Cyrus's famous decree (538 B.C.) and the instrument of divine sovereignty (Is 40). Isaiah spoke of the impatience of the interim generations that waited for the restoration of the nation, and he encouraged them in his magnificent language of grace:

> Even youths grow tired and weary,
>   and young men stumble and
>   fall;
> but those who hope in the LORD
>   will renew their strength.
> They will soar on wings like eagles;
>   they will run and not grow
>   weary,
>   they will walk and not be faint.
>   (Is 40:30–31)

At the same time, national revival was hardly devoid of monarchical hopes, as we see in Zechariah 4:6 and Haggai 2:20–23; and one wonders how a nation, deeply bound up in the trappings of kingship, could revive so quickly unless the hopes of a renewed monarchy breathed life into its dry bones. Thus we see a reflection of that hope written into this first macro-collection of the Psalms (Pss 2–89). Even those psalms that contemplated personal hopes and frustrations could be reread in the context of Israel's national crisis of 586 B.C. The individual heart, depressed and enlarged by the exigencies of life, became the microcosm of a nation's despair and optimism.

The Editorial Seams of the Book: Books 4–5 (Pss 90–150)

Book 4 (Pss 90–106)

We observed above that Psalm 89 affirms the Davidic covenant (vv. 3–4, 19–37) and asks why the Lord has broken his promises to David (vv. 38–45). This psalm closes Book 3 by asking Yahweh how long his wrath would continue against Israel, and what had happened to his former love and faithfulness to David (vv. 46, 49). The keen reminder at the end of the psalm makes the nations' hostility against the psalmist tantamount to hostility against the Lord:

> Remember, Lord, how your ser-
> vant has been mocked,
> how I bear in my heart the
> taunts of all the nations,
> the taunts with which *your enemies*
> have mocked, O LORD,
> with which they have mocked
> every step of your
> anointed one. (vv. 50–51;
> emphasis added)

Then Psalm 90 opens Book 4, quite appropriately, with an affirmation in the words of Moses, "the man of God," attesting to the powerful and secure refuge the Lord had been to Israel through the years. This psalm incorporates a spirit of humility and confession (v. 8), unlike Psalm 89, which cannot see through Yahweh's breach of the Davidic covenant to Israel's own failure. Psalm 90 sets divine wrath in the context of history and insists that, if necessary, they must wait a thousand years until the Lord settles the score with the nations.

It seems significant that, after Psalm 89 has introduced the failure of the Davidic covenant, Psalm 90 is a prayer of Moses, who acknowledges that the problem is Israel's failure, not the Lord's:

> You have set our iniquities before
> you,

Book 3 as a Theological Statement

According to Wilson, the major thrust of this collection is to put forth the following ideas: (1) Yahweh is king; (2) he was Israel's refuge long before the monarchy (i.e., in the Mosaic period); (3) he is still and will continue to be Israel's refuge even though the monarchy has disappeared; and (4) blessed are those who trust in him![1]

1. Gerald H. Wilson, *The Editing of the Hebrew Psalter*, SBL Dissertation Series 76 (Chico, Calif.: Scholars, 1985), 215.

> our secret sins in the light of
> your presence.
> All our days pass away under your
> wrath;
> we finish our years with a
> moan. (vv. 8–9)

While this psalm comes from a much earlier time than the exile, what more effective voice than Moses' to intercede for Israel in this time of distress (see Nm 14:13–19)? Israel, devastated and beaten down by the exile, now could hear their revered ancestor pray for them. Such intercession for Israel by this ancient worthy, of course, is accomplished by the masterful work of the compiler of this macro-collection of Psalms. His love for Israel and his deeply anchored faith in the Lord's steadfast love are legacies of his spiritual character, written in the seams and woven into the fabric of this collection.

Wilson proposes that Book 4 is the editorial "center" of the final edition of the Psalter. He believes this collection of psalms affirms the Davidic covenant. While I agree with Wilson that this is a critically important section of the Psalter, it nevertheless seems to me that the compiler of this section had another purpose, that is, to divert attention away from the Davidic covenant, which had so miserably failed, back to the Abrahamic and Mosaic covenants, especially the Mo-

Hosea's Appeal to the Abrahamic Covenant

In 1:8 Hosea indicates that the Lord was canceling his covenant with Israel: "After she had weaned Lo-Ruhamah, Gomer had another son. Then the LORD said, 'Call him Lo-Ammi, for you are not my people, and I am not your God.'" That disavowal actually reads, "you are not my people, and I am not *I AM* to you," obviously the unique name by which the Lord had reaffirmed His relationship to Israel in Moses' day (Ex 3:14). Although Israel had known that name for centuries, in Moses' day Yahweh renewed his relationship to them by revealing something more to Israel about his character. Then, once Hosea had signaled the cancellation of the Mosaic covenant, he immediately begins reassuring Israel in terms of the Abrahamic covenant, "Yet the Israelites will be like the sand on the seashore, which cannot be measured or counted" (Hos 1:10). These words allude to the Lord's covenant with Abraham (Gn 22:17). Therefore, the Lord was declaring that, even though Israel had broken the terms of the Mosaic covenant, he would not allow his relationship to fail, so he would revert to the foundation covenant he had established with Israel through Abraham.

saic. It is similar to the way Hosea, when Israel had violated the Mosaic covenant, shifted the focus from that covenant to the Abrahamic in order to establish Yahweh's continuing covenantal relationship to the rebellious kingdom of Israel (Hos 1:8–11). In fact, Moses' name appears seven times in Psalms 90–106 (90 [title]; 99:6; 103:7; 105:26; 106:16, 23, 32). The praying voice heard in Psalm 90 introduces the one man who could bring some semblance of hope to this despairing nation. In the prayer of Psalm 90, Moses, though dead, yet prays for Israel. The object of God's work through Moses is clearly stated in 105:44–45:

> He gave them the lands of the nations,
> and they fell heir to what others had toiled for—
> *that they might keep his precepts and observe his laws.* (emphasis added)

This becomes a signpost, pointing the people of Israel to the real reason God

had worked so marvelously in Israel's history: that they should keep the Torah.

This diversion of attention from the Davidic covenant, and thus from the defunct monarchy, may also be seen in the "kingship of Yahweh" theme that is highlighted in this collection (Pss 90–106). Psalms 93, 97, and 99 begin with the declaration, "The LORD reigns" (also 96:10), and the Lord is called "king" in 95:3; 98:6; and 99:4. The voice of David himself, Israel's model king, declares in 103:19: "The LORD has established his throne in heaven, / and his kingdom rules over all."

What more of a witness do the people of Israel need in order to turn their eyes from the earthly monarch to the heavenly! The crisis of 586 B.C. might be assuaged if this people could recognize that, although their earthly king no longer sits on his throne, their heavenly King is still sitting securely on his heavenly throne. Indeed, he is the true King, and he rules over all the nations, a fact of which the Israelite monarchy was merely a symbol. In the world of true reality, that is all that matters. Therefore, they should not harden their hearts as the people of Israel had done at Meribah when Moses led them and they rebelled against the Lord, a deed that was irreversible for that generation (95:7b–11). In this critical time of decision, they must learn the lesson their ancient history had taught them.

Psalms 106 and 107, like the sutured lines of Psalms 41 and 42 (the seam of Books 1 and 2), form a double seam that binds together Books 4 and 5. In fact, Psalm 106 is a historical psalm that provides an archetype of spiritual guidance in the Mosaic era. It begins and ends with "Praise the LORD" (*Halleluyah*). Significantly, Psalm 105, another historical psalm, reinforces the impact of Psalm 106 on Book 4. The subject of Psalm 105 is almost exclusively the Lord, and the poem draws out the meaning of the major theme found in verse 8: "He remembers his covenant forever, / the word he commanded, for a thousand generations." The terms of this verse remind us of the Ten Commandments, which extend God's love "to a thousand generations of those who love me and keep my commandments" (Ex 20:6). Indeed, the psalmist also knows this reason for God's giving the land of Canaan to Israel: "that they might keep his precepts / and observe his laws" (Ps 105:45).

But to put the issue in historical relief, the writer of Psalm 106 views the covenant, not from Yahweh's, but from Israel's perspective. In verse 6 he introduces the national confession from which the rest of the psalm flows: "We have sinned, even as our fathers did, / we have done wrong and acted wickedly." The psalm is nevertheless not forgetful of divine action, for the Lord's actions intervene in verses 8–12 and 40–46 to form a contrast with Israel's aberrant behavior. After a personal prayer of petition (vv. 1–5), the psalm becomes a corporate expression of sentiment, and we see an alternating pattern between Israel's acts and the Lord's:

Israel	vv. 6–7
the Lord	vv. 8–11
Israel	vv. 12–39
the Lord	vv. 40–46
Israel	v. 47

The nation is summoned to say the "Amen" to this powerful confession. Not only is this confession appropriate for the exile, but verse 46 infers that the poet was speaking directly out of the midst of the exile: "He caused them to be pitied / by all who held them captive."

Psalm 106 is a "hallelujah" psalm, beginning and ending with this imperative of praise, translated in the NIV as "Praise the LORD." In comparison, while Psalm 105 ends with "Praise the LORD," it does not begin with the imperative. Psalms 105 and 106, therefore, were an appropriate reappraisal of the covenant at a time when Israel's hope had failed. These poems propound the thesis that even though Israel had broken the covenant, Yahweh was faithfully compassionate. Relying upon that compassion, another historical miracle was yet possible. Just as he had heard their cry in Egypt (Ex 3:7), he was still listening in this new era of national distress:

> But he took note of their distress
>   when he heard their cry;
> for their sake he remembered his
>   covenant
> and out of his great love he
>   relented.
> He caused them to be pitied
>   by all who held them captive.
> Save us, O LORD our God,
>   and gather us from the nations
> that we may give thanks to your
>   holy name
> and glory in your praise.
>   (106:44–47)

Book 5 (Pss 107–50)

Psalm 107 picks up the thread of Yahweh's love (*khesed*) from Psalm 106 (v. 45): "Give thanks to the LORD, for he is good; / his love endures forever" (107:1). This psalm is a call to consider the great and enduring love of the Lord, and is reinforced by a recurring refrain: "Let them give thanks to the LORD for his unfailing love / and his wonderful deeds for men" (vv. 8, 15, 21, 31). The terms of this psalm are generic, with no references to historical persons. The wise are admonished to give heed to these things and consider the Lord's great love: "Whoever is wise, let him heed these things / and consider the great love of the LORD" (v. 43). Wilson makes the plausible suggestion that Psalm 107 is a response to the plea of the exiles in 106:47.[20]

The time of compilation for Book 5 seems to have been the exilic or post-exilic period, perhaps as late as the time of Nehemiah (ca. 444–432 B.C.). Psalm 137 with its references to the spiritual depression of the exiles likely indicates the earliest date of compilation, but it is not impossible that it could have been composed in the exilic period before the fall of Babylon in 539 B.C. Of course the psalms of a single book were not all written during that period but sometimes antedate the age of the collection by generations or even centuries.

The editor of Book 5 installed a group of Davidic psalms (Pss 138–45) in the place of honor at the end of his collection, evidently to balance the end of the book with the opening Davidic collection of Book 1. It would appear that he was now working with a macro-collection of psalms that may have consisted basically of Psalms 2–106. Erich Zenger has called attention to the correspondences among the four doxologies that occur at the end of the four books and suggested that by their terms they form a chiasm, the doxology of Book 1 corresponding to that of Book 4 (note "The LORD, the God of Israel" and "from everlasting to everlasting"), and the doxology of Book 2 corresponding to that of Book 3 (note "forever" and "Amen and Amen").

> **Book 1 (41:13)** Praise be to *the LORD, the God of Israel, / from everlasting to everlasting.* Amen and Amen.
>
> **Book 2 (72:18–19)** Praise be to the LORD God, the God of Israel, / who alone does marvelous deeds. / Praise be to his glorious name *forever;* / May the whole earth be filled with his glory. *Amen and Amen.*
>
> **Book 3 (89:52)** Praise be to the LORD *forever! Amen and Amen.*
>
> **Book 4 (106:48)** Praise be to *the LORD, the God of Israel, / from everlasting to everlasting.* / Let all the people say, "Amen!"

On the basis of this observation, as well as the content of the closing psalms themselves, Zenger submits that it is quite likely that these four books already existed as four distinct books when Book 5 was added.[21]

Since this book began with a major Davidic collection, it was most appropriate, in recognition of the psalmist *par excellence*, to conclude the book with another Davidic collection.

Assuming, as I believe we should, that Book 5 was compiled in the exilic period, or at the latest, in the early postexilic period (probably not later than the governorship of Nehemiah), the frequent reference to the psalmist's enemies and the wicked, identifiable in each of these psalms,[22] would be a most appropriate reference for a community depressed by conquest and exile. These psalms, written from David's personal perspective, could easily achieve relevance for this community when placed on the new grid of history and prayed through the experience of the exiles. As Israel waited for the Lord to bring judgment upon the nations, David prayed on their behalf: "May all the kings of the earth praise you, O LORD. . . . / Though the LORD is on high, he looks upon the lowly, / but the proud he knows from afar" (Ps 138:4a, 6).

Psalms 138–45 are all prayers to God, with only occasional direct addresses to the community. Of much importance, moreover, is the final affirmation of the Lord's faithfulness to the psalmist, and thus to Israel as it is applied to the new historical situation, and the decisive call to all creatures to praise the holy name of the Lord (145:21). At the end of Book 4 (106:48) "all the people," obviously a reference to Israel, are summoned to praise the Lord. Now, as Book 5 lays out the marvelous deeds of the Lord in returning his people from exile, this book summons "every creature" to praise the Lord (145:21). In effect, the whole world should marvel at what God has done. By placing these psalms at the end of the collection, in effect the compiler stations David, the greatest and most revered of all psalmists, in the belfry of the cathedral of praise, and from there he sends out this cantata of adoration to this humiliated and downcast community, a community on which the praise of God could work its transforming power. It is a befitting conclusion that honors the great psalmist and acclaims the majesty of his Lord. Now the stage is set for the grand finale of praise that is comprised of Psalms 146–50.

Iron fetters were often used to bind prisoners on the hands, feet, and neck.

To reinforce the power and effectiveness of the praise of God, the editor of the final edition of the book puts praise over against the formidable problem of Israel's enemies. Even though the return had begun or was past history when Book 5 was compiled, and Babylon, that enemy who had brought Judah to her knees, had fallen to Cyrus in 539 B.C., many of Israel's enemies still lived and prospered. In fact, the Lord's way of punishing Israel's enemies who had done so much violence to them, becomes, not a diatribe of wrath, but a paean of praise. Indeed, says the psalmist, the praise of God will become a double-edged sword to bring vengeance on the nations:

> May the praise of God be in their
> mouths,
> and a double-edged sword in
> their hands,

to inflict vengeance on the nations
and punishment on the people,
to bind their kings with fetters,
their nobles with shackles of
iron,
to carry out the sentence written
against them.
This is the glory of all his saints.
(149:6–9)

If the exile in some way had taught Israel that the praise of God was the only strong defense they had against their earthly foes, it had been then a great boon for the kingdom of God.

Summary

Book 4 shifts attention from the failed Davidic covenant and monarchy to the Mosaic covenant and the kingship of Yahweh, whose work through Moses had been directed to the end that Israel might keep his law. The voice of Moses, then, opens this book (Ps 90), and a consideration of the covenant from the Lord's perspective (Ps 105) and also from Israel's point of view (Ps 106) closes it. Quite appropriately, the people of Israel confess their sin through the various stages of their history, from Egypt to Canaan, and are called upon to say the "Amen" (106:48). When the editor of Book 4 puts this psalm in the exilic setting, it is a powerful confession on the lips of the nation that languishes in the depths of despair brought on by exile in Babylonia.

Psalm 107 begins Book 5, the final book of the collection, with a strong affirmation of God's unfailing love (khesed), and Psalm 145 concludes this collection with the same affirmation, describing Yahweh as faithful, compassionate, and loving. Chastened by the wrath of God, Israel waited in humiliation for the Lord to punish the nations whom he had used as his agents of wrath. And David himself exalts the true King Yahweh (v. 1). Just as the closing psalm of Book 4 had called upon Israel to pronounce the "Amen" of this powerful confession (106:48), Psalm 145 closes Book 5 with a universal summons to all creatures to praise the Lord's holy name (v. 21).

The Final Shape of the Book: Psalms 1 and 146–50

With the stroke of a genius, the Psalter receives its final shape. We cannot be sure whether the five books received any new psalm contributions at this time, but the bookends of the Psalter, Psalm 1 (a wisdom psalm) and the concluding cluster of euphonic praise in Psalms 146–50, highlight the book in two ways. First, Psalm 1 sets the stage for the law to become the all-encompassing paradigm of faith. Its simple contrast between the wicked and the pious sets the matter of faith in the sharp relief of wisdom teaching, with its opposite categories of the wicked and the wise. Wisdom literature virtually eliminates the middle ground and insists that one must move in the direction of wickedness or wisdom, or to put it another way, in the direction of death or life. Psalm 1 declares the way of the wicked to be as unsubstantial as chaff which "the wind blows away" (v. 4). This psalm, very likely written of individuals, now takes its place in the larger book of the Psalms as a declaration both to individuals and the nation that "the LORD watches over the way of the righteous, / but the way of the wicked will perish" (v. 6). This assurance, in a time when Israel's enemies were still grouped around them, would be a strong encouragement to this people whose life was now turning more directly toward the piety of the law they had rejected in their preexilic days.

Second, at the end of Psalm 149 the praise of the Lord becomes a sword of vengeance in Israel's hands. For a people whose armies had been humiliated and their kings deposed, the powerful weapon of praise would accomplish the task of vengeance which the military and monarchy could never do. At last the people of Israel had turned to their sovereign Lord and left vengeance in his hands (Dt 32:35). At last they had learned not to trust in horses and military hardware (Dt 17:16). At long last they had come to David's conclusion in Book 1: "Some trust in chariots and some in horses, / but we trust in the name of the LORD our God" (Ps 20:7). Whether they had reached this conclusion out of humiliation or desperation made little difference. They had at last arrived, and it was obvious that history was in God's mighty hands.

The Date of the Final Compilation of the Psalter

We have suggested above that the compositional process that resulted in Books 1–3 was well under way in the preexilic period and probably came to fruition while Israel was in Babylonian exile. Based upon the fact that 1 Maccabees 7:17 quotes Psalm 79:2–3 as Scripture, this compilation must have been fixed in the canon by the first century B.C. The argument that the Psalter, or at least Books 4 and 5, was still fluid during the time of the Qumran sect (first century B.C. to first century A.D.) is based upon the different order of the Psalms in the manuscript from Cave 4 (4QPs^a) and the other psalmic materials not found in the canonical Psalter.[23] This argument, however, is really tenuous, especially since the Qumran sect ought not be taken as a measure of standard Judaism, nor their texts as the standard for the canon. The Qumran materials are immensely informative, but the covenanters at Qumran were a "sect" and did not represent normative Jewish thought and practice. In fact, the compelling evidence that the Psalter was complete by the third century B.C. is to be found in the fact that the Septuagint, translated between 250 and 150 B.C., included the Psalms in the order and form of the Hebrew canonical version, with the exception of an additional psalm (Ps 151).

A Consideration of Authorship in the Shaping of the Book

Authorship

Another quite obvious feature of the book is the various collections that were brought together, perhaps as mini-psalters, based upon authorship or other formal criteria. While the Hebrew letter *lamedh* ("by, of, belonging to, for") has been much discussed, the most obvious meaning of the word is "belonging to," found on so many potsherds from ancient Israel. This term most naturally attributes the psalm to the person named ("of David," "of Solomon," etc.), although I would not restrict its meaning to that of authorship. It may have the sense of dedication, as it would seem in some of the Asaph and Korah psalms, for example, "For the director of music. According to *gittith*. Of Asaph" (Ps 81), and other examples. Obviously this psalm does not have two authors, but it is dedicated to the "director of music," or written for his special use.

The Davidic Psalms

The largest clusters of psalms by far are those attributed to David, consisting of the large Davidic collection in Book 1 (Pss 3–41), a sizeable collection in Book 2 (Pss 51–65, 68–70), only a single psalm in Book 3 (Ps 86), two psalms in Book 4 (101 and 103), and another large collection in Book 5 (Pss 108–10, 122, 124, 131, and 138–45). We have already observed that a significant collection of Davidic psalms (Pss 3–41) begins the book and another such collection concludes it (Pss 138–45).

The portrait of David as musician, psalmist, and liturgical innovator is composed of three pictures all put together. We find the first and the second in the Books of Samuel, which describe David as a harpist and composer of psalms. The story of the mu-

sical therapy he performs on Saul depicts him as playing the harp to soothe Saul's troubled spirit (1 Sm 16:14–23). The second reference to David's musical associations adds little to this, since it merely describes David and all Israel celebrating the transfer of the ark to Jerusalem "with songs and with harps, lyres, tambourines, sistrums and cymbals" (2 Sm 6:5). The second part of this portrait is supplied by the three poems of David in 2 Samuel. Perhaps these more than anything else fix the image of David as psalmist in biblical memory. The first is his lament over Saul and Jonathan (2 Sm 1:17–27), the second is his song of praise and victory when the Lord had delivered him from all his enemies, including Saul (2 Sm 22:1–51), and the third is his dying words (2 Sm 23:1–7).

The Book of Psalms itself gives evidence of David as psalmist. Information provided there includes (1) the ascription of seventy-three psalms to David, (2) eleven psalms whose superscriptions provide a historical setting in David's life (Pss 3, 34, 51, 52, 54, 56, 57, 59, 60, 63, 142), and (3) random information about David within the content of certain psalms (18:50; 78:70–72; 89:3–4, 20–37, 49; 132:1–5, 10–12, 17–18; 144:10). There is no question but that the historical books and the Psalms are talking about the same David. That is certainly the way the Jewish community for the most part understood it, and the way the New Testament Christians understood the book also.

The strokes of the Chronicler upon the canvas of David's life round out the portrait and provide the third component of the portrait, David as liturgical innovator. In approximately 835 B.C., Jehoiada the priest backed the counter-coup that removed the usurper Athaliah from the Judean throne and restored temple worship. Part of that restoration was returning the Levites to their duty of presenting the burnt offering before the Lord according to the law of Moses "with rejoicing and singing," as David had assigned them in his liturgical innovations (2 Chr 23:18; see 1 Chr

23:1–5). Ezra 3:10 confirms the fact that the Levites were still exercising that duty in the sixth century B.C. when Zerubbabel and his associates rebuilt the temple. The Chronicler further depicts David as an inventor of instruments, a memory that was alive as late as Hezekiah in the eighth century B.C. and Nehemiah in the fifth (1 Chr 23:5; 2 Chr 7:6; 29:26; Neh 12:36).

With the rise of modern criticism, confidence in Old Testament historicity continued to erode, until little but an aesthetic representation was left of the portrait described above, at least for those scholars of a more liberal bent. Yet there was a lingering sentiment in the minds of most critics that David must be in the Book of Psalms somewhere. Alan Cooper, citing Johannes Herder, sets out two criteria for determining whether a psalm is Davidic. The first is the *aesthetic* standard, by which the psalms are judged by the commentator's aesthetic view of David's poetic ability and moral character.[24] Although the historicity of the materials that told David's story and described his character could not be relied upon, hypothesize the critics, nevertheless an aesthetic mist arose out of this material to provide a hologram of the man, and that apparition became the basis of judgment. A good example of this is the nineteenth-century German scholar Heinrich Ewald, who thought he could detect David's essential character from the "feeble remains of historical recollection concerning him," and by this he reached the judgment that David's "peculiarly powerful genius" could be identified in thirteen psalms, in part or in whole.

The second standard is *historical correlation*. If something in the psalm can be correlated with information in other biblical books or extra-biblical sources, then the date of the psalm, its setting, or perhaps even authorship can be postulated. Cooper's example is Psalm 24:7–10. On the basis of Numbers 10:35 and 1 Samuel 4:21 interpreters infer that the ritual described here is a procession that included the ark, even though the Bible says nothing about processions with the ark. The most popular proposal is the episode found in 2 Samuel 6. Cooper, however, cites the rabbinic interpretation that this ritual was Solomon's effort to install the ark in the newly built Holy of Holies.[25] This criterion is used by most scholars, even though we must recognize that there is always an element of uncertainty about it.

I am inclined toward giving the historical titles and the Davidic ascriptions more credence, starting out with the assumption that the historical books preserve accurate information about David and his musical and poetic genius, and the Psalms are his literary and spiritual legacy. The Hebrew term *ledavid* ("to David" or "by David") in the superscription of Psalm 18 is obviously a genitive of authorship because it reads "to David who spoke to the LORD the words of this song."[26] The form-critical school, represented by Hermann Gunkel and Sigmund Mowinckel and others, shifted the focus of the discussion from the historical to the social setting. In that case, the psalm would be written *for* or *to* the Davidic king rather than *by* David.[27]

At the same time, we should not draw ourselves into a corner so that we have to defend every psalm with *ledavid* as coming from David's hand. Yet the assumption of this study is that the burden of proof should be on the negative side rather than on the positive. That is, we should not start from a default position that a psalm is not by David until proven otherwise; our default position should be that those psalms which have *ledavid* in the superscription are by David unless we can show by historical correlation that it is otherwise.

While we cannot discuss in detail all the Davidic psalms here, we should note the first Davidic collection (Pss 3–41) is largely made up of psalms that are preoccupied with political and personal struggles. From what we know about David as a man of war (1 Chr 28:3), and as a man of sometimes failing character (2 Sm 11–12), these psalms for the most part fit this description.

The second collection (Pss 51–65; 68–70), found in Book 2, closes with the colophon: "This concludes the prayers of David son of Jesse" (72:20). While some scholars, for example, Delitzsch,[28] understand this to apply to Psalms 3–72, others interpret it more restrictively, to apply particularly to the second collection of Davidic psalms (Pss 51–65; 68–70). Goulder[29] espouses this position and proposes that the psalms in this collection were written, not by David, but by one of his associates during his lifetime and dedicated to David. If this final note applied, however, only to the Davidic psalms in Book 2, we would expect it to come as a colophon to the collection itself, with the doxology of 72:18–19 following to mark the end of Book 2. However, that is not the case, which may indicate that the colophon applies to the entire macro-collection of Psalms 3–72.

Other minor collections are to be found in the Psalter, such as the kingship of Yahweh psalms (Pss 93–99) and the hallelujah psalms (Pss 104–6; 111–17; 135; 146–50). We will discuss these when we give more attention to the content of the various collections.

The Korah Psalms (Pss 42–49; 84–85; 87–88)

The second collection is a group of psalms attributed to the "sons of Korah." They are actually composed of two groups, one in Book 2 (Pss 42–49), and the second in Book 3 (Pss 84–85, 87–88). While Psalm 43 in the first collection has no title, the recurring refrain in 42:5 and 11, which is continued in 43:5, plus the same subject matter in both psalms (oppression by enemies, and the psalmist's longing for the sanctuary), lead naturally to the conclusion that Psalms 42 and 43 were originally a single psalm.

The second series is also interrupted by a psalm, Psalm 86, which is not atttributed to the sons of Korah but simply titled "A Prayer of David." Its place in that group is not as easily explained as Psalm 43. It is, however, the only Davidic psalm in Book 3, and perhaps the editor, in view of the presence of Davidic psalms in the other books with which he was working, saw a need to have David represented here too, and inserted this psalm in the concluding collection of Book 3. This would likely have completed a macro-collection of psalms, Books 1–3. Kirkpatrick pointed out that Psalm 86 is a virtual mosaic of other psalms, its quotations being almost verbatim.[30] Perhaps it should be noted also that all of these quotations, mostly short phrases, come from other Davidic psalms. While it is speculative, if the editor did compose this psalm as a representative of the Davidic psalms, he certainly was steeped in the phraseology of David's psalmody and the product could be legitimately titled, "A Prayer of David."

Korah was the great-grandson of Levi who led a levitical rebellion against Moses and Aaron, and was swallowed up by a gaping hole in the earth (Nm 16). His sons, however, were spared (Nm 26:11). The Korahites were important supporters of David (1 Chr 12:6), and when he made his revisions in the temple liturgy and personnel, he gave two families of the Korahites and one family of Merari the responsibility of keeping the temple gates (1 Chr 26:1–10), perhaps merely a confirmation of a responsibility they had fulfilled for a long time. Their long-standing temple responsibility is mentioned in Psalm 84:10: "I would rather be a doorkeeper in the house of my God / than dwell in the tents of the wicked." During postexilic times they were still gatekeepers (1 Chr 9:17–19; Neh 11:19).

The Korah psalms originated within the family of Korah ("sons of Korah") and do not have individual names attached to them. In that sense they are anonymous. But obviously their origin within the Korah family carried a great deal of weight, whoever their individual composers were.

Michael D. Goulder[31] has done a thorough analysis of these psalms and drawn attention to their similar content and vocabulary. The similar expressions are either exclusive to this group of psalms or predominant in them.

Table 3.1
Vocabulary of the Korah Psalms

	Korah Psalms	Elsewhere in the Psalter and the Old Testament
"the living God"	42:2; 84:2	Hos 1:10; Jos 3:10
"appear before God"	42:2; 84:7	common in Old Testament texts describing attendance at the festivals but does not appear anywhere else in the Psalter
"oppression" (*lakhats*)	42:9; 43:2; 44:24	occurs only in the Korah psalms
"(your) tabernacles"	43:3; 84:1; 87:2	Pss 132:5; 46:4; Ez 37:27
"(the) city of God"	46:4; 48:1; 87:3	occurs only in the Korah psalms
"LORD of hosts"	46:7, 11; 48:8; 84:1, 3, 12	Pss 24:10; 69:7
"LORD God of hosts"	84:8	Pss 59:6; 80:4, 19; 89:8

A distinguishing feature of these two sequences of Korah psalms is the use of the divine names. Table 3.2 shows that there is a predominant use of Elohim (God) in the first sequence of Korah psalms (Pss 42–49), and a predominant occurrence of Yahweh (LORD) in the second sequence (Pss 84–85, 87–88).

In a previous generation of scholarship it was customary to speak of an Elohistic Psalter composed of Books 2 and 3, excluding the second Korah sequence (thus, Pss 42–83). In this so-called Elohistic psalter, Elohim (God) occurs 200 times, while Yahweh (LORD) occurs 44 times. In comparison, Book 1 uses Yahweh 278 times and Elohim 15, while Books 4 and 5 use Yahweh 339 times and Elohim 9.[32] The question, of course, is, What should one make of this data? If, as some have supposed, an Elohistic editor went through the "Elohistic psalter" and changed the divine name from Yahweh to Elohim, he only did a partial job. One might wonder then if there is not a better explanation. Goulder proposes that, in

view of the occurrences of Yahweh in this collection, the divine name Elohim was original and not the work of an editor. An explanation for the preponderance of Elohim, therefore, should be found in the provenance of these psalms.[33] Thus, following the work of J. P. Peters,[34] he proposes the northern provenance of the sanctuary at Dan where these psalms were used in the northern Feast of Tabernacles.[35] While the kind of specificity Goulder builds into his study must remain a bit tenuous, the northern provenance does offer a better explanation than the editor hypothesis. It is certainly possible that the Israelites contributed something of their own psalmic literature to this book. We must not assume that all the north was apostate. Even Amos and Hosea, both prophets to that kingdom, saw a glimmer of hope for Israel if they would just turn to Yahweh (e.g., Am 5:4–6; Hos 6:1–3). Hosea was keenly aware that Israel's practice and belief did not correspond. When he indicted them for breaking the cove-

Table 3.2

Divine Names in the Korah Psalms

	Pss 42–49	Pss 84–85, 87–88
God (Elohim)	29	2
your, my, our God	9	1
God of Jacob	2	1
God of my refuge	1	
God of my salvation		2
God of Abraham	1	
altar of God	1	
name of our God	1	
house of God	1	
(the) city of (our) God	3	1
living God (El)	1	1
God (El) of my joy	1	
LORD God		1
Total	50	9

	Pss 42–49	Pss 84–85, 87–88
LORD (Yahweh)	4	13
LORD of Hosts	3	3
LORD God of Hosts		1
LORD Most High	1	
LORD God		1
God LORD		1
LORD God of my salvation		1
Total	8	20

nant, they remonstrated that they in fact knew the Lord:

> Put the trumpet to your lips!
>   An eagle is over the house of the LORD
> because the people have broken my covenant
>   and rebelled against my law.
> Israel cries out to me,
>   "O our God, we acknowledge you!" (Hos 8:1–2)

Assuming that the editor was working on an augmentation of Books 1–2, the installation of the second sequence of Korah psalms at the end of his collection would have brought a kind of balance to it, particularly balancing the first Korah sequence of Book 2 (Pss 42–49) with the final segment of his own augmentation (Pss 84–85, 87–88). Furthermore,

since the sons of Korah and Asaph were associates in David's worship center, it would be quite natural to install a collection of Korah psalms after a collection attributed to Asaph (Pss 73–83). We may make one last observation, which is by no means the least important. That is, on one side of the so-called Elohistic psalter that contains the first sequence of the Korah psalms, and to which the second sequence is appended, is the strongly Yahwistic Book 1, which uses Yahweh 278 times but Elohim only 15. On the other side of the Elohistic psalter is another strongly Yahwistic collection of psalms that make up Books 4 and 5, where Yahweh occurs 339 times as compared to 9 times for Elohim. At some stage of the shaping of the Book of Psalms, perhaps even at this stage, the Yahweh collections may have served to "sanctify" the Elohim collection.

The Asaph Psalms (Pss 50; 73–83)

The third collection of psalms, which may help us understand an important dimension of the composition of this book, is the Asaph psalms, found together in Psalms 73–83, the beginning of Book 3, with one lone representative in Book 2, Psalm 50, making a total of twelve Asaph psalms. It seems strange that the compiler of Book 2 would separate the Asaph collection by placing Psalm 50 right before a Davidic collection (Pss 51–65). To solve this problem, Leslie McFall has offered the plausible explanation that in sorting the Psalms by theme,[36] the compiler prefixed Psalm 50 to the Davidic collection in deference to the use of the term "adulterers" in 50:18. This topic brought Psalm 50 and Psalm 51 together. Although Psalm 51 does not mention adultery, the superscription makes it very clear that this was the sin about which David was grieved.[37] Thus the placement of the single Asaph psalm apart from the Asaph collection would make sense.

According to 1 Chronicles, David designated Heman and Jeduthun, sons of Asaph, "for the ministry of prophesying, accompanied by harps, lyres and cymbals" (25:1). The chronicler further records that Hezekiah, as part of the temple rededication, ordered the Levites, accompanied by trumpets, cymbals, harps, and lyres, "to praise the LORD with the words of David and of Asaph the seer" (2 Chr 29:30). Evidently they had songs written by Asaph in their musical repertoire. The descendants of Asaph, 128 in number, were among those who returned with Zerubbabel from Babylonian exile in the late sixth century B.C. (Ezr 2:41); and when the foundations of the temple were laid, they were among the celebrants (3:10).

Delitzsch[38] identified five distinguishing characteristics for this group of psalms:

1. They overwhelmingly use the name Elohim for God: Elohim (God) 50 times; Elohim in combination (LORD God [4], your God the LORD [1], God of Hosts [2], LORD God of hosts [2]) 9 times; Yahweh (LORD) 10 times.
2. They have a prominent prophetic character. For example, God often speaks directly in these psalms as he does in the prophets: 50:7–15, 16b–23; 75:2–5; 81:6–16. A strong historical element is present: 74:13–15; 77:15–20; 78; 80:9–12; 81:5–8; 83:10–12.
3. They frequently mention Joseph and his tribes: 77:15; 78:67; 80:2; 81:5.
4. They share common language, for example, referring to the Lord as Shepherd and Israel as his flock: 74:1; 77:20; 78:52; 79:13; 80:1.
5. They deal with Israel and the nations, or God and the nations.[39]

The Asaph psalms, much like the Davidic psalms in Book 1, are preoccupied with Israel's enemies and how the Lord will deal with them. In Psalm 73 the psalmist lays out the problem of the prosperity of the wicked (vv. 2–3), which is both a personal and an international problem, and he provides an answer, or at least a place—the sanctuary—where the problem no longer troubled him so severely (vv. 16–17). In Psalm 74:3–8 we learn that Israel's enemies have brought destruction even on the sanctuary where the psalmist found such solace. Then in Psalm 75 the psalmist praises God who judges uprightly, and when he does, "the earth and all its people quake" (vv. 2–3). Psalm 76 follows with the acclamation that God breaks the spirit of rulers; he is feared by the kings of the earth (v. 12).

Psalm 77 deals with the same problem as Psalm 73. Yet, rather than finding solace in the sanctuary, the poet reflects upon the miracles God had performed in Israel's history (vv. 11–12), a theme that Psalm 78 continues, although the focus there is on Israel's rebellion against God rather than Israel's rebellious enemies. Walter Houston has observed, particularly in reference to the Asaph psalms, that when God's goodness is not present in the contemporary situation, the psalmist is inclined to appeal to God's past goodness. As a rule, the psalms of praise do not engage much in historical reflection.[40]

In Psalm 79 the psalmist returns to the theme of the nations, calling attention to the fact that they have invaded the Lord's "inheritance," and prays that God will pour out his wrath on them (v. 6). Psalm 80 follows this appealing prayer with a passionate plea that God would restore Israel to his favor and heal the devastation caused by its enemies. The answer to this plea occurs in Psalm 81 as the Lord himself assures the people of Israel that if they would listen to him, he would

> subdue their enemies
>   and turn my hand against their
>   foes!
> Those who hate the LORD would
>   cringe before him,
> and their punishment would
>   last forever. (vv. 14–15)

In fact, the problem was internal and was traceable to their idolatry:

> Hear, O my people, and I will warn
>   you—
>   if you would but listen to me, O
>   Israel!
> You shall have no foreign god
>   among you;
>   you shall not bow down to an
>   alien god.
> I am the LORD your God,
>   who brought you up out of
>   Egypt.
> Open wide your mouth and I
>   will fill it.
> But my people would not listen to
>   me;

> Israel would not submit to me.
>   (Ps 81:8–11)

But God's judgment would not stop with the nations—it would extend all the way to the gods of the nations (Ps 82:1, 6–8). The Asaph psalms close with a plea that God would not keep silent but punish Israel's enemies as he had done in the days of Deborah and Barak (83:9–10).

This group of psalms defines Israel as a people of the covenant.[41] God summons them by that association: "Gather to me my consecrated ones, / who made a covenant with me by sacrifice" (50:5). And only they have a claim to this covenant:

> But to the wicked, God says:
> "What right have you to recite my
>   laws
>   or take my covenant on your
>   lips?
> You hate my instruction
>   and cast my words behind you."
>   (50:16–17)

In another instance the psalmist rather than God refers to the covenant as the basis of his appeal: "Have regard for your covenant, / because haunts of violence fill the dark places of the land" (Ps 74:20). The northern kingdom had been known for its rejection of the covenant (78:9–10, 37). Despite Israel's unfaithfulness to the covenant, however, God had been faithful to Israel:

> Yet he was merciful;
>   he forgave their iniquities
>   and did not destroy them.
> Time after time he restrained his
>   anger
>   and did not stir up his full
>   wrath.
> He remembered that they were but
>   flesh,
>   a passing breeze that does not
>   return. (Ps 78:38–39)

Based in part upon the observation that the Joseph tribes figure prominently in this group of psalms (Pss 77:15; 80:2), Goulder proposes a northern provenance for the Asaph psalms, perhaps during the decade when the Assyrians had cut Ephraim and Manasseh off from the Galilean tribes (732–722 B.C.).[42]

Songs of Ascents (Pss 120–34)

The criterion of authorship applies only in part to the fourth collection of psalms, the **Songs of Ascents.** Only five of these fifteen psalms have attributive titles, four to David (Pss 122, 124, 131, 133) and one to Solomon (Ps 127). Ten of them are anonymous.

The meaning of the term *hamma'aloth,* generally translated by the English versions as "ascents," has been much discussed. While there is no consensus opinion, a widely accepted view is that the word *ascents,* which comes from the verb "to go up," refers to either (1) the journey of the returning exiles from Babylon to Jerusalem in the last half of the sixth century B.C. or (2) the annual journey of pilgrims to Jerusalem at the agricultural festivals (Passover/Unleavened Bread, Weeks, and Tabernacles). The latter opinion seems to have the majority vote. That is, they are psalms that were sung by the Israelites as they journeyed to Jerusalem to attend a festival (Ex 23:14–17; 34:18–24; Lv 23:4–44; Dt 16:1–17), most likely the Feast of Tabernacles, suggested by the harvest imagery found in several of the psalms: 126:5–6; 127:2; 128:2; 129:6–8; 132:15.[43] It is quite likely that at a later time the Levites sang these psalms at the Feast of Tabernacles as they stood on the fifteen steps of the temple. The Mishnah makes the association between the fifteen steps that led from the Court of Women to the Court of Israel and the fifteen Songs of Ascents:

> Men of piety and good works used to dance before them with burning torches in their hands, singing songs and praises. And countless levites [played] on harps, lyres, cymbals and trumpets and instruments of music, on the fifteen steps leading down from the Court of the Israelites to the Court of the Women, corresponding to the Fifteen Songs of Ascents in the Psalms.[44]

A Song of Ascent in a Modern Setting

William L. Holladay relates the following story as it came to him through correspondence with a friend:

> Again, on June 7, 1967, the news announcer for The Voice of Israel in Jerusalem could find no more appropriate way to announce the taking of the eastern portion of Jerusalem, formerly held by the Arabs, than the recitation of Psalm 122 ("Our feet are standing within your gates, O Jerusalem. Jerusalem—built as a city that is bound firmly together"). The Psalms then live in Jewish consciousness in ways that defy delimitation.[1]

1. William L. Holladay, *The Psalms through Three Thousand Years: Prayerbook of a Cloud of Witnesses* (Minneapolis: Fortress, 1993), 154.

Although the Mishnah does not explicitly draw the conclusion that the levitical singers performed one of these psalms as they stood on each step, the Tosefta describes the temple liturgy during Tabernacles and appears to make the point more explicit:

> *And Levites [played] on harps, lyres, cymbals, and all sorts of musical instruments* [assuming the detail of the Mishnah that they were standing on the fifteen steps]. What did they sing? *A Song of Ascents. Come, bless the Lord, all you servants of the Lord, who stand by night in the house of the Lord* (Ps 134.1). Some of them would sing, *Lift up your hands to the holy place and bless the Lord* (Ps 134.3). And when they departed from one another, what did they say? *May the Lord bless you from Zion, he who made heaven and earth* (Ps 134.3).[45]

As to form, Erich Zenger proposes a division of these fifteen psalms into three groups of five each: Psalms 120–24; 125–29; 130–34. Each of these groups, he suggests, has a center psalm that reflects a royal theology and the theology of Zion: Psalm 122 (Jerusalem), Psalm 127 (the temple), Psalm 132 (David). Zenger concludes that with the different emphases of these center psalms, one gets a "coherent theological view" that points to Zion as the place of blessing where Israel should "go up," a kind of second exodus.[46]

We should also call attention to the repeated phrases in these psalms:

"who made the heavens and the earth"	121:2; 124:8; 134:3
"both now and forevermore"	121:8; 125:2; 131:3
use of word "peace"	120:7; 122:6; 125:5; 128:6
"May the LORD bless you from Zion"	128:5; 134:3
"O Israel, put your hope in the LORD"	130:7; 131:3

Proposing a different division, E. W. Hengstenberg[47] pointed to Psalm 127, attributed to Solomon, as the centerpiece of the collection. On either side, he observed, stands a series of seven psalms, two of which are attributed to David, and five of which are anonymous. Hengstenberg further observed that each series of seven (heptad) contains the divine name Yahweh twenty-four times. If one acccepts his division of the psalms into four sub-groups (120–23; 124–26; 128–31; 132–34), then his second observation is just as interesting: each of these connected groups contains the divine name twelve times. The shortened form of Yahweh, *Yah* (compare *Hallelujah*, which uses the shortened form—*jah* = *yah*), occurs in the third psalm of each group of seven (122:3—"tribes of the LORD [*Yah*]; 130:3—"If you, O LORD [*Yah*], kept a record of sins").[48] This kind of

distribution seems too symmetrical to be coincidental.

In recent years the purpose of the Songs of Ascents has been the topic of special study. Zenger seems to think in terms of their theological purpose within the Book of Psalms, which is largely our concern in this study too. David Mitchell follows the theological approach as well, submitting that they served an eschatological purpose in the Book of Psalms, a thesis that he seeks to extend to other collections within the Psalter. At the same time, he recognizes that they were historically recited in the Feast of Tabernacles. Michael D. Goulder[49] has carried the matter much further than the literary purpose of the collection within the Psalter, to propose a special use for these psalms in the life of ancient Israel. His hypothesis is that these psalms were composed by a Levite during the time of Nehemiah to celebrate his accomplishments. On the basis of the Nehemiah "memoirs," the first-person passages in the Book of Nehemiah, Goulder proposes that the individual psalms of ascents each celebrated one phase of his attainments. That is, Nehemiah lamented the troubles that had befallen the Judeans (Neh 1), and the levitical poet responded with Psalm 120, which reflects their troubled situation:

> I call on the LORD in my distress,
>   and he answers me.
> Save me, O LORD, from lying lips
>   and from deceitful tongues.
>   (vv. 1–2)

And so the pattern continues:

Nehemiah's lament	Ps 120
Nehemiah's journey	Ps 121
Nehemiah's arrival	Ps 122
Contempt of enemies	Ps 123
Deliverance from plot	Ps 124

Table 3.3

Attributive Titles of the Psalms of Ascents

Pss 120–26	Ps 127	Pss 128–34
Ps 120 The Song of Ascents (anonymous)	Ps 127 The Song of Ascents, **of Solomon**	Ps 128 The Song of Ascents (anonymous)
Ps 121 Song for Ascents (anonymous)		Ps 129 The Song of Ascents (anonymous)
Ps 122 The Song of Ascents, **of David**		Ps 130 The Song of Ascents (anonymous)
Ps 123 The Song of Ascents (anonymous)		Ps 131 The Song of Ascents, **of David**
Ps 124 The Song of Ascents, **of David**		Ps 132 The Song of Ascents (anonymous)
Ps 125 The Song of Ascents (anonymous)		Ps 133 The Song of Ascents, **of David**
Ps 126 The Song of Ascents (anonymous)		Ps 134 The Song of Ascents (anonymous)

Restraining of usurers	Ps 125
Walls completed	Ps 126
Building of houses and gates	Ps 127
Villagers moved into Jerusalem	Ps 128
Tobiah's confession	Ps 129
Sabbath breaking	Ps 130
Mixed marriages	Ps 131
Renewal of temple clergy purity	Ps 132
Procession to temple	Ps 133
Thanksgiving there	Ps 134

While this kind of reconstruction of the real-life situation is quite appealing, confidence begins to thin out when we go beyond positing the use of these psalms at Tabernacles.

To emphasize the theological purpose of these author collections, we may refer again to Wilson's suggestion that Books 1–3 and Book 5 are concerned with the Davidic covenant, while Book 4 is a celebration of kingship, both Israel's and the Lord's.[50] Zenger has further pointed out that Book 5 returns to the topic of the Davidic king and, in contrast to the military language of the Davidic psalms 108–10, puts the king in the service of the universal kingdom of Yahweh.[51]

Wilson proposes two periods of editorial shaping,[52] the first related to Books 1–3, and the second to Books 4–5. Books 1–3 are dominated by "author" collections, while Books 4–5 have a high number of untitled psalms. Book 4 (90–106) has 10 out of 17 untitled psalms, and Book 5 (107–50) has 16 out of 44. These books were edited in a later period when Davidic authorship had become a strong plus, but other authors had also taken a place of prominence in the collection, and even anonymous psalms found a place of honor.

Also attributed to individuals are two collections of Korah psalms that begin Book 2 (Pss 42–49) and lead toward the conclusion of Book 3 (Pss 84–85, 87–88), and a collection of Asaph psalms that heads up Book 3 (Pss 73–83). In view of the association of Korah and Asaph (and Ethan, Ps 89) with worship during David's reign, it seems quite fitting to reinforce the Davidic collections with psalms attributed to David's associates. Other authors, such as Solomon

(Pss 72, 127), Moses (Ps 90), Heman the Ezrahite (Ps 88), and the unnamed musical director, are mentioned, but these psalms do not form collections as such.

Key Terms

Torah psalms
Korah psalms
Asaph psalms
Davidic psalms
Songs of Ascents

Study Questions

1. The final editor(s) of the Psalms most likely imposed the fivefold division in order to emphasize the centrality of the Torah. What evidence demonstrates this shaping? Does it represent a formal recognition of implicit teaching or an artificial imposition?

2. At the seams of the Book of Psalms one may see the thematic editorial threads that link them. What themes tie together the outer seams of Books 1–3? The inner seams of Books 1–3? What is the overall editorial framework of this first macro-collection, and how does this help us date it?

3. Why is Moses featured so prominently in the second macro-collection (Books 4–5)? How does this powerfully answer the hanging question (in Book 3) of God's apparent abrogation of the Davidic covenant and desertion of Judah?

4. If indeed Book 4 is the editorial center of the Psalms, how does this baptize the entire collection in hope?

Part

2

Encountering the Psalms as Worship and Historical Reflection

4 The Psalms in Worship and Faith

Objectives

After reading this chapter, you should be able to

1. Recognize the power of the Psalms in human life.
2. Discuss the use of the Psalms in the New Testament.
3. Discuss the use of the Psalms in Jewish and Christian worship.

The Psalms as an Expression of Shared Humanness

There is a shared humanness in the Psalter that appeals to the strongest and the weakest of us. It takes hold of us where we are, in our personal troubles and corporate crises, when our joy is inexpressible and our pain is unutterable. This shared humanness, part of the power and the mystery of the Incarnation, undergirds us when we feel utterly abandoned, when the tensions of life capture us in an inescapable web, or when our souls surmount the pinnacle of human achievement. Calvin commented on this aspect of the Psalms in the preface to his commentary, recognizing that the Psalms will seize us and compel us into an honesty about ourselves before God:

> Or rather, the Holy Spirit has here drawn to the life all the griefs, sorrows, fears, doubts, hopes, cares, perplexities, in short, all the distracting emotions with which the minds of men are wont to be agitated. The other parts of Scripture contain the commandments which God enjoined his servants to announce to us. But here the prophets themselves, seeing they are exhibited to us as speaking to God, and laying open all their inmost thoughts and affections, call, or rather draw, each of us to the examination of himself in particular, in order that none of the many infirmities to which we are subject, and of the many vices with which we abound, may remain concealed. It is certainly a rare and singular advantage, when all lurking places are discovered, and the heart is brought into the light, purged from that most baneful infection, hypocrisy.[1]

The attraction of the church and her individual members to the Psalms through the centuries is indeed intriguing. At first it might seem almost mysterious that this book has spoken to monarchs and commoners alike and charged their lives with power and understanding. Yet the mystery dissolves when we observe that the Psalms bring us to the heart of God and to the heart of our human condition. The Psalms examine the problem in the light of the solution, and they bring the solution to bear directly on the problem. Whether it be our personal sin, or the injustice of our enemies, or the illness that stalks our once peaceful life, or emotional trauma that shakes our souls, the Psalms do not avoid the problem. They embolden us to face it and write our name on it, and with that courage to put the problem in the light of the solution.

Calvin saw David as an ancient guide who still, through the Psalms, shows us the way: "In considering the whole course of the life of David, it seemed to me that by his own footsteps he showed me the way, and from this I have experienced no small consolation."[2] From David's faith we learn the way we ought to go, and from his sin, the condition for which God has immeasurable compassion. With Calvin, we can follow David's footsteps confidently.

The Psalms as an Expression of Our Fragmentary Life

When we stand back and look at our lives, they sometimes look more like a collage of unrelated fragments than a unified picture. Indeed, that person is truly blessed who discovers a unifying center in his or her life. That center for the Jewish and Christian believer, of course, is God. But even when God is the cohering power of life, most people at some moment of their existence feel that life's fragmentary nature has overcome the unifying center, and they feel splintered into a thousand pieces. The Psalms express this sentiment well. Dietrich Bonhoeffer, whose life was more unified by the God whom he trusted than most peo-

The Psalms as Connector of Life's Fragments

Herman Wouk, in his novel *War and Remembrance*, describes how Berel Jastrow, a Jewish inmate of the death camps, was forced to do the morbid work of removing decaying Jewish bodies from the death pit to be burned. In order to keep his sanity in his fragmentary life, he recited the Psalms:

While he does this work, Berel Jastrow recites the psalms for the dead. He knows the psaltery by heart. Several times each day he goes through all hundred and fifty *t'hillim*. The dead hold no terrors for Berel. In the old days, as an officer of the burial society, the *hevra kadisha*, he washed and prepared for interment many bodies. . . .

He goes about this gruesome task with love, murmuring psalms. He cannot give these dead the orthodox purification by water, but fire purifies too, and the psalms will comfort their souls. The Hebrew verses are so graven in his memory that he can listen to Mutterperl, or even break off to argue, without missing a word of a psalm. . . .

He heaves up body after body—they are light, these long-dead Jews, one seizes a body by the waist and twitches it readily into the air, into the waiting hands above—and goes on murmuring psalms. This is how Berel Jastrow holds on to his sanity.[1]

1. Herman Wouk, *War and Remembrance* (Glasgow: William Collins Sons, 1978), 730–31.

ple's, understandably still had those moments when, imprisoned for his anti-Nazi sentiments, he saw his life as fragmentary. He articulates this point potently:

It finally comes to this, if one thinks about the fragment of our life, how the whole was really planned and thought out, and of what material it consists. There are finally fragments which still belong to the rubbish heap, and there are those fragments which are meaningful only when looked at in the perspective of centuries because their fulfillment can be only a divine matter, fragments which must remain fragments. An analogy that comes to mind is the fugue. If our life also is only a slightest reflection of such a fragment, in which at least for a short while the various themes, growing ever stronger, harmonize, and in which the

great counterpoint is held on to from beginning to end so that finally, after the breaking-off point, the chorale *"Vor deinen Thron tret ich hiermit"* can still be intoned, then we do not wish to complain about our fragmentary life, but even to be glad for it.[3]

Bonhoeffer helps us understand this phenomenon of our existense, and he found the Psalms to be the great advocate in that situation.

The Psalms as Preincarnational Revelation

The weakness of human flesh, its capacity for sin, the stark realities of life and death, and the power of grace to redeem—all of these figure prominently in the Psalms. Bonhoeffer presented this perspective on the Psalms in terms of a preincarnational view of life and the world. David prayed them, and Christ became them. David could pray them *because* Christ became them. The Incarnation of God in Jesus of Nazareth, as the New Testament attests, was central to the eternal master plan of redemption. Thus the Old Testament, and especially the Psalter, which brings together humanness and divinity as no other book does, is phrased in the overarching glow of the Incarnation. In Jesus Christ God became all that the psalmists were; he faced their temptations and encountered their enemies in the formative review of all history. Bonhoeffer states it like this:

It is the incarnate Son of God, who has borne every human weakness in his own flesh, who here pours out the heart of all humanity before God and who stands in our place and prays for us. He has known torment and pain, guilt and death more deeply than we. Therefore it is the prayer of the human nature assumed by him which comes here before God. It is really our prayer, but since he knows us better than

Qumran Scrolls from Cave 4

The order of the psalms in the scroll from Cave 4 (4QPs[a]) is as follows:

> 5:9–13—
> 6:1–4
> 25:15
> 31:24 (–25)—
> [Ps 32 lacking]
> 33:1–12
> 35:2, 14–20, 26–28—
> 36:1–9
> 38:2–12, 16–23—
> 71:1–14
> 47:2
> 53:4–7—
> 54:1–6
> 56:4
> 62:?13—
> 63:2–4
> 66:16–20—
> 67:1–7
> 69:1–19[1]

1. J. A. Sanders, *The Dead Sea Psalms Scroll* (Ithaca, N.Y.: Cornell University Press, 1967), 143–44. Dashes at the end of references mean the text continues with the following text.

Noncanonical Texts from Cave 11

The eight noncanonical texts from Cave 11 (11QPs[a]) are as follows:

> Ps 151A, B
> Ps 154
> Ps 155
> Sirach 51:13ff.
> Plea for Deliverance
> Apostrophe to Zion
> Hymn to the Creator
> David's Composition[1]

1. J. A. Sanders, *The Dead Sea Psalms Scroll* (Ithaca, N.Y.: Cornell University Press, 1967), 11.

we know ourselves and since he himself was true man for our sakes, it is also really his prayer, and it can become our prayer only because it was his prayer.[4]

At the deepest level of meaning, this is the reason the Psalms speak so powerfully and effectively to us and for us. On the divine side, they represent God praying on our behalf and speaking in our defense. On the human side, they represent the God-Man praising as humans ought and lamenting as humans will.

The Psalms in the Qumran Scrolls

The psalmic tradition is splendidly represented in the Qumran Scrolls, the first of them coming to light in 1947. Among this treasury of biblical and nonbiblical manuscripts were at least thirty manuscripts of the Book of Psalms, either complete or partial, which amounted to more manuscript evidence on the Psalms than on any other biblical book.[5] Cave 4 yielded a Psalms scroll (4QPs[a]) that contained all or parts of Psalms 6–69, pretty much in the canonical order (substantially Books 1–2).[6] In contrast, the Psalms scroll from Cave 11 (11QPs[a]), which contained all or part of thirty-nine psalms from Books 4–5, does not follow the canonical order consistently, and includes the psalm from 2 Samuel 23, plus eight other noncanonical compositions interspersed with the canonical psalms. The first four texts in the sidebar "Noncanonical Texts from Cave 11" were known, prior to the Qumran discoveries, in ancient translations (Greek, Latin, and Syriac), but now this scroll from Cave 11 gives us the original Hebrew text for these compositions. The last four were not known until the discovery of this scroll in 1956. Frank Cross believes that the general correlation with the canonical order in the Cave 4 scroll (dated in the second century B.C.) suggests that the order of the psalms in Books 1 and 2 was fixed as early as

Qumran Cave 4, where one of the Psalms scrolls was discovered.

the Maccabean period.[7] At the same time, Sanders proposes that the unconventional order of the psalms in the scroll from Cave 11 indicates the fluidity of the collections now found in Books 4 and 5. Of course, the assumption is that the Cave 11 scroll represents the state of composition of the Book of Psalms at the time, an assumption that may or may not be true.

Psalms 118–50 are contained on this scroll, with the exception of Psalm 120, which may have been lost as a result of the deterioration of the scroll.[8] While it is not our purpose to discuss the peculiarities of these scrolls in any detail here,[9] the numerous manuscripts of the canonical Psalms make it clear that the Qumran sect highly prized this collection.

In addition, the psalmic tradition continued in the thanksgiving hymns discovered in Cave 1.[10] Some twenty-five in number, they are preserved on a single manuscript, and were evidently composed by members of the Qumran community. Each one begins with the words "I thank you, O Lord," or similar words, and they incorporate terms and phrases from the biblical Psalms. While some of these hymns express the troubles of the community at large, others record the experiences of a teacher deserted by his friends and victimized by his enemies, drawing upon the model of the biblical laments.[11]

The Psalms in the New Testament

In the *Greek New Testament* (United Bible Societies, 4th ed.), the "Index of Quotations" lists a few more than four hundred quotations from the Book of Psalms.[12] Of course, this list includes phrases as well as complete verses. Another count lists fifty-five quotations, including the parallels in the Gospels.[13] Only the Book of Isaiah comes anywhere near this frequency, quoted forty-seven times in the New Testament. Of the 150 psalms, thirty-five are quoted, which is quite a significant number. Rather than doing a complete survey, we will only mention the way the Psalms are used.

The Psalms in the Gospels

The Gospels made extensive use of the Psalms to disclose Jesus' identity. As a rule, when he himself quoted the Psalms, Jesus generally used phrases or brief quotes that would require the hearer to make the connection. For example, he gave the lesson about the good tree that bears good fruit and

The Order of the Psalms in the Scroll from Cave 11

The order of the psalms in the scroll from Cave 11 (11QPs[a]) is as follows:

101:1–8	136:1–16, 26—
102:1–2, 18–29—	?118:1, 15, 16, 8, 9,
103:1	29—
109:21–31	145:1–7, 13–21
118:25–29—	154:3–19
104:1–6, 21–35—	Plea for Deliverance
147:1–2, 18–20—	139:8–24—
105:1–12	137:1, 9—
105:25–45	138:1–8
146:9–10—	Sirach 51:13–30—
148:1–12	Apostrophe to Zion—
121:1–8—	93:1–3
122:1–9—	141:5–10—
123:1–2	133:1–3—
124:7–8—	144:1–7, 15—
125:1–5—	155:1–19
126:1–6—	142:4–8—
127:1	143:1–8
128:4–6—	149:7–9—
129:1–8—	150:1–6
130:1–8—	Hymn to the Creator
131:1	2 Sam 23:7—
132:8–18—	David's
119:1–6, 15–25, 37–49,	Compositions—
59–73, 82–96, 105–	140:1–5
20, 128–42, 150–	134:1–3—
64, 171–76—	151A, B[1]
135:1–9, 17–21—	

1. J. A. Sanders, *The Dead Sea Psalms Scroll* (Ithaca, N.Y.: Cornell University Press, 1967), 144–45. Dashes at the end of references mean the text continues with the following text.

pesher

concluded that it was not the person who said, "Lord, Lord," who would enter the Kingdom, but the one who did the will of his Father. To wrap up the lesson, he quoted from Psalm 6:8, "Away from me, all you evildoers" (Mt 7:23/Lk 13:27).

At other times Jesus was more direct. He closed the parable of the vineyard with a quotation of Psalm 118:22–23, applying it to himself as a prophetic prediction:

What then will the owner of the vineyard do? He will come and kill those tenants and give the vineyard to others. Haven't you read this scripture:

"The stone the builders rejected has become the capstone; the Lord has done this, and it is marvelous in our eyes"? (Mk 12:9–11/Mt 21:42/Lk 20:17)

The use of the Psalms in the Gospels, however, is weighted heavily on the side of the writers. That is, the direct application of the Psalms to Jesus is largely due to the Evangelists' own theology. Sometimes the application consists merely of the way they put the text together. An example is the declaration of the crowd at the triumphal entry, taken from Psalm 118:26: "Blessed is he who comes in the name of the Lord" (Mt 21:9). Jesus did not openly acknowledge that he was the Messiah on that occasion. He simply went about doing what the Scriptures had said the Messiah would do, such as cleansing the temple (Mt 21:12–17/Mal 3:1–3). But when he wept over Jerusalem, he quoted from Psalm 118:26: "For I tell you, you will not see me again until you say, 'Blessed is he who comes in the name of the Lord'" (Mt 23:39). The way Matthew put the two uses of this verse together indicated Jesus' acceptance of the acclamation.

Paul's Use of the Psalms

The apostle Paul makes extensive use of the Psalms to show that the gospel was not a novelty in history, for it already existed in its Old Testament form, and the Psalms, as well as other Old Testament books, predicted what was happening in the first century A.D. For example, the spread of the gospel (Rom 10:18/Ps 19:4), the power of sin over Jews and Gentiles (Rom 3:18/Ps 36:1b), and the rejection of the gospel by the Jews (Rom 11:9–10/Ps 69:22–23) are among the topics Paul finds in the Psalms. His hermeneutic was more or less that of the *pesher*, "this is that." He saw the words of the Psalms happening before him. Their prophetic nature becomes very clear in Paul's usage.

The Scriptorium of Qumran, where the members of the sect may have copied many of the scrolls found in the nearby caves.

Hillel

qal vahomer

The Psalms in the Epistle to the Hebrews

The *Greek New Testament* (United Bible Societies, 4th ed.) indicates that there are some thirty-seven citations (quotations and allusions) from the Psalms in the Epistle to the Hebrews, all from the Septuagint.[14] Eleven psalms are quoted.[15] Sometimes the writer merely makes association with certain terms in the Old Testament, like "angels" (Heb 1:5–7/Pss 2:7; 104:4). In other instances he uses a psalm as the basis of his argument, as he does Psalm 110, arguing that Christ is a priest in the order of Melchizedek (Heb 7). It is quite obvious that he believes the Old Testament predicted Christ, and he views the Psalms as a repository of prophetic prediction.[16]

Summary

Holladay has a helpful summary of the hermeneutical function of Psalms texts (and Old Testament texts in general) in the New Testament:[17]

1. In some ways the Qumran sect and the New Testament writers share a hermeneutic. One shared attitude is that they both believed that their era was the final epoch of history, and they applied the Old Testament texts to demonstrate that. For the Qumran covenanters the Psalms

had pointed to the "teacher of righteousness," whereas the New Testament writers believed they had spoken directly of Christ. At Jesus' baptism the voice from heaven quotes Psalm 2:7 to confirm his messiahship in terms of his kingship and divine sonship: "And a voice came from heaven: 'You are my Son, whom I love; with you I am well pleased'" (Mk 1:11/Mt 3:17/Lk 3:22).

2. The New Testament writers use the Psalms to support the truth that has been revealed in Jesus Christ. This truth, which does not necessarily arise out of the Old Testament text, is supported by it. The Psalms provide affirming evidence.

3. The New Testament writers employ the seven hermeneutical rules of **Hillel** in their application of Old Testament texts. Jesus employed the first rule, which was an argument from the "light" to the "heavy" (Hebrew *qal vahomer*). That is, if one thing of less importance is true, then by analogy, another thing of weightier importance must be true. Jesus made use of this method in the Sermon on the Mount:

And why do you worry about clothes? See how the lilies of the field grow. They do not labor or spin. Yet I tell you that not even Solomon in all his splendor was

Hillel's Seven Rules of Interpretation

Hillel, born about 50 B.C., became president of the Sanhedrin during the reign of Herod the Great. Hillel introduced seven rules of interpreting Scripture, which were subsequently expanded into thirteen by Rabbi Ishmael ben Elisha of the second century A.D.

1. The inference from the *minor* to the *major* (*qal vahomer*, light and heavy).
2. The analogy of expressions.
3. The generalization of one special provision.
4. The generalization of two special provisions.
5. The effect of general and particular terms.
6. The analogy made from another passage.
7. The explanation derived from the context.

midrash

dressed like one of these. If that is how God clothes the grass of the field, which is here today and tomorrow is thrown into the fire, will he not much more clothe you, O you of little faith? (Mt 6:28–30)

4. The New Testament writers operated under the assumption that the Psalms could be interpreted midrashically (see **midrash** in glossary), which meant that there was some flexibility in how they applied the texts to their New Testament realities. That seems to be the way the writer to the Hebrews applied Psalm 110, particularly in his application of the Melchizedek reference to Jesus (Heb 7).

5. The New Testament writers take for granted that the Psalms prefigure New Testament realities. The psalmist declares about humanity, or the son of man: "You made him ruler over the works of your hands; / you put everything under his feet" (Ps 8:6). Both Paul and the writer to the Hebrews understand this Psalm to prefigure Jesus Christ, the Son of Man. The "feet" are his feet (1 Cor 15:27; Heb 2:6–9).

6. The New Testament writers were aware of a mystery revealed in their time which the Old Testament writers had predicted. Matthew applies the "parables" and "hidden things" of Psalm 78:2 to Jesus' use of parables (Mt 13:35).

The New Testament use of the Psalms, and for that matter, the Old Testament generally, is a fascinating study. The New Testament writers believed that the Psalms had spoken of Jesus of Nazareth, and Jesus himself offered a post-resurrection body of teaching on this matter: "He said to them, 'This is what I told you while I was still with you: Everything must be fulfilled that is written about me in the Law of Moses, the Prophets and the Psalms'" (Lk 24:44). We may speculate that many of the New Testament applications have their origin in those teachings which Jesus Christ gave between his resurrection and ascension.

The Psalms in Temple Worship

This topic is complicated by the fact that it is difficult to reconstruct the temple liturgy. Here, of course, we are speaking about the second temple (dedicated in 516 B.C.) and the temple of Herod (destroyed in A.D. 70), since the Psalter was incomplete while the Solomonic temple existed (destroyed in 586 B.C.). The singing of the Psalms in the first temple, however, is attested in the Psalter itself. Psalm 92 has the heading, "A Song for the Sabbath." By the time the Old Testament was translated into Greek (ca. 250–150 B.C.), Psalms 24, 48, 94, and 93 were also assigned to particular days of the week:

First Day	Psalm 24 (LXX Ps 23)
Second Day	Psalm 48 (LXX Ps 47)
Fourth Day	Psalm 94 (LXX Ps 93)
Sixth Day	Psalm 93 (LXX Ps 92)
Sabbath	Psalm 92 (LXX Ps 91)

The roster of daily psalms had probably been completed a long time before the destruction of the temple by Titus in A.D. 70. The list is given in the tractate *Tamid* of the Mishnah:

First day	Psalm 24
Second day	Psalm 48
Third day	Psalm 82
Fourth day	Psalm 94
Fifth day	Psalm 81
Sixth day	Psalm 93
Seventh day	Psalm 92[18]

The Mishnah further locates the singing of the psalm of the day after the morning and afternoon sacrifices.[19] Other uses of the Psalms are known, for example, the singing of Psalm 135 on the morning of the Feast of the Passover, but the date when certain psalms or parts of psalms were introduced into the temple service is difficult to determine.

The Psalms in Synagogue Worship

Abraham Millgram has called the Psalms "the spiritual girders of the synagogue worship."[20] The synagogue developed alongside the temple, and correlations to the temple services characterized synagogue worship. John Alexander Lamb gives six ways the Psalms were used in synagogue worship:[21]

1. The Psalms were recited in part or in whole in the services.
2. Proper Psalms, or psalms appropriate to the day or festival, were assigned. They included:

The Hallel (Pss 113–18)	New Moon
	Passover
	Pentecost
	Tabernacles
	Dedication
Psalm 7	Feast of Purim

Psalm 12	8th day of Feast of Tabernacles
Psalm 30	Feast of Dedication
Psalm 47	Feast of the New Year
Psalms 98 and 104	Feast of the New Moon
Psalms 103 and 130	Day of Atonement

3. At points, certain verses from the Psalms were recited. For example, after one puts on the *tallith* (prayer shawl), Psalm 36:7–10 is read, and after the Torah scroll is removed from the ark, the leader holds it up and says Psalm 34:3, "O magnify the Lord with me and let us exalt his name together."
4. Some scholars have suggested that the Psalms were read in the synagogue in a trienniel cycle, as the Torah was read in Palestine. The number of 150 psalms would be about adequate for a three-year lectionary cycle. Unfortunately no evidence of such a cycle has survived in the Jewish prayer book.
5. Responses from the Psalms were incorporated in the synagogue services. Certain doxologies from the Psalter were a part of the liturgy.
6. Many prayers are composed of phrases from the Psalms, some of them being a catena of psalmic terms and phrases.

The Psalms in Christian Worship

Surveying the Christian use of the Psalms in worship is as challenging as trying to survey Jewish practice. We can only highlight some of the notable works that draw heavily upon the Psalms.

The Church until the Reformation

Among those early Christian works that draw heavily from the Psalms are 1 Clement (ca. A.D. 96), which cites the Psalms thirty-two times (out of forty-nine Old Testament citations), the Epistle of Barnabas (ca. A.D. 130), with twelve citations from ten different psalms, Justin Martyr's *Apology* and *Dialogue with Trypho* (middle of the second century A.D.), with numerous citations, and Irenaeus's *Against Heresies* (second half of the second century A.D.), which also is replete with Psalm citations.[22]

In Augustine's *Confessions* he writes the story of his baptism by Ambrose and notes that the church in Milan had taken over the Eastern practice of singing hymns and psalms.[23] Further, by the time of Augustine proper psalms had come into use, and certain psalms were assigned to particular days of the Christian calendar.[24]

A further activity that evidences the popularity of the Psalms in the early church was the number of commentaries written on the book or portions of it. They include commentaries by Origen (ca. A.D. 185–254), Jerome (ca. 342–420), Theodore of Mopsuestia (ca. 350–428), and Augustine (d. 430).

The liturgies of both the Eastern and Western Church are full of the Psalms. In the Western and Eastern Orthodox Churches the recitation of the entire Psalter is part of the weekly Divine Office.[25] This was also true of the Rule of Saint Benedict (ca. A.D. 530), which became the basis for the Roman Catholic Divine Office.[26]

The Psalms in the Reformation Church

The Reformers were as much in love with the Psalms as any of the fathers and mothers of the church. Some of Martin Luther's early lectures were on Psalms 1–126. Roland Bainton has written of Luther's love

and use of the Psalms, suggesting that he lived in them so deeply that "he improved them":

> Luther so lived his way into the Psalms that he improved them. In the original the transitions are sometimes abrupt and the meaning not always plain. Luther simplified and clarified. . . . Take his conclusion to the Seventy-third Psalm. "My heart is stricken and my bones fail, that I must be a fool and know nothing, that I must be as a beast before thee. Nevertheless I will ever cleave to thee. Thou holdest me by thy right hand and leadest me by thy counsel. Thou wilt crown me at last with honor" [vv. 21–24].[27]

He comments that Luther took great liberties with the Psalms

> because here he was so completely at home. They were the record of the spiritual struggles through which he was constantly passing. . . . Where the English version of Psalm 90 speaks of "secret sins" Luther has "unrecognized sins." He was thinking of his fruitless efforts in the cloister to recall every wrongdoing, that it might be confessed and pardoned. Where the English translates, "So teach us to number our days, that we may apply our hearts unto wisdom," Luther is blunt: "Teach us so to reflect on death that we may be wise."[28]

An example well known to English speakers is Luther's hymn "A Mighty Fortress Is Our God," based upon Psalm 46. This powerful paraphrase capsulates the meaning of the psalm in potent language, reflecting Luther's own spiritual struggle.

With John Calvin a new trend in Psalm usage takes effect, the singing of **metrical psalms.** Calvin insisted that there could be no better instrument for the praise of God than the Psalms: "There can be no better songs than the psalms spoken by the Holy Spirit."[29] Convinced that worship must take place in the vernacular language and that congregational participation was highly desirable, he chose the metrical version of the Psalms as the most adaptable form. This form was simply a paraphrase of the Psalms into metrical form, following the meter and rhyme of Latin poetry, rather than the rhythmic Hebrew style, which does not have strict meter. He himself tried his hand at putting the Psalms into metrical form, without much success, and in 1539 he published a metrical version of thirteen psalms in French, composed by Clement Marot (1497–1544), and to those he added five of his own psalms, plus the Song of Simeon, and the Ten Commandments. Several editions like this appeared in the next twenty-five years, and a second edition was published by Calvin in 1541, for which Louis Bourgeois was his musical editor. It was Bourgeois who composed the tune "Old One Hundredth," to which Psalm 100 was sung and continues to be sung even today. This tune was published in an earlier edition of the Geneva Psalter in 1551. Then in 1562 the entire Psalter, all 150 psalms, reached its metrical completion at the hand of Theodore Beza, one of Calvin's colleagues in Geneva. It included 125 melodies to which the Psalms could be sung[30] and was so popular that it went through sixty-two printings within two years of its publication and was translated into twenty-four languages.[31]

On the English side of the continent, Miles Coverdale, famous for his Bible translation, published an English version of thirteen metrical psalms in 1535. In the year 1549 Thomas Sternhold and John Hopkins published a larger version containing forty-four psalms, unfortunately known for their verbosity. This book was enlarged, most likely by William Whittingham, to include all 150 Psalms and was published in London in 1562. The famous English version of Psalm 100, "All people that on earth do dwell," written by William Kethe, first appeared in this edition.[32]

In England the developing and reforming Anglican Church published its first Prayer Book in 1549, in which a method of reciting the Psalms was put forth: they should be completed in course once each month. Moreover, it prescribed how the Psalter was to be used at Matins (morning service) and at Evensong (evening service). The translation of the Psalms given in this Prayer Book was that of the Great Bible, published under the auspices of King Henry VIII in 1539.[33]

Before the Reformation the Psalms were chanted in plainsong by the priest and choir, but during the Reformation the congregation, especially under Calvin's influence, became more involved in the singing of the Psalms.

The Scottish Psalter has a rich heritage, going back to the Genevan Psalter. When John Knox returned to Scotland from Geneva in 1559, he brought back the Geneva Psalter as it had developed in that city. Two Edinburgh ministers, Robert Pont and John Craig, revised it and published the new edition in 1564 as part of the *Book of Common Order*, sometimes known as the *Psalm-Book*. It contained all 150 psalms in metrical form, plus several other metrical versions of *Veni Creator, Nunc Dimittis, Magnificat*, and the Twelve Articles of the Christian Faith (a version of the Apostles' Creed). This continued to be the metrical Scottish Psalter until 1650, and seventy editions were published between 1564 and 1644. This Psalter included more than a hundred tunes, forty-two of them being from Geneva, with no harmony provided. Calvin had preferred unison singing, and this continued for some time in the Scottish Church. The 1635 edition, however, provided harmony for all the tunes.[34]

Francis Rous had published an edition of the Psalter that made its way to Scotland, and the Westminster Assembly approved that version, on the provision that it be revised. This edition appeared in 1650 and has continued in various versions to the present day.

On the other side of the Atlantic, Psalm singing was also a popular mode of worship. Some felt that it was not fair to the Hebrew text to enlarge the Psalms with words and ideas that were not in the text, as the Sternhold and Hopkins versions had done so freely, so they urged a more faithful rendering of the Hebrew text into English metrical form. The *Bay Psalm Book*, published in Cambridge, Massachusetts, in 1640, was the product of this way of thinking.

The Psalms into the Twenty-First Century

The tradition of Psalm singing has continued in the United States, even though hymn singing tended to replace this tradition in the middle of the nineteenth century. However, in 1858 the United Presbyterian Church began to revise the old Scottish Psalter and published the *Book of Psalms* in 1871, which contained revised Scottish psalms and new versifications. A music edition was published in 1887 as *The Psalter*. This development represented a "small beginning of a revival of metrical psalmody in North America."[35] At the invitation of the United Presbyterian Church in 1893, nine different denominations came together and eventually published an ecumenical psalter in 1912, simply called *Psalter*. It was the first thoroughly North American psalter. While most of the texts were new, a few old ones from the 1887 version and older psalters survived, like Isaac Watts's Psalm 90 ("O God, Our Help in Ages Past"), and the Scottish Psalter Psalm 23 ("The Lord's My Shepherd, I'll Not Want"), and William Kethe's Psalm 100 from the Anglo-Genevan Psalter of 1561. This became the best known and most widely used psalter of the twentieth century.[36]

Eventually the United Presbyterian Church began singing hymns, and they added them to their psalter, publishing the *Psalter Hymnal* in 1927, followed by the Christian Reformed Church, which published its psalter under the same title in 1934. This latter edition revived more than thirty Genevan tunes, now set to English texts. The 1912 Psalter had virtually abandoned the Genevan Psalter. The Genevan tradition has been preserved by the Canadian Reformed Churches, which published the *Book of Praise* (1972; 2nd ed., 1984), which is the only extant complete Genevan Psalter with English texts.[37] Emily R. Brink details the revival of metrical psalm singing in the last part of the twentieth century and states three influences: (1) the publication of the *Common Lectionary* in 1983, which assigned psalms for each Sunday; (2) the publication of *Psalm Praise* in 1973 by the Jubilate Group in England; and (3) the ecumenical movement, although that influence is waning.[38] Brink also analyzed ten recent hymnals that indicated a strong psalmody influence in American churches.[39] In the last thirty years of the twentieth century the Reformed Presbyterian Church of North America published the *Book of Psalms for Singing* (1973), which preserved the Scottish Psalter tradition, and the Christian Reformed Church published a new edition of the *Psalter Hymnal* in 1987, which preserved a strong Genevan Psalter influence.[40]

Hiding the Psalms in One's Heart

Perhaps the reader may be surprised to find this kind of practical advice in a book of this nature, but the Psalms are some of the most practical literature in the Bible and they call for practical suggestions on ways to draw upon their rich spiritual resources. In that vein, I would like to say that consistent and systematic memorization of Scripture is a discipline every Christian should follow. I sometimes give my students a duo of practical advice, that (1) they should always be reading some good literature outside their own discipline, and (2) they should always be memorizing portions of Scripture and great literature. Given the power of the

Psalms, they are one of the best portions of Holy Scripture for memorization. When we fill our minds with them, hide them in our hearts, the Holy Spirit can bring them forth at the appropriate time for comfort and reassurance. We can review them when we are waiting on someone, or when we are delayed for an appointment, or when we are taking our morning jog. They can be the object of reflection and recitation when we wake in the early hours of the morning and cannot drop off to sleep again.

In addition to memorization, we should read the Psalms systematically. The method of reading the Psalms through once a month (five psalms a day for thirty days), put forth in the first Anglican Prayer Book of 1549, is still a beneficial way to make the Psalms a part of our daily devotion and a practical part of our lives. They ought not to replace the reading of other portions of the Old and New Testaments, but should be a supplement to those readings. Dietrich Bonhoeffer in his excellent little book on the Psalms wrote about the power of the Psalms to set the order of the day right:

> The entire day receives order and discipline when it acquires unity. This unity must be sought and found in morning prayer. It is confirmed in work. The morning prayer determines the day. Squandered time of which we are ashamed, temptations to which we succumb, weaknesses and lack of courage in work, disorganization and lack of discipline in our thoughts and in our conversation with other men, all have their origin most often in the neglect of morning prayer.[41]

One thing for sure, the Psalms will enrich our spiritual life and give us windows through which to look at the events of our lives. Through those windows we will see the hues of a new landscape where our help comes from the Lord, who made heaven and earth.

Study Questions

1. The Psalms examine our problems of sin, injustice, illness, and trauma "in light of the solution." Where do the Psalms inexorably center that solution? Explain how this solution can be basic without being simplistic.

2. How do the Psalms manifest a preincarnational revelation of Jesus Christ?

3. The New Testament writers grounded their understanding of the Psalms in Jesus' person, words, and works. Give three examples of their Christocentric interpretation of the Psalms.

4. By A.D. 70 psalmic use had been formalized in the worship of temple and synagogues. Describe the use of psalms in both temple and synagogue.

5. The early church adopted the practice of using psalms in worship, both in reading and singing. How did John Calvin contextualize this practice for the Western world? Give an example of this practice in worship today.

6. What practical steps might one give for allowing the Psalms to order and sanctify our lives? Why is this advice integral to even an academic approach to the Psalms?

Summary

It is hardly possible to draw together a summary of the power and use of the Psalms in Christian and Jewish worship and personal piety during the centuries of this era. However, our cursory discussion of this topic suggests the potency of the Psalms in both worship traditions. As for the Christian experience, we can say without hesitation that no book of the Bible has been more influential in shaping the worship and piety of the Church. The Reformation, especially the Reformed expression of it, perceptively seized upon the power of the Psalter and thrust it forward as its book of prayer and praise. And hopefully, the modern generation of Christians is rediscovering this powerful instrument of worship.

Key Terms

pesher
Hillel
qal vahomer
midrash
metrical psalms

5 Encountering Theology and History in the Psalms

Outline

- **Israel and Creation**
- **The Patriarchs in Retrospect**
- **The Exodus**
  Egyptian Bondage
  Crossing of the Red Sea
- **Sinai**
- **The Wilderness**
- **Conquest**
- **Life in the Land**
- **The Monarchy**
- **The Exile and Return**
- **Summary**

Objectives

After reading this chapter, you should be able to

1. Discuss theological aspects of the Psalms.
2. Summarize the views of Israel's history as presented in the Psalms.

Given the prominent position of the first eleven chapters of Genesis in the Torah and the significant names that occur there, it is rather surprising that only one person from these chapters, Ham, is mentioned by name in the Psalter, and that one only incidentally. Yet at the same time we should remember that the Psalter contains neither a systematic presentation of theology or history. When historical persons are named, the theological purpose of individual psalms and of the Psalter as a whole determines *when* and *where* such persons are mentioned. Even though history is a major component of the Book of Psalms, it is at the service of the psalmists' theology. That is not to suggest that historical data are bantered about with reckless abandon, but simply to say that the psalmists, like the Old Testament writers of history in general, do not distinguish sharply between history and theology. These writers are "painters" rather than "photographers."[1] A delicate balance exists between these two components, a balance that the Western mind may not fully appreciate since we have made them two distinct categories. In the Old Testament they tend to blend into each other and form a single category. Nevertheless, when we discuss them, there is no way we can ignore the distinction we have come to make between them. But as our discussion proceeds, we must remind ourselves that we have entered a category of the Hebrew worldview that was far more a single fabric than it is in our minds.

I have therefore chosen to discuss theology and history somewhat separately because that is the way we understand them, and quite likely we can only enter the Hebrew mind with integrity through the door of our Western categories. Yet, when we are there, thankfully, we can claim some ownership of that mind-set—the Old Testament is our testament too—while at the same time recognizing we are resident aliens in that culture.

Israel and Creation

Our discussion of creation and its place in Israel's understanding of history will come under theology. Suffice it to say at this point that in the scheme of things, creation marks the beginning of history. "In the beginning" was the point of entry into what we know as history, the realm of time and space in which the human-divine story occurs. Even though some scholars insist that the beginning of history in the Old Testament is properly that of the Abrahamic narrative, there is hardly any question that the writer of Genesis viewed the events recorded in chapters 1–11 as part of the historical narrative he set out to compose. It all began at creation. While the Psalms are not concerned with *when* history began, creation marks the boundary line between the divine and the human orders. Yet God the Creator establishes the boundary in such a way that his existence is intertwined with the created order:

> O Lord my God, you are very
>   great;
>   you are clothed with splendor
>   and majesty.
> He wraps himself in light as with a
>   garment;
>   he stretches out the heavens like
>   a tent
>   and lays the beams of his upper
>   chambers on their waters.
> He makes the clouds his chariot
>   and rides on the wings of the
>   wind.
> He makes winds his messengers,
>   flames of fire his servants. (Ps
>   104:1b–4)

The psalmist understands quite well that the Creator not only brought the world into existence, but the world is an expression of himself. It is a metaphor of his being. To use a term that will come to express this concept in the theological distance of Scripture, he *incarnates* himself in it. Thus, "The heavens declare the glory of God; / the skies proclaim the work of his hands" (Ps 19:1). And the reciprocal transaction is expected, that humanity should reflect his character: "May the words of my mouth and the meditation of my heart / be pleasing in your sight, / O LORD, my Rock and my Redeemer" (Ps 19:14).

The Patriarchs in Retrospect

As we have already observed, the psalmic memory has little information regarding the period between creation and the patriarchal age. Even so important an episode as the flood with its hero, Noah, does not demand attention, except for the mention of Noah's son, Ham, as the patriarch of the Egyptians (Ps 105:23, 27).

Yet all three patriarchs, Abraham, Isaac, and Jacob, merit mention in the Psalms. Abraham takes the place of honor as the "servant" of the Lord, where the Abrahamic covenant is the centerpiece of Psalm 105. As the psalmist writes his brief history of the **exodus,** that event which, more than any other, made the promise to Abraham a reality, the focus of the covenant is the gift of the land to Abraham and his descendants. In fact, the psalm, after a stanza of praise (vv. 1–4), recounts the covenant with Abraham, of which the central feature was the land, and then closes this brief theological history by tying together the Abrahamic covenant and the exodus, thus completing the promise that God made to Abraham and confirmed to Isaac and Jacob:

> For he remembered his holy promise
> given to his servant Abraham.
> He brought out his people with rejoicing,
> his chosen ones with shouts of joy;
> he gave them the lands of the nations,
> and they fell heir to what others had toiled for—
> that they might keep his precepts and observe his laws.
> Praise the LORD. (105:42–45)

As in the Genesis narrative, Isaac gets short shrift in the Psalms (105:9), but Jacob receives more attention, much of it due to the use of his eponym for the nation Israel. The one scene in which we see a snatch of Jacob's life is found in the synopsis of the Joseph story in 105:16–23. When Pharaoh made Joseph "ruler over all he possessed," "Then Israel entered Egypt; / Jacob lived as an alien in the land of Ham" (105:23).

The person from the patriarchal era to whom the psalmist assigns an action story of some relative length is Joseph. And just as Joseph is the link between the patriarchs and the Egyptian oppression in the story line of the Pentateuch, his story serves the same function in Psalm 105. The basic details are picked up from the Joseph story in Genesis (Gn 37–50):

- Joseph was a slave;
- Joseph was known for his predictions;
- Joseph was released from prison by the king;
- Joseph became ruler of the king's household and all he possessed (Ps 105:19–21; see Gn 41).

With slight embellishments the psalmist, using his poetic license, provides the details one would expect in a prison story: "They bruised his feet with shackles, / his neck was put in irons" (105:18). Another detail of the psalm that the Genesis narrative does not mention is Joseph's instruction of the king's princes and elders (v. 22). This too would be the prerogative of a man in Joseph's position of authority, so the psalmist is offering a slightly fuller job description for Joseph than we have in the Genesis story. It is quite likely that the psalmist had an oral tradition that had transmitted this information.

Nestled in the patriarchal narratives is the interesting and rather peculiar story of Sodom and Gomorrah. It functions as a way to show how very important to God Abraham was, and it also performs another literary duty, namely, to give the readership

History in the Psalms

The controversy over Old Testament history has itself become a long tradition, as modern criticism goes. Its beginnings were crystallized in the work of Julius Wellhausen, who viewed the Pentateuch as a composite work made up of four literary documents: J, E, D, and P. Wellhausen's conclusions regarding the composition of the Pentateuch were shaped by his acceptance of the Hegelian scheme of history, which insisted that human history and culture developed from the simple forms and ideas to the complex. Thus Wellhausen gave an order to this developmental hypothesis which placed the simplest source, "J" (called J because it used the name Jehovah = Yahweh as the name for God), first in time, and the most complex of the sources, "P" (called Priestly because it contained the code of priestly laws), last. Other scholars, like Hermann Gunkel, Martin Noth, and Gerhard von Rad, resorting to form and tradition criticism, have emphasized the traditions that stand behind these sources. Canonical criticism, championed by Brevard S. Childs, among others, has emphasized the final shape of the text as the form that we must deal with. Ironically, Old Testament criticism, which was vitalized by Hegel's development theory, from thesis to antithesis to synthesis, has undergone the process itself and in a sense reached its synthesis in the canonical approach to Scripture. That is most obvious when looking at Old Testament theology. Source criticism resulted in a fragmented text, dictating that the theologian must speak about "theologies" rather than theology. Form and tradition criticism, despite their effort to say something about the text that could hopefully enlighten the student on how the Old Testament, especially the Pentateuch, came to be, nevertheless failed to produce a theology in the singular sense. Some scholars felt that the Old Testament had therefore lost its meaning for the church. But to give up on this powerful body of literature, which had sustained the Jewish and Christian communities for so many centuries, was a radical and unwarranted turn of events. Canonical criticism, without invalidating the basic methods and conclusions of its predecessors, sought to bring synthesis to this process. By emphasizing the primacy of the final form of the text, regardless of how it had come to be, this method introduced the possibility that the Old Testament could again speak with a unified voice. Certainly that's the kind of voice the New Testament writers and the early church theologians heard in the Old Testament.

Unfortunately the canonical approach has not answered the question that conservative scholars insist must be answered: Is Old Testament history an accurate and reliable record of Israel's past? The Psalms, in my view, reflect an accurate picture of Old Testament history, based upon the following observations:

1. Basically the order of events is the same as that which is presented in the Pentateuch and the historical books.
2. The descriptions of each event are remarkably similar to what we find outside the Psalms. When additional details are included, they may be attributed to poetic license or to oral information passed down through the generations. Oral tradition should not be considered inaccurate simply because it is oral. Admittedly it runs a greater risk of inaccuracy, but the ancient memory was a powerful tool for the preservation of fact as well as fiction.
3. The balance of the historical events as seen outside the Psalms, especially in the Pentateuch, is reflected in the same proportions in the Psalter. It hardly needs to be said that the central event-complex in the Pentateuch is exodus-Sinai. Similarly this centrality is reflected in the Book of Psalms, expecially in its emphasis upon the exodus. Moreover, in the Old Testament the conquest is of such major proportions that the entire Book of Joshua is devoted to it. In like manner the Psalms treat this era as central to Israel's history.

a preview of the Canaanite sin of sexual perversion. We should recall that the writer of Genesis promised that the Israelites would be in slavery for four hundred years and only afterward possess the land of Canaan. It would not happen until the "fourth generation" because "the sin of the Amorites has not yet reached its full measure" (Gn 15:16). The picture of that sin in its full dimensions, with its depraved effect upon the Israelites, is not seen until the story of the Benjamites in Judges 19—the Benjamites had assimilated the homosexual perversion of their Canaanite neighbors. Sodom in its Genesis context did not represent the moral totality of Canaan, only an isolated example of what could happen if sexual sin were allowed to go unchecked. The Book of Judges announces the bad news that Israel did not follow God's orders to annihilate the Canaanite population, and the outcome was the assimilation of the sins of the Canaanites, of which Judges 19 is the final picture.

Psalm 107, perhaps in a concealed reference to Sodom, draws a broad contrast between the Lord's power to turn rivers into a desert, a miracle that he accomplishes "because of the wickedness of those who lived there," and his power to reverse the process:

> He turned rivers into a desert,
>   flowing springs into thirsty
>   ground,
> and fruitful land into a salt waste
>   because of the wickedness of
>   those who lived there.
> He turned the desert into pools of
>   water
>   and the parched ground into
>   flowing springs;
> there he brought the hungry to live,
>   and they founded a city
>   where they could settle.
> They sowed fields and planted
>   vineyards
>   that yielded a fruitful
>   harvest;
> he blessed them, and their num-
>   bers greatly increased,
>   and he did not let their herds di-
>   minish. (vv. 33–38)

Indeed, if one looks at verses 33–43 of this psalm, an outline of the psalmist's theology of history is evident:

- the Lord punishes wickedness by transforming a prosperous land into wasteland (vv. 33–34);
- the Lord blesses the earth (and Israel) and causes them to increase (vv. 35–38);
- the Lord causes the depletion of the population and brings calamity and sorrow (vv. 39–40);

- the Lord restores the needy and causes their numbers and the livestock to increase (v. 41).

Although Psalm 107 does not use the terms of curse and blessing, that is nevertheless the pattern we see here. If we agree that verses 33–34 are a veiled reference to Sodom and Gomorrah, then the psalmist is using that event as ethical ground zero to show how God exhibits his power and his grace.

The Exodus

Presently the tendency is to study the historical motifs according to the genres of the psalms. Erik Haglund uses the older genre divisions of the form-critical school and identifies the exodus motif in the following genres:

hymns: 68, 81, 105, 114, 135, 136
national laments: 74, 80, 106
individual thanksgivings: 66, 103
individual lament: 77
psalm of instruction: 78[2]

The simpler categories of Claus Westermann, lament and praise, comprise the basis for Clark Hyde's breakdown of the exodus motif. As a minor motif it occurs in both psalms of praise and lament:

lament: 44, 74, 77, 80
praise: 66, 68, 99, 103, 135

In the laments, the exodus forms the basis on which the people of Israel appeal to Yahweh to act now in response to their desperate situation and pleading prayer, whereas the hymns of praise offer up acclamation to God because he had delivered Israel from Egyptian bondage.[3]

Major mention of the exodus occurs in five psalms, two of which are psalms of praise, Psalms 114 and 136, and three psalms that are generally considered historical psalms, Psalms 78, 105, and 106.[4] While their discussion by genre is quite helpful, I would

The Egyptian Bondage

"During that long period, the king of Egypt died. The Israelites groaned in their slavery and cried out, and their cry for help because of their slavery went up to God. God heard their groaning and he remembered his covenant with Abraham, with Isaac and with Jacob. So God looked on the Israelites and was concerned about them." (Ex 2:23–25)

Pharaoh's Population Control

The Exodus narrative tells us that Pharaoh used three methods of population control on the Israelites. He (1) imposed forced labor upon them; (2) directed the Hebrew midwives to kill the male babies when they were born; and (3) commanded the Egyptians to throw all the male babies into the Nile River (Ex 1:9–22).

like to follow the historical lines of the Old Testament narratives and look at the events as they are described in the Psalms.

Egyptian Bondage

The historical memory of the Psalms recalls the suffering of the Israelites in Egypt. We see the picture of slave labor in Psalm 81:6–7a: "I removed the burden from their shoulders; / their hands were set free from the basket. / In their distress you called and I rescued you."

Psalms 103:6–7 and 105:23–25 contain oblique references to their suffering, in each case followed by the reference to Moses as their deliverer. Psalm 105:23–27 recalls that Egypt was an alien land for the Israelites, and the Lord made them so numerous that the Egyptians conspired against them:

> Then Israel entered Egypt;
> > Jacob lived as an alien in the land of Ham.
> The LORD made his people very fruitful;
> > he made them too numerous for their foes,
> whose hearts he turned to hate his people,
> > to conspire against his servants.
> He sent Moses his servant,
> > and Aaron, whom he had chosen.

Another feature of the story that we see in the Psalms is Yahweh's readiness, more like eagerness, to deliver his people from their bondage.

The Exodus narrative associates thunder, as does Psalm 81:7, with the plagues, but it also allies the phenomenon of thunder with the giving of the law on Sinai. Perhaps the psalm is speaking in both directions. Not only did God answer their cry with the immediacy of the plagues, which led to their political and physical emancipation (Ex 9:28–29, 33–34), but he was ready to answer their cry at a deeper level than that—with the revelation of himself on Sinai. The Hebrew term that the NIV translated as "thundercloud" (Ps 81:7) is really "secret [place] of thunder": "In your distress you called, and I delivered you, / I answered you at the secret place of thunder" (v. 7, author's trans.). The psalmist saw in the exodus God's pattern for dealing with Israel throughout history (vv. 4–7): he delivers his people when they call out to him, and in view of that, they should honor him as their one and only God. If they would do that, rather than rebel against him in the wilderness as they had done (vv. 8, 11), then he would subdue their enemies as he had subdued the Egyptians (vv. 13–15).

Though not verbatim, this psalm preserves the substance of the first commandment: "You shall have no foreign god among you; / you shall not bow down to an alien god" (v. 9). Also appended to this commandment is Yahweh's statement of self-identity that prefixes the Ten Commandments in Exodus 20 and Deuteronomy 5: "I am the LORD

The First Commandment

And God spoke all these words: "I am the LORD your God, who brought you out of Egypt, out of the land of slavery. You shall have no other gods before me" (Ex 20:1–3).

your God, / who brought you up out of Egypt" (v. 10).

The plagues are of major interest in Psalms 78 and 105. Although there are some differences in their order as compared to the Exodus narrative, neither the order nor an exhaustive list seems to be the interest of the psalmists. Rather they focus on the *fact* of the plagues as God's way of manifesting his great power before their enemies. The purpose of the list in Psalm 78 is to remind the Israelites that their ancestors rebelled against the Lord in the wilderness despite the fact that he had performed these great miracles in their midst (vv. 41–42), a sober reminder that they should not repeat this response of ingrati-

tude. Psalm 105, on the other hand, lists the plagues among God's miraculous works that were designed to teach Israel to "keep his precepts and observe his laws" (v. 45). In any case, of particular interest is the fact that the death of the firstborn, so climactic in the Exodus order of the plagues, is also the climax in both lists found in Psalms 78 and 105. More than that, the tenth plague is also mentioned in 135:8 and 136:10.

The following table does not attempt to coordinate the lists but simply indicates the order of the plagues in each case. A blank occurs in the list where the plague of the Exodus narrative is lacking in the psalm. Psalm 78 lists seven plagues (gnats, boils, and darkness are missing), and Psalm 105 names eight (death of livestock and boils are missing).

Other details matching the story in Exodus include the idea that the Israelites carried with them expensive items that they had borrowed from the Egyptians; and that even though the Egyptians had been favorably disposed toward the Israelites at one point, they were glad to see them finally go:

Table 5.1
The Order of the Plagues

in Exodus	in Ps 78	in Ps 105
1. Water to blood 7:17–21	Rivers to blood 78:44	Darkness 105:28
2. Frogs 8:2–13	Flies 78:45	Water to blood 105:29
3. Gnats 8:16–19		Frogs 105:30
4. Flies 8:21–31	Frogs 78:45	Flies 105:31
5. Death of livestock 9:1–7	Death of livestock 78:48	
6. Boils 9:8–12		
7. Hail 9:13–35	Locusts 78:46	Gnats 105:31
8. Locusts 10:1–20	Hail 78:47	Hail 105:32–33
9. Darkness 10:21–29		Locusts 105:34–35
10. Death of firstborn 11:1–10	Death of firstborn 78:51	Death of firstborn 105:36

He brought out Israel, laden with
    silver and gold
    and from among their tribes no
      one faltered.
Egypt was glad when they left,
    because dread of Israel had
      fallen on them. (105:37–38)

The story of the exodus as reflected in the Psalms, quite interestingly, and quite in keeping with the
integrity of the Exodus narratives,
contains the negative side of the story
as well. When Pharaoh assessed his
work projects and the grave need for
laborers that the departure of this
slave population had created, he had
second thoughts about his decision
and pursued them all the way to the
Red Sea. With Pharaoh's army on one
side and the Red Sea on the other—
what seemed a certain death trap—
the Israelites rebelled against Moses.
Psalm 106, which is entirely devoted
to the exodus theme, recalls that critical moment:

When our fathers were in Egypt,
    they gave no thought to your
      miracles;
they did not remember your many
    kindnesses,
and they rebelled by the sea, the
    Red Sea. (v. 7)

Crossing of the Red Sea

The graphic description of the
parting of the waters of the sea and
Israel walking through on dry
ground is not lost to the psalmists.
Whereas the Exodus narrative speaks
in terms of God's control of nature
("the LORD drove the sea back with a
strong east wind and turned it into
dry land"—Ex 14:21), Psalm 106:9
gives the event an ethical flavor, as if
the Red Sea stood in the way of the
divine will. Therefore, the Lord commanded the sea to stand aside so his
people could walk through, and walk
through on dry ground: "He rebuked
the Red Sea, and it dried up; / he led
them through the depths as through
a desert."

As one would expect, the Psalms
share the metaphorical language of

The Plunder of the Egyptians

The Egyptians urged the people
to hurry and leave the country.
"For otherwise," they said, "we will
all die!". . . The Israelites did as
Moses instructed and asked the
Egyptians for articles of silver and
gold and for clothing. The LORD
had made the Egyptians favorably
disposed toward the people, and
they gave them what they asked
for; so they plundered the Egyptians (Ex 12:33, 35–36).

---

the Song of the Sea (Ex 15). This way of
describing the event is similar to the
poetic account in Exodus 15:8, where
the east wind of 14:21 has become the
"blast" of Yahweh's nostrils:

By the blast of your nostrils
    the waters piled up.
The surging waters stood firm like
    a wall;
    the deep waters congealed in
      the heart of the sea.

Psalms 77 and 114 switch the subject from the Lord to the sea itself,
personifying the Red Sea and the
Jordan River. The waters saw God
and recoiled at his awesome presence. Then when he had led the way
through the sea, there was no doubt
that he had gone ahead of Israel,
even though no one could see his
footprints:

The waters saw you, O God,
    the waters saw you and
      writhed;
    the very depths were
      convulsed.
The clouds poured down water,
    the skies resounded with thunder;
    your arrows flashed back and
      forth.
Your thunder was heard in the
    whirlwind,
    your lightning lit up the world;
    the earth trembled and quaked.
Your path led through the sea,
    your way through the mighty
      waters,

Sinai

Death Trap at the Sea

As Pharaoh approached, the Israelites looked up, and there were the Egyptians, marching after them. They were terrified and cried out to the LORD. They said to Moses, "Was it because there were no graves in Egypt that you brought us to the desert to die? What have you done to us by bringing us out of Egypt? Didn't we say to you in Egypt, 'Leave us alone; let us serve the Egyptians'? It would have been better for us to serve the Egyptians than to die in the desert!" (Ex 14:10–12)

though your footprints were not seen. (77:16–20)

Without question, God was the force behind this event, and nature responded to him as all his creation should, and especially Israel, with fear and awe. Psalm 114, another psalm entirely devoted to the exodus, perfectly phrases this view of nature's response to the Creator:

When Israel came out of Egypt,
    the house of Jacob from a people
        of foreign tongue,
Judah became God's sanctuary,
    Israel his dominion.
The sea looked and fled,
    the Jordan turned back;
the mountains skipped like rams,
    the hills like lambs.
Why was it, O sea, that you fled,
    O Jordan, that you turned back,
you mountains, that you skipped
        like rams,
    you hills, like lambs?
Tremble, O earth, at the presence of
        the Lord,
    at the presence of the God of Jacob,
who turned the rock into a pool,
    the hard rock into springs of
        water.

In the literary sense of the word, such a personification of nature—the fleeing of the Red Sea and the Jordan River at the majestic appearance of the Lord, and the skipping of the mountains and hills like rams—is a potent way to represent the reality of God's special relationship with Israel, but it is more than that. Theologically, it is a witness to the awesome power of God over nature. Metaphor incarnates the realities of life in images that are familiar—that is part of the power of metaphor. But in the Old Testament, metaphors not only encapsulate abstract realities in everyday language, they also transport theological truth along paths that theological abstractions cannot imitate. In that way they connect the created order and the Creator in language that leaves little doubt that God is supreme over his creation. Here we have such an instance. The graphic image of the Red Sea and the Jordan recoiling at the presence of God, and the hills, perhaps the hills of Canaan, dancing in anticipation of his taking up residence in that land, needs no other language to proclaim the majesty of God.

In summary fashion Psalm 136:11–12 announces God's deliverance of Israel with an "outstretched arm," the same characteristic term the Exodus narratives employ (e.g., Ex 6:6). It is not an overstatement to say that the Psalms are replete with the imagery and terminology of the exodus event. Yahweh's performance in this era of history was fixed in the national memory. Ongoing crises and triumphs replayed the footage of that drama to evoke Israel's praise and to call them to spiritual introspection.

Sinai

It may seem surprising that **Sinai,** as important as it was in the faith of ancient Israel, should have such a low profile in the Psalms, mentioned only twice in Psalm 68. When it does occur by name, one of those two references is to God rather than the place. The term "the One of Sinai" occurs in Psalm 68:8 (also Jgs 5:5). In a fusion of images, the psalmist draws together the events of saving history:

A general view of the granite mountains of the Sinai, where God revealed his law to Moses.

wilderness

conquest

the exodus, Sinai, **wilderness,** and **conquest:**

> When you went out before your
>   people, O God,
>   when you marched through the
>   wasteland,
> the earth shook,
>   the heavens poured down rain,
> before God, the One of Sinai,
>   before God, the God of Israel.
> You gave abundant showers, O
>   God;
>   you refreshed your weary
>   inheritance.
> Your people settled in it,
>   and from your bounty, O God,
>   you provided for the poor.
>   (vv. 7–10)

The ability the psalmist had for theological fusion is quite impressive. Just as he compressed together the saving events, he also fused together Yahweh's descent upon Sinai and his entrance into the sanctuary in Jerusalem. They form the seamless robe of God's revelation as he enters into Israel's national consciousness:

> Why gaze in envy, O rugged
>   mountains,
>   at the mountain where God
>   chooses to reign,
>   where the LORD himself will
>   dwell forever?
> The chariots of God are tens of
>   thousands

and thousands of thousands;
    the Lord has come from Sinai
    into his sanctuary.
When you ascended on high,
    you led captives in your train;
    you received gifts from men,
even from the rebellious—
    that you, O LORD God, might
    dwell there. (vv. 16–18)

Yahweh's determination to dwell in his sanctuary surpassed all other human designs. He took captives when necessary and received tribute from conquered peoples along the way, so that he might dwell in his sacred place. The enactment of the entrance ritual at the temple, so beautifully and rarely described in verses 24–27, was a moment of actualization, when the Lord made himself as present to Israel then as he did to Israel at Sinai. Each new generation needed to be present at the Lord's mighty manifestation of himself on that mountain.

The thrust of Psalm 99 is much the same as that of Psalm 68. The psalmist declares the Lord's sovereignty (vv. 1–2) and calls Israel to worship him (vv. 3, 5), reminding them that Moses, Aaron, and Samuel were among his priests, and they kept his statutes and decrees (vv. 6–7). Then the psalmist summons Israel to worship at his holy mountain.

The Saving Character of God

Theological fusion of the saving works of God is a common practice in the Old Testament and the New. God's saving work, while concentrated more in one event than another—for example, the Cross and the Resurrection—is really the revelation of his saving character. It is God who saves, not events. He simply chooses to reveal his saving nature in particular events of history. This is the reason why Paul can speak of God's having chosen us in Christ before the foundation of the world, and the writer of Hebrews can say that God's work was finished since the foundation of the world. Peter clarifies this concept by saying that Christ was chosen for his saving work before the foundation of the world, but he has been revealed in the last times for our sake (1 Pt 1:20). This seems also to be Paul's intent when he declares, after having acknowledged the atoning work of Christ on the cross, that we are saved by his life (Rom 5:10). His life, or the character of God, sums it all up. Thus we see how the Scriptures teach that the God who existed before the foundation of the world, the God who planned salvation when he created the world—it is this God who saves. His works are manifestations of his saving character. The "One of Sinai," therefore, is the God who saves, and his saving work can be summed up in the manifestation of himself in historical events.

Psalm 78 also takes a retrospective glance to Sinai, not by name, but by the laws the Lord established there, all for the sake of future generations, that they might keep God's commandments (vv. 5–8).

With this worship theology of actualization, one might think of the powerful and passionate theology of the old spiritual, "Were You There When They Crucified My Lord?" Israel's worship experience should re-actualize the great saving event of Sinai. In a liturgical sense—more than liturgical—in a spiritual sense, its people could stand there on Sinai in that indescribable moment of revelation and participate in the scene of glory unmatched by any other revelatory event until God should reveal himself on another mountain in another Servant and by another seismological event (Mt 27:51–53).

Included in the historical review of Psalm 106 are the levitical rebellion led by Dathan and Abiram (Nm 16) and the golden calf incident (Ex 32). In the psalmist's view, the rebellion of Dathan and Abiram was another installment in the ongoing rebellion of Israel against God and his appointed servants. Yet, God continued to spare rebellious Israel for his own sake (v. 8) as well as Israel's (v. 45), and to honor his servant Moses (v. 23). The psalmist was aware of the details of that story, which included the earth swallowing up the rebels, and the fire consuming their followers:

> In the camp they grew envious of
>   Moses
> and of Aaron, who was conse-
>   crated to the LORD.
> The earth opened up and swal-
>   lowed Dathan;
>   it buried the company of
>   Abiram.
> Fire blazed among their followers;
>   a flame consumed the wicked.
>   (vv. 16–18)

The poet theologian of Psalm 106 also reminisced about the golden calf incident when the Israelites engaged in a cheap transaction and "exchanged their Glory / for an image of a bull, which eats grass" (v. 20). Their actions were a result of forgetting the miracles God had done for them in Egypt, and, had not Moses stood in the breach on their behalf, God would have destroyed them (vv. 19–23).

We can see that the presence of Sinai and the spirit of Israel that prevailed there are far more pervasive in the Psalms than the place itself. And most of all, it is the God of Sinai who reveals himself at every turn of history.

The Wilderness

The psalmists for the most part put a negative spin on Israel's experiences in the wilderness and give this era a negative assessment generally.

The Wilderness of Paran near Kadesh-Barnea where the Israelites spent thirty-eight years of their forty-year wilderness "wandering."

Psalm 95 offers the clearest assessment of the wilderness era:

> For forty years I was angry with
>   that generation;
>   I said, "They are a people whose
>   hearts go astray,
>   and they have not known my
>   ways."
> So I declared on oath in my anger,
>   "They shall never enter my
>   rest." (vv. 10–11)

Indeed, the observations on the wilderness that we find in the Psalms are much in line with the negative view of the same era that we find in the Books of Exodus and Numbers. On the other hand, the prophets Hosea and Jeremiah put Israel's wilderness experience in a favorable light:

> Therefore I am now going to allure
>   her;
>   I will lead her into the desert
>   and speak tenderly to her.
> There I will give her back her
>   vineyards,
>   and will make the Valley of
>   Achor a door of hope.
> There she will sing as in the days of
>   her youth,
>   as in the day she came up out of
>   Egypt. (Hos 2:14–15)

> I remember the devotion of your
>   youth,
>   how as a bride you loved me

and followed me through the
      desert,
   through a land not sown. (Jer
      2:2)

The wilderness was a transition era, and despite the negative developments that occurred there, Hosea and Jeremiah could see something positive coming out of that time. That is easy to see if we include, and certainly we should, Sinai in the broad scope of the wilderness era. Thus if we block out the other events that receive a negative assessment, then the covenant and its laws, which established a special relationship between Israel and the Lord, cast a bright spot on the wilderness. Psalm 78 recognizes this perspective on the wilderness era: God gave them the laws on Sinai so they (the future generations) would keep his commandments and not be like their forefathers who had been rebellious. But they also sinned against him and put him to the test (vv. 17–18). The psalmist is intent on magnifying God's patience and goodness, and he recalls how the Israelites of the wilderness era demanded the food they craved, but yet God blessed them with the bread of angels, giving them more than they could eat (v. 25). Despite such grace, however, they did not remember the miraculous deeds that God had per-

Baal of Peor

formed on their behalf in Egypt. But he still delivered them from their enemies by leading them through the Red Sea (vv. 52–53), and he brought them to the border of the Holy Land, subduing the nations before them. Yet, they still rebelled against him (v. 56).

And then with time, once they were in the Promised Land, God took a different strategy toward their rebellion, not the tender mercy of the wilderness, but a severe mercy: he rejected Israel and abandoned his tabernacle at Shiloh, sent the ark into captivity, and delivered them into enemy hands (vv. 59–64). Then on reflection, God realized how awful the punishment had been. He turned from the Rachel tribes (Saul being from the tribe of Benjamin, descended from Rachel) to the Leah tribes (David being from the tribe of Judah, descended from Leah) for a new start, and built his sanctuary on Mount Zion, choosing David as his servant (vv. 65–72).

The wilderness era was a time of instructing Israel for the sake of future generations, but alas, those generations had learned nothing from the example of their ancestors in the wilderness. Thus Yahweh made a radical change in the way he dealt with his people.

One of the characteristic phrases of the Pentateuchal narratives describing the Lord's relationship to Israel in the wilderness era flows from the pen of the psalmists. God led them with a "cloud by day and fire by night" (78:14; 105:39); and in reference to his revelation, he spoke to Moses and Aaron from the pillar of cloud (99:7; cf. Ex 19:9).

The individual episodes in the wilderness that are fixed in the psalmic memory are water from the rock, manna, quails, and Israel's apostasy with the Canaanite god, **Baal of Peor.** The "water from the rock" incident references the story of Exodus 17:1–7, in which Moses struck the rock and water came out of it. The abundance of the water is the topic of Psalms 78:15–16 and 105:41—the water flowed like a river. The place name,

Meribah, stuck in the psalmic memory and is mentioned three times (81:7; 95:8; and 106:32).

Theologically, it is of particular interest that when these psalms refer to the "rock" incident, Moses is never the subject of the action. Rather the stress falls upon the Lord as the actor in that scene. Psalm 78 illustrates this:

> They spoke against God, saying,
> "Can God spread a table in the desert?
> When he struck the rock, water gushed out,
> and streams flowed abundantly.
> But can he also give us food?
> Can he supply meat for his people?" (vv. 19–20)

Moses moves to the background of the incident so that the psalmist may present God as the Actor on that critical occasion when Israel could have taken a turn in the right direction but did not.

The second "rock" incident (Nm 20:1–13), for whatever reason, does not come up for mention at all, unless, of course, the plural form "rocks" in 78:15 should be taken as inclusive of both stories. Basically the psalmists use this story as a warning to Israel, admonishing them to obey and to learn from the past rather than to repeat history's errors.

Psalm 78 combines the miracles of manna, quails, and water from the rock in much the same way as the three incidents occur in succession in the Exodus narrative (Ex 16:1–17:7). But it would appear that the interpretation of the quails is shaped by the negative assessment of the second incident of quails. Both Psalms 78:30–31 and 106:13–15 reflect the punishment of the plague that followed the second quail incident (Nm 11:33–34), a detail not included in the narrative of Exodus 16:

> But before they turned from the food they craved,
> even while it was still in their mouths,
> God's anger rose against them;

he put to death the sturdiest
among them,
cutting down the young men of Israel. (78:30–31)

But they soon forgot what he had
done
and did not wait for his counsel.
In the desert they gave in to their
craving;
in the wasteland they put God
to the test.
So he gave them what they asked
for,
but sent a wasting disease upon
them. (106:13–15)

The last incident of the wilderness era that we find in the Psalms takes place in the final days of the wilderness when Israel was encamped at Shittim on the Moabite plain (Nm 25). Psalm 106:26–31 records the sordid fact that these people became involved with the worship of Baal of Peor, counterbalanced by the fitting information that Phinehas, the grandson of Aaron, stayed the plague that followed this incident by his intervention. The psalmist observes that this era too had its "Abrahamic" figure of faith, for he declares in the words of Genesis 15:6 that "this was credited to him as righteousness" (106:31).

In summary, except for Phinehas's action and God's patience and grace, the wilderness era, as the psalmists recall it, has few pleasant memories. Yet, it was a time from which Israel could receive much instruction, even from their ancestors' disobedience, for their ongoing history and relationship to God.

Conquest

Next to the exodus, the most frequently mentioned period of history in the Psalms is the conquest. Psalm 105 recalls the Lord's covenant with Abraham in which he promised him the land of Canaan: "To you I will give the land of Canaan / as the portion you will inherit" (v. 11).

Date of the Exodus

Using the early date of the exodus (ca. 1447), based upon the chronology of 1 Kings 6, the conquest began soon after Moses' death in approximately 1406 B.C. The Book of Joshua records the exploits of this era. If it was completed within a decade or so, Israel would have been planted in the land by around 1390 B.C.

Yahweh both initiated the promise and fulfilled it—that is the way the Psalms look at the conquest. This is illustrated clearly in Psalm 44:2–3, where the psalmist extols Yahweh for the conquest of the land and attributes the credit directly and only to him:

It was not by their sword that they
won the land,
nor did their arm bring them
victory;
it was your right hand, your arm,
and the light of your face, for
you loved them. (v. 3)

Just as we saw the tendency of the Psalms to obscure the honor that could have been given to Moses and rather credit it directly to God's account, so again we see how Psalm 44 deflects any credit from Joshua and Israel and attributes the honor to the Lord. The background of this psalm of Korah is a humiliating defeat the nation has suffered, and the psalmist laments that it is undeserved:

If we had forgotten the name of our
God
or spread out our hands to a foreign god,
would not God have discovered it,
since he knows the secrets of the
heart?
Yet for your sake we face death all
day long;
we are considered as sheep to be
slaughtered. (vv. 20–22)

In contrast to the innocence of Israel on this occasion, the poet of Psalm 80 acknowledges that the nation is

Jericho was the Israelites' gateway to Canaan. The weaponless conquest of Jericho was a symbol of the Lord's power to subdue Canaan without human agency: "It was not by their sword that they won the land, / . . . it was your right hand, your arm, / and the light of your face, for you loved them." (Ps 44:2–3)

guilty and their humiliation deserved (v. 16—"at your rebuke"; v. 18—"Then we will not turn away from you"). In parabolic language much like that of Isaiah's Song of the Vineyard (Is 5), he describes the Lord's careful and gentle planting of his vineyard whose healthy vines spread out over the mountain-trellised land of Israel:

> You brought a vine out of Egypt;
>   you drove out the nations and
>   planted it.
> You cleared the ground for it,
>   and it took root and filled the
>   land.
> The mountains were covered with
>   its shade,
>   the mighty cedars with its
>   branches.
> It sent out its boughs to the Sea,
>   its shoots as far as the River.
>   (80:8–11)

The poet-singer of Psalm 68 describes the land of Canaan as a place where the Lord refreshed his "weary inheritance" and provided for the poor from its bounty (vv. 9–10). When he had scattered the kings of the land, a peace fell upon the land like "snow fallen on Zalmon" (v. 14).

Yahweh as Conqueror of the land forms the backdrop of Psalm 78:54–64. He brought Israel to the border of the "hill country his right hand had

taken" (v. 54). But the lament over their ungrateful behavior in the land describes them "as unreliable as a faulty bow" (v. 57), building pagan high places and provoking the Lord's jealousy with their idols (v. 58).

Psalms 135 and 136 remember how the Lord struck down powerful kings, Sihon of the Amorites and Og of Bashan among them, and gave their land to Israel as an inheritance (135:10–12; 136:17–21). Again it should not escape our attention that the Lord did all of this. Joshua and the Israelite army are not even mentioned.

The crossing of the Jordan is only alluded to in Psalm 114, where the psalmist relates that God came out of Egypt and made Judah his sanctuary. This psalm revels in the sheer delight of the presence of God among his people:

> When Israel came out of Egypt,
>   the house of Jacob from a people
>   of foreign tongue,
> Judah became God's sanctuary,
>   Israel his dominion. (vv. 1–2)

> Tremble, O earth, at the presence of
>   the Lord,
>   at the presence of the God of
>   Jacob (v. 7).

In summary, the conquest, like the wilderness era, was a series of events

Incarnational Theology

While we do not want to make the Old Testament out to be the New Testament in disguise, we do want to recognize that the Old Testament sometimes provides the substance out of which the great doctrines of the New Testament are made. Here in Psalm 114 we have evidence of that. Incarnational theology, which is at the center of New Testament theology, underlies the theology of this psalm. God takes up residence in his people Israel before he takes up residence in Jesus Christ his Son, who represented Israel. This motif can be seen in Matthew's story of the "exodus" of Jesus and his mother and Joseph from Egypt (Mt 2:13–15). Matthew quotes Hosea 11:1, "Out of Egypt I called my son," to connect this "exodus" with the exodus under Moses. Jesus recapitulated Israel's history and performed it in a truly saving and perfectly obedient manner, much in contrast to ancient Israel.

Idolatry and Military Defeat

John Milton in "Paradise Lost" (Book 1) describes the false gods that led Israel astray, suggesting that Israel's bowing down to the pagan gods resulted in their defeat in battle:

For those the race of Israel oft
    forsook
Their living Strength, and unfrequented left
His righteous altar, bowing lowly
    down
To bestial gods; for which their
    heads as low
Bow'd down in battle, sunk before the spear
Of despicable foes.

that the Lord himself performed. It was both a fulfillment of his covenant with Abraham and a manifestation of his power on Israel's behalf.

Life in the Land

The psalmic reservoir of memories, as one would expect, includes reflections about the victories the Israelites had won against the Canaanite nations and images of the depraved influence the Canaanites exercised over the settling tribes. The victories come from the period of the Judges and represent some of the great military moments of the past. As the poet of Psalm 83 faced the threatening problem of present enemies, he prayed that God would do to them as he had done to the princes and kings of Midian and to Jabin, the king of Hazor, and his general, Sisera:

Do to them as you did to Midian,
    as you did to Sisera and Jabin at
      the river Kishon,
who perished at Endor
    and became like refuse on the
      ground.
Make their nobles like Oreb and
    Zeeb,

all their princes like Zebah and
    Zalmunna
who said, "Let us take possession
    of the pasturelands of God"
    (83:9–12; Jgs 4; 5; 7:25;
    8:21).

In the collective memory of Israel, past events became the example of what God could do.

Psalm 78 provides a general view of life in the land, a very negative one in fact. It sounds prophetic in its description of the high places that Israel built and their practice of idolatry (vv. 56–59). While the date of this psalm is debated, its composition must be well into the monarchy, since God's choice of David concludes the psalm. In fact, the reference to the sanctuary in verse 69 would suggest that the psalm was written after the construction of the temple. Israel's inclination to embrace the religion of Canaan was quite apparent when the psalmist wrote this theology of history:

But they put God to the test
    and rebelled against the Most
      High;
They did not keep his statutes.
Like their fathers they were disloyal and faithless,

as unreliable as a faulty bow.
They angered him with their high
    places;
they aroused his jealousy with
    their idols. (vv. 56–58)

The description of Israel's life in the land in 106:34–43 is a summary view of the Book of Judges. The Israelites did not destroy the Canaanites as the Lord had commanded them to do, but instead they adopted their customs, worshiped their idols, and even sacrificed their children to the gods of Canaan. The result was that the Lord handed them over to their enemies.

The Monarchy

The one king whom the psalmists were interested in was David. For the most part the **monarchy** comes off very well in the Psalms because of the psalmists' great respect for David and his line. This reverence climaxes Psalm 78, where God's choice of David is a drastic change in history, a turn from the Rachel line, represented by Saul from the tribe of Benjamin, to the Leah line, represented by David from the tribe of Judah.

He chose David his servant
    and took him from the sheep
        pens;
From tending the sheep he brought
    him
    to be the shepherd of his people
        Jacob,
    of Israel his inheritance.
And David shepherded them with
    integrity of heart;
    with skillful hands he led them.
        (vv. 70–72)

With a beautiful turn of the phrase, David the shepherd is made the shepherd of Israel.

The singer of Psalm 89 references the Davidic covenant as the still point in a turning world. When the exile occurred, however, that stable point of reference began to flit to and fro in the theological mind. The fall of Jerusalem and the end of the monar-

chy thus raised the question of the validity of the Davidic covenant. How could this tragedy happen in light of Yahweh's covenant with David to establish an everlasting kingship to rule on his throne (89:4, 36–37; 2 Sm 7)? Psalm 132:11–12 affirms that promise and makes it contingent upon Israel's keeping the Lord's covenant and observing his statutes. On David's behalf, and on Israel's, Psalm 89 interprets the failure of the Davidic dynasty as the Lord's renunciation of that covenant and an affront to David (vv. 38–51). The psalmist took the event quite personally.

At some important temple celebration the poet of Psalm 132 recalled David's determination to establish a place for the Lord's house. While 2 Samuel 7:2 and 1 Chronicles 17:1 agree on David's resolve, neither expresses it in terms of an oath. Yet the psalmist has clearly understood—it was as strong as an oath.

The Exile and Return

No event in Israel's history was so devastating and yet so profoundly reforming as the exile to Babylonia. Psalm 106:44–47 preserves words that were inscribed upon the suffering hearts of the Israelites of that time:

But he took note of their distress
    when he heard their cry;
for their sake he remembered his
        covenant
    and out of his great love he
        relented.
He caused them to be pitied
    by all who held them captive.
Save us, O LORD our God,
    and gather us from the nations,
that we may give thanks to your
        holy name
    and glory in your praise.

While the return had not yet occurred, the psalmist anticipated it and called Israel to praise the Lord

(v. 48). The following psalm joyfully celebrates the return:

> Let the redeemed of the LORD say this—
> those he redeemed from the hand of the foe,
> those he gathered from the lands,
> from the east and west, from north and south. (107:2–3)

The psalmist describes the hopeless and depressed condition of exiles:

> Some wandered in desert wastelands,
> finding no way to a city where they could settle.
> They were hungry and thirsty,
> And their lives ebbed away. (vv. 4–5)

> Some sat in darkness and the deepest gloom,
> prisoners suffering in iron chains,
> for they had rebelled against the words of God
> and despised the counsel of the Most High.
> So he subjected them to bitter labor;
> they stumbled, and there was no one to help. (vv. 10–12)

> Some became fools through their rebellious ways
> and suffered affliction because of their iniquities.
> They loathed all food
> and drew near the gates of death. (vv. 17–18)

The exile was the Egyptian oppression all over again—God subjected his people to bitter labor. And God's reaction to it was the exodus all over again—the people cried to the Lord and he delivered them (vv. 6/7–9; 13/14–16; 19/20–22; 28/29–42). The praise that Psalm 106 calls for is rendered by Psalm 107, and it is for the miraculous deliverance from captivity that Psalm 106 believed would come. Whatever reason Israel gave in the past for the captivity is modulated clearly into the self-serving sins of Israel (v. 17).

If Psalm 107 was written on the verge of the return, Psalm 137 was composed in the bowels of captivity itself. The exiles are taunted by their captors and derided for their faith. It was the lowest moment of despair as they remembered Jerusalem and mused painfully on the pillaging of the city by the Edomites (see the Book of Obadiah). In their unrequited hearts they contemplated the curses that might repay their enemies for the cruelties done to them:

> By the rivers of Babylon we sat and wept
> when we remembered Zion.
> There on the poplars,
> we hung our harps,
> for there our captors asked us for songs,
> our tormentors demanded songs of joy;
> They said, "Sing us one of the songs of Zion!"
> How can we sing the songs of the LORD
> while in a foreign land?
> If I forget you, O Jerusalem,
> may my right hand forget its skill.
> May my tongue cling to the roof of my mouth
> if I do not remember you,
> if I do not consider Jerusalem my highest joy.
> Remember, O LORD, what the Edomites did
> on the day Jerusalem fell.
> "Tear it down," they cried,
> "tear it down to its foundations!"
> O Daughter of Babylon, doomed to destruction,
> happy is he who repays you
> for what you have done to us—
> he who seizes your infants
> and dashes them against the rocks.

The indescribable joy of the return to Judah in approximately 537 B.C. is the subject of Psalm 126. As the exiles formed the lines that led home, they were filled with laughter, and songs of joy wafted along the road of their plodding feet. Now they could see their exile in the form of a spiritual relief. They had left home in tears, realizing there was seed to sow even in this arid time of history, and now they were on their way home carrying the sheaves of their harvest with them. It was so much like a dream:

> When the LORD brought back the
>   captives to Zion,
>   we were like men who
>   dreamed.
> Our mouths were filled with
>   laughter,
>   our tongues with songs of joy.
> Then it was said among the na-
>   tions,
>   "The LORD has done great
>   things for them."

> The LORD has done great things for
>   us,
>   and we are filled with joy.
> Restore our fortunes, O LORD,
>   like streams in the Negev.
> Those who sow in tears
>   will reap with songs of joy.
> He who goes out weeping,
>   carrying seed to sow,
> will return with songs of joy,
>   carrying sheaves with him.

The Psalms follow Israel's history to the joyful end. The nightmare of the oppression had ended in the miraculous events of the exodus, and they awakened from the bad dream of exile to find that they were home.

Study Questions

1. In the Hebrew worldview, history and theology were part of the same fabric. Describe how, for the psalmists, history could be viewed as theology.

2. In terms of the Psalms, what does it mean to say that the "world is a metaphor of God's being"? How is the personification of nature (Pss 77 and 114) and the attribution of Moses' actions to God (Ps 78:19, 20) consistent with this concept?

3. Describe how the psalmists use history as a theological compass for the future. Give one example each from the exodus, Sinai, wilderness, and conquest of their theological appropriation of history—relationship past informing relationship future on the basis of the character of God.

4. Psalms 106, 107, 126, and 137 likely give different snapshots of the exile, emotions of despair, hope, confession, and utter joy at restoration. Compare and contrast these different emotions and their relation to exilic events. Is there a natural application to believers of every age for their times of sin, exile, and restoration?

5. The Psalms in themselves are not an adequate source of Israel's history, but as a supplement they are a great enhancement. Give two examples of how the Psalms poetically enhance the historical record, painting the role of God in exponentially vivid colors.

Summary

We have seen that the order of events, when that order can be discerned in the Psalms, is the same as we see in the historical narratives: the exodus, Sinai, wilderness, and conquest. Except for the psalmists' occasional embellishments, which may be merely poetic license, or in some instances represent an oral tradition, they describe these events with remarkable accuracy when compared to the narrative accounts.

Further, we have observed the psalmists' inclination to describe the Lord as the initiator and executor of historical events, sometimes at the expense of moving the human actors like Moses and Joshua to the background.

Another transaction the psalmists sometimes make is, in poetic style, to personify the forces of nature in order to show how God's creation responds obediently to him and stands in awe of his presence.

While the Psalms would not be an adequate source for Israel's history if taken by themselves, they are nevertheless a great enhancement to our understanding of this history and the God who orders it.

Part

3

Encountering the Psalms as Literary and Theological Types

6 "Praise the LORD, O My Soul; All My Inmost Being, Praise His Holy Name"

The Psalms of Praise

Outline

- **The Anatomy of Praise**
- **Form and Description of the Psalms of Praise**
- **Major Themes of the Psalms of Praise**
    - Creation
        - Creation by the Word of Command
        - Creation by Deed
        - Creation by Understanding
        - Creation by Power
        - The Beauty and the Language of Creation
        - Universality of God's Presence and Reign
    - God's Work in Israel's History
- **Summary**

Objectives

After reading this chapter, you should be able to

1. Analyze the forms of the praise psalms.
2. Describe the psalms of praise by form and theme.
3. List the major themes of the psalms of praise.

The Anatomy of Praise

A case can be made on the basis of the Psalms that the purpose of human existence is to praise God. In a world that has become increasingly more human-centered, that may sound like an anomaly. How could anyone realize self-fulfillment and achieve his or her goals in life by praising God! First off, we should say that we are not speaking about isolating ourself in a monastery and praying all day—although that too has a respectable place in the Christian tradition. Rather we have in mind the principle commended by Paul to the Corinthian church: "So whether you eat or drink or whatever you do, do it all for the glory of God" (1 Cor 10:31). It is obviously a difficult challenge for any human being, but one from which the Christian cannot disengage himself or herself. To do so is to turn one's back on God and deny that he is our Creator and Redeemer. Further, to disengage oneself from the vocation of praise is to deny one's own human existence. It was nothing short of divine inspiration that the Westminster divines began the Shorter Catechism on this note: "What is the chief end of man?" "The chief end of man is to glorify God and to enjoy Him forever."[1] They recognized that "glorifying" God, the comprehensive notion of praising, is the proper mode of human existence and the only mode that can lead to happiness in this world.

The centrality of praise in the Jewish and Christian faiths is integral to fulfilling one's duty to God. The prophets sometimes tried to reduce the Hebrew faith to its essential duty (Mi 6:8; 1 Sm 15:22), as did our Lord himself (Mt 22:36–40). Indeed, Jesus said the law and the prophets hung on the two commandments to love the Lord with all one's heart and to love one's neighbor as oneself. David had his moments when he was also engaged in that search for the essence of faith in God, and he declared that God was more pleased with praise than sacrifice:

> I will praise God's name in song
>   and glorify him with
>   thanksgiving.
> This will please the LORD more
>   than an ox,
>   more than a bull with its horns
>   and hoofs. (Ps 69:30–31)

Normally the psalmists do not examine the anatomy of praise in any kind of detail—they merely do it. But there are thankfully those occasions when they take a close look at the form of praising God. Psalm 22:3 declares that the holy God is enthroned (Hebrew "sitting" or "inhabiting") on the praises of Israel.[2] That means that our praises become the royal throne for God, and there he sits to reign. Our praises are like the cherubim who support God's throne. This signifies God's willingness to enter into a relationship with us. Or we might render this verse, "For you are holy, inhabiting the praises of Israel." In that case, he takes up residence in our praises. That is how close he is! And that is how much he esteems our humanness—that he would allow our human praise to support his majestic throne, or that he would assume residence in our praises. This truth is only a few short steps from the doctrine of the incarnation.

In our discussion of the psalms of the kingship of Yahweh we note that the universality of God is a prominent theme in those psalms.[3] One might say that the Psalms in their general theological thrust, like Isaiah 40–55, turn Old Testament theology in that direction. The praise language of the Psalms gives us two memorable ways to express God's universality. In one of the Songs of Zion, the psalmist, relating how the Lord puts the weapons and personnel of war out of commission, proclaims, "Surely the wrath of men shall praise thee" (Ps 76:10, RSV). This is another way of saying, "If God is for us, who can be against us?" (Rom 8:31). This perspective, which looks at human wrath from the Lord's vantage point, turns to the perspective of the people of God in Psalm 149 as the psalmist considers the power of praise on their lips:

> May the praise of God be in their
> mouths
> and a double-edged sword in
> their hands,
> to inflict vengeance on the nations
> and punishment on the peoples,
> to bind their kings with fetters,
> their nobles with shackles of
> iron,
> to carry out the sentence written
> against them.
> This is the glory of all his saints.
> Praise the LORD. (vv. 6–9)

The parallel construction in verse 6 would suggest that praise in this psalm becomes the weapon of choice to bring the enemies of God's people to their knees. This vivid hope, if viewed in the context of a defeated nation languishing among their unrequited enemies, reveals the secret weapon of God's people. The monarchy and its army had long been vanquished, but the most powerful weapon of all, the praise of God, was still available to his people; and this, rather than kings and armies, was their glory.

On occasion the psalmist addresses his own soul and summons himself to the majestic activity of praise:

> Praise the LORD, O my soul;
> all my inmost being, praise his
> holy name.
> Praise the LORD, O my soul,
> and forget not all his benefits.
> (Ps 103:1–2)

Given our human frailty and thus cumbersome way of approaching God, it becomes necessary at times to summon our inner self to the tabernacle of praise. Too often we come reluctantly. Moreover, it is mandatory that we withhold nothing as we offer this service to God. J. Clinton McCann has appropriately described praise as the "offering up of the whole self to God."[4]

Most often, however, the psalmists could not contain their spirit of praise within the bounds of their own souls. They seemed both unable and unwilling to keep the majesty and power of praise to themselves. So they sent out the summons to God's people to join them. At times it simply takes the form of an imperative, as in the **hallelujah psalms** (*hallelujah* means "Praise the LORD"): "Praise the LORD. / Give thanks to the LORD, for he is good; / his love endures forever" (Ps 106:1).

Any worshiper could not keep anything so good, so freeing, so exalting, as praise, to himself. But C. S. Lewis draws out yet another characteristic of praise in his excellent discussion of the subject. Once he had discovered the power of praise that drives the Book of Psalms, he commented:

> I had not noticed either that just as men spontaneously praise whatever they value, so they spontaneously urge us to join them in praising it: "Isn't she lovely? Wasn't it glorious? Don't you think that magnificent?" The Psalmists in telling everyone to praise God are doing what all men do when they speak of what they care about.[5]

There is a saying that if all Jews perfectly kept one Sabbath, the Messiah would come. In an analogous way, we might suggest that if all of God's people would praise him with their whole hearts in one simultaneous moment, God's kingdom would immediately materialize before their eyes. Lewis ventures a comment on this topic also:

> If it were possible for a created soul fully (I mean, up to the full measure conceivable in a finite being) to "appreciate," that is to love and delight in, the worthiest object of all, and simultaneously at every moment to give this delight perfect expression, then that soul would be in supreme beatitude. It is along these lines that I find it easiest to understand the Christian doctrine that "Heaven" is a state in which angels now, and men hereafter, are perpetually employed in praising God.[6]

123

The author of Psalm 150, while he does not say it in quite the same way, knows that the majesty of the Lord calls forth the praise of all creatures, and he closes the Psalter with this summons to praise: "Let everything that has breath praise the LORD. / Praise the LORD" (v. 6).

It should not surprise us, then, to hear, at the climax of history, the whole creation praising God (Rv 19:1–10). C. S. Lewis reminds us concerning the anatomy of praise, "I think we delight to praise what we enjoy because the praise not merely expresses but completes the enjoyment; it is its appointed consummation." Indeed, the imagery of final redemption is that of the whole creation praising God:

> Then I heard what sounded like a
> great multitude, like the
> roar of rushing waters and
> like loud peals of thunder,
> shouting: "Hallelujah!
> For our Lord God Almighty
> reigns.
> Let us rejoice and be glad
> and give him glory!" (Rv 19:6–
> 7a)

To paraphrase the thesis we have outlined above, we could say that to praise God is to live, and to live is to praise God. Anything less than that is a substandard existence. Westermann warns us:

> Exalting is a part of existence. It is so much a part of it, that when one has ceased to exalt God, something else must be exalted. Then God can be displaced by a man, an institution, an idea. Exalting remains a function of existence. World history demonstrates this. Man *must* exalt something, and without such exalting there can apparently be no existence. . . . If the praise of God, as the Psalms express it, belongs to existence, then the directing of this praise to a man, an idea, or an institution must disturb and finally destroy life itself. The Psalms say that only where God is praised is there life.[7]

Form and Description of the Psalms of Praise

It is not coincidental that the Hebrew title for the Book of Psalms is *tehillim*, "praises." Even though the psalms of lament and complaint outnumber the psalms of praise in Books 1–3, praise dominates in Books 4–5. This movement from lament to praise seems to be a pattern that has developed consciously in the compilation of the Psalter. Praise is the goal toward which the whole book moves. The doxologies that conclude each book, and especially the doxological aggregate at the end of the book, confirm this fact: Psalms 41:13; 72:18–19; 89:52; 106:48; and 146–50. They are the pediments that highlight the architecture of the book.

Westermann has shown that the two poles of the Psalter are *lament* and *praise*, with an inner force that moves both individual psalms and the book as a whole toward praise. Indeed, the lament of the individual and the lament of the people[8] incorporate words of trust and a vow to praise the Lord, both belonging in an integral way to the category of praise. Thus, even lament has an inner movement in the direction of praise.

A helpful distinction in Westermann's study of the **psalms of praise** is his differentiation between **declarative praise** and **descriptive praise**. The first involves generic language like "Praise the LORD" (Hebrew *hallelu* = praise [imperative] + *yah*, the shortened form of Yahweh or LORD = Praise the LORD), without the details of why or for what the psalmist is praising God. Descriptive praise, as the term implies, involves the details. One can see the transition from declarative to descriptive praise in a number of instances. Psalm 113 is one of those psalms that illustrates the transition, and in this psalm, it occurs at verse 5 (indicated by the italics):

Table 6.1

Distribution of the Psalms of Praise in the Psalter

Book 1 (1–41)	Book 2 (42–72)	Book 3 (73–89)	Book 4 (90–106)	Book 5 (107–50)
4	4	0	9	13

Praise the LORD.
Praise, O servants of the LORD,
   praise the name of the LORD.
Let the name of the LORD be
      praised,
   both now and forevermore.
From the rising of the sun to the
      place where it sets,
   the name of the LORD is to be
      praised.
The LORD is exalted over all the
      nations,
   his glory above the heavens.
Who is like the LORD our God,
   the One who sits enthroned on high,
who stoops down to look
   on the heavens and the earth?
He raises the poor from the dust
   and lifts the needy from the ash
      heap;
he seats them with princes,
   with the princes of their people.
He settles the barren woman in her
      home
   as a happy mother of children.
Praise the LORD.

The psalms of praise are the hymns that Gunkel isolated as a distinct genre, those identified by Westermann as descriptive psalms of praise.[9] Hans-Joachim Kraus, following the work of F. Crüsemann,[10] gives a helpful breakdown of the psalms of praise. His list is the following: Psalms 8, 19A, 29, 33, 47, 65, 66A, 68, 93, 96, 97, 98, 99, 100, 104, 105, 106, 111, 113, 114, 117, 134, 135, 136, 145, 146, 147, 148, 149, 150. They fall into two divisions:

(1) those hymns that can be differentiated by form-critical methods:
   a. The imperative hymn, modeled on that of Exodus 15:21. The reason for praising is characteristically introduced by the word "because" (Hebrew *ki*).

These include Psalms 96, 98, 100, and 136.
   b. The participial hymn, which has its examples in Isaiah 40–55.
   c. The hymn of the individual, examples of which are Psalms 8 and 104.
(2) those hymns that must be differentiated by theme rather than form:
   a. Psalms of praise of the Creator: Psalms 8, 19A, 33, 104, and 136.
   b. Psalms of Yahweh as king: Psalms 47, 93, 96, 97, 98, and 99.
   c. Harvest psalms: Psalms 65 and 145.
   d. Historical psalms: Psalms 105; 106; 114; 135; 136.
   e. Entrance psalms: Psalms 24, 95, and 100.[11]

It is difficult to identify the life situation of these psalms. Some may have been written specifically for temple worship (for example, Ps 136), while others were personal expressions of gratitude for God's mighty deeds and goodness (perhaps Ps 8), and later incorporated in temple worship, if they were incorporated at all. We should not assume that all of the psalms were used in the temple. In a sense the psalms were the "hymnbook" of the temple, but not in the sense that a modern hymnbook is written for the express purpose of worship in the church. The Psalter was a book of corporate *and* private worship. The psalms were written both for private and public use, and psalms in each category moved in the other direction, from private to public, and from public to private.

125

Major Themes of the Psalms of Praise

The range of themes found in the psalms of praise is rather broad, but four themes have a high profile: creation, the universality of Yahweh's presence and sovereignty, Israel's history, and God's awesome deeds.

Creation

We will consider the topic of creation to some extent in our discussion of the kingship of Yahweh psalms,[12] which, as one can see in the list above, are included, for the most part, in the category of psalms of praise. The fact that a subcategory like this is included in this major category of hymns illustrates how broad is the category of the psalms of praise.

It is obvious why the topic of creation or the Creator should be a major object of attention in the psalms of praise—creation marked the beginning of world history, and all of God's awesome deeds in history must be seen in the light of his majestic work of creation. When the psalmists spoke of God's work in creation, it was an unobtrusive way of saying that the world belonged to him. The God who ruled over kings, nations, and the gods of the human imagination was the Creator of the world, and that gave him certain rights and privileges.

One might think that the major reason for praising God would be his loving care as a shepherd, or his protection as a fortress, or any number of real-life reasons. Yet the psalms of praise often point to creation, historical events, Yahweh's universal reign, and his awesome deeds as the initial reasons for praising God. John Goldingay explains it this way: "The Psalm's own logic is less predictable but more profound. We glory in the fact that God is the creator but then kneel in reverence in the light of the fact that this creator and sovereign has condescended to be our maker and shepherd."[13]

Part of the majesty of the psalms of praise is that they fix our eyes upon the exalted realities, those that can transfer their majesty to the things of earth and transform the shepherd into a God-figure, make the sheep God's people, and transfigure the pasture into the life with God. They accomplish that, not by beginning with those earthly figures, but by beginning with the heavenly realities.

It is not coincidental that the doctrine of creation is the introductory chapter of the story of Israel (Gn 1–2). That signals the fact that it has a major place in the theological system of the Old Testament, and thus the central place of this doctrine in the Psalms should not surprise us. When one reads the first two chapters of Genesis, one recognizes that. The creation narratives present God's creative work in two ways. First, he creates by his Word of command, and second, by his personal deed. In Genesis 1 God speaks and creation comes into being, whereas in Genesis 2 he forms man from the dust of the ground and woman from the man's rib. The latter is more the hands-on approach, by which the Lord becomes personally involved with his creation. In fact, Genesis 2 gives a hint of this personal touch by the use of the divine name, LORD God. In Genesis 1 the consistent divine name is 'Elohim (God), while in Genesis 2 it is Yahweh 'Elohim (LORD God), with the addition of the tetragrammaton (LORD). While the proponents of the documentary hypothesis have explained the different names for God as a result of different literary sources, the Jewish tradition was to view the context of the different names as determinative. That is, when 'Elohim occurred, it suggested God in his power, and when Yahweh occurred, it implied his compassion and personal presence. The generic 'Elohim connoted the God who stood above the world, while the unique name Yahweh implied his nearness. Thus we can see that in Genesis 1 God brings his creation into existence by his Word of command, "Let there be light," while in Genesis 2 he is personally and immanently involved, "The LORD God formed the man from the dust of the ground and breathed into his nostrils the breath of life."

The Psalter expresses the Lord's creating in two other ways, giving us four ways by which he created: (1) by his Word or command, (2) by his personal deed, (3) by his attribute of wisdom or understanding, and (4) by his strength.

Creation by the Word of Command

After the psalmist calls the sun, moon, stars, and waters to praise the Lord, he recalls: "For he commanded and they were created. / He set them in place for ever and ever; / he gave a decree that will never pass away" (Ps 148:5b–6).

The unique verb "create," used also in Genesis 1, is used here in conjunction with the verb "he commanded." The latter verb does not occur in the Genesis narrative, but the effect of God's speaking creation into existence is the same. We should also observe that the noun "word" does not occur in the Genesis narrative either, but it is quite evident that it is the Word of the Lord that brings creation into existence. That is the way Psalm 33:6 puts it: "By the word of the LORD were the heavens made, / their starry host by the breath of his mouth."

This same psalm puts the verb "spoke" in parallel with the verb "command," recognizing the synonymity of the two ideas: "For he spoke, and it came to be; / he commanded, and it stood firm" (v. 9).

Creation by Deed

The second way of describing God's creating activity, by his deed, is not lost on the psalms of praise either. Whereas this metaphorical way of speaking about creation is more often than not implied, we do see it explicitly in Psalm 147:4 as the Lord brings the stars into existence and calls them each by name as he takes his inventory: "He determines the number of the stars / and calls them each by name." The anthropomorphism of

Genesis 2 lies behind this description. The Lord's personal interest in his creation can be seen in his naming of the stars, an activity that may also suggest his authority over the creation (cf. Gn 2:19–20; 3:20).[14]

Creation by Understanding

The wisdom movement introduced its own vocabulary to speak about creation, or at least it borrowed vocabulary from the other literatures and capitalized on it. The theology of the Psalms is infused with wisdom thought in many places. While creation in the Psalms has the imprimatur of wisdom thought, wisdom nevertheless does not seem to have significantly reshaped this doctrine. In wisdom thought, the terms "wisdom" (*hokhmah*) and "understanding" (*tevunah*) were virtually synonymous. Just as Proverbs describes wisdom as God's *craftsman* in creating the world (Prv 8:30), the terms "wisdom" and "understanding" occur in parallel lines to describe the creating activity of God in Proverbs 3:19: "By wisdom the LORD laid the earth's foundations, / by understanding he set the heavens in place."

Jeremiah, who may also have experienced some wisdom influences on his thinking, draws out this same idea when he speaks of creation: "He made the earth by his power; / he founded the world by his wisdom / and stretched out the heavens by his understanding" (Jer 51:15).

In the same mode of thought, the psalmist calls upon Israel to give thanks to the Lord:

> who by his understanding made
>   the heavens,
> *His love endures forever.*
> who spread out the earth upon the
>   waters,
> *His love endures forever.*
> who made the great lights—
> *His love endures forever.*
> the sun to govern the day,
> *His love endures forever.*
> the moon and stars to govern the
>   night;
> *His love endures forever.* (Ps
>   136:5–9)

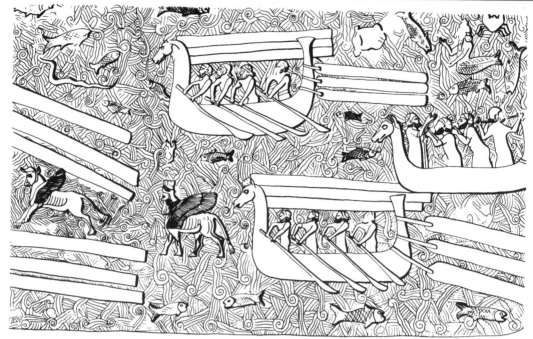

Ships carrying Phoenician wood. The troubled waters plus the various creatures rising out of the sea represent the treacheries of seafaring.

Psalm 104, a beautiful creation hymn, also describes creation in wisdom terms:

> How many are your works, O
>   LORD!
>   In wisdom you made them all;
>   the earth is full of your
>   creatures.
> There is the sea, vast and spacious,
>   teeming with creatures beyond
>   number—
>   living things both large and
>   small.
> There the ships go to and fro,
>   and the leviathan, which you
>   formed to frolic there.
>   (vv. 24–26)

Here we have an ethical connection between God's *steadfast love* (*khesed*) and his creation. The creation experiences the nature of the Creator. A line of divine love runs from the creation throughout history. According to Psalm 145, the same link exists between the Lord's righteous nature and the relationship to his creation:

> The LORD is righteous in all his
>   ways
>   and loving toward all he has
>   made.
> The LORD is near to all who call on
>   him,

to all who call on him in truth.
> He fulfills the desires of those who
>   fear him;
>   he hears their cry and saves
>   them.
> The LORD watches over all who
>   love him,
>   but all the wicked he will de-
>   stroy. (vv. 17–20)

Psalm 146 continues to focus on the link between the "Maker of heaven and earth, the sea, and everything in them," and the application of his faithfulness (*'emeth*) in history. In a similar vein, Psalm 147 draws out the link between the Lord's care and compassion for his people and his creation of the world. He created the stars and called them by name, and in an analogous way

> He heals the brokenhearted
>   and binds up their wounds.
> He determines the number of the
>   stars
>   and calls them by name.
> Great is our Lord and mighty in
>   power,
>   his understanding has no limit.
> The LORD sustains the humble
>   but casts the wicked to the
>   ground. (vv. 3–6)

The association of power and understanding with the ethical demeanor of the Creator gives us a rather full character description. He is not arbitrary, although he is powerful, and he exercises justice for the oppressed and the wicked alike. This is the nature of the Creator, and therefore his righteous acts in history are to be expected.

Creation by Power

Jeremiah used three instrumental ideas to describe creation: by power, by wisdom, and by understanding (Jer 51:15). While all three do not occur together in the Psalms, power and understanding do occur in different contexts. In Psalm 65 the brute strength of the Creator becomes the instrument by which the Lord brought the mountains into existence.

Moreover, in this context we see an interesting link between worship and creation:

> You answer us with awesome
> deeds of righteousness,
> O God our Savior,
> the hope of all the ends of the earth
> and of the farthest seas,
> who formed the mountains by
> your power,
> having armed yourself with
> strength,
> who stilled the roaring of the seas,
> the roaring of their waves,
> and the turmoil of the nations.
> Those living far away fear your
> wonders;
> where morning dawns and
> evening fades
> you call forth songs of joy. (Ps
> 65:5–8)

In Psalm 134 the psalmist forges the same link between worship and the "Maker of heaven and earth":

> Praise the LORD, all you servants of
> the LORD
> who minister by night in the
> house of the LORD.
> Lift up your hands in the sanctuary
> and praise the LORD.
> May the LORD, the Maker of
> heaven and earth,
> bless you from Zion.

We find this link again in Psalm 149:

> Praise the LORD.
> Sing to the LORD a new song,
> and his praise in the
> assembly of the saints.
> Let Israel rejoice in their
> Maker;
> let the people of Zion be
> glad in their King.
> (vv. 1–2)

The Hebrew participial noun that stands behind *Maker* (*'oseh*) comes from the word *to do* or *make* that introduces the creation narrative of Genesis 2 (v. 4b), "When the LORD God made the earth and the heavens," and suggests the deed-creation of that narrative. In distinction, the word-of-command creation of Genesis 1 employs the word *to create* (*bara'*). Actually the term *Maker* occurs several times in the Psalter as part of what may be a standard liturgical phrase, *Maker of heaven and earth* (115:15; 121:2; 124:8; 134:3; 146:6). It certainly has become part of the Christian liturgy, and its repetition in the Psalter might suggest that it was standard in the Hebrew liturgy as well.

The Beauty and the Language of Creation

Two other ideas regarding the Creator and the creation occur in the psalms of praise. One is the sheer beauty of the creation, lauded by the psalmist in the immortal language of Psalm 8:

> O LORD, our Lord,
> how majestic is your name in all
> the earth!
> You have set your glory
> above the heavens.
> From the lips of children and
> infants
> you have ordained praise
> because of your enemies,
> to silence the foe and the
> avenger.
> When I consider your heavens,
> the work of your fingers,
> the moon and the stars,
> which you have set in place,
> what is man that you are mindful
> of him
> the son of man that you care for
> him?

129

Feeling Unworthy of a Weed

G. K. Chesterton in his autobiography comments on the human sense of unworthiness: "The only way to enjoy even a weed is to feel unworthy even of a weed." Chesterton calls it

the strange and staggering heresy that a human being has a right to dandelions; that in some extraordinary fashion we can demand the pick of all the dandelions in the garden of Paradise; that we owe no thanks for them at all and need feel no wonder at them at all; and above all no wonder at being thought worthy to receive them. Instead of saying, like the old religious poet, "What is man, that Thou carest for him, or the son of man that Thou regardest him?" we are to say like the discontented cabman, "What's this?" or like the bad-tempered Major in the club, "Is this a chop fit for a gentleman?"[1]

1. G. K. Chesterton, *Autobiography* (London: Hutchinson, 1937), 332.

You made him a little lower than
> the heavenly beings
> and crowned him with glory
> and honor.
You made him ruler over the
> works of your hands;
> you put everything under his
> feet:
all flocks and herds,
> and the beasts of the field,
the birds of the air,
> and the fish of the sea,
all that swim the paths of the
> seas.
O LORD, our Lord,
> how majestic is your name in all
> the earth!

The beauty of God's creation dwarfs human existence and thus elevates the wonder that the Creator should be mindful of humans at all.

The second idea in the psalms of praise is that creation has its own language of praise and lauds the Creator's glory:

The heavens declare the glory of
> God;
> the skies proclaim the work of
> his hands.
Day after day they pour forth
> speech;

night after night they display
> knowledge.
There is no speech or language
> where their voice is not heard.
Their voice goes out into all the
> earth,
> their words to the ends of the
> world. (19:1–4b)

Not only has the Creator by his creation of the world established his reputation for justice and compassion, but he has recorded his character in the works of his creation in such a way that they, by their very existence, proclaim the Creator's glory in a universal scope.

Universality of God's Presence and Reign

As with creation, we will discuss later the universal scope of the Psalms as it is expressed in the psalms of the kingship of Yahweh. But a further word on this matter in the context of the psalms of praise is in order. The universal perspective on God and his relationship to all peoples in the Psalter is parallel to Isaiah 40–66, although we should not anticipate that the perspective of the Psalter will be as theologically consistent as that of Isaiah. Yet, the parts of the whole can be found in the Psalms.

We have already observed that Psalm 19 announces that God has endowed the world with a language that proclaims his glory. It follows that the human inhabitants of the world, all nations included, should also proclaim his glory "from the rising of the sun to the place where it sets" (Ps 113:3). The shortest psalm in the book, Psalm 117, is a summons to all nations and peoples to praise the Lord. The fundamental reason that all peoples should praise the Lord is found in his awesome deeds, including the creation of the world (Ps 33:6–9) and his deeds done on Israel's behalf (Ps 65:5–8). It is not surprising to hear creation, of which all peoples are beneficiaries, acclaimed as the basis for praising God, but the focus on his works done on Israel's behalf is quite another matter. Why should the na-

Psalm 66 in John Bunyan's Writings

Rowland E. Prothero comments on the autobiographical nature of John Bunyan's writings and his use of Psalm 66:16 to declare the transforming grace of Christ in his life:

[Bunyan] describes his own experience: he paints, with vivid realism, the picture of his own inner self; the struggle of Christian is a transcript of his own spiritual conflict. He has himself been plunged into the Slough of Despond, himself fought hand-to-hand with Apollyon, himself passed through the Valley of the Shadow of Death, himself reached the Heavenly landing-place. In his *Grace abounding to the Chief of Sinners*, which bears the motto, "Come and hear all ye that fear God, and I will declare what he has done for my soul" (Ps. lxvi., verse 14 [sic 16]), he has recorded, with a pen of iron and in letters of fire, his own passage from death to life.[1]

1. Rowland E. Prothero, *The Psalms in Human Life* (New York: E. P. Dutton, 1905), 245.

let the sound of his praise be
heard;
he has preserved our lives
and kept our feet from slipping.
For you, O God, tested us;
you refined us like silver.
You brought us into prison
and laid burdens on our backs.
You let men ride over our heads;
we went through fire and water,
but you brought us to a place of
abundance.
I will come to your temple with
burnt offerings
and fulfill my vows to you—
vows my lips promised and my
mouth spoke
when I was in trouble.
I will sacrifice fat animals to you
and an offering of rams;
I will offer bulls and goats. Selah
Come and listen, all you who fear
God;
let me tell you what he has done
for me. (vv. 1–16)

Not only Israel but the whole earth bows in obeisance to God and in honor of his awesome deeds on Israel's behalf.

The universal reign of Yahweh is not simply a reign in power over the world, but a reign that draws the world into salvation. God is seated on his throne, and all the kings of the earth belong to him. His universal reign is such that he puts his claim on all peoples, drawing them to himself as "the people of the God of Abraham" (Ps 47:7–9). God's universal reign then represents a saving sovereignty, not merely a sovereignty of power.

God's Work in Israel's History

In view of our lengthy discussion of the historical perspectives on Israel's history in the Psalms,[15] we will only briefly mention some of the historical events and eras which become the reasons for praising the Lord in the great hymns of the Psalter. The story of Joseph (Ps 105:16–22), the sojourn in Egypt (vv. 23–27), the plagues (vv. 28–36), the exodus (vv. 37–38, 43), the wilderness (vv. 39–42), and the conquest (v. 44) are pictures in the memory of the writer of Psalm 105. Egypt, the Red Sea, the

tions be glad about the Lord's awesome deeds performed in Israel's history? Psalm 66 puts the two together, first acknowledging God's awesome acts on humanity's behalf as reason for praise, and then his works in Israel as the second reason:

Shout with joy to God, all the earth!
Sing the glory of his name;
make his praise glorious!
Say to God, "How awesome are
your deeds!
So great is your power
that your enemies cringe before
you.
All the earth bows down to you;
they sing praise to you,
they sing praise to your name."
Come and see what God has done,
how awesome his works in
man's behalf!
He turned the sea into dry land,
they passed through the waters
on foot—
come, let us rejoice in him.
He rules forever by his power,
his eyes watch the nations—
let not the rebellious rise up
against him.
Praise our God, O peoples,

Study Questions

1. In keeping with the psalmists' understanding of praise as the throne of God and the invincible weapon of believers, the suggestion is made that "if all of God's people would praise him with their whole hearts in one simultaneous moment, God's kingdom would immediately materialize before their eyes." Is praise really this powerful? Comment.

2. C. S. Lewis speaks of praise as more than expressing enjoyment, but rather completing enjoyment, being its own "appointed consummation." In this understanding, praise is more a state of being and direction of life than a few words during worship. How do the Psalms convey this "praise as state of soul" concept? Have we lost this in our modern age? Comment.

3. Proponents of the documentary hypothesis look at the different names used for God as indicative of different sources, while the rabbinic tradition views the context of the different names as determinative: 'Elohim suggesting the power or transcendence of God, and Yahweh his compassion, nearness, and personal presence. How does this Jewish approach give a positive direction to interpreting the Psalms? Specifically, how does it help us understand the doctrine of creation given here?

4. Think about the exalted place the Psalter gives to creation, and the ascription of praise to God as Creator. What are the various ways in which the Psalms express the Lord's creation, and why is it such a prominent theme? Answer in an essay that links with other wisdom thought.

5. Closely related to the theme of creation is the understanding of Yahweh as King—a King whose reign is universal. How does this concept of Yahweh as ruling King speak to the salvation of the world as a whole and the salvation of Israel specifically?

wilderness, and the exile each have their spot on the canvas of history painted by the writer of Psalm 106. The historical repertoire of Psalm 114 includes the exodus, the Red Sea, and the Jordan, while Psalm 135 encloses Israel's history between the tenth plague and the conquest (vv. 8–12). In a powerful combination of creation and history, Psalm 136 extols the God who created the world (vv. 5–9) and then skips to the sojourn in Egypt, followed by the Red Sea, the wilderness, and the conquest (vv. 10–26). God has acted on his people's behalf in a continuous chain of awesome events, and for that he deserves high praise. While the psalmists do not always enumerate Yahweh's deeds by name, using generic terms, they extol them nevertheless. "Awesome deeds" (nora'oth, Ps 65:5), "works" ('aliloth, Pss 105:1; 66:5 [sing.]), "wonderful acts" (nifle'oth, Pss 105:2, 5; 136:4), "mighty acts" (gevuroth, Pss 106:2; 145:4,12), and "great deeds" (gedolim, a combination of the adjective "great" and the noun "works," Pss 111:2; 136:4) are among the generic terms that convey the message of the Lord's works in creation and history. They elicit the response of praise from Israel and the nations alike.

Summary

The psalms of praise dominate Books 4–5. In the Psalter praise is the nerve center of the spiritual life. Even lament moves in the direction of praise. The Psalms themselves, while they do not consciously anatomize praise, do inform the reader from time to time how central praise is in the faith of Israel, and thus in the Christian faith. God is enthroned on (or inhabits) the praises of Israel, another way of informing us how very close he is to the person of faith.

The psalms of praise, or those psalms that have sometimes been called hymns, extol the Lord for what he has done in creation and in history. They fall into two categories: (1) those that can be identified by form, and (2) those that can be identified only by theme. The basic hymn engages in the praise of God and then gives the reasons for praising him. Westermann has subdivided praise into the rubrics of *declarative* and *descriptive* praise, the first being rather generic forms of praise and the second filling in the details of what God has done.

While the major themes in the psalms of praise are not exclusive to them, they are nevertheless dominant themes in these psalms: God the Creator and his creation, the universality of God's presence and reign, God's awesome deeds in history, and the historical events in which God has shown himself faithful and powerful.

Key Terms

hallelujah psalms
psalms of praise
declarative praise
descriptive praise

7 "My God, My God, Why Have You Forsaken Me?"

Psalms of Lament

Outline

- Definition and Description of the Psalms of Lament
- Subcategories of the Psalms of Lament
- Identity of the Enemies/Evildoers in the Psalms
- Summary

Objectives

After reading this chapter, you should be able to

1. Assess the psalms of lament as a category.
2. Summarize the literary aspects of the psalms of lament.
3. Describe the major contents of the psalms of lament.

If we looked from a distance at the canvas of life, we would see the contrasting colors. The joy and sorrow, the hope and despair—those emotional states representing the extreme situations of life would appear in black and white. Of course, there are obviously many colors in between, and they are just as real as the opposites, but our eyes naturally fall on the points where the contrast is greatest. It is like looking at a Rembrandt painting and seeing the focal point of light which immediately sets the darker parts of the canvas in contrast to this focal center. That is an analogy of life. How many times have we been asked to share the most common experience we ever had? No, we want to hear about the highs and lows. And when we have retold the story, we have given our audience some sense of the extremes of our lives but not the real center of attention, which is where most of us live out our daily existence. Yet, the contrasts of our lives do give an orientation to who we are, even though they are not the heart of our autobiography. They are like the index of a book—they tell us a lot about its contents, but we have to read the book to understand the story. That is the way the psalms of praise and the **psalms of lament** function in the Psalter. They are the index to the spiritual personalities of the psalmists. We know what really moves them at either end of the spectrum of life, even though we may not have read the heart of their autobiography. Nevertheless, we can deduce a lot about them from those extremes, about their values and reason for being. Thankfully for us, the psalmists do fill the canvas with other colors and fill in the gaps of our understanding in regard to who they are and what their relationship to God and humanity is. And even those intermediate colors are fuller because we also have the contrasts from either end of their lives.

Definition and Description of the Psalms of Lament

In our discussion of the psalms of praise, we observed that they are primarily composed of a word of praise and the reasons for praising. In comparison, the psalms of lament include the lamentation and the reasons for lamenting, even though the precise nature of what causes the psalmist to lament may be left to a bit of ambiguity, a matter we will consider later in our discussion. Yet it is more complex than that. Westermann, who follows Gunkel's[1] lead in dividing the psalms of lament into **laments of the people** and **laments of the individual,** identifies five component parts of the laments of the people:

1. address and introductory petition
2. lament
3. confession of trust
4. petition
5. vow of praise[2]

In some of these psalms, observes Westermann, the confession of trust is so prominent that one can speak of a psalm of trust for the people, and he gives Psalms 46, 123, and 126 as examples. Further, the vow to praise seldom occurs in the lament of the people, probably because vows were made by individuals.[3]

The lament of the individual, by Westermann's accounting, has the following components:

1. address, with introductory cry for help and/or turning to God
2. lament
3. confession of trust
4. petition
5. assurance of being heard
6. wish or petition for God's intervention
7. vow of praise
8. praise of God when petition has been heard[4]

The Cry of Dereliction

Elizabeth Barrett Browning catches the essence of this God-forsaken cry of the psalmist when she takes note of Jesus' cry of dereliction from the cross. In her poem "Cowper's Grave" she expresses the idea that "Immanuel's orphaned cry" was echoless, so that no other human being would ever have to utter that cry again:

> Deserted! God could separate from His own essence rather;
> And Adam's sins *have* swept between the righteous Son and Father;
> Yea, once, Immanuel's orphaned cry His universe hath shaken—
> It went up single, echoless, "My God, I am forsaken!"
>
> It went up from the Holy's lips amid His lost creation,
> That, of the lost, no son should use those words of desolation!
> That earth's worst phrensies, marring hope, should mar not hope's fruition,
> And I, on Cowper's grave, should see his rapture in a vision.[1]

1. Elizabeth Barrett Browning, "Cowper's Grave," in *The Poetical Works of Elizabeth Barrett Browning* (London: John Murray, 1914), 143.

We should understand that not all laments include all of the above components, nor do they necessarily follow the above order. There are considerable deviations from this pattern, but we are still left with the two basic components, the lament itself and the reason for lamenting.

To simplify the matter, Westermann has further pointed out that the structure of the psalm of lament usually deals with three dimensions: (1) a complaint against God (problem is God), (2) a complaint against an enemy (problem is external), and (3) and the psalmist's complaint against himself (problem is internal),[5] even though these three are not often found in the same psalm. A psalm which does contain all three is Psalm 22. First, the complaint is against God:

> My God, my God, why have you
>   forsaken me?
>   Why are you so far from saving
>   me,
>   so far from the words of my
>   groaning?
> O my God, I cry out by day, but
>   you do not answer,
>   by night, and am not silent.
>   (vv. 1–2)

Second, the psalmist voices a complaint against his enemies:

> All who see me mock me;
>   they hurl insults, shaking their
>   heads:
> "He trusts in the LORD;
>   let the LORD deliver him,
> Let him deliver him,
>   since he delights in him." (vv. 7–8)
>
> Many bulls surround me;
>   strong bulls of Bashan encircle
>   me.
> Roaring lions tearing their prey
>   open their mouths wide against
>   me. (vv. 12–13)

Third, his complaint is also against himself: "But I am a worm and not a man, / scorned by men and despised by the people" (v. 6).

This is also true of Psalm 38, which sets forth complaints against God, the psalmist's enemies, and himself (vv. 2–3—against God; vv. 4–5, 18—against himself; vv. 11–12, 19—against his enemies). In Psalm 41, David indicts himself (v. 4) and his enemies (vv. 5–9) but not God (see table 7.2 for an analysis).

These psalms are basically prayers, as the psalmists lay their problems out on the table before God. As they do, they lay their spiritual in-

137

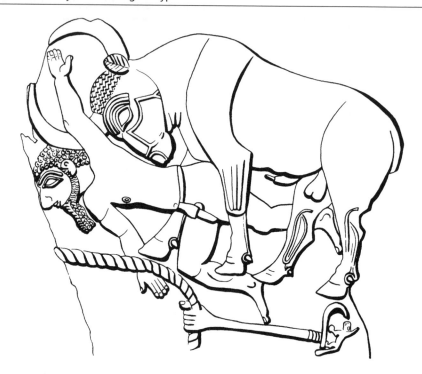

Bulls were considered powerful and fierce animals, thus an appropriate image to describe the psalmist's enemies.

songs of prayer

hibitions aside as they deal with the crises that have interrupted their lives and created physical pain and spiritual consternation. While the boldness and naked honesty of the psalmists may shock us, this attitude is nevertheless instructive for our own spiritual lives. We sometimes hold back too much from God, conceal our true feelings in prayer, and create a false image of ourselves at the heavenly throne of grace. What would happen to us and to our relationship to God if we were truly honest with him and with ourselves? Thankfully there is a place in the biblical faith for this kind of boldness before God. The psalms of lament carve out a spiritual niche for us where we can use the colloquial language of life's hurts and still stay within the vocabulary of faith. John Goldingay remarks that Psalm 22, with its range and depth of complaint (and psalms similar to it), invite us into "an extraordinary freedom in our speech with God."[6] Goldingay is right—this freedom is indeed extraordinary, and we can use it to great benefit, as Job did. But it is also a dangerous freedom that can too easily move us, on the divine level, in the direction of

spiritual defiance and mutiny. On the human level, it can direct us down the path of insolence and hatred of our enemies. So we must use this freedom—and use it we should!—with great precaution and humility.

Subcategories of the Psalms of Lament

In Kraus's taxonomy of the Psalms, he uses the phrase **songs of prayer** as a broad classification, and includes both community and individual songs in this category, which contains the largest number of psalms in the Psalter. It subdivides into prayer songs of the individual, community prayer songs, and thanksgiving songs.[7] The first of these subcategories, prayer songs of the individual, can be analyzed by literary form[8] and further broken down into subcategories:

1. The prayer song of the sick. The psalms which he with some con-

Table 7.1

Distribution of Individual Laments and Thanksgiving Songs in the Psalter

	Bk 1 (1–41)	Bk 2 (42–72)	Bk 3 (73–89)	Bk 4 (90–106)	Bk 5 (107–50)
Individual Psalms of Lament	19	5	1	3	1
Community Psalms of Lament	0	2	6	2	3
Individual Psalms of Thanksgiving	5	2	0	1	3

fidence assigns to this category are Psalms 38, 41, and 88.

2. The prayer songs of the sick with modifications. A much longer list of psalms belongs, in varying degrees, to this group, either by form or theme: Psalms 6, 13, 22, 30, 31, 32, 35, 39, 51, 69, 71, 91, 102, and 103.

3. The prayer song of the persecuted and the accused, to which category belong Psalms 3, 4, 5, 7, 11, 17, 23, 26, 27, 57, and 63.

4. The prayer song of a sinner. While Kraus acknowledges that this is a disputed subcategory, he would include Psalms 51 and 130 in it.[9] The early church included these two psalms in the category of the seven penitential psalms, which were Psalms 6, 32, 38, 51, 102, 130, and 143.

The second of Kraus's subcategories, the community prayer songs, identified in Psalm 80:4 as "prayer of the people," includes Psalms 44, 60, 74, 77, 79, 80, 83, 85, 90, 94, 123, 126, and 137.

The third subcategory, according to Kraus's classification, is the thanksgiving song of the individual, which is closely associated with the prayer songs of the individual but is distinguished from it in that a turn of events in the psalmist's situation, or rescue from his distress, has taken

place. It includes Psalms 18, 30, 31, 32, 40A, 52, 66B, 92, 116, 118, and 120.[10]

Perhaps there is some significance in the fact that the individual psalms of lament are concentrated (nineteen out of twenty-nine) in Book 1, the core collection of Davidic psalms. Indisputably, David had his share of problems with individuals and nations, and we should expect expressions of his complaint and grief among the Davidic psalms. At the same time, no community laments occur in Book 1, but they are distributed throughout Books 2–5 where a national or community consciousness rises to the surface of the literary consciousness of the Psalter.

Table 7.2 is an attempt to provide an analysis of the psalms of lament that clearly arise from an illness suffered by the psalmist. In all three of these psalms (Pss 38, 41, 88), the psalmist is in the very depths of his suffering and cannot see the light at the end of the tunnel. His hope is that God has or will deliver him from the crisis:

Blessed is he who has regard for
    the weak;
    the LORD delivers him in times
        of trouble.
The LORD will protect him and preserve his life;
    he will bless him in the land
    and not surrender him to the desire of his foes.

139

Table 7.2

Individual Psalms of Lament: Songs of the Sick

	Ps 38	Ps 41	Ps 88
Problem	vv. 7, 11, 17–18 illness and spiritual anguish, perhaps caused by sin	vv. 3–5 illness, perhaps caused by sin	vv. 3–5 illness and spiritual anguish
Complaint against God	vv. 2–3 "Your arrows have pierced me."		vv. 6–9, 14–18 "Your wrath lies heavily upon me."
Complaint against Self	vv. 4–5 "My guilt has overwhelmed me."	v. 4 "I have sinned against you."	
Complaint against Enemies	vv. 11, 12, 19–20 "My friends and companions avoid me"; "Those who seek my life set their traps"; "Those who seek me without reason are numerous."	vv. 5–9 "My enemies say of me in malice, 'When will he die.'"	
Petition	vv. 1, 16, 21–22 "Do not rebuke me in your anger."	vv. 4, 10 "But you, O Lord, have mercy on me."	vv. 1–2, 9b, 13–14 "Day and night I cry out before you."
Solution	v. 18 confession of sin	vv. 4, 10–12 confession of sin, the Lord's mercy, and the psalmist's integrity	

The LORD will sustain him on his
sickbed
and restore him from his bed of
illness. (Ps 41:1–3)

In this small group of psalms physical illness and spiritual anguish are inseparable, as they are also in table 7.3 (psalms of the sick and anguished). We can readily understand this, particularly in light of our knowledge of and experience with the interconnections between the physical and psychological. Even those who have suffered from only minor illnesses will recognize that a bit of "anguish," or at least a feeling of having been inconvenienced, is often an accompaniment of these occasions.

In two of these psalms the psalmist attributes the cause of his illness to God (38:2–3; 88:6–9, 14–18), even though in Psalms 38 and 41 there is reason to believe that sin lies at the base of the poet's affliction, for he confesses his guilt (38:4–5; 41:4). If that is not complicated enough, the psalmist also turns toward his enemies as a source of his anguish (38:11–12, 19–20; 41:5–9). We see, therefore, that the psalmist finds himself in difficult straits, and his physical malady is complicated by the spiritual anguish he feels.

Table 7.3 breaks down the individual psalms of lament, songs of the sick and anguished, into their major parts. I have added to this table Psalms 51 and 130, which Kraus calls "Songs of the Sinner," because sin is so much a part of this category (see Pss 32:3, 5–6; 51:1–14; 69:5; 103:3; 130:3–4), and it is difficult, as observed in the previous category, to keep physical illness, spiritual anguish, and sin distinct from one another. They form a complex. The reason this group is distinct from the psalms in table 7.2 is

Table 7.3

Individual Psalms of Lament: Songs of the Sick and Anguished

	Ps 6	Ps 13	Ps 22	Ps 30	Ps 31	Ps 32	Ps 35	Ps 39	Ps 51	Ps 69	Ps 71	Ps 91	Ps 102	Ps 103	Ps 130
Problem	vv. 2–3 illness and spiritual anguish	vv. 1–2 spiritual anguish	vv. 14–15, 17–18 illness and spiritual anguish	vv. 1–3, 8–9 illness and spiritual anguish	vv. 7, 9b–10 illness and spiritual anguish	vv. 3, 5–6 illness and spiritual anguish, perhaps a result of sin	vv. 1, 3, 20–21 persecution/false accusations	vv. 2–3, 13 illness and spiritual anguish	vv. 1–14 spiritual anguish (and perhaps illness, v. 8) as a result of sin	vv. 2–3, 5, 19 persecution, spiritual anguish, sin (and perhaps illness v. 3)	vv. 9, 19–21 illness (old age) and spiritual anguish	vv. 3–7 pestilence	vv. 2–11, 13–17 spiritual anguish, illness, national humiliation	vv. 3–4, 10 illness (and perhaps sin)	vv. 3–4 sin
Complaint against God	v. 5 "No one remembers you when he is dead."	v.1 "How long, O LORD? Will you forget me forever?"	vv. 1–2, 15c "My God, my God, why have you forsaken me?"	vv. 5a, 7 "When you hid your face, I was dismayed."		v. 4 "For day and night your hand was heavy upon me."	vv. 13c–14 "My prayers returned to me unanswered."	vv. 9–11 "Remove your scourge from me."			v. 20 "You have made me see troubles, many and bitter."		vv. 9–11, 23 "You have taken me up and thrown me aside."		
Complaint against Self			vv. 6–8 "I am a worm and not a man."						vv. 3–5 "For I know my transgressions."	v. 5 "My guilt is not hidden from you."					
Complaint against Enemies	vv. 7, 10 "My eyes grow weak with sorrow; they fail because of all my foes."	vv. 2b, 4 "My enemy will say, 'I have overcome him.'"	vv. 7–8, 12–13, 16 "All who seek me mock me."	v. 1c "[You] did not let my enemies gloat over me."	vv. 1b, 11–13, 18 "Because of all my enemies, I am the utter contempt of my neighbors."		vv. 1, 3–8, 11–17 "Ruthless witnesses come forward."			vv. 4–5, 14, 18–19, 21 "Those who hate me without reason outnumber the hairs of my head."	vv. 10–11 "For my enemies speak against me."	v. 8 "You will only observe with your eyes and see the punishment of the wicked."	v. 8 "All day long my enemies taunt me."		
Trust	vv. 4, 10	vv. 5–6	vv. 3–5, 9–10, 24, 26–31	vv. 5, 7a	vv. 1a, 6, 14–15a, 19–20, 21–24	vv. 10	vv. 10, 24		vv. 1–2, 17	vv. 13, 16, 33	vv. 1, 6, 7b–8, 14–21	vv. 1–13	vv. 12–22, 25–28	vv. 8–18	vv. 3–8
Petition	vv. 1–4 "O LORD, do not rebuke me in your anger."	vv. 1–4 "Look on me and answer, O LORD my God."	vv. 11, 19–21 "Do not be far from me."	v. 10 "Hear, O LORD, and be merciful to me."	vv. 1b–5, 9a, 15b–18 "Let me never be put to shame."		vv. 1–8, 17, 19, 22–27 "Contend, O LORD, with those who contend with me."	vv. 4–13 "Show me, O LORD, my life's end and the number of my days."	vv. 1–2, 7–12, 14, 18 "Have mercy on me, O God."	vv. 1, 6, 13–18, 22–29 "Save me, O God, for the waters have come up to my neck."	vv. 2–4, 9, 12–13 "Rescue me and deliver me in your righteousness."		vv. 1–2, 24 "Do not take me away, O my God, in the midst of my days."		v. 2 "Let your ears be attentive to my cry for mercy."

	Ps 6	Ps 13	Ps 22	Ps 30	Ps 31	Ps 32	Ps 35	Ps 39	Ps 51	Ps 69	Ps 71	Ps 91	Ps 102	Ps 103	Ps 130
Solution	vv. 2–4 trust in the Lord's unfailing love	vv. 5–6 trust in the Lord's unfailing love	vv. 4–5 trust in the God who saved their ancestors	vv. 2, 10 the Lord's mercy	vv. 9a, 15b–20 the Lord's mercy and goodness	vv. 1–2, 5 confession and divine forgiveness	vv. 4–10 divine judgment	vv. 4–6, 7–8 recognition of the brevity of life, and the Lord's mercy	vv. 3–12 confession and divine forgiveness	vv. 13–18 goodness of the Lord's love	vv. 19–21 the Lord's salvation	vv. 9–13 make the Most High your dwelling	vv. 1–2, 13–20 the Lord's mercy and intervention	vv. 7–18 trust in the Lord's mercy	vv. 3–4, 7–8 the Lord's forgiveness and mercy
Vow to Praise		v. 6 "I will sing to the LORD."	vv. 22, 25 "I will declare your name to my brothers."	vv. 1, 12b "O LORD my God, I will give you thanks forever."	vv. 7–8 "I will be glad and rejoice in your love."		vv. 9–10, 18, 28 "My tongue will speak of your righteousness and of your praises all day long."		v. 15 "My mouth will declare your praise."	vv. 30–31 "I will praise God's name in song."	vv. 6c, 14–16, 22–24 "I will praise you with the harp for your faithfulness."		vv. 21–22 "So that the name of the LORD will be declared in Zion and his praise in Jerusalem."	vv. 1, 2a, 20–22 "Praise the LORD, O my soul."	
Vow to Service									vv. 13–14 "Then I will teach transgressors your ways."						
Appeal to History/ God's Mighty Works			vv. 3–4 "In you our fathers put their trust."								vv. 16–17 "I will . . . proclaim your mighty acts, O Sovereign LORD."			v. 7 "He made known his ways to Moses."	
Oracle to Psalmist/ Israel						vv. 8–10						vv. 14–16	vv. 18–20		

that there is more ambiguity in table 7.3 regarding the psalmist's problem. It may be physical illness, but his physical suffering and spiritual anguish merge so perfectly that it is difficult to tell which lies at the base of his lament. In the case of table 7.2, we are pretty certain that the psalmist's problem is physical illness, even though spiritual anguish is an accompaniment.

In ten out of fifteen of these psalms the worshiper turns to God as the cause of his suffering, and in as many again he files complaints against his enemies as being the problem, although in three of them the psalmist acknowledges his own sin (22:6–8; 51:3–5; 69:5). It should be noted that despite the trouble, these psalms point to a solution to the problem, which is basically trust in the unfailing character of Yahweh. Whether the specific solution is located in the Lord's mercy (e.g., 6:2–4), the psalmist's confession of sin (e.g., 32:1–2, 5), or divine judgment (e.g., 35:4–10), the essence of the psalmist's trust is in the true character of Yahweh. In table 7.3 this solution can be seen in its broader dimensions in the psalmist's frequent expressions of faith and trust.

It is certainly helpful to take account of the power of confession as the Psalms deal with the matter of sin and guilt. Yet it is not the power of confession alone, but confession coupled with divine forgiveness. This certainly sets the theology of the Psalms off from any modern therapy that would stress confession apart from God's forgiveness. In this group of psalms, confession, which is a mighty therapeutic recourse, has its complement in divine forgiveness:

> Then I acknowledged my sin to you
>   and did not cover up my iniquity.
> I said, "I will confess
>   my transgressions to the LORD"—
> and you forgave
>   the guilt of my sin.
> Therefore let everyone who is godly pray to you
>   while you may be found;

> surely when the mighty waters rise,
>   they will not reach him.
> You are my hiding place;
>   you will protect me from trouble
> and surround me with songs of deliverance. (Ps 32:5–7)

It is quite evident from this psalm that the source of healing is the Lord, however therapeutic the process of confession may be.

Some form of the vow to praise the Lord occurs in ten out of fifteen of these psalms, either using the personal pronoun "I" or a metonymous noun, "My mouth will declare your praise" (51:15), or a future declarative statement, "So the name of the LORD will be declared in Zion and his praise in Jerusalem" (102:21), or an imperative call to praise, "Praise the LORD, O my soul" (103:1, 2a, 20–22). The vow to praise reveals the psalmist's confidence in the Lord's unfailing love.

An interesting feature of three of these psalms is that there is an answer of sorts, either in the form of the psalmist's own word of admonition (32:8–10; 102:18–20), or a divine message in the form of an oracle (91:14–16) given to the psalmist. The latter also occurs in Psalm 60:6–8, as noted in table 7.5.

Table 7.4 includes those psalms that arise out of circumstances when either personal or national enemies have persecuted the psalmist. While the identification of the enemies or evildoers in the Psalms will be discussed below, suffice it to say at this point that the nature of these psalms suggests that many of these conflicts were interpersonal rather than international. Psalm 27 may be an exception in this group of psalms.

Interestingly there is only one complaint against God in this group (Ps 17:3). The psalmist has the sense that God is looking for some reason to blame him, but, like Job, he claims his innocence. In the same vein, we note that there are no self-indictments as we find in tables 7.2 and 7.3. A personal innocence per-

Table 7.4
Individual Psalms of Lament: Songs of the Persecuted and Accused

	Ps 3	Ps 4	Ps 5	Ps 7	Ps 11	Ps 17	Ps 23	Ps 27	Ps 57	Ps 63
Problem	vv. 1–2, 6 enemies	vv. 2–3 distress caused by others	v. 8 enemies	vv. 1–9 enemies	vv. 1–3 enemies	vv. 7–12 enemies	v. 5 enemies	vv. 2–3, 6, 10–12 enemies and war	vv. 3–4, 6 enemies	vv. 9–10 enemies
Complaint against God						v. 3 "Though you probe my heart and examine me at night, . . . you will find nothing."				
Complaint against Self										
Complaint against Enemies	vv. 1–2 "How many are my foes."	v. 2 "How long, O men, will you turn my glory into shame?"	vv. 9–10 "Not a word from their mouth can be trusted."	vv. 6, 14–16 "Rise up against the rage of my enemies."	vv. 1b–3 "The wicked bend their bows."	vv. 7–12 "They close up their callous hearts."	v. 5 "You prepare a table before me in the presence of my enemies."	vv. 2–3, 6, 12 "False witnesses rise up against me."	vv. 4, 6 "I am in the midst of lions."	vv. 9–10 "They who seek my life will be destroyed."
Trust	vv. 3–6	vv. 3b, 8	vv. 3–7	vv. 1, 9–11	vv. 1a, 4–7	vv. 6–8, 14b–15	vv. 1–6	vv. 1–3, 5, 13–14	vv. 1–3, 10	vv. 3–5
Petition	vv. 7–8 "Arise, O Lord! Deliver me, O my God!"	vv. 1, 6b "Be merciful to me and hear my prayer."	vv. 1–3, 8, 10–11 "Listen to my cry for help, my King and my God."	vv. 1–9 "Save and deliver me from all who pursue me."		vv. 1–2, 6–9, 13–14a "Rise up, O Lord, confront them."		vv. 4, 7–12 "One thing I ask of the Lord, . . . that I may dwell in the house of the Lord all the days of my life."	v. 1 "Have mercy on me, O God, have mercy on me."	
Solution	vv. 3–5, 7 trust in the Lord, and his intervention	vv. 5–8 trust in the Lord and right sacrifices	v. 10 the Lord's judgment	vv. 1–2, 8, 10–13 refuge in the Lord and personal integrity	vv. 1, 4–7 trust in divine justice and personal integrity	vv. 13–14a the Lord's judgment	vv. 5–6 the Lord's goodness and intervention	v. 4 the Lord's mercy and dwelling in his house	vv. 1–3, 7 the Lord's mercy and personal integrity	vv. 1–2 worship of and trust in God
Vow to Praise			v. 11 "Let all who take refuge in you be glad; let them ever sing for joy."	v. 17 "I will give thanks to the Lord."				v. 6b "I will sing and make music to the Lord."	vv. 7b, 9 "I will praise you, O Lord, among the nations."	vv. 3–8 "I will praise you as long as I live."

vades these psalms. Rather, complaints against the psalmist's enemies, of which he has plenty, are found in all of these psalms, and that is their qualifying characteristic. The solution to the problem is again found, rather surprisingly, in view of the psalmist's innocence, in the character of God, even though his personal integrity is quite important (7:8; note his oath to that effect in vv. 3–5; 11:5, 7; 57:7). Either the Lord's mercy, his sense of justice, or his power to intervene comes into focus as the more immediate way out of the psalmist's crisis. The psalmist's confidence in God and his hope for a solution to his problem can be seen in the "Solution" line of table 7.4 as well as in the psalmist's various expressions of trust in God, and also in the five instances of the vow to praise.

Perhaps it is of some significance that all except two of these psalms occur in Book 1, a book dominated by David's conflicts with his enemies, and all of them are Davidic psalms. We should not, however, conclude that these enemies were all national, for we know from the historical books that David had many personal enemies.

Table 7.5 presents an analysis of the community laments, or the laments of the people. The plural pronouns and frequent references to the nation characterize these psalms. In most cases these thirteen psalms focus on some national crisis. In eight of these poems the psalmist's attention turns toward God who, by his assessment, has rejected Israel or is angry with them. There are no self-indictments, while the enemies get a pretty good tongue-lashing. The national consciousness appears prominently in these psalms, particularly in the appeal to Yahweh's work in history. Eight out of thirteen include references to the past (44:1–3; 74:2–3, 13–17; 77:5, 10–20; 80:8–11; 83:9–12; 85:1–3; 90:1; 126:1–3). The solution to the national problem is most often divine intervention in much the same way as has occurred in the past (see "Solution" line in table 7.5). But even Yahweh's intervention is not merely a naked display of his power but is a positive expression of his character. He is a God of mercy and justice.

The vow to praise is, like the language of this group of psalms, phrased in the plural, occurring in only three cases (44:8; 79:13; 80:18), with a variation in 74:21. As has been observed above, the vow to praise was basically an individual activity, but there is certainly no reason why the nation could not also pledge itself to the praise of God. Indeed, it was most appropriate.

Identity of the Enemies/Evildoers in the Psalms

One of the challenges of this category is to identify the external perpetrators of the psalmists' distress, or the enemies and evildoers who victimize the psalmists. Suggestions have ranged widely:

1. a party of godless Jews who opposed the pious in the post-exilic era (Alfred Rahlfs);[11]
2. those who insisted, like Job's friends, that the psalmist was the object of divine punishment, and thus must have committed some grievous sin; or those who denied divine justice in the world and insisted that the psalmist was suffering despite his piety (Hermann Gunkel);[12]
3. those who, observing the psalmist's suffering, falsely accuse him of sin (so far, in agreement with Gunkel), and in the cases when the psalmist insists on his innocence, he is expected to undergo some cultic ceremony to prove it (Schmidt);[13]
4. those who worked sorcery on the psalmists (Mowinckel)[14]
5. foreign powers who threaten Israel as the covenant people (who are the pious) (Birkeland);[15]

Table 7.5
Community Psalms of Lament

	Ps 44	Ps 60	Ps 74	Ps 77	Ps 79	Ps 80	Ps 83	Ps 85	Ps 90	Ps 94	Ps 123	Ps 126	Ps 137
Problem	vv. 9–16 defeat in war	vv. 1–3, 10 defeat in war	vv. 1, 3–8 defeat in war, destruction of sanctuary	vv. 1–2, 5–9 distress, perhaps defeat in war	vv. 1–4 defeat in war	vv. 13–17 defeat in war	vv. 2–8 threat by enemies	vv. 4–7 defeat in war	vv. 7–10 brevity of life and perhaps defeat in war	vv. 4–7 defeat in war	vv. 3–4 perhaps defeat in war	vv. 1–2a humiliation of exile	vv. 1–4 Babylonian exile and challenge of captors
Complaint against God	vv. 9–14, 23–24 "You have rejected and humbled us."	vv. 1–3, 10 "You have rejected us, O God."	vv. 1, 10–11 "Why have you rejected us forever, O God?"	vv. 7–9, "Will the Lord reject forever?"	vv. 5–6, 12–13 "How long, O LORD? Will you be angry forever?"	vv. 4–17 "How long will your anger smolder against the prayers of your people?"		vv. 4–7 "Will you be angry with us forever?"	vv. 7–10 "We are consumed by your anger and terrified by your indignation"				
Complaint against Self													
Complaint against Enemies					vv. 1–4 "O God, the nations have invaded your inheritance."	vv. 6, 13 "Our enemies mock us."	vv. 2–8 "See how your enemies are astir, how your foes rear their heads."			vv. 4–11 "They crush your people, O LORD; they oppress your inheritance."	vv. 3–4 "We have endured much ridicule from the proud."		vv. 7–9 "Happy is he who repays you for what you have done to us."
Trust	vv. 1–8	vv. 4, 12	vv. 12–17	vv. 10–20	v. 13	vv. 1–2a, 3, 7, 19	v. 18	vv. 1–3, 8–13	vv. 1–2	vv. 9–14, 18–19, 22–23	v. 2		
Petition	vv. 23–26 "Rouse yourself! Do not reject us forever!"	vv. 5, 11 "Save us and help us with your right hand."	vv. 2–3, 18–23 "Remember the people you purchased of old."		vv. 6–12 "Pour out your wrath on the nations that do not acknowledge you."	vv. 1–3, 7, 14–15, 19 "Restore us, O God; make your face shine upon us, that we may be saved."	vv. 1–3, 9–18 "Do to them as you did to Midian."	vv. 4, 7 "Restore us again, O God our Savior."	vv. 12–17 "Relent, O LORD! How long will it be?"	vv. 1–3 "Rise up, O Judge of the earth; pay back to the proud what they deserve."	vv. 3–4 "Have mercy on us, O LORD, have mercy on us, for we have endured much contempt."	v. 4 "Restore our fortunes, O LORD, like streams in the Negev."	v. 7 "Remember, O LORD, what the Edomites did on the day Jerusalem fell."
Solution	vv. 4–9, 23–26 the power and mercy of God	vv. 5–12 divine intervention	vv. 13–23 divine intervention	vv. 5, 10–20 remembering God's mighty acts	vv. 9–12 divine intervention and forgiveness of sins	vv. 3, 7, 19 divine intervention and favor	vv. 1, 9–18 divine intervention	vv. 4–7 divine intervention	vv. 11–17 divine intervention	vv. 14–23 the Lord's mercy and justice	v. 3 the Lord's mercy	vv. 2b–3 divine intervention	
Vow to Praise	v. 8 "We will praise your name forever."		v. 21 "May the poor and needy praise your name."		v. 13 "Then we your people, the sheep of your pasture, will praise you forever."	v. 18 "Revive us, and we will call on your name."							
Appeal to History/God's Mighty Acts	vv. 1–3		vv. 2–3, 13–17	vv. 5, 10–20		vv. 8–11	vv. 9–12	vv. 1–3	v. 1			vv. 1–3	
Oracle		vv. 6–8											

6. the language is open and metaphorical, allowing readers to adapt the psalm to their individual situations (Miller).[16]

It takes a long stretch of the imagination to come to the conclusion of proposal 1 above. The language of the laments is pretty literal, even though metaphorical terms are frequent. For example, the enemies are called bulls, roaring lions, and dogs. In Psalm 7:1–2, to illustrate, the psalmist's pursuers threaten to tear him up like a lion and rip him to pieces (see also Pss 17:12; 22:12–13, 16; 57:4), but the evidence hardly points to some godless party of Jews who have made the psalmists the object of their scorn.

On the basis of these psalms, proposal 2—that God is punishing the psalmist because of his sin—has merit in some cases, although it certainly is not the general explanation for understanding the opposition the psalmists were experiencing. In this regard, however, we encounter two situations in these psalms. In the first situation the psalmist freely admits his sin (51; 38:18; 32:5–6), and in the second, the psalmist believes he has been falsely accused (27:10–12). But in between these two positions is that situation where the psalmist admits his sin (69:5) but also feels that the accusations against him are baseless (vv. 4–5). It is difficult to know what is going on here, unless the psalmist is admitting that there may be some wrong in his life, but certainly not of the proportions his enemies claim. Or, it may be a situation similar to Job's, and he is simply prefixing his statement with an unexpressed *if*: "[*If* I have sinned] You know my folly, O God; / my guilt is not hidden from you" (v. 5). In fact, in this particular instance, David was convinced he was suffering for the Lord's sake, which implies that he believed he was not suffering for his own sin (v. 7). Gunkel suggests that the confusion may arise out of the fact that the psalmist was not absolutely sure

that there was a causal connection between his sin and illness.[17]

Then there are those instances when the psalmist strongly and without question affirmed his innocence, such as Psalm 7:3–5, where David took an oath to establish his innocence, and Psalm 17:4–5, where he distinguished his way from that of violent persons.

This discussion raises the question with which the Book of Job deals extensively, the relationship between sin and illness or suffering. The common theological tenet put forth by Job's friends, that sin begets physical and emotional suffering, sometimes undergirds the Psalms too. That is obvious when one looks at the table of psalms that deal with sickness (table 7.2). The connection between sin and physical illness is at times clearly attested. This may fall outside the boundaries of what we think is theologically admissible, but the Old Testament does indeed make the connection. From my point of view, this means that such a relationship, however unpalatable to our sensitivities, does exist. For centuries, and especially in our modern world, we have come so far as to recognize the existence of psychosomatic illness. That may in part explain the connection that the psalmists are aware of, but it cannot explain the entire phenomenon. If we take this theological tenet as normative in Old Testament theology, then we have to make an allowance for physical illness as an expression of divine punishment.

The problem we have with this is the same problem Job had. Only God and the person who is suffering can know whether the connection has any validity, and even the sufferer may not always know. Of course, in Job's case he insisted that he was innocent, and therefore no such connection between sins he had not committed and his suffering could exist. Job's friends worked with the assumption that sin always begets suffering, and they also thought the formula could be reversed: where there is suffering, one can presuppose that there is sin. There is a question in my mind whether Job went so far as to deny a connection altogether, or whether he was merely denying the absolute, without-exception principle his friends propounded. I tend to believe the latter.

Proposal 3 espouses Job's theology—that those who observe his suffering, assuming that sin always begets suffering, falsely accuse him of sin. This position is quite clear in the case of David's accusers in Psalm 41. They observe his physical suffering ("A vile disease has beset him"—v. 8) and falsely accuse him:

> My enemies say of me in malice,
>   "When will he die and his name
>   perish?"
> Whenever one comes to see me,
>   he speaks falsely, while his
>   heart gathers slander;
>   then he goes out and spreads it
>   abroad. (vv. 5–6)

Proposal 3 as augmented by Schmidt—that the psalmists are anticipating some kind of innocence ritual—has little evidence to support it. Certainly they are concerned at times about their innocence, but the Psalms provide little substance for such a ritual.

Proposal 4, set forth by Mowinckel—that the enemies in the Psalms were those who worked sorcery or black magic on the psalmists—is hardly more commendable as a substantive hypothesis than Schmidt's. In fact, Mowinckel came to alter his view as a result of the work of his student, Harris Birkeland.

Proposal 5, put forth by Harris Birkeland, suggests that the enemies of the Psalms were foreign powers, or Gentiles, who threatened the covenant people Israel. Birkeland worked from the more explicit to the less explicit, beginning with those individual psalms of lament (9–10, 42–43, 54, 56, 59) that were clearly not royal psalms, in which the king spoke with a royal "I" and intended the nation by it. His method led him to posit the view that both the individual and community laments refer to Gentile enemies. Admittedly, there

is a lot of evidence in the psalms of lament that enemy powers were a great threat to Israel, a fact we know from the rest of the Old Testament. This seems to be more likely in the case of the community psalms of lament. That is the issue in Psalm 83, for example:

> "Come," they say, "let us destroy
>   them as a nation,
>   that the name of Israel be re-
>   membered no more."
> With one mind they plot together;
>   they form an alliance against
>   you—
> the tents of Edom and the
>   Ishmaelites,
>   of Moab and the Hagrites,
> Gebal, Ammon and Amalek,
>   Philistia, with the people of
>   Tyre.
> Even Assyria has joined them
>   to lend strength to the descen-
>   dants of Lot.
> Do to them as you did to Midian,
>   as you did to Sisera and Jabin at
>   the river Kishon,
> who perished at Endor
>   and became like refuse on the
>   ground.
> Make their nobles like Oreb and
>   Zeeb,
>   all their princes like Zebah and
>   Zalmunna,
> who said, "Let us take possession
>   of the pasturelands of God." (vv.
>   4–12)

The extreme position, however, that the enemies or evildoers in the Psalms can be generally identified as Gentiles, is, in my view, more difficult to demonstrate.

In the case of proposal 6, set forth by Patrick Miller, the identity of the psalmists' enemies remains an open question. That is not to suggest that we should make no effort to find out who the enemies were, but it simply recognizes the stalemate that has resulted from the research of the past. In view of that, Miller suggests that it ultimately makes no difference how we identify the enemies and evildoers in these psalms. The lack of identity, in fact, leaves the hermeneutical question open for each new reader and each new generation: "The enemies are an open category, and the content of the category is filled by the predicament and plight not only of the psalmist but also by that of the contemporary singer of the psalm."[18]

I have sometimes felt a bit awkward when I have walked into a hospital room to minister to a suffering parishioner and recited the opening verses of Psalm 27, and I have even wondered if that person might feel as awkward as I did in view of the non-belligerent circumstances. But then I have reasoned that the disease which had attacked that person's body was, *mutatis mutandi*, an awesome foe:

> When evil men advance against me
> to devour my flesh,
> when my enemies and my foes attack me,
> they will stumble and fall. (v. 2)

When the suffering individual makes that mental translation, then the ending of the Psalm has all the more meaning:

> I am still confident of this:
> I will see the goodness of the LORD
> in the land of the living.
> Wait for the LORD;
> be strong and take heart
> and wait for the LORD. (vv. 13–14)

Summary

The psalms of lament, the largest category in the Psalter, are an expression of one of the extremes of human life. Yet, standing opposite of praise, it is not entirely alien to it but is drawn in its direction. It should not surprise us that the laments contain so much praise, or that they are so often accompanied by a vow to praise the Lord for his mercy and deliverance. The basic components of the laments have been recognized and labeled by the form critics, but their presence in these psalms is not always predictable, nor is the order in which they occur.

The crisis from which the psalmist prays for deliverance is sometimes sickness, but rarely is it disassociated from spiritual or psychological anguish caused by the psalmist's own doubts and uncertainty, or the criticism of his friends and foes, and the gloating of his enemies. These enemies, while they are national in the community laments, are often personal in the individual laments. Metaphorical language often picks up the imagery of war, hunting, and animals enraged by hunger and fear to express the terrible pain and suffering the psalmist undergoes.

The very fact that lament figures so prominently in a collection of religious literature like the Psalms means that the Hebrew faith drew the circle wide enough to accommodate human complaint. In this respect, our New Testament faith is more sterile than the Old Testament faith. But since the Old Testament is *our* testament too, the Christian believer can operate within that frame

---

Study Questions

1. Westermann divides the psalms of lament into individual and corporate categories. Compare his component parts of the lament of the people to those of the lament of the individual. What examples of psalms can you give for each category?

2. How do the psalms of lament promote "freedom of speech" with God? Do you consider this comforting or dangerous?

3. In the individual psalms of lament labeled "Songs of the Sick and Anguished" (table 7.3), demonstrate how confession necessarily is complemented by divine forgiveness. How does this stand in stark contrast to modern therapies?

4. Suggestions have ranged widely as to the identity of the enemies or evildoers in the Psalms. What are the six options mentioned in this textbook, and which one(s) do you find most appealing? Why?

5. How do the psalms of lament show us that "lamentation is never very far away from praise"?

of mind without fear of condemnation. Obviously, however, that is not where he or she ought to stay for very long, and as the psalms of lament attest, lamentation is never very far away from praise.

Key Terms

psalms of lament
laments of the people
laments of the individual
songs of prayer

8 "I Love the LORD, for He Heard My Voice; He Heard My Cry for Mercy"

Psalms of Thanksgiving

Outline

- **Description of Form and Content**
  Introduction
  Report of Crisis
  Deliverance as an Accomplished Fact
  Conclusion
- **The Life Situation (*Sitz im Leben*) of the Psalms of Thanksgiving**
- **Content of the Individual Psalms of Thanksgiving**
- **Community Psalms of Thanksgiving**
- **Theological Implications of the Psalms of Thanksgiving**
- **Summary**

Objectives

After reading this chapter, you should be able to

1. Describe the form and content of the psalms of thanksgiving.
2. Show how these features are reflected in this group of psalms.
3. Discuss the theological implications of the psalms of thanksgiving.

psalms of thanksgiving

On the opposite ends of the emotional and theological spectrum of the Psalter stand the psalms of lament and the **psalms of thanksgiving.** We have already observed that even when the psalmists of the laments are overwhelmed with sorrow and anguish, they often still express their deep trust in Yahweh and his mercy. So while the distance between lament and thanksgiving might seem long, it is really much shorter than this set of opposites would imply. At least, the distance, however far it may be, is traversed, sometimes with lightning speed, as thoughts of Yahweh's gracious deeds and compassionate nature launch the psalmist on a trajectory of joy and grateful elation. This joy, as noted, grows out of the character of Yahweh himself, an observation we have already made in our discussion of the psalms of lament. As any normal human being knows, our spiritual experience ranges between these two poles, hovering at moments over one more than the other.

Ps 30:1 describes a person being drawn up out of a well or pit with a bucket, such as the one shown here.

Description of Form and Content

If the reader has not already discovered the frustration of trying to classify the psalms, this particular genre ought to bring that experience to reality. Kraus is certainly correct when he says the literary form of the psalms of thanksgiving is "not always clear and unambiguous."[1] However, there are some essentials that make this category distinct. The two components essential to the genre are: (1) the psalmist's report about his crisis, and (2) the statement or declaration that the crisis has passed and his deliverance is an accomplished fact. The latter element is that which distinguishes these psalms from the lament. Whereas the crisis of the lament is current in the poet's life, the psalm of thanksgiving reports a crisis that, while it is still very real in the psalmist's memory,

has in fact passed. The following elements may be found in psalms of thanksgiving.

Introduction

This may take the form of the intention to worship and the reason why. A good example is the opening statement in Psalm 30:1: "I will exalt you, O LORD, / for you lifted me out of the depths / and did not let my enemies gloat over me." David states his intention to praise the Lord, which rises out of his gratitude that the Lord has lifted him "out of the depths," an expression that may have its clarification in the following line, "and did not let my enemies gloat over me."

The introduction also takes other forms. For example, Psalm 92:1–4 is a statement regarding the appropriateness of worship:

> It is good to praise the LORD
>   and make music to your name,
>   O Most High,
> to proclaim your love in the
>   morning
>   and your faithfulness at night,
> to the music of the ten-stringed lyre
>   and the melody of the harp.
> For you make me glad by your
>   deeds, O LORD,
>   I sing for joy at the works of
>   your hands.

In the final statement the psalmist offers the reason why he believes worship to be appropriate—he was awed by Yahweh's actions in history. In other cases, the introduction takes the form of an injunctive call to thanks or praise, as is the case of Psalm 118:1: "Give thanks to the LORD, for he is good; / his love endures forever."

As verse 2 makes clear, the worshiper addresses the congregation, Israel, which responds to the singer's words by affirming Yahweh's lovingkindness: "Let Israel say: / 'His love endures forever.'"

Thus, the introduction is not a standard formula, although in some way it introduces the psalmist's intention to thank the Lord or to enter into the act of worship.

Report of Crisis

As stated above, this is one of the two essential elements of the psalm of thanksgiving. Psalm 52, for example, a psalm that some scholars list among the psalms of thanksgiving, may imply that the psalmist has been delivered from the deceitful and arrogant (vv. 1–7), but it does not take the form of a report. The psalmist is more likely stating an ethical principle. In any event, his words do not take the form of the report of a personal experience he has had. Even though this poem includes a form of the vow to praise ("I will praise you forever for what you have done," v. 9), I have excluded it from the psalms of thanksgiving simply because the report form is not clear.[2]

This report may be brief, as it is in some of these psalms (32:3–4; 40:2–3; 92:10–11; 120:1, 6), or a rather extended narrative as it is in others (18:4–5, 7–19; 30:2–3, 6–9, 11–12a; 31:9–13, 21–22; 66:5–12). In any event it records the nature of the crisis.

Deliverance as an Accomplished Fact

This element sets the report of the psalm of thanksgiving apart from that of the psalm of lament, as we have already pointed out. Yahweh's powerful deliverance from the psalmist's crisis is the turn of events that really sets

A sacrificial animal being slaughtered with a vessel below to collect the blood.

him in the direction of praise. This element, which does not have to be part of the report, is nevertheless an essential component of the psalm of thanksgiving, as is the report itself. Together they form the heart of the genre. It is out of gratitude for this deliverance that the intention to worship grows.

Conclusion

This element is as fluid as the introduction. It may take the form of the psalmist's vow to praise the Lord or make a sacrifice, as in Psalm 116:17–19:

> I will sacrifice a thank offering to
>   you
>   and call on the name of the
>   LORD.
> I will fulfill my vows to the LORD
>   in the presence of all his people,
> in the courts of the house of the
>   LORD—
>   in your midst, O Jerusalem.
> Praise the LORD.

It may also pick up on the worshiper's intent to praise the Lord and sound more like the introduction, as is the case of Psalm 118:28–29, which closes the psalm with the same injunction to praise as is found in the opening verse:

> You are my God, and I will give
>   you thanks;
>   you are my God, and I will exalt
>   you.
> Give thanks to the LORD, for he is
>   good;
>   his love endures forever.

In a similar way, Psalm 32:11 closes with a call to praise: "Rejoice in the LORD and be glad, you righteous; / sing, all you who are upright in heart!"

A statement of the psalmist's resolution to praise God closes Psalm 30, summing up what the Lord has done for him:

> You turned my wailing into
>   dancing;
>   you removed my sackcloth and
>   clothed me with joy,
> that my heart may sing to you and
>   not be silent.
> O LORD my God, I will give you
>   thanks forever. (vv. 11–12)

Other forms that the conclusion takes are a statement on Yahweh's faithfulness (18:50; 92:15) and an admission of the psalmist's need coupled with a petition (40:17).

Wisdom sayings or words of instruction also occur in some of these psalms. Mowinckel thinks this linkage to wisdom was only natural, given the tendency of the psalms of thanksgiving to tie confession to personal experience.[3] The word of instruction is central to Psalm 32:

> I will instruct you and teach you in
>   the way you should go;
> I will counsel you and watch
>   over you.
> Do not be like the horse or the
>   mule,
>   which have no
>   understanding
> but must be controlled by bit and
>   bridle
> or they will not come to you.
> Many are the woes of the wicked,
>   but the LORD's unfailing love
>   surrounds the man who trusts
>   in him. (vv. 8–10)

Other such words occur in Psalms 18:25–36; 32:8–10; and 92:6–7, 12–15.

Lists of the **individual psalms of thanksgiving** vary considerably. The lists of Gunkel, Mowinckel, Westermann, and Kraus have only three psalms in common: Psalms 30; 40:2–12; and 116. If one leaves out Mowinckel and compares only

Gunkel, Westermann, and Kraus, the list enlarges from three to six: Psalms 18; 30; 40:2–12; 66; 116; and 118. So the variation is evident. In view of the two criteria I have called "essential," the list of the individual psalms of thanksgiving becomes Psalms 18, 30, 31, 32, 40, 66, 92, 116, 118, and 120.[4] Examples outside the Psalter are Isaiah 38:10–20 and Jonah 2:3–9.

The Life Situation (Sitz im Leben) of the Psalms of Thanksgiving

Those who study the Psalms generally acknowledge that we do not know much about the ritual that accompanied the psalm of thanksgiving. Two things seem clear, however: a personal or national crisis occasioned the psalm; and the worshiper performed the ritual, whatever form and order it took, in the temple, most likely in the presence of the congregation, or at least the presence of friends and family. That the place of performance was the temple is explicit from Psalms 66:13 and 116:19, while Psalm 92:13 may imply that the ceremony took place there.

The Book of Leviticus speaks of making the peace offering (sometimes called the well-being offering) as an expression of thanksgiving (*todah*), but it does not seem to be the **thank offering** spoken of in these psalms. The thank offering of the Psalms appears to be one pledged by the worshiper during or after some zero hour of his life. On the basis of Psalm 107 the rabbis spoke of four occasions when the thank offering was appropriate: safe return from a voyage (vv. 23–32), safe return from a desert journey (vv. 4–9), recovery from illness (vv. 17–22), and release from prison (vv. 10–16).[5] In fact, Psalm 107, which Westermann explains as a combination of four indi-

Table 8.1

Individual Psalms of Thanksgiving

	Ps 18	Ps 30	Ps 31	Ps 32	Ps 40	Ps 66	Ps 92	Ps 116	Ps 118	Ps 120
Introduction	vv. 1–3, 6 "I call to the LORD, who is worthy of praise, and I am saved from my enemies."	v. 1 "I will exalt you, O LORD, for you lifted me out of the depths."			v. 1 "I waited patiently for the LORD; he turned to me and heard my cry."	v. 17 "I cried out to him with my mouth; his praise was on my tongue."		vv. 1–2 "I love the LORD, for he heard my voice"; "I will call on him as long as I live."	vv. 1–4 "Give thanks to the LORD, for he is good."	v. 1 "I called on the LORD in my distress, and he answered me." (author's translation)
Report	vv. 4–5, 7–19 "The cords of death entangled me; the torrents of destruction overwhelmed me."	vv. 2–3, 6–9, 11–12a "You healed me. O LORD, you brought me up from the grave."	vv. 9–13, 21–22 "I am the utter contempt of my neighbors; I am a dread to my friends."	vv. 3–4 "When I kept silent, my bones wasted away through my groaning all day long."	vv. 2–3 "He lifted me out of the slimy pit, out of the mud and mire; he set my feet on a rock and gave me a firm place to stand."	vv. 5–12, 16–19 "Come and see what God has done" (national); "I cried out to him with my mouth" (personal).	vv. 9–11 "You have exalted my horn like that of a wild ox"; "My eyes have seen the defeat of my adversaries."	vv. 8–9 "For you, O LORD, have delivered my soul from death."	vv. 5, 10–13 "In my anguish I cried to the LORD"; "All the nations surrounded me."	vv. 1, 6 "Too long have I lived among those who hate peace."
Company of Those Hearing Report		v. 4 "saints"	v. 23 "saints" v. 24 "all you who hope in the LORD."	v. 11 "righteous"		v. 16 "all you who fear God"		vv. 14, 18–19 "in the presence of all his people" in the temple.		
Problem	vv. 3, 17, 47–48 hostility of enemies	vv. 2–3, 9 illness	vv. 8–11 contempt of friends related to psalmist's illness	vv. 3–5 psalmist's sin and refusal to confess it	vv. 12, 14 psalmist's sin and those who pursue him	vv. 10–12, 14 personal distress ("When I was in trouble") and national distress ("You brought us into prison and laid burdens on our backs.")	vv. 10–11 opposition of enemies	vv. 3, 8 illness and spiritual anguish	vv. 7, 10–13, 18 psalmist's enemies and prospect of death	vv. 2–3, 7 deceitful people who encourage war
Deliverance an Accomplished Fact	vv. 6, 16–19, 43 "From his temple he heard my voice"; "He reached down from on high and took hold of me."	vv. 2–3 "O LORD my God, I called to you for help and you healed me. O LORD you brought me up from the grave; you spared me from going down in the pit"; "You turned my wailing into dancing."	vv. 7–8, 21–22 "You saw my affliction"; "You have not handed me over to the enemy"; "Yet you heard my cry for mercy when I called to you for help."	v. 5 "You forgave the guilt of my sin."	vv. 2–3 "He lifted me out of the slimy pit, out of the mud and mire; he set my feet on a rock."	vv. 9, 19 "He has preserved our lives and kept our feet from slipping"; "God has surely listened and heard my voice in prayer."	v. 11 "My eyes have seen the defeat of my adversaries."	vv. 1–2, 6, 8, 16 "He heard my voice; he heard my cry for mercy. . . . He turned his ear to me."	v. 5, 13, 18, 21, 23 "He answered by setting me free."	v. 1 "He answered me." (author's translation)
Reason for Deliverance	vv. 20–24 psalmist's righteousness and obedience to the law	v. 10 the Lord's mercy	vv. 7, 19 the Lord's goodness; "You saw my affliction and knew the anguish of my soul."	vv. 5, 10 confession, the Lord's forgiveness and unfailing love	v. 11 the Lord's love and truth	v. 20 God's love	v. 2 the Lord's love and faithfulness	vv. 5, 7, 12 the Lord's grace and compassion	v. 1, 29 the Lord's goodness	

	Ps 18	Ps 30	Ps 31	Ps 32	Ps 40	Ps 66	Ps 92	Ps 116	Ps 118	Ps 120
Petition		v. 10	vv. 1–5, 14–18		vv. 11, 13–16, 17c			v. 4	v. 25	v. 2
Wisdom/Teaching	vv. 25–36			vv. 8–10			vv. 6–7, 12–15			
Conclusion			vv. 21–24	vv. 8–11		v. 20			vv. 25–29	
Praise	vv. 46–48		vv. 21–22			v. 20	vv. 1–5, 8, 15		vv. 1–4, 26–28	
Vow to Praise	v. 49 "Therefore I will praise you among the nations, O LORD."	v. 12 "O LORD my God, I will give you thanks forever."				vv. 13–15 "I will come to your temple."	vv. 1–3 "It is good to praise the LORD" (an adaptation of the vow to praise).	vv. 13–14 "I will lift up the cup of salvation and call on the name of the LORD."	vv. 17, 19, 21, 28 "I will give you thanks, for you answered me."	
Invitation to Praise		vv. 4–5 "Sing to the LORD, you saints of his."	v. 23 "Love the LORD, all his saints!"	v. 11 "Rejoice in the LORD and be glad, you righteous; sing, all you who are upright in heart!"		vv. 1–9 "Shout with joy to God, all the earth!"			v. 29 "Give thanks to the LORD, for he is good."	
Vow to Sacrifice						vv. 13–15		vv. 17–19		

Emaciated by famine, these Egyptians illustrate the tragedy described in Ps 107:4–5: "Some wandered in desert wastelands / finding no way to a city where they could settle. / They were hungry and thirsty, / and their lives ebbed away."

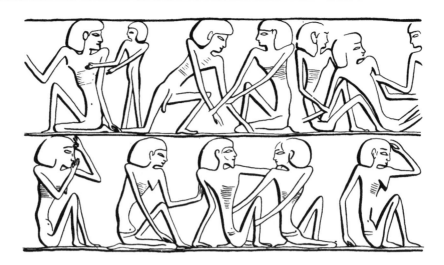

vidual psalms of thanksgiving,[6] lays out the pattern by which the psalm of thanksgiving came into being: the individual experienced a crisis and was then summoned to give thanks for deliverance:

> Some wandered in desert
>   wastelands,
>   finding no way to a city where
>   they could settle.
> They were hungry and thirsty,
>   and their lives ebbed away.
> Then they cried out to the LORD in
>   their trouble,
>   and he delivered them from
>   their distress.
> He led them by a straight way
>   to a city where they could settle.
> Let them give thanks to the LORD
>   for his unfailing love
>   and his wonderful deeds for
>   men,
> for he satisfies the thirsty
>   and fills the hungry with good
>   things. (vv. 4–9)[7]

A bit of the ritual itself may be preserved in Jeremiah 33, which describes the joy of the restoration of Jerusalem as characterized by throngs of people coming to the city to bring their thank offerings:

> Yet in the towns of Judah and the streets of Jerusalem that are deserted, inhabited by neither men nor animals, there will be heard once more the sounds of joy and gladness, the voices of bride and bridegroom, and the voices of

those who bring thank offerings to the house of the LORD, saying, "Give thanks to the LORD Almighty, / for the LORD is good; / his love endures forever" (vv. 10–11).

The liturgy reflected here is a close duplicate of Psalms 118:1 and 29. Some are of the opinion that the psalm of thanksgiving, sung by the worshiper or a temple singer, preceded the animal sacrifice. As a rule the thank offering that accompanied the psalm was the result of a vow that the worshiper had made when he was in trouble (66:13–15). Yet Psalm 40 may suggest that the worshiper confessed, at least on that occasion, that it was not sacrifice that the Lord wanted, but obedience. After briefly reviewing his crisis (vv. 2–3) and then confessing that the Lord had done so many things for him that he could not relate them all, he sought to put his confession of gratitude and spiritual posture in light of the sacrifice:

> Many, O LORD my God,
>   are the wonders you have done.
> The things you planned for us
>   no one can recount to you;
> were I to speak and tell of them,
>   they would be too many to
>   declare.
> Sacrifice and offering you did not
>   desire,
>   but my ears you have pierced;
> burnt offerings and sin offerings
>   you did not require.

Then I said, "Here I am, I have
     come—
it is written about me in the
     scroll.
I desire to do your will, O my God;
     your law is within my heart.
          (vv. 5–8)

Another bit of information we can glean from the text is that the worshiper performed this ritual and sang his song of gratitude in the presence of other worshipers, perhaps his family and close friends. This congregation of people are referred to as "saints" (Pss 30:4; 31:23), the "righteous" (32:11), those "who fear God" (66:16), and the Lord's "people" (116:14, 18). They shared the joy of the occasion, as they would also have shared portions of the meal that followed.

But did every individual who escaped a life-threatening crisis compose a psalm as an expression and instrument of his gratitude? It is hardly possible that the capabilities of the common worshiper would have come up to that level of literary accomplishment. What we have in the Psalter is most likely samples of songs that accomplished composers had provided for use in the temple for the purpose of the thanksgiving ritual, even though some of these writers could have been common worshipers. Of the ten psalms I have listed among the individual psalms of thanksgiving, five of them are attributed to David (18, 30, 31, 32, 40), as we might expect since they are included in the Davidic collection of Book 1, and the authors of the last five are anonymous (66, 92, 116, 118, 120).

Content of the Individual Psalms of Thanksgiving

The language of this group of psalms generally includes a form of the verb "to thank" (Hebrew *yadah*), or the noun "thanks" or "thanksgiv-ing" (*todah*). This verb and noun occur in other psalms that do not fall within the classification of the psalms of thanksgiving, since giving thanks was a broader category of religious experience than the specific ritual represented here. The sentiment can be expressed another way—the language of thanksgiving is not limited to the use of this verb and noun, since it can be expressed with other vocabulary terms of praise. In fact, it can simply take the form of a recital of Yahweh's deeds. So we do not in fact have these particular vocabulary terms in all of the psalms of thanksgiving. Of the ten psalms in our list, Psalms 31, 66, and 120 do not use any form of the root *ydh*, but they qualify under the other essential conditions listed above.

Gunkel described the psalm of lament and the psalm of thanksgiving as complementing one another like the "two shells of a mussel."[8] We have already observed that in the psalms of lament the crisis is in progress, whereas in the psalms of thanksgiving the crisis is past. The psalm itself is the grateful product of escape from the crisis. As we have also noted above, sometimes the psalmist details the crisis in his report, but in other instances he merely summarizes the event. In any case, Leopold Sabourin is right in his observation that the psalm of thanksgiving is the "final act in a human drama."[9] It is the destination of the human heart as it moves from complaint to trust to thanksgiving.[10] We only see the tip of the iceberg in most instances. In some cases we hear a bit more detail about the psalmist's urgent circumstances, but even then we only have the outline. In still other instances he only speaks about his crisis in metaphors:

He lifted me out of the slimy pit,
     out of the mud and mire;
he set my feet on a rock
     and gave me a firm place to
          stand. (40:2)

Yet, like many instances celebrated by the psalms of lament, the description is quite literal and awesome, both in its physical and social details, with a few graphic metaphors thrown in to amplify the account:

> Be merciful to me, O LORD, for I am
> in distress;
> my eyes grow weak with
> sorrow,
> my soul and my body with
> grief.
> My life is consumed by anguish
> and my years by groaning;
> my strength fails because of my
> affliction,
> and my bones grow weak.
> Because of all my enemies,
> I am the utter contempt of my
> neighbors;
> I am a dread to my friends—
> those who see me on the street
> flee from me.
> I am forgotten by them as though I
> were dead;
> I have become like broken
> pottery.
> For I hear the slander of many;
> there is terror on every side;
> they conspire against me
> and plot to take my life. (31:9–
> 13)

Among the dreadful experiences of the psalmist were illness and the prospect of death, spiritual and emotional anguish, hostility and contempt by friends as well as enemies, banishment from his home, and the threat of war, to name only some.

In one instance the psalmist reflected upon God's great acts on the nation's behalf (Ps 66:5–12). He saw them as a parallel on a personal level with the national events of deliverance, and he drew inspiration from that analogy (vv. 8–12). But not only was his deliverance a microcosm of the great deliverance Yahweh had wrought for Israel, it also reflected the character of Israel's God, a God of mercy and goodness (30:10; 31:19; 32:5, 10; 40:11; 66:20; 92:2; 116:5, 7, 12; 118:1, 29). Yet the psalmist was not reluctant at times to remind the Lord that he was innocent and had kept his law (18:20–24).

Community Psalms of Thanksgiving

The essential criteria defining the **community psalms of thanksgiving** are the two mentioned above—(1) the report of the crisis, and (2) the acknowledgment that the crisis has passed—plus the community aspect, which may take the form of plural pronouns (e.g., Ps 65:3, "When we were overwhelmed by sins, you forgave our transgressions"); an address to Israel (e.g., 124:1, "If the LORD had not been on our side—let Israel say"; also 129:1); or clear indicators that the first person singular pronouns ("I," "my," "me") refer to Israel (e.g., 118). Two of the six psalms that I have identified as community thanksgiving songs, Psalms 66 and 118, incorporate individual psalms of thanksgiving into a corporate setting. Psalm 66:1–12 is a community song, while 66:13–20 is a song of the individual. As I have indicated above, the individual worshiper may find the inspiration for his own faith in the experience of the nation as it is reported in verses 5–12.

Psalm 118 is an especially interesting psalm. It contains the report of an individual, or perhaps even the community, and uses the singular pronoun "I." My inclination is to view the "I" report as that of a royal person. He is rehearsing Israel's experience of warfare and refers to the army as "the tents of the righteous" (v. 15). It is quite obvious from verses 1–4 and the conclusion of verse 29 that the community is joining the worshiper in this song of thanksgiving. In fact, in the individual psalms of thanksgiving we hear the psalmist's call for his fellow Israelites to join him in this service of thanksgiving, and here we may have an illustration of that in verses 22–27, where the congregation joins in worship. The Psalm even includes one of those rare eyewitness pictures of the procession as it makes its way, boughs in hand, to the altar (v. 27b).

159

As with the individual psalms of thanksgiving, there is much disagreement on which psalms qualify as community psalms of thanksgiving. Westermann found only two in the entire Psalter, Psalms 124 and 129, and called them declarative psalms of praise of the people. He further wonders why there are so few and offers the explanation that since they tend to glorify past events of history, this type of poem did not find its way into the postexilic collection due to the more recent concerns of the postexilic community.[11] According to the criteria set forth above, there are a few more psalms in the category than Westermann avows, but still the number is not large. In table 8.2 below we have designated six psalms as community psalms of thanksgiving: Psalms 65, 66, 107, 118, 124, 129. It seems to me, however, that the small number may stem from the fact that the thanksgiving vow and offering were more an individual than a community procedure.

Theological Implications of the Psalms of Thanksgiving

Mays has pointed out that the cycle of trouble-prayer-help is not complete without "specific and public acts of gratitude."[12] Gratitude is a spiritual virtue that opens the door of the soul to the world around us. It creates a centrifugal force that causes the individual to look away from the self to God and to fellow human beings. It is not self-generating but stems from something outside oneself. The psalmists found Yahweh's works on Israel's behalf to be a source of inspiration and reason to believe that he would accomplish personal deliverance in their own lives. That is the function of Psalm 66:5–12, which summarizes the Lord's mighty works in Israel's history from the Red Sea

("He turned the sea into dry land," v. 6) to the entrance of Canaan, or perhaps even to the return from exile ("you brought us to a place of abundance," v. 12). Based on those powerful works, which were the macrocosm of the worshiper's own personal deliverance, the singer of this song recounted what the Lord had done for him personally: "Come and listen, all you who fear God; / let me tell you what he has done for me" (Ps 66:16).

If the Old Testament ever loses sight of the individual, it is certainly not in the Psalms. There is, in fact, an easy movement from the nation to the individual. Here we see that directional movement, but in other psalms we can detect the opposite direction from the person to the nation (see 25:22; 51:18–19; 130:7–8).

Something should be said also about the importance of grace in the individual's life to the community.[13] As Mays has noted, the cycle represented by the psalms of thanksgiving is only completed when the worshiper comes to the temple and makes his public witness. The importance of "public" is noteworthy. Just as the congregation received inspiration from the Lord's works in history, they also identified with the personal experience of fellow Israelites. The value of substitution may be operative in this temple ritual—the fellow worshipers saw themselves in that or similar situations and entered empathetically into the singer's joy of deliverance. Or the call for the saints to join him in praise and celebration may be motivated by the psalmist's desire to spread the joy and evoke a response of faith from his comrades.

While the vertical dimension of the Old Testament faith—God and humanity—cannot be overestimated, the horizontal dimension is of the utmost importance also. The command to "love your neighbor as yourself" (Lv 19:18) is a central feature of Old Testament theology. Grace that is truly grace radiates outwardly in its environment. No community of faith can see itself as a community unless grace is shared. And as we have ob-

Table 8.2

Community Psalms of Thanksgiving

	Ps 65	Ps 66	Ps 107	Ps 118	Ps 124	Ps 129
Introduction	vv. 1–2 "Shout with joy to God, all the earth!"	vv. 1–2 "Praise awaits you, O God, in Zion; to you our vows will be fulfilled. O you who hears prayers, to you all men will come."	vv. 1–3 "Give thanks to the LORD, for he is good; his love endures forever."	vv. 1–4 "Give thanks to the LORD, for he is good."	vv. 1–2 "If the LORD had not been on our side—let Israel say."	
Report	v. 3 "When we were overwhelmed by sins, you forgave our transgressions."	vv. 5–12 "Come and see what God has done"; "You refined us like silver."	vv. 4–7, 10–14, 17–20, 23–30 "Some wandered in desert wastelands, finding no way to a city where they could settle."	vv. 5, 10–13, "In my anguish I cried to the LORD"; "All the nations surrounded me" (the king is evidently speaking, and the people identify with the danger he describes.)	vv. 2b–3a "When men attacked us, when their anger flared against us."	vv. 2–3 "They have greatly oppressed me from my youth."
Company of Those Hearing Report	v. 4 "Those you choose and bring near to live in your courts."	v. 16 "All you who fear God."				
Problem	v. 3 sins of the community	vv. 10–12 national distress; "You brought us into prison and laid burdens on our backs."	vv. 4–5, 10–12, 17–20, 23–27 lost in the desert, imprisoned, sickness, threatened at sea	vv. 7, 10–13, 18 the psalmist's enemies and the prospect of death	vv. 2b–3 Israel threatened by enemies	vv. 1–3 foreign oppression
Appeal to History/God's Mighty Works	vv. 5–8 "Who formed the mountains by your power, having armed yourself with strength, who stilled the roaring of the seas."	vv. 5–12 "He turned the sea into dry land, they passed through the waters on foot."	vv. 33–41 "He turned the desert into pools of water and the parched ground into flowing springs."		v. 8 "Maker of heaven and earth."	
Deliverance an Accomplished Fact	v.3 "When we were overwhelmed by sins, you forgave our transgressions."	v. 9 "He has preserved our lives and kept our feet from slipping."	vv. 2–3, 6b–7, 13b–14, 19b–20, 28b–30 "He delivered them from their distress."	vv. 5, 13, 18, 21, 23 "He answered by setting me free."	vv. 6–7 "Praise be to the LORD, who has not let us be torn by their teeth. We have escaped like a bird out of the fowler's snare."	vv. 2b, 4b "But they have not gained the victory over me."
Reason for Deliverance	vv. 9–13 God cares for the earth out of love for his people	v. 20 God's love	vv. 1, 43 the Lord's goodness and mercy	vv. 1, 29 the Lord's goodness	vv. 1–2, 8 the Lord's favor of Israel ("If the LORD had not been on our side"); and the "Maker of heaven and earth" was strong enough to deliver.	v. 4a the Lord's justice
Petition				v. 25		
Wisdom/ Teaching	vv. 9–13 God's care of the earth					vv. 6–7
Conclusion		v. 20 "Praise be to God, who has not rejected my prayer or withheld his love from me!"	v. 43 "Whoever is wise, let him heed these things and consider the great love of the LORD."	vv. 25–29	v. 8 "Our help is in the name of the LORD, the Maker of heaven and earth."	v. 8 "May those who pass by not say, 'The blessing of the LORD be upon you; we bless you in the name of the LORD.'"
Praise	v. 13c	vv. 3–4, 20		vv. 1–4, 26–28		
Vow to Praise	v. 1b "To you our vows will be fulfilled."			vv. 17, 19, 21, 28 "I will give you thanks, for you answered me."		
Invitation to Praise			vv. 1–3, 8, 15, 21, 31–32, 43	v. 29 "Give thanks to the LORD, for he is good."		
Vow to Sacrifice			v. 22			

served, it moves in both directions, from the community to the individual, and from the individual to the community. In Old Testament theology there is no such thing as individuality in isolation from community, nor is there community apart from the individual. The one contributes to the nature of the other and shapes its life. Have you ever seen a grateful community made up of ungrateful persons? Impossible! Admittedly, there may be grateful persons within a basically ungrateful community, but as gratitude pervades the ranks, it will change the nature of the community. Gratitude is infectious. There was no way that Israel could remain ungrateful when a stream of individuals flowed into the temple giving testimony to the Lord's marvelous grace. The scene of joy in Jeremiah 33:11, describing the returnees to Zion bringing their thank offerings to the temple, would be truly trans-forming to a community that had languished in despair. Indeed, Yahweh's deliverance had been directed to the nation, but individuals saw themselves as defined by the nation and shaped by the liberating grace. It was not so much the nation that returned to Zion but individuals, fathers and mothers, brothers and sisters, grandparents and grandchildren. Their restoration, a grace that knew no rival, was one that called for individual thank offerings to express their gratitude. The line between their joy as individuals and their joy as a restored community was invisible.

The psalms of thanksgiving tap one of the great spiritual resources of Holy Scripture and offer us a spiritual home where the passions of life can find their moorings in a source outside the human self. One of the great tragedies of the human spirit is to become a prisoner of ingratitude, for ingratitude shuts the human spirit up in a world lightened only by the self, which is no light at all. It creates a dark dungeon of selfishness because there is no horizon to give perspective to an individualistic world. Ingratitude is a closed system that prohibits the individual from opening up to God and neighbor. Gratitude, on the other hand, throws the door to this prison wide open and liberates the soul to thank God for what he has done and to share this spirit of grateful elation with fellow human beings. The individual psalms of thanksgiving easily outnumber the community psalms of thanksgiving. Maybe that is only coincidental, but given the simple fact that gratitude is basically an individual virtue before it is a community one, the presence of the individual psalms of thanksgiving may be a witness to this truth.

Study Questions

1. What are the two components essential to the psalms of thanksgiving? Give an example of a psalm of thanksgiving, including the introduction and conclusion.

2. The psalms of lament deal with a crisis in progress, while in the psalms of thanksgiving, the crisis is past. They thus complement one another like "two shells of a mussel." One must go through the context of lament to reach the thanksgiving. What theological application can be made from this principle?

3. What verb or noun often accompanies the psalms of thanksgiving? What criterion defines the community psalms of thanksgiving?

4. As suggested, the psalms of thanksgiving offer us a "spiritual home where the passions of life can find their moorings in a source outside the human self." How did the completed cycle of thanksgiving psalms necessarily lift one outside of oneself?

Summary

The individual psalms of thanksgiving have two basic criteria. First, the psalmist reports on a crisis he has experienced, a report that may take the form of an extended recital of events or only a clause reporting the matter. Second, the psalmist in some way will also testify that the crisis has passed. It is always the passing of the crisis for which he praises Yahweh. In view of these criteria, we have designated Psalms 18, 30, 31, 32, 40, 66, 92, 116, 118, and 120 as individual psalms of thanksgiving.

The psalms of community thanksgiving add a third criterion, the use of plural pronouns or some other clear indicator that the congregation of Israel, rather than the individual, has undergone the crisis. In my view, Psalms 65, 66, 107, 118, 124, and 129 exhibit these three traits. These psalms are the literary version of a drama that has taken place in the psalmist's life, and the deliverance has occurred as a consequence of the Lord's mercy and goodness. In comparison to the laments, which represent the crisis as current, the psalms of thanksgiving are the worshiper's gift of praise to God for the deliverance he has received.

Key Terms

psalms of thanksgiving
individual psalms
    of thanksgiving
thank offering
community psalms
    of thanksgiving

9 "The LORD Is My Shepherd, I Shall Not Want"

Psalms of Trust

Objectives

After reading this chapter, you should be able to
1. Define and describe the psalms of trust.
2. Explain why individual psalms are classified as psalms of trust.
3. Explicate more fully certain psalms of trust.

Many of the psalms express a deep confidence in God and his goodness. Such expressions are numerous in the Psalter, and can be found in various types of psalms. However, the sentiment of trust dominates a few psalms and singles them out as special expressions of confidence in God. Experience is the master teacher of trust. In fact, the spirit of trusting seems more often than not to be directly proportional to the intensity of distress or the depth of trouble. One person's level of trust may not have achieved the level or matured to the quality of another's. Often in human experience, and most often in the psalms of trust, or the psalms of confidence, the difference is the depth and intensity of trouble.

Definition and Description of the Psalms of Trust

Somewhere in the shadows of the psalms of trust trouble is lurking. We cannot always determine what crisis prompted the psalmist to declare his trust in the Lord, but generally speaking, some trouble had lain in ambush along the psalmist's path. Unlike the psalms of thanksgiving, which state the crisis and also add a word of assurance that the crisis has passed, this group of psalms makes their declaration of trust in the Lord, but do not always clarify the occasion that provoked the statement of confidence. They are more likely to provide only hints. Psalm 27, for example, seethes with allusions to combative circumstances, which had likely cultivated the psalmist's deep confidence in Yahweh:

> Though an army besiege me,
>   my heart will not fear;
> though war break out against me,
>   even then will I be confident.
>   (v. 3; also v. 6)

Similarly, Psalm 23 depicts the psalmist as surrounded by enemies ("You prepare a table before me / in the presence of my enemies," v. 5). Perhaps that was the "valley of the shadow of death" from which he had emerged, very much alive and victorious. While these crisis descriptions are not explicit, they are still helpful hints of the circumstances that taught the psalmist to trust in God.

In a few instances, however, the occasion is clear. That is the case of Psalm 62, where the psalmist exposed those people who actively sought his downfall:

> How long will you assault a man?
>   Would all of you throw him
>   down—
>   this leaning wall, this tottering
>   fence?
> They fully intend to topple him
>   from his lofty place;
>   they take delight in lies.
> With their mouths they bless,
>   but in their hearts they curse.
>   (vv. 3–4)

We find the same unambiguous language in Psalm 73, which describes how troubled the psalmist had become over the prosperity of the wicked:

> But as for me, my feet had almost
>   slipped;
>   I had nearly lost my foothold.
> For I envied the arrogant
>   when I saw the prosperity of the
>   wicked. (vv. 2–3)

Unquestionably that was the problem that drove him into the sanctuary of trust, where he found spiritual solace (73:17).

With the kind of problems the psalms of trust introduce, we might expect to encounter a strong lament, but that is seldom the case. Rather, the lament seems to have faded into the background of the psalmist's life. He has moved beyond lament to confidence, even though, in contrast to the psalms of thanksgiving, the crisis may not yet have passed. But the psalmist can face it now because experience has taught him that Yahweh

Table 9.1
Individual Psalms of Trust

	Ps 4	Ps 16	Ps 23	Ps 27	Ps 62	Ps 73
Declaration of Trust	vv. 3, 8 "The LORD will hear when I call to him"; "I will lie down and sleep in peace, for you alone, O LORD, make me dwell in safety."	vv. 1b, 2, 7b–9, 9–10 "In you I take refuge"; "You are my Lord; apart from you I have no good thing"; "Even at night my heart instructs me. I have set the LORD always before me. Because he is at my right hand, I will not be shaken"; "Therefore my heart is glad and my tongue rejoices; my body also will rest secure, because you will not abandon me to the grave."	vv. 1–3 "The LORD is my shepherd, I shall not be in want. He makes me lie down in green pastures."	vv. 1a, 2a, 3, 5b–6a, 8, 9b, 10, 13 "The LORD is my light and my salvation"; "The LORD is the stronghold of my life"; "even then will I be confident"; "He will keep me safe in his dwelling"; "My heart says of you, 'Seek his face!' Your face, LORD, I will seek"; "You have been my helper"; "though my father and mother forsake me"; "I am confident of this: I will see the goodness of the LORD in the land of the living."	vv. 1–2, 5–7, 11–12 "My soul finds rest in God alone"; "One thing God has spoken, . . . that you, O God, are strong"; "Find rest, O my soul, in God alone."	vv. 1, 17, 18–20, 23–28 "Surely God is good to Israel"; "till I entered the sanctuary of God"; "Surely you place them on slippery ground"; "Yet I am always with you; . . . I have made the Sovereign LORD my refuge; I will tell of all your deeds."
Invitation to Trust	vv. 4–5 "In your anger do not sin; when you are on your beds, search your hearts and be silent. Offer right sacrifices and trust in the LORD."			v. 14 "Wait for the LORD; be strong and take heart and wait for the LORD."	vv. 8, 10 "Trust in him at all time, O people"; "Do not trust in extortion."	
Basis for Trust	v. 7 "You have filled my heart with greater joy than when their grain and new wine abound."	vv. 5–6, 11 "LORD, you have assigned me my portion and my cup; . . . The boundary lines have fallen for me in pleasant places"; "You have made known to me the path of life."	v. 1 "The LORD is my shepherd."		vv. 11–12a "One thing God has spoken, . . . that you, O God, are strong, and that you, O Lord, are loving."	
Petition	vv. 1, 6b "Answer me when I call to you. . . . Give me relief from my distress; be merciful to me and hear my prayer"; "Let the light of your face shine upon us, O LORD."	v. 1a "Keep me safe, O God."		vv. 4, 7, 9, 11 "One thing I ask of the LORD, this is what I seek: that I may dwell in the house of the LORD all the days of my life"; "Hear my voice when I call, O LORD; be merciful to me and answer me"; "Do not hide your face from me, do not turn your servant away in anger; . . . Do not reject me or forsake me, O God my Savior"; "Teach me your way, O LORD; lead me in a straight path because of my oppressors."		
Vow to Praise		v. 7 "I will praise the LORD, who counsels me."		v. 6b "At his tabernacle will I sacrifice with shouts of joy; I will sing and make music to the LORD."		
Interior Lament (implied or expressed)	vv. 1, 2 "My distress"; "How long, O men, will you turn my glory into shame? How long will you love delusions and seek false gods?"	v. 4 "The sorrows of those will increase who run after other gods."	vv. 4–5 "Even though I walk through the valley of the shadow of death, I will fear no evil, for you are with me; your rod and your staff, they comfort me. You prepare a table before me in the presence of my enemies. You anoint my head with oil; my cup overflows."	vv. 1b, 2–3, 5, 11b, 12 "Whom shall I fear?"; "Of whom shall I be afraid?"; "when evil men advance against me"; "though an army besiege me"; "though war break out against me"; "in the day of trouble"; "because of my oppressors"; "the desire of my foes"; "False witnesses rise up against me."	vv. 3–4 "How long will you assault a man?"	vv. 3–15, 21–22 "But as for me, my feet had almost slipped"; "when my heart was grieved."

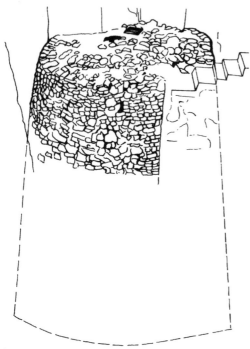

The Psalms use the terms "tower," "fortress," and "refuge" to suggest height and security. While this picture represents a human-built tower, when the term "refuge" occurs in the Psalms, it generally is a natural fortress.

community psalms of trust

interior lament

individual psalms of trust

is good and answers when his children call. These psalms are expressions of faith, not cries of victory. They sketch out the path that leads to victory, to be sure, but they do not necessarily lead all the way. The psalms of trust bare the hearts of these ancient worshipers and reveal the spiritual buoys that kept them afloat amidst their world of pain and turmoil. Along the landscape of their lives one may see the banners of faith flying above the adversities, and lining the road the writer to the Hebrews described in his backward glance at history (Heb 11). The psalms of trust plot this map of faith.

The psalms of trust fall into the categories of individual and community. Those that articulate the individual psalmist's faith are Psalms 4, 16, 23, 27, 62, and 73, while the **community psalms of trust** include Psalms 90, 115, 123, 124, 125, and 126. As we have already observed, sentiments of trust occur in numerous psalms, but the expansive tone of trust characterizes this group of poems. The psalms of trust are written for the express purpose of declaring the psalmist's trust in God. Some-

times the Hebrew root verb *trust* (*btkh*) or *to have faith* (*'mn*) occurs to express the idea, but not always. In addition to the language of faith, the psalmists use many metaphors and expressions to represent their sense of trusting, like lying down to rest (23:2) and to sleep (4:8), and enjoying safety in the presence of one's enemies (23:5). Metaphors depicting the Lord as light (27:1), as rock (62:2, 6), and fortress or refuge (16:1; 27:1; 62:8), and the metaphor of walking in a straight path (27:11), are taken from the landscape of the psalmist's world. The physical landscape provided him with common but powerful images to describe his spiritual life.

The essential elements in these psalms are the *declaration of trust,* which may open the psalm or close it, or may punctuate the poem at various points, and the **interior lament,** which may be only a memory of the trouble that shaped and directed the psalmist's sense of trust in God. Neither element has a fixed place in the order of the psalm. They can occur at various points. Psalm 27, for example, has words of trust at all of these positions. It opens with "The LORD is my light and my salvation," and virtually closes with the affirmation of confidence in the future goodness of the Lord: "I am still confident of this: / I will see the goodness of the LORD / in the land of the living" (v. 13).

Confidence also meets the reader at the internal junctions of the poem (27:5, 8a, 9b, 10), thus making the element of trust pervasive in this psalm.

Obviously, the *declaration of trust* is the first and most important component of the individual and community psalms of trust. As stated above, this declaration casts its hue over the whole psalm.

A second element of the psalms of trust or confidence is the *invitation to trust* issued to the community. It is not always present, but it does occur in Psalms 4:4, 5; 27:14; and 62:8 (**individual psalms of trust**), and in Psalm 115:9–11 (community psalm of trust). Sabourin has observed that this feature gives even the individual psalms

Table 9.2
Community Psalms of Trust

	Ps 90	Ps 115	Ps 123	Ps 124	Ps 125	Ps 126
Declaration of Trust	vv. 1–2 "Lord, you have been our dwelling place throughout all generations."	vv. 1, 9b, 10b, 11b "Not to us, O LORD, not to us but to your name be the glory"; "He is their help and shield."	vv. 2–3 "As the eyes of slaves look to the hand of their master, . . . so our eyes look to the LORD our God."	v. 6 "Praise be to the LORD, who has not let us be torn by their teeth."	vv. 1–2 "Those who trust in the LORD are like Mount Zion, which cannot be shaken."	vv. 1–3 "When the LORD brought back the captives to Zion, we were like men who dreamed. Our mouths were filled with laughter."
Invitation to Trust		vv. 9a, 10b, 11b "O house of Israel, (Aaron, you who fear him) trust in the LORD."				
Basis for Trust		vv. 12–13 "The LORD remembers us and will bless us: He will bless the house of Israel"; "The highest heavens belong to the LORD."	v. 1 "I lift up my eyes to you, to you whose throne is in heaven."	v. 8 "Our help is in the name of the LORD, the Maker of heaven and earth."	v. 2 "As the mountains surround Jerusalem, so the LORD surrounds his people both now and forever."	vv. 5–6 "Those who sow in tears will reap with songs of joy. He who goes out weeping . . . will return with songs of joy, carrying sheaves with him."
Petition	vv. 12, 13, 14, 15, 17 "Teach us to number our days"; "Relent, O LORD! . . . Have compassion"; "Satisfy us in the morning with your unfailing love"; "Make us glad"; "May the favor of the LORD our God rest upon us; "Establish the work of our hands."	vv. 14–15, 18b "May the LORD make you increase, both you and your children. May you be blessed by the LORD"; "Praise the LORD."	v. 3 "Have mercy on us, O LORD, have mercy on us."		vv. 4–5 "Do good, O LORD, to those who are good. . . . Peace be upon Israel."	v. 4 "Restore our fortunes, O LORD, like streams in the Negev."
Vow to Praise		vv. 17–18 "It is not the dead who praise the LORD. . . . It is we who extol the LORD. . . . Praise the LORD."				
Interior Lament (implied or expressed)	vv. 3–11 "You turn men back to dust. . . . Who knows the power of your anger?"	v. 2 "Why do the nations say, 'Where is their God?'"	vv. 3b–4 "For we have endured much contempt. We have endured much ridicule from the proud."	vv. 1–5, 7 "If the LORD had not been on our side—the raging waters would have swept us away"; "We have escaped like a bird."	v. 3 "The scepter of the wicked will not remain over the land allotted to the righteous."	

of trust a collective meaning.[1] Personal trust was not enough for the psalmist. He wanted Israel to share it with him.

A third element of this group of psalms is *the basis for trust*. That is, sometimes the psalmist recounted a point of knowledge, a spiritual principle he had observed, or an experience that had taught him the lesson of faith. Apart from the crisis that shaped his faith, the psalmist had discovered the structure of faith. He was well aware of the mountains that surrounded Jerusalem, and he had observed that the Lord's protection of Jerusalem was as constant and defen-

sively certain as that geographical fact: "As the mountains surround Jerusalem, / so the LORD surrounds his people / both now and forevermore" (125:2).

The theological tenets of the psalmist's faith taught him about the majesty of Yahweh, and that he could trust in him: "I lift up my eyes to you, / to you whose throne is in heaven" (123:1). And not only was he enthroned in heaven, but he was the Maker of heaven and earth, the Creator of the universe (124:8). This was enough to assure any troubled soul that God was powerful and could deliver from the most threatening circumstances.

A fourth element in the psalms of trust is *petition*. These are prayers of faith. The psalmist, for example, knows God is a God of mercy, and he can show mercy again:

> As the eyes of slaves look to the
>   hand of their master,
>   as the eyes of a maid look to the
>   hand of her mistress,
> so our eyes look to the LORD our
>   God
>   till he shows us his mercy.
> Have mercy on us, O LORD, have
>   mercy on us,
>   for we have endured much con-
>   tempt. (123:2–3)

Given the nature of the psalmist's faith, it is not surprising that in at least two instances a fifth element enters the psalm. The worshiper makes a *vow* or *promise to praise the Lord* (16:7; 27:6b; 115:17–18). This promise arises out of the depths of his faith that God will hear his cry and come to his rescue.

The sixth element, and next to the *declaration of trust*, the most frequent component of the psalms of trust, is the *interior lament*. It is not a lament as such, but the remnant of one. In virtually all of these psalms, as mentioned above, the language suggests some crisis that the psalmist has endured that taught him to trust in the Lord. It was an experience that shaped the faith of the psalmist, and out of it grew a faith that could help him stand against the adversities of life.

These six components of the psalms of trust compose the texture of this group, even though they do not all occur with the same consistency. The *declaration of trust* and the *interior lament* are the consistently recurring elements. The others are auxiliary, and their presence highlights the purpose of the psalms, which is to give a faithful witness to the psalmist's trust in God.

The Individual Psalms of Trust

Psalm 4

Given the association of Book 1 with David, it is not surprising to find five of the six individual psalms of trust in this book. The first of them, Psalm 4, begins and ends on the note of trust:

> Answer me when I call to you,
>   O my righteous God. (v. 1a)

> I will lie down and sleep in peace,
>   for you alone, O LORD,
>   make me dwell in safety. (v. 8)

This expression of trust was evidently aroused by those who followed false gods (v. 2) and were a bit skeptical about religion in general (v. 6a). The psalmist's response to that attitude was a petition that God would cause his face to shine upon the community of faith (v. 6). His faith was not lived out in a vacuum, but in his community, and he summons them to "offer right sacrifices / and trust in the LORD" (v. 5). Faith interfaces in two directions, toward God and toward one's community.

Psalm 16

This psalm is replete with affirmations of trust. Every verse, except verse 5, is such an affirmation. So pervasive is the psalmist's faith in God that it is difficult to detect any crisis that might have evoked this discourse of confidence. Perhaps it was through contemplation of those who "run after other gods," but one cannot be sure. The psalmist certainly saw his behavior in contrast to theirs, for he had fastened his attention upon Yahweh, and Yahweh had stationed himself at the suppliant's right hand: "I have set the LORD always before me. / Because he is at my right hand, / I will not be shaken" (v. 8).

Psalm 23 in American Culture

William Holladay, in his intriguing study of the use of Psalm 23 in American culture, concludes that before the Civil War the psalm was not often used as a deathbed psalm. However, by 1880, he writes, the psalm had gained popular usage for this time of need, a phenomenon to which he believes Henry Ward Beecher's tribute to Psalm 23 gave great impetus.[1] That tribute is printed below:

The Twenty-Third Psalm is the nightingale of the psalms. It is small, of a homely feather, singing shyly out of obscurity; but, oh, it has filled the air of the whole world with melodious joy, greater than the heart can conceive! Blessed be the day on which that psalm was born!

What would you say of a pilgrim commissioned of God to travel up and down the earth singing a strange melody which, when once heard, caused him to forget whatever sorrow he had? And so the singing angel goes on his way through all the lanes, singing in the language of every nation, driving away trouble by the pulses of the air which his tongue moves with divine power. Behold just such an one! This pilgrim God has sent to speak in every language on the globe. It has charmed more griefs to rest than all the philosophy of the world. It has remanded to their dungeon more felon thoughts, more black doubts, more thieving sorrows, than there are sands on the seashore. It has comforted the noble host of the poor.

It has sung courage to the army of the disappointed. It has poured balm and consolation into the hearts of the sick, of captives in dungeons, of widows in their pinching griefs, or orphans in their loneliness. Dying soldiers have died easier as it was read to them; ghastly hospitals have been illuminated; it has visited the prisoner and broken his chains, and, like Peter's angel, led him in imagination, and sung him back to his home again. It has made the dying Christian slave freer than his master, and consoled those whom, dying, he left behind, mourning not so much that he was gone as because they were left behind and could not go too.

Nor is its work done. It will go on singing to your children and my children, and to their children, through all the generations of time; nor will it fold its wings till the last pilgrim is safe, and time ended; and then it shall fly back to the bosom of God, whence it is issued, and sound on, mingled with all those sounds of celestial joy which make heaven musical forever.[2]

1. William L. Holladay, *The Psalms through Three Thousand Years: Prayerbook of a Cloud of Witnesses* (Minneapolis: Fortress, 1993), 359–69.
2. Henry Ward Beecher, quoted by Leslie D. Weatherhead in *A Shepherd Remembers* (London: Hodder and Stoughton, 1937), 15–16.

Psalm 23

No psalm in the entire Psalter is more loved than Psalm 23. Against the memory of pursuing enemies, David recounts his experience with his Shepherd Yahweh, who had led him to green pastures and quiet waters, and there restored him. Instead of pursuit by the psalmist's enemies, the attendants of the Good Shepherd, goodness and mercy, gently pursue him on his way to the house of the Lord: "Surely goodness and mercy will follow [*pursue*] me all the days of my life" (v. 6).

The psalm traverses the distance from the shepherd's field (vv. 1–4) to the house of the Lord (v. 6), even though the Lord's house had no exclusive claim to God's presence. He was just as present in the shepherd's field where the sheep grazed as he was in the tabernacle. Generally speaking, the imagery of the Lord as Shepherd in the Old Testament is in reference to the Lord as Israel's Shepherd, but Psalm 23 confesses him as David's personal Shepherd.[2] This note of personal piety is not strange to the Psalms, and, in fact, is one of the noted features that makes this book so powerfully effective as a source of personal piety and worship. Patrick Miller makes this point in the following words:

This is not a communal credo. It is the song of trust of someone who knows in the midst of the vicissitudes of her or his personal life and over the course of the years that he or she has been carried in the bosom of God, sheltered from harm, and given rest. That is why the psalm has had such a central place in personal piety and the devotional life.[3]

Some commentators see Psalm 23 in two parts: the Lord as Shepherd (vv. 1–4), and the Lord as Host (vv. 5–6),[4] while others insist that the shepherd imagery follows through the whole psalm.[5] The theology of this psalm arises out of the practice of life, the practice of the lowliest of occupations, shepherding sheep. In the broad outline of biblical theology, it

En Gedi where David hid out from Saul, and a place where he learned much about the quiet waters that restore the soul (Ps 23:2–3).

is not an exaggeration to say that this imagery is a hint of the incarnation of God in human flesh, in Jesus of Nazareth. That God would condescend to the level of a shepherd is remarkably assuring, affirming his love for humanity. Isaiah saw the shepherding aspect of Yahweh's nature and reassured Israel that

> He will feed his flock like a
>   shepherd,
>   he will gather the lambs in his
>   arms,
> he will carry them in his bosom,
>   and gently lead those that are
>   with young (Is 40:11 RSV).

Leslie D. Weatherhead makes an interesting and accurate observation about this psalm: "It strikes a positive note. It is not beseeching God to be something or to do something. It is stating positively that He *is* and *does* all that is required by man. The writer does not say, 'O Lord, be my Shepherd! Make me to lie down in green pastures: lead me beside the still waters.' He is asserting these very things and glorying in them."[6]

Psalm 23 is the psalm of trust par excellence. The psalmist has rested his whole life in the loving care of the divine Shepherd.

Psalm 27

The element of trust in this psalm is overpowering. If one looks at table 9.1, one sees a string of affirmations undergirding this poem as an expression of deep faith in God. With the exception of *basis for trust*, it contains all of the elements mentioned above that may be found in the psalms of trust. The occasion for the psalm seems to have been war:

> For in the day of trouble
>   he will keep me safe in his
>   dwelling;
> he will hide me in the shelter of his
>   tabernacle
>   and set me high upon a rock.
> Then my head will be exalted
>   above the enemies who sur-
>   round me. (vv. 5–6a)

Some scholars believe that the first part of the psalm (vv. 1–6) is a separate psalm distinguished from the last part (vv. 7–14).[7] Yet the last half continues the theme of opposition, even though the military setting may not appear as strongly as it does in the first part, and it affirms a faith as strong as that of verses 1–6.

Psalm 62

Psalm 62 qualifies as a psalm of trust by its structure and content. Part 1 (vv. 1–7) is framed by affirma-

The Valley of the Shadow of Death

In John Bunyan's *Pilgrim's Progress*, the central character, Christian, on his journey to the Celestial City, came upon the Valley of the Shadow of Death. There he met others who had come that far and decided they could not navigate the treacheries of this frightful place. So as they retreated they warned Christian, like the spies warned the Israelites, that the land ahead was good, but the way was too formidable for travel. Christian, however, in his determination to reach his destination, pressed on ahead, hearing voices that spoke blasphemous words, even to the point that he thought they were coming from his own mouth. Then Bunyan describes his forward journey:

When Christian had travelled in this disconsolate condition some considerable time, he thought he heard the voice of a man, as going before him, saying, *'Though I walk through the Valley of the Shadow of Death, I will fear none ill, for thou art with me.'*[1]

1. John Bunyan, *The Pilgrim's Progress*, ed. with an introduction and notes by Roger Sharrock (London: Penguin, 1965), 58.

tions of trust (vv. 1–2 and vv. 5–7), with verses 1 and 5 virtually expressing the same idea, the first instance (v. 1) as an affirmation, and the second (v. 5) as a summons to trust. Part 2 (vv. 8–12) is composed of a summons to trust (v. 8) based on the observation that human life is transitory (v. 9) and ill-gotten gain is no basis for confidence (v. 10).

Structurally, the repetition of the word "only" (Hebrew *'ak*) constitutes the pillars that support the thought of this psalm. The psalmist uses this adverb to stress the exclusiveness of the thought:

Only in God does my soul wait in silence, from him is my salvation (v. 1)

Only he is my rock and my salvation (v. 2)

Only do they scheme to thrust him down from his high place (v. 4)

Only in God does my soul wait in silence, because from him is my hope (v. 5)

Only he is my rock and my salvation (v. 6)

Only are men a breath, the sons of men a lie (v. 9) [author's trans.]

In the Hebrew text the word for *only* stands at the beginning of the line, making each of these declarations that much more poignant.

Psalm 73

Elsewhere in this book I have typed this psalm as a psalm of wisdom[8] because it deals with a common problem found in wisdom literature, the prosperity of the wicked. But based on its strong affirmations of trust (vv. 1, 17, 18–20, 23–28), it can also be classified as a psalm of trust. We should remember that the psalmists, while working with general categories of psalms, were not working with our categories in the strict sense of the word. In fact, they often mix and match ideas.

The psalmist begins with an affirmation of God's goodness (v. 1), and then with verses 2 and 17 he frames the problem that troubles his heart, acknowledging that this is the problem that has almost caused him to lose his trust in God (v. 2). He knows and describes the problem well (vv. 3–12), and for him it was not merely philosophical but very personal (vv. 13–16). He tended to look at his own life and wonder why his innocence had not been rewarded, while the wicked seemed to be rewarded lavishly by prosperity. And then, he found a solution in the sanctuary of God:

Surely you place them on slippery ground;
you cast them down to ruin.
How suddenly are they destroyed, completely swept away by terrors!
As a dream when one awakes,
so when you arise, O Lord,
you will despise them as fantasies. (vv. 18–20)

The solution amounts to an admission that, though the wicked may prosper for a time, divine judgment will come (compare Ps 92:6–7). While the psalmist found this solution quite satisfactory, he did so in the context of the worship of the God who is "good to Israel" (vv. 1, 17). The goodness of God both opens and closes this psalm, and in view of verse 17 we should understand verse 28 in the context of worship too. It is the spiritual sentiment of Psalm 122:1: "I rejoiced with those who said to me, / 'Let us go to the house of the LORD.'"

Even though Psalm 73 puts a heavy burden of expectation on worship, it is not too heavy for the God who guides the psalmist with his counsel (v. 24). The psalmist, like Job (Jb 16:19; 19:25), had passed through the valley of despair and had emerged with the joyful disclosure that God was in heaven and had not forsaken him: "Whom have I in heaven but you? / And earth has nothing I desire besides you" (v. 25). This witness to the heavenly Advocate and the psalmist's confidence in him stands shoulder to shoulder with the great affirmations of faith in the Old Testament.

The Community Psalms of Trust

We have observed that the individual psalms of trust also have a communal nature. It was against the disposition of the psalmists to derive spiritual benefits from their relationship to Yahweh and withold them from the community. Yet there are those psalms that basically use plural pronouns and verbs and speak on behalf of the community of Israel. These community psalms of trust are Psalms 90, 115, 123, 124, 125, and 126. The essential element of *declaration of trust* is the same in these psalms as those of the individual psalms of trust. Further, the *interior lament* is also a consistent component.

Psalm 90

This psalm has a way of calming the soul. When human beings have a sense of their tenuous place in the universe and their transitory existence, they need to see themselves in view of the God of time and eternity. That is the effect of Psalm 90. It is very much a psalm of Israel, attributed to Moses,[9] and there are no good reasons why Moses could not have written the psalm. He spoke, of course, not for himself alone, but for Israel. As a community psalm of trust, it contains a strong affirmation of God's abiding presence with Israel (vv. 1–2):

> Lord, you have been our dwelling place
> throughout all generations.
> Before the mountains were born
> or you brought forth the earth and the world,
> from everlasting to everlasting you are God.

This word of trust comes against the backdrop of a serious lament (vv. 3–11) in which the brevity of life is set up against the totally different way God looks at time:

> You turn men back to dust,
> saying, "Return to dust, O sons of men."
> For a thousand years in your sight
> are like a day that has just gone by,
> or like a watch in the night.
> You sweep men away in the sleep of death;
> they are like the new grass of the morning—
> though in the morning it springs up new,
> by evening it is dry and withered. (vv. 3–6)

Then follows a transition in verses 12–13, petitioning God to help Israel judge the length of their life so that they may live it wisely. The conclusion of the psalm is a series of petitions in which Moses prays that their joy may counterbalance their affliction and that the favor of the Lord may distinguish their lives (vv. 14–17).

Psalm 115

Some call this psalm a communal complaint,[10] and complaint is certainly an element, brief though central. The nations tauntingly mock Israel: "Why do the nations say, / 'Where is their God?'" (v. 2). But the psalmist has a ready answer: "Our God is in heaven; / he does whatever pleases him" (v. 3).

And then the psalmist turns the taunt on the nations, exposing the idiocy of idolatry (vv. 4–8), much like Isaiah 44. The potent truth of his conclusion is that people become like their gods: "Those who make them will be like them, / and so will all who trust in them" (v. 8).

In contrast to those who trust in idols and become like them, the worshiper summons Israel to trust in the Lord:

O house of Israel, trust in the
LORD—
he is their help and shield.
O house of Aaron, trust in the
LORD—
he is their help and shield.
You who fear him, trust in the
LORD—
he is their help and shield.
(vv. 9–11)

This strong summons to trust in the Lord combines with the beginning affirmation of verse 1 to give Psalm 115 its expansive tone of trust, while the *interior lament* seems to have grown out of the taunting of the nations.

Psalm 123

The center of this psalm is confidence:

As the eyes of slaves look to the
hand of their master,
as the eyes of a maid look to the
hand of her mistress,
so our eyes look to the LORD our
God,
till he shows us his mercy. (v. 2)

Behind this word of trust lies a lament about the trouble Israel has seen (vv. 3–4), a rather generic kind of contempt from the arrogant, with no supporting details. It is this interior lament that gives rise to the plea for mercy in verse 3: "Have mercy on us, O LORD, have mercy on us, / for we have endured much contempt." While the psalm begins like Psalm 121 (v. 1), the "I" of verse 1 turns to the "our" of verse 2 (*our eyes*) and verse 4 (*our soul*), and the "us" and "we" of verse 3, putting the psalm quite comfortably in the category of the community psalms of trust.

Psalm 124

The "if—then" stanza of this psalm (vv. 1–5) is the "what if" of history, a question we cannot always answer, but one that definitely is sobering in its full dimensions (compare Isa 1:9). The psalmist was working with the worst possible scenario, and the very thought that God had been on Israel's side caused him to break out in the praise of verses 5–8. Not only did they have Yahweh's help when their crises came, but their Helper was the "Maker of heaven and earth" (see also Ps 121:2).

The consistent plural language of Psalm 124 puts it in the community category, although some have insisted that this language is more characteristic of individual than community psalms.[11]

Psalm 125

This psalm begins with a strong declaration of trust:

Those who trust in the LORD are
like Mount Zion,
which cannot be shaken but endures forever.
As the mountains surround
Jerusalem,
so the LORD surrounds his
people
both now and forevermore.
(vv. 1–2)

On the basis of verses 3 and 5, it would appear that the interior lament is over those who do evil. That is, the psalmist's contemplation of the problem of the wicked, somewhat like Psalm 73, had led him to a deep trust in Yaweh. Indeed, the geographical setting of Jerusalem reminded him of the surrounding presence and protection of the Lord. The clues that this is a community psalm of trust are found in the use of the plural participles of verse 1 ("*Those who trust* in the LORD") and verse 5 ("*those who turn* to crooked ways"), the word "people" (v. 2), the plural nouns that refer to Israel ("the righteous," v. 3b; "those who are good" and "those who are upright in heart," v. 4a), and, of course, the final pronouncement of peace upon Israel (v. 5b).

Psalm 126

Trust permeates this psalm. The remembrance of God's restoration to Zion, recalled by Israel and the nations (vv. 1–3), gives rise to the petition that he will again restore his people's fortunes (vv. 4–6). Some believe the psalmist was recalling some past miracle of restoration to Jerusalem, and now, in the midst of the exile he prays that God will give a repeat performance. If verses 1–3 reference a past restoration, we do not know what it was. Then there are those, on the other hand, who view the restoration of verses 1–3 to be the return from Babylonian exile and the petition of verses 4–6 as a prayer that God would restore them out of another crisis. If they have already returned to Zion, we do not know what that new crisis was. Yet, we should keep in mind that once the exiles had returned to Zion, the crisis was not over. They still faced repatriation, which involved reclaiming their property, rebuilding the temple, reinstituting worship, finding work to do, and reintegrating themselves into the society generally. Psalm 126 could very well, then, celebrate the return from exile and be a prayer for full restoration that was coming slowly, with much hardship and opposition (see Haggai and Ezra-Nehemiah).

Summary

The psalms of trust, both individual and community, carry a tone of deep faith in God and in his providence. For the most part, they arise out of some crisis in the psalmist's or Israel's life, a crisis whose hardship and testing shaped the psalmist's faith. This crisis is generally visible in the words of the psalm. Although it does not give rise to a lament as such, it nevertheless leaves its mark on the psalmist's memory (I have called this the *interior lament*). Thus, the two essential elements of the psalms of trust are the *declaration of trust* and the *interior lament*. These psalms often do not give evidence that the crisis has passed, but they exhibit the faith that can see one through the crisis. The psalms of trust are the girders of the Psalter, for they crisscross the book with expressions of the faith of the Old Testament in its finest form.

Key Terms

community psalms of trust
interior lament
individual psalms of trust

Study Questions

1. How do the psalms of trust compare with the psalms of thanksgiving?

2. What two elements are consistently present in the psalms of trust?

3. What is meant by *interior lament?*

4. How may the psalms of trust instruct believers today?

10 "You Are My Son; Today I Have Become Your Father"

Psalms of the Earthly King

Outline

- **Identifying the Royal Psalms**
- **The Setting of the Royal Psalms**
- **The Royal Psalms and the Messiah**
- **Summary**

Objectives

After reading this chapter, you should be able to

1. Recognize the royal psalms.
2. Examine the relationship of the king to God.
3. Discuss the messianic interpretation of the royal psalms.

royal psalms

The monarchy was, along with the priesthood and prophecy, one of Israel's three fundamental institutions, and it takes a far more central place in the Psalms than either of the other two. That, of course, is not surprising since David, Israel's ideal king, had such an active hand in producing the Psalter. With seventy-three psalms attributed to him, the monarchy obviously leaves its imprint on this book. The reader sees reflections of Israel's king and kingship not only in the "of David" superscriptions, but also in the content of the Psalms. As we explained in chapter 3, concern for the monarchy appears also in the way the editor(s) has put the book together.

The vision of Israel's future was shaped more out of the elements of kingship than either priesthood or prophecy. We may see this in the Old Testament canon with its massive histories of the monarchy, Samuel, Kings, and Chronicles. As we have observed earlier regarding Israel's history as represented in the Book of Psalms, the importance and the proportionality of the central events, as seen in the rest of the Old Testament, are accurately reflected in the Psalter. Likewise, the importance of kingship in Israel also finds its proper ratio in the Psalms. If the Book of Psalms takes any one institution and holds it up as the ideal paradigm of the future, it is kingship. In fact, the messianic interpretation of the Psalms, as we shall see, found its center of gravity in the psalms that deal with Israel's kings.

Identifying the Royal Psalms

Hermann Gunkel isolated the **royal psalms** as a special group, even though he did not think "royal psalms" to be a proper genre. Instead he proposed that they had been composed of other genres, like individual thanksgiving songs and complaint songs. His list of ten psalms (he in-

Wisdom, the Third Force

The third force in ancient Israel was wisdom, which can hardly be described as an institution. While the sages were highly influential, particularly in certain eras of history, their influence came largely through the infiltration of their ideas into the thought structures of Israelite society. As a formal movement they did not constitute anything like the well-defined institutions of priesthood and prophecy. We tend to talk about the wisdom schools, but this is often more a term of convenience than a claim that an organized, widely disseminated structure of wisdom teachers and students existed.

cludes Ps 89 only tentatively) has become rather standard, with a few people now and then breaking ranks. Including Psalm 89, we will consider the following eleven psalms as royal psalms: Psalms 2, 18, 20, 21, 45, 72, 89, 101, 110, 132, and 144.

The common thread that holds these psalms together is the subject of kingship. The most obvious criteria are that they (1) refer to the "king," (2) mention the "anointed" one as a noun or make use of the verb, and (3) they refer to David by name. In fact, seven of the psalms do refer to the "king" (1, 18, 20, 21, 45, 72, 89), while six of them (2, 18, 20, 45, 89, 132) refer to the "anointed" (Hebrew *mashiakh*, or English "messiah"). In the four that do not use the word "king" at all, David is nevertheless mentioned in the content of two of them (132 and 144), while neither king nor David is mentioned in two of them (101 and 110). That obviously means there are other criteria holding these psalms together as a group, since two of them (101 and 110) have none of the three criteria. That is, some of these psalms clearly describe the power, paraphernalia, and activities of the king, even though they do not mention his name. Psalm 101 sat-

Table 10.1

The Royal Psalms and Their Royal Terms

	Ps 2	Ps 18	Ps 20	Ps 21	Ps 45	Ps 72	Ps 89	Ps 101	Ps 110	Ps 132	Ps 144
King	X	X	X	X	X	X	X	O	O	O	O
Anointed (*mashiakh*)	X	X	X	O	O#	O	X	O	O	X	O
David	O	X	O*	O*	O	O	X	O*	O*	X	X

Key to Table

X occurs
O does not occur
* appears in superscription or colophon
# appears as verb

isfies the "royal" criteria in that the psalmist promises to "cut off every evildoer from the city of the LORD" (v. 8), a kind of power over Jerusalem that no one other than the king would possess. Psalm 110 uses language that obviously refers to the king, speaking of him as "my lord" (v. 1) and referring to his "scepter" (v. 2).

The relationship of the king to the Lord is an interesting feature of these psalms. The Lord, who himself is enthroned as King in heaven (Ps 2:4), has installed his earthly representative in Jerusalem: "I have installed my King / on Zion, my holy hill" (v. 6).

The same psalm implies an intimate relationship, Father-son, between God and the king: "He said to me, 'You are my Son; / Today I have begotten you'" (v. 7 RSV).

The Lord reaffirms this declaration when the psalmist reviews his covenant with David in Psalm 89:

> He will call out to me, "You are my Father,
> my God, the Rock my Savior."
> I will also appoint him my firstborn,
> the most exalted of the kings of the earth. (vv. 26–27)

The psalmists remembered the Father-son relationship that the Lord had made an intrinsic part of his cov-

enant with David (2 Sm 7:14). Other allusions or direct references to the Davidic covenant occur in Psalms 2:7; 89:3–4, 19–37, 49.

These psalms speak quite often of the king's military exploits but without attributing the victory to him. Since the heavenly King is in control of the earthly kingship, this heavenly King is also the power behind Israel's conquests. In Psalm 18:7–19 the real warrior is the Lord himself:

> He shot his arrows and scattered the enemies,
> great bolts of lightning and routed them.
> The valleys of the sea were exposed and the foundations of the earth laid bare
> at your rebuke, O LORD,
> at the blast of breath from your nostrils. (vv. 14–15)

None other than Yahweh gives the king his victories (21:1). His very active part in the conquests of Israel's kings appears not only in the battles themselves but in the preparation for battle as he trains the king's hands for war (144:1). There is never any question of who will win the battle when the Lord is the Commander-in-Chief. As the threat of war looms dark on the horizon, the Lord announces that he will "make your enemies / a footstool for your feet" (110:1). This view

179

Egypt's enemies, the Nubians and Asiatics, have already become a footstool for the boy king as he sits on his nurse's lap. The imagery of Ps 110:1 depicts the Messiah sitting in the privileged position at God's right hand until he has made his enemies a footstool (Ps 110:1).

of the Lord's hands-on role in Israel's military activity follows the deuteronomic thesis about war:

> When you go to war against your enemies and see horses and chariots and an army greater than yours, do not be afraid of them, because the LORD your God, who brought you up out of Egypt, will be with you. When you are about to go into battle, the priest shall come forward and address the army. He shall say: "Hear, O Israel, today you are going into battle against your enemies. Do not be fainthearted or afraid; do not be terrified or give way to panic before them. *For the LORD your God is the one who goes with you to fight for you against your enemies to give you victory.*" (Dt 20:1–4, emphasis added)

Not only do the royal psalms describe the king and his conquests, but they also paint a picture of the monarchical era as one of justice and righteousness. First, God's heavenly throne, the archetype of Israel's, is founded on justice (89:14). So justice is intrinsic to God's nature (45:7). The second observation follows from the first: the Israelite monarch, whom God himself had set on his throne, will rule by the scepter of justice (45:6). That is, justice will characterize the king's rule. The prayer that the

psalmist, probably David himself, prays on his son's behalf is that God would endow Solomon with justice and righteousness (72:1). It sounds very much like Solomon's own petition to God that he might have "a discerning heart" to govern Israel (1 Kings 3:9). Yet the royal psalms go beyond these generic terms and fill in the details of justice and righteousness. The king will defend the afflicted, save the children of the needy, and crush the oppressor (72:4, 12–14). Israel's monarchs were not mere symbols of justice; they were its guarantors in the real circumstances of life.

The Setting of the Royal Psalms

The form-critical school has generally assigned the royal psalms to a court or temple setting. In fact, Gunkel was so certain of it that he recorded his mental picture of the typical occasion on which these psalms were sung:

> They were performed in the presence of the king and his dignitaries in the palace or in the sanctuary.

The majestic wonder of the room is evident in its venerable splendor, in the expensive, colorful garments of all of the gathered nobles, including the first person of the state in all his ornate dress, in the glittering weapons of his body guards, and in the whirling clouds of expensive incense.[1]

That is to say, the setting was a ritual that took place either in the king's court or in the temple surrounded by the trappings of royalty. If it was the temple setting, then the so-called enthronement festival, surmise many form critics, was the occasion. The enthronement festival is a scholarly extrapolation from a Babylonian festival in which the god Marduk was annually reenthroned in pomp and circumstance at a special event in the fall agricultural festival. The comparable occasion in Israel, or so thought Sigmund Mowinckel, was the Feast of Tabernacles in the seventh month.[2] However, the direct biblical evidence for such an Israelite festival is virtually nil. It has essentially grown out of a "parallelomania" in bibical studies that shapes Israelite religion in the form of the neighboring cultures' religions. One can identify parallels, to be sure, but the imposition of whole institutions on Israelite religion merely because echoes of such institutions from other cultures can be heard in the Psalms is questionable.

Of course, it is quite possible that the royal psalms were used in some ritualistic function, but it is at best a guess as to what that function was. The one thing we can say for certain, which the form critics do not care to admit, is that these psalms find their setting in a historical situation. The subject of the king's conquests, his concern for justice and the oppressed, the theme of the Davidic covenant, and other historical elements point in that direction, not to say, of course, that these could not be celebrated in a moment of ritual recital. Yet, the concept of ritual recital, that is, actualizing a past event in the present by reciting the story or details about the event, was probably foreign to the Israelite concept of worship. Admit-

tedly, the Old Testament gives plenty of evidence that past events were "celebrated" within Israel, but "actualized" is another matter. The **actualization** of past events involved a mysticism that was alien to the Israelites. They "celebrated" the past in basically two ways: by (1) analogy and (2) telescoping.[3] The idea of **analogy** involved seeing a present or future event as equivalent to or even surpassing a past event. This is how Jeremiah interpreted Israel's return from Babylonian exile, drawing an analogy to the exodus:

> "However, the days are coming," declares the LORD, "when men will no longer say, 'As surely as the LORD lives, who brought the Israelites up out of Egypt,' but they will say, 'As surely as the LORD lives, who brought the Israelites up out of the land of the north and out of all the countries where he had banished them.' For I will restore them to the land I gave to their forefathers." (Jer 16:14–15; also 23:7–8)

The other way Israel "celebrated" past events was by **telescoping** the past and present, and, sometimes, the past, present, and future. That is, the present was merely a continuation of the past, and in that sense present and future Israel participated in the benefits of God's marvelous works in the past. This is the sense of Deuteronomy, as Moses called the second generation of the exodus to observe the covenant that the Lord had made at Horeb: "The LORD our God made a covenant with us at Horeb. It was not with our fathers that the LORD made this covenant, but with us, with all of us who are alive here today" (Dt 5:2–3).

Israel was to see itself on the continuum of God's relationship with his people. Like the cross and the resurrection, the great events of Israel's past were unrepeatable. There was a once-for-all finality about them.[4] However, in the lives of each new generation and each person, these events took on a conscious realism. In this way God demonstrated to Israel that he was not a God of the dead but of the living. Indeed, that is the point

Jesus makes in his exchange with the Sadducees about the resurrection. He quoted Exodus 3:6 ("I am the God of Abraham, the God of Isaac, and the God of Jacob") to say that God would not make such a relational statement if the patriarchs were merely dead men with no hope of resurrection (Mt 22:31–32).

There is a deep need in the human soul to enter into the experience of past saving events and thus lay claim to their spiritual benefits. Yet, both in Judaism and in New Testament Christianity this did not take place by some mystical "actualization." In the case of the New Testament we may go beyond the ideas of analogy and telescoping, and say that the Holy Spirit effects a mystical transfer of those benefits, but it is not the same as the mystical actualization that the form critics have imagined Israel experienced in worship.

One might also wonder why, if the royal psalms had a connection to the court and temple, they were not collected in a special group by themselves. The fact is that they are distributed somewhat evenly throughout the Psalter, with four in Book 1, two in Book 2, one each in Books 3 and 4, and three in Book 5. Three of these psalms do occur in important compositional locations. Psalm 2 opens Book 1 with the announcement that the nations have conspired against the Lord and his "anointed one" to set the tone for David and his struggle against his enemies, a major topic of Book 1. This psalm announces at the beginning of this collection that David's enemies will not succeed because the Lord has set him on the throne and has a special Father-son relationship to him. Therefore, at the very beginning, this psalm prescribes a program of victory for David and ultimately for Israel, and more than that, lays the foundation for Yahweh's relationship to the kingdoms of the world: "Ask of me, / and I will make the nations your inheritance, / the ends of the earth your possession" (v. 8). Out of this setting, and for this purpose, the Anointed One

will arise. "Blessed are all who take refuge in him" (v. 12c).

Both Psalms 72 and 89 close their respective books, stamping a royal seal on those collections. Perhaps as much as anything, the royal psalms, once the Davidic dynasty had fallen, helped to keep alive the hope that it would rise again, although that was not likely their original purpose. And when that hope did not materialize in its historical form, it turned into a hope for the appearance of the Messiah, the **Anointed One.** Obviously this hope, begun as the record of David's kingship and reign, and idealized in the Messiah, could be celebrated in individual hearts as well as in the worship experience of the community. Thus a temple setting (or even a court setting) is only one of the venues where such hope can spring up and stay alive. In fact, it cannot stay alive there unless it invigorates the soul of the individual. In my view, there is no good reason why the royal psalms should have originated in the temple or royal court rather than the venue of individual loyalty to God and the king.

The Royal Psalms and the Messiah

As we have observed above, the royal psalms are a major source of messianic hope. The noun *messiah* ("anointed one") occurs nine times in these eleven psalms, and twice in verbal form ("to anoint"). Here we may speak of two levels of understanding: the *historical* level and the *eschatological*. By the *historical* level we simply refer to the literal meaning: the king is the Israelite king, and David is the David of Old Testament history. By *eschatological* level we refer to a future person: the king is a superhuman figure, designated by Yahweh to accomplish a superhuman task, and ultimately he is the Messiah, the Christ of the New Testament. The New Testament quoted from this group of psalms at least fifteen times, all of those quotations taken from Psalms 2 (6 times), 18, 45, and 110 (7 times).

We can say that consistently when the royal psalms refer to the king and David, they directly reference the historical figures of the Old Testament. This is the ground level of hermeneutics, the starting point for the eschatological. History is very important to God, and any vision of a future that supercedes history is unrealistic. For example, when John describes heaven and the life of the redeemed church, he does so in terms of a new Jerusalem coming down out of heaven, and a renewed Garden of Eden where trees of life border the river of life.

Taking an example from the Psalms, when the psalmist declared "You are my Son; / today I have become your Father" (Ps 2:7), he referred to the special relationship between God and the king who reigned in Jerusalem. On the other hand, when the apostle Paul stood up in the synagogue of Pisidia to give his famous sermon, he quoted this verse and applied it to the resurrection of Christ (Acts 13:33). Obviously many years and various levels of hope intervened between the psalm and the first-century application. The messianic vision, while not complete in the Psalms, develops somewhere in between. We can see this development more clearly in the prophets than in the Psalter. In fact, there is a self-contained messianism in the prophets that we do not find in the Psalms. In contrast, the messianic application of the Psalms develops within the interpretive process of the Jewish and Christian communities, although it is important to recognize that the raw material for the messianic vision is already laid out in the Psalms and is not merely an invention of those communities. Jesus himself recognized this when he dealt with the matter of his divine sonship. On that occasion, cited by all three Synoptics, he quoted Psalm 110:1:

> "What do you think about the Christ? Whose son is he?"
> "The son of David," they replied.

He said to them, "How is it then that David, speaking by the Spirit, calls him 'Lord'? For he says,

> 'The Lord said to my Lord:
>   "Sit at my right hand
> until I put your enemies
>   under your feet."'

If then David calls him 'Lord,' how can he be his son?" (Mt 22:42–45/ Mk 12:35–37/Lk 20:42–44).

In this psalm Jesus heard one Lord speaking to another Lord, and this did not imply that David was the second Lord, since the heavenly Lord would hardly call an earthly monarch "Lord." Rather it implied divinity. So while the raw material for Jesus' messianic interpretation lies within the psalm itself, it is developed outside the psalm. Generally speaking, then, what we have in the Psalter is the raw material for the messianic vision that captured the attention of the Jewish synagogue and the Christian church.

This is not to suggest that the eschatological level of interpretation was an addendum with no relationship to the text or the historical circumstances. In fact, the idea of the Messiah arose out of the debris and ashes of history scattered over the hapless eras of Israel's past. So many hopes had burst into flame from the embers of expectancy and died away again, hopes of victory and universal sovereignty, of king and kingship devoted to God and his purpose for the monarchy. Israel's checkered experience in this regard reinforced the eschatological hope that the God of Israel would someday raise up a King who would truly fulfill the righteous reign God intended, and he would hold dominion over all the nations of the world as God had designed. While this notion may have in its early stages been hardly more than the idea of political sovereignty over the nations, in time it came to represent saving sovereignty. This is the way Paul uses Psalm 18:49 in Romans 15:9:

> Therefore I will praise you among
>   the nations, O LORD;
> I will sing praises to your name.

183

Anointing kings was a feature of Syria-Palestine monarchies.

He gives his king great victories;
He shows unfailing kindness to
his anointed,
to David and his descendants
forever.

God the sovereign Ruler of the nations became God the sovereign Savior of the nations.

Thus, out of the disappointment of history and the subsequent yearning for something better, the eschatological hope takes shape and substance. Thus the eschatological hope is endemic to the historical circumstances. God had intended from the beginning what the New Testament writers affirmed had taken place in Jesus Christ, even though the first lines of this hope clung to the historical institution of kingship in such a way that we cannot say for certain if the psalmists saw the historical and eschatological meanings as distinct. Nevertheless, in time this hope rose above the historical dimension and soared to the elevated heights of God's grace revealed in Jesus of Nazareth.

The royal psalms readily lend themselves to the New Testament messianic view. We can understand their readiness in that the New Testament writers were intent on declaring and affirming the exaltation of Jesus Christ and his victory over the powers of evil. What better source than those psalms which deal with Israel's king, his victories, and his exaltation over the nations. The universal sovereignty of Israel's king, which takes its place in the royal psalms,

The Gospel in Psalm 110

Martin Luther used Psalm 110 as the subject of his sermons in the spring of 1538. In it he saw the Christian gospel:

This is the high and chief Psalm of our dear Lord Jesus Christ, in which His Person, and His Resurrection, Ascension, and His whole kingdom are so clearly and powerfully set forth, that nothing of a similar kind is to be found in all the writings of the Old Testament. It is therefore meet and right that it should always be sung and expounded at such festivals of our Lord as Easter, Ascension, and Whitsuntide.[1]

1. Quoted by Jane T. Stoddart, *The Psalms for Every Day* (London: Hodder and Stoughton, 1939), 267.

was a pliable concept in the hands of Jesus himself and the New Testament writers as they sought to address the issue of Christ's sovereign rule over the world and all its powers. Consequently, the New Testament draws upon these psalms to affirm Christ's superiority: over angels, over David, and over the Aaronic priesthood. The writer to the Hebrews quotes Psalm 45:6–7 to attest to Christ's superiority over angels (Heb 1:8–9). He also draws upon Psalms 2:7 and 110:1 for the same purpose (Heb 1:5 and 1:13 respectively). Jesus himself, as noted above, cites Psalm 110:1 to affirm that he is superior to David. Stopping short of declaring himself God, he takes his listeners to the brink of it, leaving it to logical deduction. The writer to the Hebrews continues this superiority theme in his declaration that Christ occupies the office of the Melchizedekan priesthood that is superior to the Aaronic office (Heb 5:5/Ps 2:7; Heb 5:6; 7:17, 21/Ps 110:4).

The royal aspect of these psalms plays into the hands of the New Testament writers again in the sense that they become a source to affirm Christ's exaltation over the powers of the world and ultimately over death. In Peter's powerful sermon on the Day of Pentecost, he quoted Psalm 110:1 and proclaimed that God by raising Christ from the dead "has made this Jesus, whom you crucified, both Lord and Christ" (Acts 2:36). Paul, in his sermon at Pisidia of Antioch, heard the same forward thrust in Psalm 2:7 and declared:

> We tell you the good news: What God promised our fathers he has fulfilled for us, their children, by raising up Jesus. As it is written in the second Psalm:
> "You are my Son;
> today I have become your Father." (Acts 13:32–33)

In the apostle Paul's immortal words about the resurrection, he proclaims Christ's dominion, not only over the nations opposed to his lordship, but over the ultimate enemy, death: "Then the end will come, when he hands over the kingdom to God the Father after he has destroyed all dominion, authority and power. For he must reign until he has put all his enemies under his feet. The last enemy to be destroyed is death" (1 Cor 15:24–26).

Quoting Psalm 2:9, John affirms that Christ will extend his sovereign rule over the nations to all of those who overcome (Rv 2:26). Thus the themes of victory and sovereignty shape the messianic vision of the New Testament and proclaim

Study Questions

1. The monarchy, priesthood, and prophetic office formed Israel's three fundamental institutions. Which of these three takes a central place in the Psalms? What are the authorial and editorial reasons for this?

2. Name the three criteria that generally define a royal psalm. What other characteristics can define a royal psalm even if these three are missing? Give one example of a royal psalm with the three criteria and one without.

3. One fascinating feature of the royal psalms is the relationship it presents between earthly king and heavenly King, or between earthly ruler of God's people and God himself. How do these psalms correctly prioritize the exploits of the earthly king? Write a one-page essay detailing the treatment of this Father/son (or King/king) relationship in the royal psalms.

4. How do the subjects of the king's conquests, his concern for justice and the oppressed, and the theme of the Davidic covenant all point us toward a historical setting for the royal psalms? In what two ways did Israel celebrate the past? How does this stand over against the form critics' attempt to de-historicize the worship and history of Israel?

5. How do the royal psalms readily lend themselves to the New Testament messianic view?

Christ's exaltation and sovereign rule over the universe.

Summary

The royal psalms focus on the historical king of Israel and his kingdom. Yet, clinging to the historical institutions, and nurtured by the frustrations and failed expectations, they laid out the claim for a greater person and institution that would rise above the human disappointments and realize the hopes that mere history, unaided by the divine King, could not deliver. This future vision, while it lay in the arms of the historical circumstances, only came into its own reality as the Jewish synagogue and Christian church reflected on these psalms and read out of them the hope of a kingdom whose King would accomplish all and more than Israel's king had done or ever could.

Key Terms

royal psalms
actualization
analogy
telescoping
Anointed One

11 "The LORD Reigns"

Psalms of the Heavenly King

Outline

- **Description**
- **Thematic Emphases**
  The Lord Is Sovereign in Righteousness and Justice
  The Lord Is Sovereign in Creation
  The Lord Is Sovereign in Judgment
  The Lord Is the Sovereign King of the Future
- **The Messianic Overtones of the Kingship of Yahweh Psalms**
- **Dating the Kingship of Yahweh Psalms**
- **Summary**

Objectives

After reading this chapter, you should be able to
1. Define and describe the kingship of Yahweh psalms.
2. Suggest a purpose for the kingship of Yahweh psalms.
3. Explain the nature and purpose of the kingship of Yahweh psalms.
4. Describe the theological emphases of the kingship of Yahweh psalms.
5. Suggest a date for the kingship of Yahweh psalms.

yhwh malak

kingship of Yahweh psalms

Description

Earlier in our study we observed that Psalm 89, concluding Book 3, dealt with the apparent failure of the Davidic covenant, a theological crisis occasioned by the fall of Jerusalem and the end of the Davidic kingship in 586 B.C. When Psalm 89 had set the stage on which that theological drama should play itself out, Book 4 put the issue in context by refocusing it. The compiler of Book 4 answered the question raised in Psalm 89 in two ways: (1) an aggregate of psalms emphasizing the kingship of Yahweh, the really important Monarch of Israel and the world, and (2) a shift of attention away from the Davidic to the Mosaic and Abrahamic covenants. In this chapter we will concern ourselves with those psalms that emphasize Yahweh's kingship.

This group of psalms, which the form critics generally call the "enthronement" psalms, does not represent a formal psalm genre as such. Like the royal psalms, they are linked together by subject matter. The characteristic clause that binds them into a group is the Hebrew declaration **yhwh malak,** which can mean either "The LORD [Yahweh] reigns," or "The LORD [Yahweh] has become king." It is found in Psalms 93:1; 97:1; 96:10; and 99:1, and in 47:8 the clause occurs as "'elohim [God] malak." Those who follow Gunkel and Mowinckel translate these two Hebrew words as "The LORD has become king." To review, Mowinckel was convinced that the Hebrews celebrated an enthronement festival like that in Babylonia during which Marduk was reelevated to his pantheonic throne at a fall festival. This was a reflection of the agricultural cycle in which the earth and its herbage languished in the hot, dry summer heat and entered a period of tranquility (mythically the netherworld) and then began to prepare for new life again with the autumn rain, and eventually flourished with grain and flora in the growing season between October and April.

The climax came with the harvest in the springtime before the cycle—and thus the god behind the forces of fertility—began all over again. Mowinckel proposed that a great festal procession to the temple in Jerusalem, like that in Babylonia, marked the event and was accompanied by singing and dancing. The ark of the Lord, he further surmised (based on his reading of Pss 24 and 132), was the symbol of Yahweh's presence in the festival, and the destination of the procession was to return the ark to its place in the temple, symbolizing Yahweh's reenthronement.[1]

As we have already said above, there is virtually no evidence in the Old Testament for the existence of such a festival. In fact, the summer was not entirely devoid of agricultural growth because the vineyards, nurtured by the heavy dew, produced grapes during the hot and dry summer season. Thus, the translation of yhwh malak as "The LORD reigns!" fits Old Testament theology more precisely and accurately. Kidner has called this formula the language of "loyal acclamation."[2] I would prefer, then, to call these psalms the **kingship of Yahweh psalms,** rather than enthronement psalms, and would include Psalms 47, 93, and 95–99.[3] They announce and proclaim the kingdom of God. That acclamation is particularly powerful and effective in the context of the failed Davidic covenant, with its implications that the Lord had lost his sovereign rule over the world, now that a Davidic king no longer sat on Judah's throne, and his holy city and temple lay in ruins. What Israel needed was not a declaration that the Lord had become king, but that the Lord still reigned in his power and majestic glory. These psalms are a declaration of that fact. They praise the God who still reigns in spite of the appearance of circumstances to the contrary. In fact, to throw the light of realism upon the pathetic scene painted for us in Psalm 89, these psalms not only declare the present reality of Yahweh's reign but incorporate a picture of the future kingship of Yahweh (96:12–13; 98:7–

9). As if in recognition that Judah's history at the moment might contradict the declaration, however well intended, these psalms paint the picture of the future reality of the kingdom of God alongside the present tragedy, which only faith can rise above and transform. Some can believe that the Lord reigns even when the debris of life lies around their feet. Others need more vivid reassurance and hope-filled pictures that the kingdom for which faith hopes, yet unrealized, will someday burst into historical reality.

In addition to the characteristic formula, "The LORD reigns!" the kingship of Yahweh psalms, as one would expect, refer to the Lord as King. This is the case with Psalms 95 and 98, neither of which use the formula, but both of which reference God as King (95:3; 98:6). Of course, there are many other psalms in the Psalter that refer to God as King but do not fit the other qualifying criteria. J. D. W. Watts has set forth the following characteristics of these psalms:

1. Universal concern for all peoples and the whole earth
2. References to other gods
3. God's characteristic acts, such as judging, establishing, making
4. Physical and spiritual protocol of the attitude of praise before the heavenly King

This led him to define this group as Psalms 47, 93, and 95–99.[4]

David M. Howard Jr. has done a careful form and vocabulary study of this group of psalms and proposed that Psalms 47 and 93–100 belong to this collection. He considers Psalm 93 as the introductory psalm, with Psalms 95 and 100 bracketing the heart of the group, which is Psalms 96–99. He insists that even Psalm 94—which has neither the formulaic declaration or references to Yahweh as King—shows noteworthy ties to the group.[5] He further points out that Psalms 93–100 are psalms of the community, and this group is bounded by two psalms of the individual, Psalms 92 and 101. Whether or not

that has any bearing on whether we include all of these psalms in Howard's grouping, it is admittedly peculiar that Psalm 94 stands among them. Howard finds that structurally and lexically Psalm 94 is most closely related to Psalm 95.[6] In fact, its relationship to the psalms on either side, Psalms 92 and 93 on the one side, and Psalm 95 on the other, is impressive. In a similar way, Psalm 96 has close ties to its next-door neighbors, Psalm 95 on the one side, and Psalms 97–99 on the other.[7] While we do not fully understand the dynamics of compilation that brought the Psalter together, it may be that the compiler was working with small groupings of psalms that he did not want to separate for various reasons (respect for the context from which he took them, for instance). We may hypothesize that he had received Psalms 92–95 as a minigroup, only one of which has the declaration formula (93), and only one of which refers to Yahweh as King (95). His second mini-collection was Psalms 96–99, all of which contain the formula (98 has the nominal form, "The LORD is the King"). Rather than taking Psalm 93 and moving it to the first position of the concentrated grouping, which would produce a group of five psalms in a row, he honored the position of Psalm 93 in the smaller grouping as it had come to him and put the two mini-collections together, leaving the obvious link between them to the reader's astuteness (that is, 93 linked the first hypothetical group to the second, 96–99). While I recognize that there is a strong element of speculation involved here, I believe that somewhere in the recesses of the art and logic of the compilation of this marvelous and complex book there is an explanation to be found, whether or not there is a scholar wise enough or astute enough to find it.

After having said all of this, I would still prefer to restrict the criteria of the kingship of Yahweh psalms to the two I have outlined above, the formulaic declaration ("Yahweh reigns") and references to Yahweh as king, and would include in this group Psalms

47, 93, and 95–99. The most important of the two criteria is the formulaic declaration, which is the reason I include Psalm 47 in a psalmic neighborhood so distant from Book 4. The reference then to Yahweh as King is secondary, but in the psalmic neighborhood of Psalms 93 and 96–99 there is no reason to exclude those psalms that share the theme of Yahweh's kingship and kingdom. The obvious question left, then, is why we do not include the other psalms that refer to Yahweh as King.[8] The answer is that the theme of Yahweh's kingship, while common in the Psalter as a whole, serves a special purpose here in Book 4: to offset the disappointment Israel had experienced in the failure of the earthly kingship, especially in the ostensible failure of the Davidic covenant. It is the compiler's way of pointing to a powerful truth of which David's dynasty was only a symbol: "The Lord reigns, let the earth rejoice" (97:1 RSV).

Thematic Emphases

The point of this small collection of psalms, as we have indicated, is to stress the kingship of Yahweh in view of the failure of the earthly kingship represented by the Davidic dynasty. When the human institution had failed, there was no greater reassurance than to point Israel to the One who had established the institution of kingship and who represented a higher kingship that was everlasting and secure. Thus, the compiler of Book 4 interjects this declaration, "The LORD reigns!" It is not without precedent in the literature about Israel's origin, where it is found in the poetic expressions of Yahweh's work on behalf of his people. We hear it in the Song of Moses (Ex 15:18), the Blessing of Moses (Dt 33:5), and the Oracle of Balaam (Nm 23:21). Thus the idea of Yahweh's kingship was basic to Israel's self-understanding, even though they probably relegated it to the geniza of their memory. As long as an earthly king sat on the

throne, it was all too easy to forget that he merely represented a greater and higher kingship and monarch. But when that institution had floundered, there was hardly a greater word of assurance than the declaration formula of these psalms, "The LORD reigns!"

The Lord Is Sovereign in Righteousness and Justice

For a people chafing under the humiliation and suffering of foreign conquest, talk of **justice** was a healing balm. Where there is no injustice, there is little need to speak of justice. The frequency of the topic of justice in these psalms would therefore suggest that they were intended to deal with circumstances where injustice had become rife. The absolute standard of justice was not arbitrary. Rather the throne of Yahweh itself was the point of reference by which justice was determined: "Clouds and thick darkness surround him; / Righteousness and justice are the foundation of his throne" (Ps 97:2). The divine throne and the Lord of that throne superseded time and history: "Your throne was established long ago; / You are from all eternity" (93:2).

Even though these psalms do not locate the divine throne in heaven, it is nevertheless implied, and other psalms outside this collection do make the point explicitly (103:19; 123:1). Yet, this God of righteousness and justice does not stand apart from his creation, and as an earthly symbol of his heavenly throne he is enthroned between the cherubim of the ark of the covenant (99:1).

As we should expect of a king, this King loves justice (99:4). And as we would expect of a King who reigns over the whole world, his righteous **judgment** applies to all nations. It even goes beyond the sphere of humanity. As Creator who endows his creation with something of himself, the creation also proclaims his righteousness:

The heavens proclaim his
    righteousness,

Bowing before God was a gesture of fear and awe. It may have its origins in the prohibition to see God's face.

creation

and all the peoples see his glory.
(97:6)

Say among the nations, "The Lord
reigns."
The world is firmly established,
it cannot be moved;
he will judge the peoples with
equity.
Let the heavens rejoice, let the earth
be glad;
let the sea resound, and all that
is in it;
Let the fields be jubilant, and everything in them.
Then all the trees of the forest will
sing for joy;
they will sing before the Lord,
for he comes,
he comes to judge the earth.
He will judge the world in
righteousness
And the peoples in his truth.
(96:10–13)

The Lord Is Sovereign in Creation

Perhaps the relationship of the **creation** to justice may elude us, but in
the psalmists' thinking it was a natural connection. To begin with, we
should deduce from these psalms the
affirmation that the Creator of the
world is in control of his world:

For the Lord is the great God,
the great King above all gods.
In his hand are the depths of the
earth,
and the mountain peaks belong
to him.
The sea is his, for he made it,
and his hands formed the dry
land. (95:3–5)

These verses, while speaking of the
earth as the Lord's possession, imply
that he is Lord of the earth and thus in
control of its operation. When the
Psalms speak of God's ownership
and control of the earth, they refer

not merely to the physical, but also to
the moral operation of the world. His
creation of the world and creation of
humanity belong together, and the
fact of his creation stamps Yahweh's
claim upon the world and Israel:

Come, let us bow down in worship,
let us kneel before the Lord our
Maker;
for he is our God
and we are the people of his
pasture,
the flock under his care. (95:6–7)

The Lord not only established the
world but installed his firm decrees
to govern it:

The Lord reigns, he is robed in
majesty;
the Lord is robed in majesty
and is armed with strength.
The world is firmly established;
it cannot be moved.
Your throne was established long
ago;
you are from all eternity.
(93:1–2)

Your statutes stand firm;
holiness adorns your house
for endless days, O Lord. (93:5)

Even the waters (literally, "rivers")
that roar and pound out their pro-
tests are no match for God (93:3–4),
who is "mightier than the thunder of
the great waters, / mightier than the
breakers of the sea— / the Lord on
high is mighty" (93:4).[9]
Psalms 96 and 98 order the singing
of a "new song" whose content proclaims that the Lord is the King of the
world:

Sing to the Lord a new song;
sing to the Lord, all the earth.
Sing to the Lord, praise his name;

191

The Sovereignty of God

At the beginning of 1939, the editor of the *British Weekly* invited G. Campbell Morgan to write one of the messages of the New Year for the paper's readers, and the truth of God's reign was the main thrust:

What is the message that was in the past, and is still, the one all-inclusive word that I am attempting to utter? It is that, to quote the old-fashioned phrase, of the Sovereignty of God. I am firmly convinced that what I once heard you say is an abiding and inescapable truth, namely, "The one fact is God, all other things are circumstances."[1]

1. G. Campbell Morgan, *British Weekly*, Jan. 12, 1939. Quoted by Jane T. Stoddart, *The Psalms for Every Day* (London: Hodder and Stoughton, 1939), 231.

sovereignty

The "new" song proclaims Yahweh's **sovereignty** over the nations, both in judgment and salvation. It announces a new era in history, when Yahweh's sovereignty in the world will be finally and universally acclaimed. In that spirit the psalmist summons Israel, the earth and its inhabitants, and nature to join their voices in a choir of praise to the Lord who comes to judge the world:

> proclaim his salvation day after
>   day.
> Declare his glory among the
>   nations,
>   his marvelous deeds among all
>   peoples. (96:1–3)

> Sing to the LORD a new song,
>   for he has done marvelous
>   things;
> his right hand and his holy arm
>   have worked salvation for him.
> The LORD has made his salvation
>   known
>   and revealed his righteousness
>   to the nations. (98:1–2)

> Shout for joy to the LORD, all the
>   earth,
>   burst into jubilant song with
>   music;
> make music to the LORD with the
>   harp,
>   with the harp and the sound of
>   singing,
> with trumpets and the blast of the
>   ram's horn—
>   shout for joy before the LORD,
>   the King.
> Let the sea resound, and every-
>   thing in it,
>   the world, and all who live in it.
> Let the rivers clap their hands,
>   let the mountains sing together
>   for you;
>   let them sing before the LORD,
>   for he comes to judge the earth.
> He will judge the world in
>   righteousness
>   and the peoples with equity.
>   (98:4–9)

The Central Benjamin Plateau with its surrounding mountains that are summoned to "sing together for joy" with the earth in praise of God as he comes to judge the earth. Even nature, to use the psalmist's personification, had witnessed injustice in the world and rejoiced to see God coming to right earth's wrongs.

The lamp was a common source of light in the world of the Psalms, often described as radiating from God (Ps 27:1). In Ps 97:11 the life of the righteous ("those who love the LORD") is the source of light.

The God who created the world has become the God of the world, and it is his right to be so acknowledged.

The fact that Yahweh created the world sets him apart from the gods of the nations: "For all the gods of the nations are idols, / but the LORD made the heavens" (96:5). When Israel, the world and its population, and nature pay homage to the Lord, there is only one entity left, the gods themselves, if we should even acknowledge their supposed existence. Sometimes the Old Testament plays along with the henotheistic tendencies of the Israelites and speaks of the gods as if they really existed. If they did, then their bowing in worship before Yahweh would be the last and most telling evidence that their idols were powerless and meaningless. This is the sense of Psalm 97:7: "All who worship images are put to shame, / those who boast in idols— / worship him, all you gods."

Such is the awesome epiphany of the divine King whose royal cortege includes the earth and its peoples (97:1, 6), nature and its effects (97:5, 6), Israel and its constituents (97:8), the worshipers of idols, and their gods too (97:7)! Is there any justification then for withholding homage from a God like this?

> Let those who love the LORD hate evil,
> for he guards the lives of his faithful ones
> and delivers them from the hand of the wicked.

> Light is shed upon the righteous
> and joy on the upright in heart.
> Rejoice in the LORD, you who are righteous,
> and praise his holy name.
> (97:10–12)

The Lord Is Sovereign in Judgment

If one is to talk about justice, one must also speak of judgment, for justice is the standard by which all actions and attitudes are measured, and any breach of the standard calls forth divine judgment. This group of psalms sets forth the judgment of Yahweh on Israel and the world. Psalm 95 finds Israel in the wilderness of decision again, much like the critical moment when Moses led them in the wilderness where they saw God's mighty works and still did not believe (Ex 17:1–7):

> Come, let us bow down in worship,
> let us kneel before the LORD our Maker;
> for he is our God
> and we are the people of his pasture,
> the flock under his care.
> (vv. 6–7)

The generation to whom the compiler of this small group of psalms is speaking faced the same kind of decision, and their hearts were much like the hearts of their wilderness ancestors. By using this psalm, the compiler issues this warning again to Israel and pauses on the brink of judgment. If the Israel of his generation would only hear the Lord's voice *today*!

> Today, if you hear his voice,
> do not harden your hearts as you did at Meribah,
> as you did that day at Massah in the desert,
> where your fathers tested and tried me,
> though they had seen what I did.
> For forty years I was angry with that generation;
> I said, "They are a people whose hearts go astray,
> and they have not known my ways."

So I declared on oath in my anger,
"They shall never enter my
rest." (vv. 7c–11)

This was a powerful word of warning, and only heeding the great King's voice could turn Israel away from the precipice of disaster. This final announcement of judgment was issued against the first generation of the wilderness, and the psalmist reissues this warning without reissuing the word of judgment—"Today, if you will hear his voice. . . ."

These psalms pronounce a second word of judgment—against the nations. The psalmists join the prophets in announcing the advent of the divine Judge. Prophetic thinking can be instructive here. The prophets were concerned about the nations, not righteous in the least, whom the Lord had used to punish disobedient Israel. They were convinced that with time, even though it might be delayed, the Lord would also punish Babylonia and the other enemies of Israel. In the historical context of Judah's fall, the pronouncement of judgment upon the nations would be most reassuring. When the Lord makes his indescribable appearance to judge the earth, even nature joins the jubilant song of joy (96:10–13; 98:7–9).

The Lord Is the Sovereign King of the Future

The reality of Judah's fall was overwhelming for some, so overwhelming that they needed a clear vision of the future kingdom of God to sustain them through the crisis. For them it was not enough to issue a declaration of his present lordship, "The LORD reigns!" Their faith needed the reinforcement of the future vision of his kingdom. In fact, the description of the Lord's appearance in 97:2–7 is composed of the Hebrew imperfect and the prophetic perfect,[10] implying that his future epiphany was being described. Similarly, Psalm 98:9 describes the kingdom of the Lord as future:

Let them sing before the LORD,
for he comes to judge the earth.

He will judge the world in
righteousness
and the peoples with equity.

The Messianic Overtones of the Kingship of Yahweh Psalms

Both John Calvin and Franz Delitzsch consider these psalms to be a description of the messianic kingdom. Calvin comments that the summons to the nations to ascribe glory to the name of the Lord in Psalm 96:7 suggests the kingdom of Christ:

We must infer from this, that it has reference to the kingdom of Christ. God's name could not be called upon in any other part of the world than Judea, until it had been revealed; and the heathen nations were at that time necessarily altogether incapacitated for any such exercise. Yet it is evident that the Holy Spirit stirred up the saints who were under the Law to celebrate the Divine praises, till the period should arrive when Christ, by the spread of the Gospel, should fill the whole earth with his glory.[11]

Delitzsch remarks that the reader may see in these psalms the future messianic kingdom in two ways: the parousia of the human king and the parousia of Yahweh himself.[12] He observes that the Lord's advent in Psalms 96–98 moves in the direction of the incarnation:

Pss. xcvi-xcviii. Are more Messianic than many in the strict sense of the word Messianic; for the centre of gravity of the Old Testament proclamation of redemption does not lie in the Messiah, but in the Parousia of Jahve—a fact which is explained by the circumstance that the mystery of the Incarnation remains outside the Old Testament knowledge of salvation. . . . No doubt the mystery of the revelation of God in the flesh, the nearer the actual manifes-

Table 11.1

Distribution of Themes in the Kingship of Yahweh Psalms

	Ps 47	Ps 93	Ps 95	Ps 96	Ps 97	Ps 98	Ps 99
The LORD (God) Reigns	v. 8 "God reigns"	v. 1		v. 10	v. 1		v. 1
The LORD Is King	vv. 2, 6, 7		v. 3			v. 6	v. 4
The LORD Is Sovereign in Righteousness and Justice				vv. 10–13	vv. 2, 6		v. 4
The LORD Is Sovereign over the Gods/Idols			v. 3	vv. 4–6	vv. 7, 9		
The LORD Is Sovereign in Creation		vv. 1b, 4	vv. 4–6	vv. 1–5, 10–13	vv. 6, 9	vv. 7–9	
The LORD Is Sovereign in Eternity		v. 2					
The LORD Is Sovereign Over the Nations	vv. 2–3, 7–9			vv. 1, 3, 9	vv. 1, 5–7	vv. 2–9	vv. 1–3
The LORD Is Sovereign in His Choice/Care of Israel	v. 4		vv. 6–7			v. 3	vv. 6–8
The LORD Is Sovereign in Judgment			vv. 7c–11	v. 13	v. 8	v. 9	
The LORD Is Sovereign in His Holiness	v. 8	v. 5		v. 9	v. 12	v. 1	vv. 3, 5, 9
The LORD Is Sovereign over the Future					vv. 2–7	v. 9	

tation of it comes, does cast beams of its rising upon prophecy, but the sun itself remains below the horizon: redemption is hoped for as a deed performed by Jahve Himself, and "Jahve cometh" is still the watchword of even the last prophet (Mal. iii.1).[13]

We should note, however, that none of these psalms, except Psalm 95, is quoted in the New Testament. The writer to the Hebrews quotes Psalm 95 to warn his generation that they should heed the voice of God speaking to them through Christ, and that the gospel heard by the second wilderness generation was still available. The writer to the Hebrews heard that availability in the word "today" of Psalm 95, introducing the nearness and accessibility of the gospel of Jesus Christ (Heb 3:7–4:11). Like the Book of Hebrews, both Calvin and Delitzsch hear the pro-

phetic voice in these psalms, announcing the coming kingdom of the Lord.

Dating the Kingship of Yahweh Psalms

With the exception of Psalm 47 (which is a psalm of the sons of Korah) and a brief heading to Psalm 98 (*mizmor*, "song"), the kingship of Yahweh psalms do not have titles. Thus an attempt at dating them depends entirely on the content of these psalms. We should admit in the beginning that dating literature by the presence or absence of certain ideas is a tenuous business. In our discussion above we have outlined the purpose for which the compiler used these psalms, to shift the focus away from the failed Davidic covenant and defunct dynasty to the kingship of Yahweh, which is the really important kingship in the world. That, of course, does not mean that these psalms were written during the exile. Neither does it mean that they were written for that purpose. We are simply suggesting that the compiler used them for that purpose. Their date of composition is another matter.

Since we are dealing with a disparate collection of poems, connected largely by their content, each of these psalms has to be treated individually.[14] Psalm 93 has been dated in a broad range from the tenth century B.C. to the postexilic era. Based on linguistic and poetic considerations, however, Howard dates this poem in the tenth century B.C., or even in the twelfth.[15] In view of connections with the Song of Moses in Deuteronomy 32, Howard dates Psalm 95 broadly in the preexilic and possibly the early monarchical period.[16] The universal perspective in Psalms 96–99 suggests to some scholars that they may have been dependent upon Isaiah 40–66 and thus may originate in the postexilic era. This is the position of Delitzsch.[17] Of course, it is possible that Isaiah could have been dependent on these psalms, rather than the opposite. And it is also possible that both Isaiah and the psalmists could have drawn upon a theological tradition of universalism which, as Dahood points out,[18] was known in the ancient Near East from the third millennium on. In fact, Howard finds reasons to consider a preexilic dating for all of these psalms.[19] Admittedly dating is not critical to our understanding them.

Summary

We have defined and delimited the kingship of Yahweh psalms by two criteria. The first is the formulaic declaration, "The LORD reigns!" found in Psalms 47 ('elohim [God] reigns!), 93, 96, 97, and 99. The second criterion is the reference to Yahweh as King, which occurs in Psalms 95 and 98. The formula is the magnet that has attracted these psalms into this rather loose grouping. While other psalms refer to Yahweh as King, Psalms 95 and 98 belong to this group because they likely were part of two smaller groupings (92–95 and 96–99) that the compiler drew into Book 4. In addition, they incorporate themes which are common to those psalms containing the formula, for example, of Yahweh's universal reign. Based on these two criteria, we define the kingship of Yahweh psalms as including Psalms 47, 93, and 96–99.

Even though some scholars have made much of the supposed existence of a festival in Israel that enthroned Yahweh, virtually no evidence in the Psalms or elsewhere in the Old Testament supports this view. It is drawn largely from the Babylonian festival. Thus the clause *yhwh malak* is better translated "Yahweh reigns!" rather than "Yahweh has become king!"

While the composition dates of these psalms may have a wide range, they have been placed in Book 4 in order to put the fall of Jerusalem and the accompanying failure of the Davidic covenant in theological relief. In a time when the Judean monarchy had come to an end, these psalms point behind that system to the enduring reality that "Yahweh reigns!" And that fact has universal implications: "Let the earth rejoice!" (97:1 RSV). The implication, of course, is that Israel too should be rejoicing that its King the Lord is on his throne and rules over the whole world, despite the chaotic appearance of the historical realities. This universal perspective could and should radically change the way Judah looked at its latest reversal of fortune. If the Lord reigns, then everything else—Babylon and all her devastation, with the parceling out of Judah's life into havoc at home and hopelessness in exile—should fade into insignificance around the margins of this relief where the Lord's reign is the central focus.

All the supporting themes of these psalms reinforce the general theme of divine sovereignty. *The Lord is sovereign in justice* could be a "balm in Gilead" for this wounded nation. His justice was an expression of his true character, upon which his reign (throne) was based.

The topic of justice, of course, naturally raised another: the topic of judgment. There is no vindictive spirit in these psalms, such as we see in Psalm 137, but there certainly is the strong belief that the God of justice issues his decrees of judgment against evildoers, and the list was long. Therefore, *the Lord is sovereign in judgment.*

If anyone had any doubts about his right to exercise his sovereign reign in justice and judgment, then the theme that *the Lord is sovereign in creation* should settle the matter. The Creator of the world holds and exercises all the rights and privileges in his creation. Let no one doubt his motive or his will to act.

Of this group of psalms, only Psalm 95 is quoted in the New Testament. Yet it definitely weaves the theme of Yahweh's reign into the tapestry of the kingdom of God, which is so central to the gospel of Christ. As John tells the story of the climax of history, we hear a multitude of voices like roaring waters and peals of thunder crying out the announcement for which all creation has anxiously waited:

> "Hallelujah!
> For our Lord God Almighty reigns.
> Let us rejoice and be glad
> and give him glory!" (Rv 19:6b–7a)

It is the answer to the summons of Psalm 97: "The LORD reigns! / Let the earth rejoice" (v. 1 RSV). Is there any wonder that Calvin and Delitzsch heard messianic tones in the words of these psalms!

Key Terms

yhwh malak
kingship of Yahweh psalms
justice
judgment
creation
sovereignty

Study Questions

1. The kingship of Yahweh psalms, like the royal psalms, are linked by subject matter. They announce and proclaim the kingdom of God, united by a characteristic Hebrew clause, *yhwh malak*, or, "the LORD reigns!" How does the title "kingship of Yahweh psalms" better convey this content than the form-critical "enthronement" title?

2. In addition to the two criteria above, several other psalms sharing a special function in relating Yahweh's kingship to the future hopes of Israel may be included in the collection. Which psalms are these? Exactly how do they theologically reassure Israel?

3. How do the kingship of Yahweh psalms orient the concept of justice along absolute lines rather than on mere arbitrary fate? What then does this say about the certain advent of judgment? How does this link with the message of the prophets?

4. With what doctrines do the kingship of Yahweh psalms thoroughly advance the concept of God's sovereignty?

5. What makes dating the kingship of Yahweh psalms so challenging? These probably have a wide range of dates, but that in no way prohibits our understanding of them or of the intentions of the editors. Why should we be more concerned with their meaning than their composition dates?

12 "My Mouth Will Speak Words of Wisdom"

The Wisdom Psalms

Outline

- Wisdom Psalms
- Definition and Description of Wisdom Psalms
- Identifying Wisdom Psalms
- Structure and Motif in the Wisdom Psalms
- Summary

Objectives

After reading this chapter, you should be able to

1. Explain the nature of wisdom in the biblical literature.
2. Define a wisdom psalm and explain how that is determined.
3. Discuss the theological implications of the wisdom psalms.

wisdom psalms

proverbial wisdom

reflective wisdom

prophecy

Many of the psalms are prayers to God, and we have seen examples of this in the psalms of lament and the psalms of thanksgiving. But many of them are reflections rather than prayers. Sometimes these psalms are called *didactic* because they teach on various themes. Even if they do not engage in admonitions, the psalmists may teach by merely giving their readers the advantage of reflecting with them on particular topics. There are three groups of psalms that fall into the category of didactic psalms. They are (1) wisdom psalms, (2) Torah psalms, and (3) historical psalms (78, 105, and 106). We will discuss the first two but not the third, since we have included a chapter on history in the Psalms.

Wisdom Psalms

The **wisdom psalms** represent influences of a certain way of conceptualizing life and faith. This way of thinking or theologizing is best represented in the biblical books of Job, Proverbs, and Ecclesiastes. Two modes of wisdom thinking are identifiable in these books. The first is a mode of teaching by the use of proverbs, best represented in the Book of Proverbs and known as **proverbial wisdom.** The proverb represents a concentrated expression of the truth. It teaches the obvious because it is a slice out of real life. Because the application was so obvious, the students would immediately understand its application to their situation or problem. When the teacher says, "A gossip betrays a confidence, / but a trustworthy man keeps a secret" (Prv 11:13), those who have had the slightest experience with tattlers will be able to recognize the truth of this proverb. It requires little reflection and yields its truth effervescently. There are other proverbs, however, that, while cut out of life's experience, will require a bit more reflection. The wisdom sage says, "The truly righteous man attains life, / but

a cruel man brings trouble on himself" (Prv 11:17). Even though it has the ring of truth and experience, experience has taught us that righteousness does not always lead to the ideal life, and cruelty does not always bring self-destruction. Job was a witness to that. Thus, this proverb will require more extended reflection and create more debate than the former one. This proverbial type of wisdom teaching is sometimes called *lower* wisdom.

The second type of wisdom, the type represented by Job and Ecclesiastes, is basically reflective. This **reflective wisdom** puts forth problems that arise out of real life, but it does not have the pat answers that proverbial wisdom offers. When Job's friends insisted that the righteous prosper and the wicked suffer, Job raised strong objections to their thesis out of his own tragic experience. This type of wisdom teaching is sometimes called *higher* wisdom. The Psalms actually contain both types.

To set wisdom in its wider context, we might observe that there are basically three worldviews represented in the Old Testament, all related and interrelated, but each having its own distinctives. They are Torah, **prophecy,** and wisdom. While we cannot discuss this matter in detail here, we can outline briefly these three ways of looking at the world and describing its vertical and horizontal dimensions.

In the Old Testament we have three major religious offices, each having its corresponding body of literature: the priest and the Torah, the prophet and prophecy, the sage and wisdom. Each of these represents a *paradigm* of faith, that is, a way of describing God and his relationship to the world and the horizontal network of relationships in the world itself. The Torah laid down the basic precepts of Old Testament faith, including numerous laws that regulated the human-God relationship and human-human relationships. The prophets, while not abandoning the Torah, built on the covenantal relationship of God and Israel, and laid greater emphasis on the relational aspect, de-emphasizing the legal aspect, although not renouncing it altogether. Micah 6:6–8 is an example of the prophetic reduction of the legal system of the Torah to a simple vertical (God/Israel) and horizontal (Israelite/Israelite) set of relationships:

> With what shall I come before the LORD
>   and bow down before the exalted God?
> Shall I come before him with burnt offering,
>   with calves a year old?
> Will the LORD be pleased with thousands of rams,
>   with ten thousand rivers of oil?
> Shall I offer my firstborn for my transgression,
>   the fruit of my body for the sin of my soul?
> He has showed you, O man, what is good.
>   And what does the LORD require of you?
> To act justly and to love mercy
>   and to walk humbly with your God.

In fact, the general assumption of the prophets was that God designed the legal system of the Torah to encourage and support Israel's relationship to him and their relationships to each other. It was not so much obedience to the letter of the law that Yahweh demanded, but moral obedience to the spirit of the law.

The wisdom paradigm, like that of the prophets, laid the emphasis on moral obedience. However, for the most part, the sages shifted their attention from the nation Israel to the individual. Perhaps it was their conviction that if the nation would be changed, the epicenter of transformation would have to be located in the individual rather than the nation. The prophets and Torah had worked in the opposite direction, from the nation to the individual. Further, like prophecy, the wisdom movement did not disregard the central features of the Torah, like sacrifice, but simply moved it from the center of soteriology, and moved moral obedience, or

a right relationship with God and neighbor, to the center. In fact, they probably did not see themselves as making any kind of shift. Rather they were merely recognizing the true meaning of sacrifice or the real center of faith in Yahweh.

Wisdom was a worldview that conceptualized reality in terms of the two ways, sometimes called by the terms of ultimate reality, "life" and "death," or by the terms "wisdom" and "folly," that is, the means of achieving or failing to achieve life's goals. The two ways may also take the names of their personal representatives, the wise and the foolish or the righteous and the wicked. Wisdom as a philosophy of living did not try to mediate between the two ways—they were kept in a dichotomous relationship. Rather it conceptualized the meaning of life in terms of the two extremes and the path by which each could be reached. There could be no compromise. If one followed the precepts of wisdom, one became wise and achieved life; if one followed the precepts of folly, one became foolish and moved along the path to death. This was the way the patrons of *lower wisdom* conceptualized life and faith.

As regards *higher wisdom*, the two ways were not as distinctly marked. Although there was a consciousness of them, human experience had taught the patrons of higher wisdom that the case of life and death, or the wise and the fool, was not black and white, but gray. The righteous sometimes suffer and the wicked sometimes prosper. In the light of that dilemma, figuring God out was the task of wisdom reflection. Or to put it another way, figuring out what difference a right belief in God and right behavior toward one's neighbor really made was the task of wisdom reflection. That was Job's situation. As the reader will observe in table 12.2, some of the wisdom psalms briefly introduce these reflective motifs.

Definition and Description of Wisdom Psalms

Sigmund Mowinckel believed that 140 out of the 150 psalms were written for cultic purposes or worship in the temple.[1] The other ten he called "learned psalmography," which originated in the circle of the sages. Five wisdom psalms (1, 37, 49, 112, 127) fall among his non-cultic psalms. While we may not accept Mowinckel's basic hypothesis, that most of the psalms were written for use in temple worship, he nevertheless recognized the presence of wisdom psalms in the Psalter.

From the work of Hermann Gunkel, the criteria of style, structure, and motif have characterized the description of the wisdom psalms. Roland Murphy's helpful study essentially reduced these two criteria to style and motif, since wisdom literature did not assume distinctive structural characteristics.[2] In regards to literary style, some distinctive features, identifiable in the wisdom books of Proverbs, Job, and Ecclesiastes, are identifiable in the wisdom psalms.

First, and perhaps most distinctive of wisdom literature, is the proverb. Psalm 37 has a string of proverbs, much like those of the Book of Proverbs. An example is Psalm 37:1–2:

> Do not fret because of evil men
>> or be envious of those who do wrong;
> for like the grass they will soon wither,
>> like green plants they will soon die away.

A second feature is the presence of wisdom admonitions or teachings, often taken from nature. Psalm 37:9, for example, admonishes the reader not to "be like the horse or the mule, which have no understanding." While the wisdom teachers were fond of drawing comparisons with animals and nature, this was not an exclusive feature of wisdom (see Is 1:3). When we compare wisdom with the prophets, for example, it is a matter of the frequency of such comparisons rather than kind.

A third feature is the use of similes (introduced by "like" or "as"), especially those that draw comparisons with nature. The blessing of children is the theme in Psalm 128, and the psalmist says of those who fear the Lord:

> Your wife will be like a fruitful vine
>> within your house;
> your sons will be like olive shoots
>> around your table. (v. 3)

Another nature simile occurs also in Psalm 37:2, where evil men are compared to withering grass: "*like the grass* they will soon wither." Table 12.2 gives other examples.

A fourth feature is the "blessed" (*'ashre*) formula, which occurs in Psalms 1:1; 34:8b; 112:1b; 127:5; and 128:1. It is a way of pronouncing divine approval on a particular way of life or action.

A fifth feature is the teacher's address to his students as "sons" or "children." This is a frequent occurrence in Proverbs, but it only occurs once in the Psalms (34:11).

A sixth feature is the use of "better" sayings, which measure the value of one thing or action over against another. It goes beyond the simile, which merely compares two things, and gives a preference to one item or behavior over another. Psalm 37:16, for example, compares the paucity of the righteous to the wealth of the wicked and declares the former "better": "Better the little that the righteous have / than the wealth of many wicked."

As observed above, *structure* is not a prominent criterion of the wisdom psalms. Some scholars have associated the acrostic poem with wisdom (e.g., Prv 31:10–31), but it is not necessarily a structural feature of wisdom. Rather it is a common mnemonic structure. Of course, the same could be said for some of the other features above. The determi-

128	128	128	128
133		133	133
(139)			

Wisdom's Male Perspective

The third motif divulges the fact that wisdom literature was written from a male perspective. That, of course, was true because the women of Israelite society were the bearers of children and homemakers, and the men of the society were the laborers and students. That says nothing about the intellectual capability of women. It is merely a reflection of the categories of ancient Israelite society. Nor should we think disparagingly about that structure, however our society may have changed. We are hardly in a position to pass judgment upon such a social order. Ours is not necessarily superior to theirs. It is different, admittedly. But it is social and intellectual snobbery to pass a judgment of inferiority upon that society. Abuse of women, the kind we find in Judges 19, or any other form, is quite another matter and is always morally wrong. With the widening of the biblical norm so that all men and women and all peoples are clearly the objects and recipients of the gospel (see Jl 2:28–32; Acts 2:14–21; Gal. 3:28), the wisdom literature is just as applicable to women as to men.

wisdom motifs nation of a psalm as wisdom depends upon a combination of these features and criteria, and there is no agreed-upon mixture that moves the psalm over into the wisdom column. It is a judgment call. This is the reason the lists of wisdom psalms vary so much from one scholar to another. The following will show the variance:

Table 12.1

Wisdom Psalm Designations

Sabourin[3]	Murphy[4]	Kuntz[5]	Scott[6]
1	1	1	1
			19B
	32	32	32
	34	34	34
37	37	37	37
49	49	49	49
(73)			
			78
(91)			
112	112	112	112
119			119
127		127	127

As the reader will observe, Psalms 1, 37, 49, 112, and 128 are common to all four lists. Adding other such lists will only highlight the variations among them.

Wisdom motifs or *themes* are by far the most important features of wisdom poetry. After all, the content of wisdom is what made it distinctive. First, wisdom literature frequently contrasts the two ways or the lifestyles of the wicked and righteous (Ps 1; Prv 3:33; 10:3, etc.). A second feature is a preoccupation with the problem of retribution. The Book of Job is the best treatment of this topic, but it also occurs many times in the Book of Proverbs, where the theology is basically one of the punishment of the wicked and the reward of the righteous. Job challenges this basic theological premise and insists that sometimes it works the other way—the righteous suffer and the wicked are rewarded. The third motif in the wisdom psalms is the occurrence of certain practical advice, such as the encouragement to be diligent in one's personal actions, to be responsible in all one's dealings, and to avoid evil women. The fourth motif is the fear of the Lord, a phrase that denotes one's general relationship to God, a relationship that shapes how one deals with one's neighbors.[7]

Identifying Wisdom Psalms

I have taken R. B. Y. Scott's list of seventy-seven wisdom vocabulary terms,[8] added some of my own, and used this list to analyze the wisdom psalms (see sidebar "Wisdom Terms"). However, the question is, How many of the criteria outlined above should be iden-

Wisdom Terms[1]

1. *'evil*	obstinate fool
2. *'awen*	evil, wickedness
3. *'omnam*	truly
4. *'orakh*	path
5. *'ashre*	happy, blessed (is)
6. *bin*	to understand
7. *binah*	understanding
8. *ba'ar*	brutish, stupid
9 *da'ath*	knowledge
10. *de'ah*	knowledge
11. *derek*	way
12. *hevel*	breath, emptiness
13. *hiqshiv*	to pay attention
14. *ho'il*	to profit, gain
15. *horah*	to teach, direct
16. *khidah*	riddle
17. *khiwwah*	to inform
18. *hokhiakh*	to decide, reprove
19. *khatta'*	sinner
20. *khush*	to hasten
21. *khakham*	to be wise
22. *khakham*	wise
23. *khokhmah*	wisdom
24. *khanef*	godless
25. *khefets*	pleasure; thing, affair
26. *khaqar*	to investigate
27. *kheqer*	investigation
28. *kheherish*	to be silent
29. *khashav*	to think, devise
30. *yir'at Yahweh*	fear of Yahweh
31. *yare*	to fear (Yahweh)
32. *yadha'*	to know
33. *yasar*	to admonish, disicipline
34. *yisser*	to admonish, discipline
35. *ya'ats*	to give counsel
36. *yashar*	upright, straight
37. *yosher*	uprightness
38. *kazav*	lie
39. *ka'as*	trouble, vexation
40. *kesil*	insolent, stupid
41. *limmad*	teach
42. *lev*	heart, mind
43. *levav*	heart, mind
44. *la'ag*	to mock
45. *lets*	insolent, scoffing
46. *leqakh*	learning
47. *madhon*	strife
48. *musar*	training, discipline
49. *mezimmah*	scheme, scheming
50. *mashal*	proverb, wise saying
51. *naval*	vulgar fool
52. *nevalah*	folly
53. *navon*	discerning
54. *nakhoakh*	straightforward
55. *nethivah*	path
56. *sod*	council; counsel
57. *sakhal*	fool
58. *'awlah*	wickedness
59. *'iwweth*	to make crooked
60. *'amal*	toil, trouble
61. *'etsah*	advice, counsel
62. *'atsel*	lazy
63. *'arum*	clever, prudent
64. *'ormah*	cleverness
65. *pethi*	simple, uninstructed
66. *tsaddiq*	righteous
67. *tsedeq*	righteousness
68. *tsedaqah*	righteousness
69. *qalon*	contempt
70. *rasha'*	wicked
71. *riv*	to contend, dispute
72. *riv*	dispute, accusation
73. *remiyyah*	neglect, deceit
74. *ratson*	wish, favor
75. *siakh*	to muse, complain
76. *siakh, sikhah*	complaint, musing
77. *ta'avah*	desire
78. *tevunah*	insight
79. *tokakhath*	rebuke, blame
80. *takhan*	estimate, measure
81. *tikken*	to estimate, measure
82. *tam*	blameless
83. *tamim*	blameless, righteous
84. *tamak*	to grasp
85. *tushiyyah*	ability, success

1. This list, which I have expanded and numbered for easy reference, is from R. B. Y Scott, *The Way of Wisdom* (New York: Macmillan, 1971), 121–22.

tifiable in a given psalm before we designate it a wisdom psalm? Admittedly any answer to this question is rather arbitrary. For example, if a psalm uses the "blessed" formula and speaks of the reward of the righteous and the wicked, is it a wisdom psalm? Perhaps the best way to answer that question is to say it depends on the preponderance of wisdom ideas (motifs), which is really the primary criterion for determining whether a psalm is a wisdom psalm. Yet, these topics were not the exclusive right of the wisdom movement.

Table 12.2 Psalms of Wisdom

	Ps 32	Ps 34	Ps 37	Ps 49	Ps 73	Ps 112	Ps 127	Ps 128	Ps 133
Formal Features/Style									v. 1
Proverbs		vv. 6, 7, 8	vv. 16, 21	vv. 12, 20			vv. 2, 3 see Prv 16:3, 9; 17:6		v. 1 family unity
Wisdom Precepts			v. 31 law and wisdom brought together			v. 1 the person who fears the Lord delights in his commandments.	vv. 1–2, 3–5 "Unless the LORD builds the house, its builders labor in vain"; children are a heritage from the LORD.	vv. 1–4 the fear of the Lord; many children are the Lord's blessing.	
Admonitions	v. 9 "Do not be like the horse or the mule, which have no understanding."	vv. 11–14 "Whoever of you loves life and desires to see many good days, keep your tongue from evil and your lips from speaking lies."	vv. 1, 3, 4, 5, 8 "Do not fret because of evil men"; "Trust in the LORD and do good"; "Delight yourself in the LORD and he will give you the desires of your heart"; "Commit your way to the LORD; trust in him and he will do this"; "Refrain from anger and turn from wrath."	vv. 16–19 "Do not be overawed when a man grows rich, when the splendor of his house increases; for he will take nothing with him when he dies."					
Similes	v. 9 *Like the horse or the mule.*		vv. 2, 6, 20, 35 *Like the grass they will soon wither, like green plants they will soon die away*; "He will make your righteousness shine *like the dawn, the justice of your cause like the noonday sun*"; "The LORD's enemies will be *like the beauty of the fields, they will vanish*—vanish *like smoke*"; "I have seen a wicked and ruthless man flourishing *like a green tree*."	vv. 14, 20 *"Like sheep they are destined for the grave"; "A man who has riches without understanding is like the beasts that perish."*	v. 20 *"As a dream when one awakes."*		v. 4 *"Like arrows in the hands of a warrior are sons born in one's youth."*	v. 3 "Your wife will be *like a fruitful vine* within your house; your sons will be *like olive shoots* around your table."	vv. 2, 3 Family unity is *like precious oil* poured on the head, running down on the beard, running down on Aaron's beard"; "It is as if (Hebrew *like*) the dew of Hermon were falling on Mount Zion."
Illustrations from Nature			vv. 2, 6, 20, 35 "Like the grass they will soon wither, like green plants they will soon die away"; "He will make your righteousness shine like the dawn, the justice of your cause like the noonday sun"; "The LORD's enemies will be like the beauty of the fields, they will vanish—vanish like smoke"; "I have seen a wicked and ruthless man flourishing like a green tree."		v. 22 "I was a brute beast before you."			v. 3 "Your wife will be like a fruitful vine within your house; your sons will be like olive shoots around your table."	
Addressees	vv. 6–7, 11 God and the righteous.	vv. 3, 9, 11 the afflicted (see v. 2) or the congregation; "his saints"; and "my children" (sons).		v. 1 "all you peoples"; "all who live in this world, both low and high, rich and poor alike."				vv. 5–6 the one who fears the Lord (implied) "May the Lord bless you from Zion all the days of your life; may you see the prosperity of Jerusalem, and may you live to see your children's children."	
"Blessed" (*ashre*) Formula	vv. 1, 2	v. 8b				v. 1	v. 5	v. 1	v. 1 "How good and pleasant" is equivalent to "blessed" or "happy"—see Prv 15:23 ("how good").
"Better" Sayings			v. 16						

	Ps 32	Ps 34	Ps 37	Ps 49	Ps 73	Ps 112	Ps 127	Ps 128	Ps 133
Acrostic Poem		yes	yes						
Antithetical Ways of Life		vv. 14, 15 "Turn from evil and do good"; "The eyes of the LORD are on the righteous . . . ; the face of the LORD is against those who do evil."	vv. 7, 9, 10–11, 12–13, 14–15, 16–17, 18–20, 21, 22, 32–33, 34, 37–38 "Be still before the LORD and wait patiently for him; do not fret when men succeed in their ways, when they carry out their wicked schemes"; "For evil men will be cut off, but those who hope in the LORD will inherit the land."		Contrast of two ways: vv. 3–12 wicked, v. 13 righteous (psalmist), v. 27 wicked, v. 28 righteous (psalmist).	vv. 1–9, 10 "Blessed is the man who fears the LORD"; "The wicked man will see and be vexed."			
Rewards and Retributions	v. 10 "Many are the woes of the wicked, but the LORD's unfailing love surrounds the man who trusts in him."		vv. 10–20		vv. 18–20, 27 (wicked); vv. 23–26 (righteous)	vv. 2–9 "Even in darkness light dawns for the upright, for the gracious and compassionate and righteous man."		vv. 2–6 The Lord blesses the one who fears him with many children and a long life.	
Qualities of the Righteous	v. 11 upright in heart		vv. 21, 26, 30–31 "The wicked borrow and do not repay, but the righteous give generously."						
Worth/Benefits of the Righteous/Righteousness		vv. 15, 17, 19 Lord's ears are "attentive to their cry"; "The righteous cry out, and the LORD hears them; he delivers them from all their troubles."	vv. 6, 16, 17, 25, 29, 30–31, 39–40 "He will make your righteousness shine like the dawn, the justice of your cause like the noonday sun"; "Better the little that the righteous have than the wealth of many wicked; for the power of the wicked will be broken, but the LORD upholds the righteous."			vv. 3, 4, 6–8, 9 "Wealth and riches are in his house, and his righteousness endures forever"; "Even in darkness light dawns for the upright, for the gracious and compassionate and righteous man"; "A righteous man will be remembered forever. He will have no fear of bad news; his heart is steadfast, trusting in the LORD. His heart is secure, he will have no fear; in the end he will look in triumph on his foes."			
Search for Understanding of Life's Problems				vv. 5–20 The prosperous die like all humans. The lesson is summed up in v. 20: "A man who has riches without understanding is like the beasts that perish."	vv. 2–3, 16–17 "For I envied the arrogant when I saw the prosperity of the wicked"; "When I tried to understand all this, it was oppressive to me till I entered the sanctuary of God; then I understood their final destiny."				
Wisdom Vocabulary by Number (See "Wisdom Terms")	v. 1 no. 5 v. 2 nos. 5, 73 v. 8 no. 15 v. 10 no. 70 v. 11 nos. 33, 66	v. 7 no. 31 v. 8 no. 5 v. 11 no. 30 vv. 15, 17, 19 no. 66 v. 21 nos. 66, 70	v. 1 no. 58 vv. 4, 15, 31 no. 42 vv. 5, 23, 34 no. 11 v. 6 no. 67 v. 7 nos. 11, 49 vv. 10, 12, 14, 16, 20, 21, 28, 32, 34, 35, 38, 40 no. 70 v. 14 no. 11 vv. 14, 37 no. 36 v. 18 nos. 32, 83 v. 30 no. 23 v. 37 no. 82	v. 3 nos. 23, 42, 78 v. 4 nos. 16, 50	v. 3, 12 no. 70 v. 11 nos. 10, 32 vv. 13, 21, 26 no. 43 v. 16 nos. 9, 60 v. 17 no. 6 v. 22 no. 32	v. 1 nos. 5, 31 v. 2 no. 36 v. 3 no. 68 v. 4 nos. 36, 66 v. 6 no. 66 vv. 7, 8 nos. 31, 42 v. 9 no. 68 v. 10 nos. 39, 70, 77	v. 5 no. 5	v. 1 nos. 5, 31 v. 4 no. 31	

The Penitential Psalms

The case can be made that great men and women throughout the Bible and church history have been men and women of repentance. The more we see of God and his glory, the more we become aware of indwelling sin, and therefore the more we find repentance to be a way of life. As George Whitefield said, "The indwelling of sin in the heart is the burden of a converted person; it is the burden of a true Christian."[1] Therefore it follows that the so-called penitential psalms were often on the lips of great people of God. Psalm 32 was Augustine's favorite, even setting it above his bed that he might immediately see it upon waking.[2] Of this psalm he said, "The beginning of understanding is to know thyself a sinner."[3] Even on his deathbed he asked that the penitential psalms be written out and placed where he could see them.[4] According to Martin Luther, the greatest of psalms were the "Psalmi Paulini" (Pauline Psalms). He considered these to be Psalms 32, 51, 130, and 143, which were all penitential psalms.[5] Of course, Scripture does not attach these psalms to the apostle Paul, yet its propriety cannot be doubted for the man who considered himself the chief of sinners.

1. George Whitefield, *Select Sermons of George Whitefield* (Carlisle, Pa.: Banner of Truth, 1997), 81.
2. Rowland E. Prothero, *The Psalms in Human Life* (New York: E. P. Dutton, 1905), 38.
3. John Ker, *The Psalms in History and Biography* (Edinburgh: Andrew Elliot, 1888), 58.
4. Prothero, *The Psalms in Human Life*, 18.
5. Ker, *The Psalms in History and Biography*, 58.

They were the common property of human beings, and any worldview could make them a topic of discussion. The difference, of course, is that wisdom tended to concentrate on certain themes and prophecy on others. Thus, it seems appropriate to type a psalm as a wisdom psalm when it meets both criteria, style and motif, outlined above. On the basis of this, I have identified Psalms 32, 34, 37, 49, 73, 112, 127, 128, and 133 as wisdom psalms. In table 12.2, I have not included Psalms 1, 19, and 119, even though they exhibit wisdom characteristics, because I will include them in the Torah psalms, nor have I included Psalm 78, which would be included in the psalms of history.

Structure and Motif in the Wisdom Psalms

Psalm 32 qualifies as a wisdom psalm both in *style* and *theme*. Right off, the use of the "blessed" formula in verses 1 and 2 suggests a stylistic feature of wisdom. The use of the simile (v. 9) with its comparison from nature ("like the horse or the mule") is a second stylistic feature. The wisdom *theme* of reward and retribution also characterizes the psalm (v. 10). While the theme of the psalm is divine forgiveness and mercy, a theme that could belong particularly to the psalms of lament and the psalms of praise, the psalm uses ample wisdom vocabulary to reinforce this classification (see table 12.2).

Craigie[9] has pointed out that the poem exhibits a chiastic structure, with wisdom and thanksgiving providing the points of the "Chi":

A Wisdom (vv. 1–2)
  B Thanksgiving (vv. 3–5)
  B′ Thanksgiving (vv. 6–8)
A′ Wisdom (vv. 9–10)
Concluding praise (v. 11)

The early Christian church had its own system of classifying the Psalms, and Psalm 32 was the second in a list of seven penitential psalms (6, 32, 38, 51, 102, 130, 143). While they are not all strictly "penitential," Psalms 51 and 130 are definitely prayers of penitence, and Psalms 32 and 102 are laments related to an illness, perhaps stemming from the psalmist's sin (32:3). The tone of all seven penitential psalms, however, is one of submission to the almighty God, a necessary disposition for anyone who would seek God's forgiveness.[10]

Psalm 34 is the second of the wisdom psalms. Stylistically, it contains proverbs (vv. 6, 7, 8), a substantive wisdom admonition on the good life as compared to the evil way (vv. 11–14), an address to the psalmist's students as "sons" (v. 11), and the *blessed* formula (v. 8b). In addition to these characteristics, the alphabetic acrostic lends itself to the wisdom mode. Thematically, the psalm discusses the antithetical ways of life (vv. 14, 15) and has a generous sprinkling of wisdom vocabulary (see table 12.2).

Psalm 37 is replete with wisdom traits. Thematically, the striking characteristic of the psalm is its contrast between the righteous and the wicked. But stylistically it also has many features of wisdom. Proverbial statements (vv. 16, 21), wisdom admonitions (vv. 1, 3, 4, 5, 8), similes drawing upon nature (vv. 2, 6, 20, 35), one "better saying" (v. 16), and a generous use of wisdom vocabulary (see table 12.2) outfit this psalm with the features of wisdom. The contrast between the two ways, that of the wicked and that of the righteous, clearly gives Psalm 37 the mark of wisdom thought. In addition, the alphabet acrostic style of poetry lends assistance to wisdom's thought. All twenty-two letters of the Hebrew alphabet inscribe the thoughts of wisdom in this psalm with a sense of completion.

Psalm 49 lays out its thematic emphasis on wealth and poverty, with death as the great equalizer:

> Why should I fear when evil days come,
> > when wicked deceivers surround me—
> those who trust in their wealth
> > and boast of their great riches?
> > (vv. 5–6)

Wealth may seem to make a great difference in life, but death equalizes whatever advantages the wealthy had and whatever disadvantages the poor endured. It cannot create a differential that will matter when that awesome moment comes:

> But man, despite his riches, does not endure;
> > he is like the beasts that perish.
> This is the fate of those who trust in themselves,
> > and of their followers, who approve their sayings.

> Like sheep they are destined for the grave,
> > and death will feed on them.
> The upright will rule over them in the morning;
> > their forms will decay in the grave,
> > far from their princely mansions.
> But God will redeem my life from the grave;
> > he will surely take me to himself. (vv. 12–15)

There is in fact a differential, but it is on the side of wisdom, and it applies to life as well as death. It applies to life in that wisdom ("understanding") makes a difference in the hope that the wise person has, and vice versa; it is a constant deficiency in the soul of the wealthy: "A man who has riches without understanding / is like the beasts that perish" (v. 20). And it applies to death in that the wise have hope that the foolish do not have. Although the psalmist did not have the fuller understanding of life after death that we have because of the resurrection of Christ and the New Testament teaching, he nevertheless believed death would not end his existence. The point of contrast is in fact the decay of the rich person's body in the grave and God's redemption of the poor wise person from the grave (vv. 14–15). He had come to that plateau of faith to which Job ascended and on which he rejoiced and exclaimed:

> I know that my Redeemer lives,
> > and that in the end he will stand upon the earth.
> And after my skin has been destroyed,
> > yet in my flesh I will see God;
> I myself will see him
> > with my own eyes—I, and not another.
> How my heart yearns within me!
> > (Jb 19:25–27)

Psalm 73 exhibits stylistic features of wisdom in two ways: (1) vocabulary (see table 12.2) and (2) the contrast of the two ways, the latter done quite descriptively. The psalmist provides a context for his words by an affirmation at the beginning and the end of the psalm:

> Surely God is good to Israel,
>> to those who are pure in heart.
>>> (v. 1)

> But as for me, it is good to be near God.
>> I have made the Sovereign LORD my refuge;
> I will tell of all your deeds. (v. 28)

In that context, the psalmist lays the problem on the table:

> But as for me, my feet had almost slipped;
>> I had nearly lost my foothold.
> For I envied the arrogant
>> when I saw the prosperity of the wicked. (vv. 2–3)

The problem was as much the psalmist's inner struggle with his own envy as with the question of why the wicked prosper. His observation of the wicked's life was much like Job's—their prosperity was unmistakable:

> They have no struggles;
>> their bodies are healthy and strong.
> They are free from the burdens common to man;
>> they are not plagued by human ills. (vv. 4–5)

Their prosperity led them to a sense of security and well-being, exhibited in their arrogant spirit, however false its promptings were:

> Therefore pride is their necklace;
>> they clothe themselves with violence.
> From their callous hearts comes iniquity;
>> the evil conceits of their minds know no limits.
> They scoff, and speak with malice;
>> in their arrogance they threaten oppression.
> Their mouths lay claim to heaven,
>> and their tongues take possession of the earth.
> Therefore their people turn to them
>> and drink up waters in abundance.

> They say, "How can God know?
>> Does the Most High have knowledge?"
> This is what the wicked are like—
>> always carefree, they increase in wealth. (vv. 6–12)

In this psalm the contrast of the two ways is a contrast of two lifestyles, or two character types. After the description of the wicked, the psalmist sketches his own innocence, which has done him very little good, as far as he can discern:

> Surely in vain have I kept my heart pure;
>> in vain have I washed my hands in innoccence.
> All day long I have been plagued;
>> I have been punished every morning. (vv. 13–14)

In the absence of understanding, the psalmist's ethical system was thrown out of focus by his observations of the prosperity of the wicked until he entered the "sanctuary of God." The new understanding that began to dawn upon him was more a change in his own spirit, which was the problem from the beginning ("I envied the arrogant," v. 3), than it was a change in the realities of the world around him. In worship he found affirmation of the confidence he expressed in the first and last verses of the psalm, a position to which his worship experience contributed. His subsequent confession, a reminder of Job's confession (Jb 42:1–6), was a post-worship recognition:

> When my heart was grieved
>> and my spirit embittered,
> I was senseless and ignorant;
>> I was a brute beast before you.
>>> (vv. 21–22)

The psalmist, enlightened and relieved of his anxiety in worship, draws a further contrast between the outcome of the condition of the wicked and that of the innocent, in this case, himself:

> The wicked:
> Surely you place them on slippery ground;

you cast them down to ruin.
How suddenly are they destroyed,
  completely swept away by
    terrors!
As a dream when one awakes,
  so when you arise, O Lord,
  you will despise them as fanta-
    sies. (vv. 18–20)

The innocent (righteous):
Yet I am always with you;
  you hold me by my right hand.
You guide me with your counsel,
  and afterward you will take me
    into glory.
Whom have I in heaven but you?
  And earth has nothing I desire
    besides you.
My flesh and my heart may fail,
  but God is the strength of my
    heart
  and my portion forever.
    (vv. 23–26)

In verse 25 the psalmist receives the answer to his real problem, the problem of envy. Now his real desire has turned away from the wicked and their easy life to the object of all desire, God himself: "And earth has nothing I desire besides you." Not only does the psalmist's experience put his problem in a new perspective, but his heart has been changed and his greed transmuted to a longing after God. The prosperity of the wicked and the benefits of righteousness is one of the major themes of wisdom literature, and the solution put forth here in Psalm 73 is one of the grandest of the literature. It equals the God speeches in the Book of Job (Jb 38–41), where Job's attention was refocused on the Lord himself rather than the wicked and their estate in life, however tenuous or temporary, and upon the joy of knowing him: "My ears had heard of you / but now my eyes have seen you" (Jb 42:5).

The psalmist's experience was qualitatively no less powerful and life-changing than Job's. The wicked still existed, but he no longer focused upon them. His attitude had undergone a spiritual overhauling, and finally he was aware that God held him by his right hand and guided him with his counsel (73:23b, 24a).

Psalm 112 stylistically has little to commend it as a wisdom psalm, apart from the one occurrence of the "blessed" formula in verse 1. But that alone turns the reader's mind to the thought of Psalm 1, where the psalmist's "delight is in the law of the LORD" (v. 2), just as the anonymous poet of Psalm 112 pronounces that person "blessed" (see also 1:1) "who fears the LORD, / who finds great delight in his commands." The theme of these psalms is identical, even though they develop that theme differently. Psalm 1 draws the contrast between the two ways more evenly, while Psalm 112 fixes its sight on the blessings of the one who fears the Lord. In comparison to Psalm 49, Psalm 112 capitalizes on the life of the righteous rather than the life of the fool. Verses 2–9 form that description, while the contrast is completed in the last verse: "The wicked man will see and be vexed, / he will gnash his teeth and waste away; / the longings of the wicked will come to nothing" (v. 10).

The theme quite interestingly turns the tables on the problem. The concern of wisdom literature was often the prosperity of the wicked as it raised questions in the minds of the righteous—why do the wicked prosper and the righteous suffer? Why do the wicked enjoy so many good things while the righteous have so little? This psalm turns from the ponderings of the righteous about this problem to put the ponderings in the mind of the wicked. He will be troubled by the great blessings he sees in the life of the righteous. It is indeed a pleasant turn of thought.

Psalm 127, attributed to Solomon, represents an expression of faith that agrees with Solomon's great wisdom and his dependence upon God found in 1 Kings 3 and 8. The use of proverbs in this poem (vv. 2, 3; see Prv 16:3, 9; 17:6) and the occurrence of wisdom admonitions (vv. 1–2, 3–5) are the most that can be said in favor of its stylistic kinship to wisdom. The wisdom factor lies largely in the theme of the psalm: human efforts are of little value unless the Lord has his hand on the project:

Gudea of Lagash sits before his god and on his knees holds the plans of the sanctuary he expects to build, a reminder to the god, Ningirsu, of all his preparations for the task of building.

Unless the LORD builds the house,
  its builders labor in vain.
Unless the LORD watches over the
  city,
  the watchmen stand guard in
  vain. (v. 1)

The psalm deals with three major institutions of Israel's life, and declares all human activity useless unless the Lord is the Architect. That applies to the temple, the city, and the home. By extension, unless God is the Designer/Architect of society, then all human effort is in vain.

Psalm 128 is a companion psalm to Psalm 127, reinforcing its theme of children as the Lord's special blessing on the human family. Stylistically, it features the blessings of those who fear the Lord, and it opens with the "blessed" formula (v. 1). Thematically it continues the thought of Psalm 127 regarding children and the central place of the temple and the city (Zion) from which the Lord blesses Israel (vv. 5–6). It gives a fuller picture of the blessing that accrues when the Lord is the Designer/Architect of the social order.

Psalm 133, while it does not begin with the "blessed" formula, does nevertheless introduce an equivalent pronouncement in its phrase, "How good and pleasant" (v. 1; see Prv 15:23). This psalm of David puts forward the theme of family unity. The modifications of this theme had shaped David's life for both good and ill. It recalls the worth of the precious oil poured generously on Aaron at his ordination to the priesthood (v. 2) and the pleasantness of the Mount Hermon dew should it fall on Jerusalem (v. 3). It is there on Mount Zion that the Lord bestows his blessing.

Summary

The wisdom psalms are not prayers as such but reflections on life and life's problems. They belong to a broad category of literature, *didactic*, that seeks to instruct the readers on a particular issue or way of life. The wisdom psalms represent a way of thinking and conceptualizing the Hebrew faith that, alongside priesthood and prophecy, composed the expanse of Old Testament theology. The wisdom movement stressed the importance of the individual, in comparison to the more corporate orientation of the priests and prophets. Moreover, in line with the prophets, wisdom reduced the religious life to its lowest common denominator, moral obedience, as opposed to the more perfunctory observance of the law that Israel commonly believed was sufficient to please God. The wisdom teachers taught that the whole of faith could be summed up in the fear of the Lord. And this was not merely an emotion but a spiritual disposition, not merely a theological precept but the principle of the good life, not merely a way of knowing but a way of being. The wisdom psalms express this view of faith and life in various ways.

The two criteria that mark a psalm as wisdom are the *formal criteria* relating to literary style, such as proverbs, wisdom admonitions, the use of similes, the occurrence of the "blessed" formula (*'ashre*), the address to students as "sons" or "children," and the occurrence of "better" sayings. The second criterion is *thematic.* Of course, here we are dealing with content, and we determine these wisdom motifs on the basis of the wisdom literature as we have it in the wisdom books of Job, Proverbs, and Ecclesiastes. Some of the wisdom motifs identifiable there are the contrast of the two ways of life, the problem of retribution for good and evil deeds,

Key Terms

wisdom psalms
proverbial wisdom
reflective wisdom
prophecy
wisdom motifs

practical advice on living, and the all-encompassing notion of the fear of the Lord. On the basis of these criteria, both of which should characterize the psalm in varying degrees, we have typed the following psalms as wisdom psalms: Psalms 32, 34, 37, 49, 73, 112, 127, 128, and 133. While Psalms 1, 19, and 119 also belong in the wisdom genre, these share the Torah label too, and we will discuss them under that rubric.

Study Questions

1. Wisdom thinking occurs within the wider Hebraic context of Torah and prophecy. Each of these three offices represents a "way of describing God, his relationship to the world, and the horizontal networks in the world itself." Describe the role of wisdom within a religious life governed by Torah and prophecy. How does wisdom fill a kind of lacuna between Torah and prophecy?

2. Wisdom literature contains both proverbial and reflective wisdom, often called "lower" and "higher" wisdom. What would be an example of each type? Give an example from the Psalms where each differently addresses the prosperity of the wicked.

3. Wisdom psalms are essentially characterized by style and motif. What are six stylistic features of the wisdom psalms?

4. Although the style is certainly evident in wisdom psalms, motif or theme is "by far the most important feature of wisdom poetry." What four wisdom motifs define the wisdom psalms?

5. Practically, the wisdom psalms reduce religious life to its lowest common denominator: moral obedience. How did this offer a corrective to the "perfunctory observance of the law that Israel commonly believed was sufficient to please God"? Would an emphasis on this wisdom message have changed the way Jesus was treated by the ceremonial guardians of Torah in his day?

13 "The Law of the LORD Is Perfect, Reviving the Soul"

The Psalms of Torah

Objectives

After reading this chapter, you should be able to
1. Define and describe the psalms of Torah.
2. Describe the spiritual provenance of the Psalter.
3. Summarize the theology of Torah as set forth in Psalm 119.

piety

Torah

Torah psalms

In wisdom literature two mind-sets stood opposite each other: the way of the wicked and the way of the righteous. As individual **piety** developed in the direction of postexilic wisdom thought, the way of the righteous became synonymous with the way of **Torah**. It was a natural development of theology as it capitalized upon the spiritual essence of the Torah. While it is an oversimplification to say that the Torah, or law, of the Old Testament can be broken down into two parts, the ceremonial and the ethical, that is nevertheless a helpful way to look at the Torah. We should further observe that the prophets and the Psalms sought to distill the essence of the Torah, and they put forth the thesis that it is found, not in sacrifice or ritual, but in doing the will of God, or in a right relationship to God and one's fellow human beings (Mi 6:8; Pss 40:6; 50:23; 51:16–17; 141:2). More and more that essence came to be identified as the Torah, just as the prophets had sought to do. So by the time the Psalter had reached its final stage of composition, meditating on the Torah was the essence of the pious life. The theological high road the prophets attempted to draw out for Israel had become the path along which the individual walked with God. The Torah, the body of law that revealed God's will to Israel, had become the individual's prescribed program of doing the will of God. What the Old Testament, especially wisdom literature, called *righteousness*, could be achieved along this path of meditation on and implementation of the Torah. The Psalter thus opens with a pronouncement of blessedness on those who meditate constantly upon the Torah:

> Blessed is the man
>> who does not walk in the counsel of the wicked
> or stand in the way of sinners
>> or sit in the seat of mockers.
> But his delight is in the law of the LORD,
>> and on his law he meditates day and night. (Ps 1:1–2)

As we have recognized elsewhere, Psalm 1 was most likely installed as an introduction to the final collection, giving the imprint of Torah to the entire book and labeling the kind of piety this collection cultivates in the soul. Psalm 2, which forms a companion poem to Psalm 1,[1] sketches an outline of the eschatological era that results from a Torah-centered life: by such meditation, the Messiah of Israel will be firmly established on the world stage, and through him the sovereign reign of God will become reality.

Description of the Torah Psalms and Definition of Torah

Description of the Torah Psalms

The **Torah psalms,** as the name suggests, focus upon the Torah with its multiple facets of theological expression. Only three psalms, Psalms 1, 19, and 119, can be called Torah psalms in the true sense of the word; that is, their major concentration is the Torah. Torah psalms do not comprise a literary genre of the Psalms, since there is no standard literary pattern comparable to what we have seen with some other literary genres. On the basis of their content, however, they nevertheless form a legitimate category.

Other psalms dealing with the notion of Torah, although it is not their key idea, are Psalms 18, 25, 33, 68, 78, 81, 89, 93, 94, 99, 103, 105, 111, 112, 147, and 148. Our definition of Torah in the following section is based upon these nineteen psalms.

As we have discussed, Psalms 1 and 2 form a pair of psalms in the composition of the Psalter, even though they might have been composed and installed in their present contexts at different times. As they now stand in mutual relationship, Psalm 2 puts Psalm 1 in an eschatological setting, anticipating the day when the Torah and its power to

A Scottish Paraphrase of Psalm 1

The Scottish love for the Psalms is very deep and goes a long way back into history. The earliest version of Psalm 1 known in Scotland is by Alexander Montgomery, who lived in the time of King James VI. The following paraphrase shows the beauty of Alexander's poetry and the tendency of the Scottish tradition to stay close to the original text of the Psalms. The language has been modernized:

I.

That man is blest,
And is possessed
Of truest rest,
Who from ungodly counsel turns his feet;
Who walks not in
The way of sin,
Nor comes within
The place where mockers take their shameful seat;
But in God's law to go
He doth delight;
And studies it to know
Both day and night.
That man shall be—like to a tree
Which by the running river spreads its shade;
Which fruit does bear—in time of year;
Whose root is firm, whose leaf shall never fade.

II.

His actions all
Still prosper shall;
So doth not fall
To wicked men; whom, as the chaff and sand,
Winds, day by day,
Shall drive away;
Therefore I say
The wicked in the judgment shall not stand:
Neither shall sinners dare,
Whom God disdains,
To enter the assembly where
The just remains.
For God most pure, keeps record sure;
He knows the righteous' heart and converse aye:
But like the fire—kindles his ire
'Gainst wicked men, till they consume away.[1]

1. John Ker, *The Psalms in History and Biography* (Edinburgh: Andrew Elliot, 1888), 18–19.

18 and 118 respectively. Like Psalm 2, Psalm 18 sets Israel's national troubles in the arena of world history and Israel's salvation within that history. Even though the "I" of the original psalm is David, when read in the context of Israel's national experience, as the Psalter came to be read, this personal pronoun has come to have a corporate nuance, and David's deliverance from Saul to adumbrate eschatological salvation. Both psalms sketch out the divine theophany, Psalm 18:2–19 in terms of God's manifestations in the exodus and at Sinai (redemption), resulting in the salvation of the nation, and Psalm 19:1–6 in terms of the natural order (creation), resulting in the salvation of the individual through the power of Torah.

Psalm 118 celebrates the deliverance of a righteous one who has been rejected, and Psalm 119 is a prayer for salvation by those who have been rejected because of their devotion to Torah.[2] The eschatological context that Psalm 118 opens up (e.g., v. 22) puts Psalm 119 in the larger arena of the kingdom of God, functioning in a very similar relationship to that of Psalms 18 and 19. Mays has proposed that this contextualization is intentional: "In all three cases, the purpose of the pairing seems to be the provision of an eschatological context for a piety based in Torah. . . . The reason is the eschatological context of the Torah piety—the hope for the coming kingdom of God."[3]

Definition of Torah

At the heart of Torah is the law God imparted to Israel on Mount Sinai. This law, which was to govern all aspects of Israel's life, was already written on the heart of Israel's revered ancestor, Abraham. Long before Moses received the law on Sinai, the Lord had declared that "Abraham obeyed me and kept my requirements, my commands, my decrees and my laws" (Gn 26:5). His life of faith pleased God (Gn 15:6), and the relationship between God and Abraham was a living example of the law written in human flesh, a relationship

change lives will eventuate in a new era of the Lord's sovereign reign through his Messiah. Mays has pointed out that Psalms 19 and 119 also have an eschatological relationship to their prior neighbors, Psalms

An ancient Torah ark sculptured in stone from the fourth or fifth century A.D. at Capernaum. In the synagogue, the written scroll of the Torah was kept in an ark such as this. In the Psalms, however, the concept of Torah is much broader than a written document. It is a way of life and virtually synonymous with our notion of a worldview.

to which the Lord would eventually restore Israel in the eschatological day (Jer 31:31–34).

The word "Torah" has many companion terms in the Psalms. The sum total of this concept is that it is God's will for human life divinely revealed and historically implemented in the story of Israel and mankind. In the Psalms God's law, or Torah, takes at least three forms: God's ways, God's works, and God's words.

God's Ways

The Psalms call attention to God's actions in history, sometimes called "the ways of the LORD" or his "paths" or "deeds," which simultaneously teach his character. That is the meaning of the term in Psalm 103, where David affirmed that Yahweh had "made known his ways to Moses, / his deeds to the people of Israel" (v. 7). And then the poet laureate of Israel moved into a description of the Lord's character, evidently expressed through his actions: "The LORD is compassionate and gracious, / slow to anger, abounding in love" (v. 8).

We would call this *natural theology*, meaning that, to some extent, one can know God through nature. But in the final analysis, we only know the true character of God through the interpretation of the mighty acts of God in

history as found in Scripture. Psalm 103 draws upon that knowledge as laid out in the Torah.

The "ways of the LORD," which are sketched along the lines of history, come to be so closely associated with the personality of God that they prescribe the mode of life that should characterize those who do his will:

> Blessed are they who keep his
>   statutes
>   and seek him with all their
>   heart.
> They do nothing wrong;
>   they walk in his ways.
>   (Ps 119:2–3)

Here God's "ways" are equivalent to his "statutes," suggesting that the written law of God was an inscripturation of his character. When one obeyed God's statutes, one lived according to his ways. Psalm 25 uses the two words "ways" and "paths" in parallel lines and summarizes the concept they embody in the phrase "your truth":

> Show me *your ways*, O LORD,
>   teach me *your paths*;
> guide me in *your truth* and teach
>   me,
>   for you are God my Savior,
>   and my hope is in you all day
>   long. (vv. 4–5, emphasis
>   added)

God's Works

The Psalms also present the concept of Torah in terms of God's works. The vocabulary of Torah ethics, such as "justice," "righteousness," and "truth," comes into prominence in the Psalms as an expression of God's revelation of his will and character. The all-but-invisible seam between God's "ways" and his works of justice and goodness can be detected in Psalm 25:8–9:

> *Good* and *upright* is the LORD;
>   therefore he instructs sinners in
>   his *ways*.
> He guides the humble in *what is*
>   *right* [*mishpat*]
>   and teaches them his *way*. (emphasis added)

As the Lord performs his works in history, he reveals himself in their character. Psalm 111 uses the nouns "truth" and "justice" as complements to "precepts": "The *works* of his hands are *faithful* and *just*; / all his *precepts* are trustworthy" (v. 7, emphasis added).

While the NIV describes God's precepts with the adjectives "faithful" and "just," the words are actually the nouns "truth" and "justice." That suggests that God's truth and justice are written into the divine precepts. Indeed, his precepts are equivalent to the justice and truth that he dispenses. While the Hebrew word for "just" (*mishpat*, from the verb *shaphat*, "to judge") may carry the meaning of law or decree, in company with the noun "truth" (*'emeth*), it likely carries the nuance of "justice" in this instance. Psalm 119 employs the word "justice" (*mishpat*) with the ethical noun "righteousness" to form the phrase "righteous laws" (vv. 7, 62, 106, 164), implying the ethical nature of the law. Thus God reveals himself and his character in the works he performs in the social order.

God's Words

When we think of Torah, we think of words, both oral and written. This is the category where we have the richest vocabulary: word(s) [*davar*,

'omer, *'imrah*] decrees/statutes [*khoqim*], precepts [*piqqudhim*], testimony [*'edhuth*], commandments [*mitsvoth*], covenant [*berith*], and law [*torah*]. These words generally denote a spoken or written communication. While some critics believe that the Torah or the laws of Israel were written rather late, we know that written codes of law were quite common in the ancient world. Regardless of the auxiliary modes of revelation mentioned above, God's *ways* and *works*, his main mode of communication is verbal. The terms for this mode occur numerous times in the Torah psalms.[4] Psalm 119, with its prolific vocabulary of Torah, declares "blessed" those who "walk according to the law of the LORD" (v. 1). These oral and written words of revelation are the source of the psalmist's joy and knowledge of the Lord, even though the auxiliary modes also figure into the larger picture.

Torah Piety as the Spiritual Provenance of the Psalter

It is my view that personal piety was a spiritual phenomenon that characterized Hebrew religion from the very beginning. There can be no corporate piety that is not undergirded by the personal. Further, the stories of Enoch, Noah, Abraham, and Joseph that form the bulk of the Genesis narrative are cut from the cloth of ancient history. Yet, in view of the collective personality of ancient Israel, evidenced by the fact that the Torah and the prophets addressed the nation as a whole, rather than individuals, personal piety was probably a subset of corporate piety. Not until the individual moved to a more prominent place in the Hebrew religion, during the Babylonian exile and afterwards, did personal piety take center stage in worship. Even then it shared that position with corporate piety. When the nation had ceased to exist as a kingdom, personal piety became the dominant mode of religious expression. This kind of piety drew from the preexilic psalms and shaped the psalms of the exile and postexilic era. In that spiritual climate the Book of Psalms was hastened on its way toward expansion and eventual completion in the postexilic era. The life setting for the development of the Psalms was religious piety, and even when corporate piety took center stage, personal piety undergirded and validated it. Mays reminds us that "the Psalms were reread in the light of this piety and it in turn was constantly shaped by the use of the Psalms."[5]

Torah and Wisdom

In the broad view, Torah and wisdom represent two paradigms of faith, with wisdom complementing and rephrasing the shape of faith as found in Torah. For example, as already alluded to above, the perspective of Torah was focused on the nation of Israel, while that of wisdom was turned on the individual. Strangely, the wisdom books of the Old Testament do not capitalize on history as the medium of divine revelation as do the Torah and the Prophets. God's revelation, in the view of the wisdom writers, is written in nature and human conscience. But we have to admit that the wisdom teachers spoke out of their theological context that was steeped in the teachings of Torah. Divine revelation, which they identified as coming forth from the natural order and found in human conscience, was a product of creation. God had, when he created the world, endowed nature and human conscience with clear traces of his personality and purpose.

The wisdom writers did not want to overemphasize the details of the Torah paradigm of faith, like sacrifice, vows, and other functional features. Nor were they ignorant of them (e.g., Eccl 5:1–7). Rather they sought to highlight the ethical content of the Torah, just as the prophets

did. It may not be coincidental that the Torah psalms do not have specific references to historical events, as is also the case with the wisdom books, even though some of the psalms in the Torah constellation mentioned above certainly do draw upon the details of history (e.g., 78, 89, 103, 105).

It is an irony that just as the demands and the restrictions of Torah brought wisdom to a place of prominence, so wisdom in time gave way to the demands and statutes of Torah, which it was designed to serve. In fact, this is indeed the triumph of wisdom: that the theological paradigm it sought to serve became in time the basic paradigm of Israel. Wisdom accomplished its purpose. Yet, the centrality of Torah and its legalistic domination of Israel's thought and life after the exile represented an overextension of wisdom's goal.

The Torah Psalms

Psalm 1

We have already dealt with Psalm 1 as an introduction to the Psalter.[6] Now we need to say another word about the psalm as a Torah psalm. Some have suggested, quite hypothetically, that Psalm 1 and Psalm 119 began and concluded an earlier edition of the book. It is difficult to say why Psalms 19 and 119 are placed in their present position in the collection. Psalm 1, as observed above, is another matter. Quite likely, the kind of Torah piety that brought the Psalter to its final form was the impetus for the installment of Psalm 1 as the title page of the book. Meditation on the Torah was the key to the blessed life, and such a demeanor stamped the entire collection with its piety. The way of the wicked is set in sharp contrast to the way of those who meditated on the Torah (vv. 1–2). In this sense it belongs to the category of the wisdom psalms.

As the postexilic community of Israel sought stability after the traumatic loss of kingdom and dignity,

At winnowing time, the grain is thrown into the air, and the wind drives away the chaff while the heavier grain falls to the ground.

Psalm 1 put forth the prescription of meditating on the Torah. The ground level of meaning should be viewed in dimensions of personal piety. Yet, as the frontispiece of the book, and in view of the ongoing political austerity to which the nation was subjected, meditating on the Torah of the Lord was more than a way of life for the individual. It was a way to deal with the problem of injustice. The problem is set in the context of the solution, meditating on the Lord's Torah. The permanence of those who meditate on the Torah ("like a tree planted by streams of water") is placed over against the impermanence of the wicked ("like chaff that the wind blows away"). The two images are quite different, but the contrast between the stability of the righteous person and the instability of wicked is quite striking. The person who follows the admonition of the psalm is "blessed," whereas the person who lives the sinner's life "will perish." These two terms stand at the opposite poles of the psalm as symbols of the two ways they describe. Thus the two ways contrasted in this poem lead in two opposite directions, the one to blessedness and delight, and the other to disrepute (v. 5) and disappearance.

The psalmist describes what it means to be blessed—it means having a solid foundation to stand on, and that foundation is delighting in and meditating on the Torah.[7] This path leads to spiritual maturity.

Psalm 19

C. S. Lewis thought this psalm to be the greatest poem in the Psalter and one of the greatest lyrics of the world.[8] Its cadences move from creation to redemption, from the world

The tree "planted by streams of water" (Ps 1:3) is a graphic image of the life of those who meditate on the Torah day and night.

to the Torah, from the sky to the earth. The poet assigns six verses to the wonders of creation (vv. 1–6), five to the transforming nature of the Torah (vv. 7–11), and three to his own spiritual musings (vv. 12–14). Although some assign this psalm to two different authors, Craigie is inclined toward a single author, or at least a poet who has utilized an older hymn of creation and made it a solid piece with his hymn on the Torah. It proclaims the ubiquitous presence of the word of God, first proclaimed by the heavens in all the cosmos, and second proclaimed by the Torah in human society. The same word (*'omer*) occurs for "speech" in the first stanza (v. 2) and in the psalmist's prayer that his "words" (*'imre*, from same root) be heard (v. 14), binding the two stanzas together.

> The heavens declare the glory of
>   God;
>   the skies declare the work of his
>   hands.
> Day after day they pour forth
>   speech [*'omer*];
>   night after night they display
>   knowledge.
> There is no speech [*'omer*] or
>   language
>   where their voice is not heard.
>   (vv. 1–3)

> May the words (*'imre*) of my mouth
>   and the meditation of my
>   heart
> be pleasing in your sight,
> O LORD, my Rock and my Re-
>   deemer. (v. 14)

Craigie has remarked that the poem moves from macrocosm to microcosm, from universal wonder to individual humility before God,[9] and the climax is in the microcosmic beauty and power of the Torah. Just as the heavens declare God's glory universally in the everyday cadences of nature, so the Torah of the Lord speaks the transforming word of grace:

> The law of the LORD is perfect,
>   reviving the soul.
> The statutes of the LORD are
>   trustworthy,

> making wise the simple.
> The precepts of the LORD are right,
>   giving joy to the heart.
> The commands of the LORD are
>   radiant,
>   giving light to the eyes.
> The fear of the LORD is pure,
>   enduring forever.
> The ordinances of the LORD are
>   sure
>   and altogether righteous.
> They are more precious than gold,
>   than much pure gold;
> they are sweeter than honey,
>   than honey from the comb.
> By them is your servant warned;
>   in keeping them there is great
>   reward. (vv. 7–11)

Lewis has pointed out that the link between the two stanzas occurs in verse 7, "nothing is hidden from its heat."[10] The Torah dominates human life as the sun dominates the daytime sky.[11] Under that scrutiny David poses the rhetorical question, "Who can discern his errors?" And the petition that follows implies the answer that no one, under the scrutiny of the Torah as under the heat of the sun, can escape the consciousness of his or her sins.[12]

Psalm 119

This psalm is an alphabetic acrostic, the best of the craft. A poem of twenty-two strophes, equal to the number of letters in the Hebrew alphabet, it begins with the first letter and proceeds systematically through the alphabet, letter by letter. Each strophe is eight lines long, and each of those lines begins with the same letter of the alphabet appropriate to that strophe. One older commentator calls this psalm "a holy alphabet for Zion's scholars." Lewis describes this poem in these words:

> this poem is not, and does not pretend to be a sudden outpouring of the heart like, say, Psalm 18. It is a pattern, a thing done like embroidery, stitch by stitch, through long, quiet hours, for love of the subject and for the delight in leisurely, disciplined craftsmanship.[13]

Each verse, except verse 122, contains at least one word for the Torah. The fact that the poem exhausts the alphabet to describe and praise the Torah would suggest that the poet intended to describe its all-encompassing nature. He has worked over the Torah from "A" to "Z," as it were, and looked at it from the linguistic angle of every single Hebrew letter. This is coupled with the fact that each strophe sustains the same letter in each of its eight verses, intensifying the extensive nature of the Torah. After the alphabet had been exhausted and each letter used as the first letter of eight continuous verses, what more could be said about the Torah! What more need be said!

As one might expect, due to the sustained literary pattern, the poem does not fit into a single literary genre (other than the acrostic poem), but contains traces of several genres, like the individual lament (v. 107), the song of trust (v. 42), the song of thanksgiving (v. 7), the hymn (e.g., vv. 71–72), and the wisdom aphorism (vv. 9, 99).[14]

One might think that the verses of any given strophe of Psalm 119 are strung together like beads on a necklace, but there are many instances in which the strophe begins on a Torah subtheme and sustains the subject throughout the strophe, even if the theme begins to grow thin before the strophe is done. The *Lamedh* strophe (vv. 89–96), for example, sounds the chord of the eternality and enduring nature of the Word of the Lord (vv. 89–90), then modulates into the enduring quality of God's laws in the world (v. 91), embellished by the psalmist's delight in the Torah and his faithful observance of it (vv. 92–93). It reaches a thematic summit in his prayer that the Lord would save him from the wicked in view of his loyalty to the Torah (vv. 94–95). The climax comes in verse 96 where he declares that all perfection has its boundaries, but God's commands are boundless. While this concluding theme is different from the opening theme of the eternality of the Torah, it nevertheless describes the Torah's infinite nature, and a case can be made for coherence of theme in this strophe.

To give one other example, the *Qoph* strophe of verses 145–52 puts forth the psalmist's intense search for God (vv. 145–49), and, like the *Lamedh* strophe discussed above, it ponders the schemes of the wicked that have come near the psalmist, and then observes that the wicked themselves are "far from your law. / Yet you are near, O LORD, / and all your commands are true" (vv. 150b–51). Unlike the conclusion of the *Lamedh* strophe, however, where the theme is at least in the broad spectrum of the subtheme, this strophe concludes with the idea that Yahweh has established his statutes to last forever (v. 152), hardly a return to the original idea of the search for God. Given the poet's rigid adherence to the alphabetic structure, the subject matter sometimes had to surrender to the literary form.

Date of Composition of Psalm 119

We have basically two criteria by which to date this psalm. First, based on that period of time in which the Torah began to move to the center stage of theology as a description and program of the good life, the psalm likely belongs in the postexilic era. By the time of Jesus Ben Sira in the early second century B.C., the Torah had certainly become the main focus of Jewish theology. This psalm, however, should not be dated as late as Ben Sira, because the Psalter seems to have been completed earlier than that. But Psalm 119 was likely one of the last compositions of the collection.

Second, the political and cultural situation of the poet was one of difficult circumstances. While verses 61–62 could describe a hypothetical situation, the writer seems rather to be laying out a real piece of his life:

> Though the wicked bind me with ropes,
> I will not forget your law.
> At midnight I rise to give you thanks
> for your righteous laws.

In that case, the psalmist is likely a victim of political adversity, and in the midst of it he rises in the middle of the night to give God thanks for his righteous laws. This may represent a daily pattern of piety, like Daniel's custom of praying three times a day (Dan. 6:10), although that observation alone may not help all that much in our effort to date the psalm. The theme of political adversity occurs in other places in the psalm, giving the impression of the rule of a hostile power. The psalmist has experienced hostility and probably expects more:

> Though rulers sit together and slander me,
> your servant will meditate on your decrees. (v. 23)

> I will speak of your statutes before kings
> and will not be put to shame. (v. 46)

> Rulers persecute me without cause,
> but my heart trembles at your word. (v. 161)

This situation, however, characterized Israel's history from the exile of 586 B.C. down to the Hasmonean era, beginning in 142 B.C. The evidence, therefore, does not permit a precise dating of the psalm, even though the centrality of the Torah seems to be the most substantive evidence. Psalm 119, then, might have been composed as early as the governorship of Ezra, which began in 457 B.C. Further, it certainly seems plausible that, with the intentional emphasis on the Torah, this was the era in which the Psalter was given its fivefold division to reflect the five books of the Torah.[15]

A Profile of the Author of Psalm 119

The composer of Psalm 119 was a young or perhaps even a middle-aged man (v. 9) whose earlier life had been marked by youthful passions. Yet, he had learned that the really needful thing in life was keeping the Torah. Indeed, the Lord had used affliction to lead him back into the fold (vv. 67, 71, 75), and the psalmist looked upon that as a blessing: "It was good for me to be afflicted / so that I might learn your decrees" (v. 71). So thorough and genuine was his conversion that the Torah came to be his greatest delight, and he constantly meditated on it (vv. 97, 99). And it was more than meditation, it was the driving force of his life, for it drew him like streams of water draw the thirsty (v. 131; cf. 42:1).

Yet, while the poet's life in the Torah had been a great delight, it had not been easy. He had encountered much opposition from others, even though the opposition was not a reaction to his devotion to the Torah. It seems much more political than religious. In fact, the psalmist described that opposition in terms of the wicked binding him with ropes (v. 61), and waiting to destroy him (v. 95). His foes were numerous (v. 157), but when suffering had come upon him (vv. 143, 153), the Torah had been his mainstay. The psalmist had turned his life of trouble into a life of praise (vv. 7, 62, 108, 164, 171, 175).

It is to the psalmist's credit, or more accurately, to the credit of the Torah, that he held no animosity toward his persecutors. They had wronged him without cause (vv. 78, 86–87, 110, 161), and he still did not turn to curse them. If he held any ill will toward them, it was mild compared to the curses of the imprecatory psalms (v. 78). Jane T. Stoddart writes of this author and poem:

A German mystic of the early eighteenth century, Gottfried Arnold, wrote a short poem entitled "An Angel throws all other flowers behind him and keeps the rose." The writer of the longest Psalm has renounced earthly delights, except the sure possession of that Divine Law which for him was like an everlasting rose. Behind the artistic arrangement of words and paragraphs the Church has discerned in his work such a depth of sincere and passionate feeling that many of his thoughts have lived in the history and literature of two thousand years. A. C. Benson supposed that he was a young and wealthy man. Apart from the question, "Wherewithall shall a young man cleanse his way?" internal evidence points to undiminished energy at the crown of manhood. Repeated references to the persecution of princes give a clearer indication of his social position than the mention of gold and silver. Princes do not usually trouble those who are obscure and "quiet in the land."[16]

The depth of the psalmist's devotion to the Torah becomes visible in his lament over those who do not delight in it as he does: "Streams of tears flow from my eyes, / for your law is not obeyed" (v. 136). While that measures the depth of his commitment, it also measures the depth of his concern for others, for he wanted them to share his devotion to the Torah.

So in this psalm we see a model of Torah piety that could be transforming, and we further see that kind of piety modeled in the psalmist himself. The theoretical and the practical converged in the poet's life to produce this literary and spiritual masterpiece.

The Torah Theology of Psalm 119

It may be overambitious to speak of a theology of Torah based upon Psalm 119. However, this psalm takes up the vocabulary and the ideas of Psalms 1 and 19, and looks at numerous other facets of the Torah concept. Further, since this psalm comes out of the climate of a well-developed Torah piety, we certainly have a mature stage of that religious expression described here. Artur Weiser makes an interesting observation in this regard:

> It is possible to deduce from the psalm a full-fledged "theology" of the law, in both its theoretical and its practical aspects. The simple form of the diction makes it unnecessary to expound the psalm in detail. It only remains to point out that the kind of piety, based on the law, such as is presented to us in the psalm does not yet exhibit that degeneration and hardening into a legalistic form of religion to which it succumbed in late Judaism and which provoked Jesus' rebuke. On the other hand, however, one cannot fail to realize that a piety such as is expressed in the psalm, according to which God's word and law take the place of God himself and his wondrous works (v. 13), are even worshipped (v. 48), and become the source of that comfort which as a rule is bestowed upon man by the divine saving grace (vv. 50, 92), carries with it the germs of a development which was bound to end in the self-righteousness of the Pharisees and scribes.[17]

Weiser's assessment is quite accurate. In view of the mature stage of Torah piety out of which this psalm arises, I would like to discuss this matter under two headings, the nature of Torah and the purpose of Torah.

PSALM 119 AND THE NATURE OF TORAH

Despite its preoccupation with the Torah, Psalm 119 does not articulate a legalistic theology. In fact, the psalmist sets the stage for the larger theme by equating the keeping of the Torah with seeking the Lord:

> Blessed are they whose ways are
>   blameless,
>   who walk according to the law
>   of the LORD.
> Blessed are they who keep his
>   statutes
>   and seek him with all their
>   heart. (vv. 1–2)

God has issued the Torah in a world that is filled with his love (khesed), and in that context he teaches his laws:

> The earth is filled with your love, O
>   LORD;
>   teach me your decrees. (v. 64)

> Preserve my life according to your
>   love,
>   and I will obey the statutes of
>   your mouth. (v. 88)

> Deal with your servant according
>   to your love
>   and teach me your decrees.
>   (v. 124)

In view of the larger context of love (*khesed*) in which the Torah was given, one can more readily understand why the psalmist would fall in love with God's decrees and delight in them. They were given in love and administered in love.

While Psalm 119 does not draw a direct relationship between the giving of the law and the creation of the world, that connection nevertheless lies behind his understanding of the Torah. In the first place, the psalmist acknowledges that God created him, and to the Creator God he appeals for a knowledge of the Torah: "Your hands made me and formed me; / give me understanding to learn your commands" (v. 73).

The connection between Torah and creation appears again in verse 90, where he uses the word "faithfulness" (*'emunah*) as a synonym for Torah and draws a parallel between the enduring earth and the enduring Torah: "Your *faithfulness* continues through all generations; / you established the earth, and it endures" (v. 90, emphasis added).[18]

It is not surprising then that the poet sets forth the idea that the Torah is eternal:

> Your word, O LORD, is eternal;
>   it stands firm in the heavens.
>   (v. 89)

> Long ago I learned from your
>   statutes
>   that you established them to last
>   forever. (v. 152)

> All your words are true;
>   all your righteous laws are eter-
>   nal. (v. 160)

Another dimension of Torah theology in Psalm 119 is the relationship of the Torah to truth. The Torah was the standard of truth, even truth itself. The "way of truth" and the "laws" of Yahweh are parallel ideas: "I have chosen the *way of truth*; / I have set my heart on *your laws* [*mishpateka*]" (v. 30, emphasis added).

The same parallel construction occurs in verse 43, equating truth with the Torah: "Do not snatch the *word of truth* from my mouth, / for I have put my hope in *your laws*" (emphasis added).[19]

This standard of truth lays the foundation for conduct, a standard from which any deviations are deserving of condemnation. The standard can be violated in both lifestyle or attitude and personal behavior. Violation in attitude is particularly evident in those persons who assume an arrogant spirit:

> You rebuke the arrogant, who are
>   cursed
>   and who stray from your com-
>   mands. (v. 21)

> The arrogant dig pitfalls for me,
>   contrary to your law. (v. 85)

The arrogant were among the psalmist's opponents, but he did not allow them to deter him from his Torah-keeping conduct: "The arrogant mock me without restraint, / but I do not turn from your law" (v. 51).

The psalmist had come to esteem the Torah above every other treasured possession or pleasure:

> The law from your mouth is more
>   precious to me
>   than thousands of pieces of sil-
>   ver and gold. (v. 72)

> Because I love your commands
>   more than gold, more than pure
>   gold,
> and because I consider all your
>   precepts right,
> I hate every wrong path.
>   (vv. 127–28)

How sweet are your words to my
taste,
sweeter than honey to my
mouth! (v. 103)

The Torah was, therefore, the delight of the poet's life, and the way that Yahweh had prescribed for his people to live. It was not a burden but a joy, and no pleasure or activity could compare with the life of the Torah.

Study Questions

1. The psalmists interpreted the essence of Torah as doing the will of God, rather than mere ritual and sacrifice. By the final composition of the Psalter, meditating on the Torah had become the prescribed program of doing the will of God, or walking in righteousness. How did this bring faith to a very personal level? How do we see this emphasis reflected in the introduction to the final collection (Ps 1)?

2. Content decides the Torah psalms since there is no stylistic pattern or literary genre standard to Torah discussion. What three psalms have the Torah as their primary concentration? On what basis should Psalm 16 and other psalms be included in this category? Read these other psalms in light of their Torah emphasis.

3. The sum concept of the Torah in the Psalms is that God's will for human life is divinely revealed and historically implemented in the story of Israel and humanity. What three forms does God's Law, or Torah, take in the Psalms? Describe these three forms in detail.

4. What factors shifted the emphasis in Hebraic worship from corporate to personal? How did this personal piety undergird Judaic religion from its very beginning?

5. Psalms 1, 19, and 119 form the heart of the Torah psalms. Write a two-page essay detailing a theology of Torah from these three psalms.

PSALM 119 AND THE PURPOSE OF TORAH

While the purpose of Torah can already be seen in the psalm's description of its nature, something more should be said in regard to its purpose. Not only did the psalmist delight in the laws of God, but he considered them his counselors who guided his life: "Your statutes are my delight; / they are my counselors" (v. 24).

Out of the sense of Torah-keeping represented by this psalm, a community of the faithful begins to take shape and create a place of fellowship and a sense of identity:

I am a friend to all who fear you,
to all who follow your precepts.
(v. 63)

May those who fear you rejoice
when they see me,
for I have put my hope in your
word. (v. 74)

May those who fear you turn to me,
those who understand your
statutes. (v. 79)

In this community, as well as in the individual life, the observance of the Torah is a preventative to sinning. It builds a wall around the observant and gives a sense of security against evil conduct:

I have hidden your word in my
heart
that I might not sin against you.
(v. 11)

Direct my footsteps according to
your word;
let no sin rule over me. (v. 133)

And in a context of threat and danger, the Torah can preserve the observant's life: "I will never forget your precepts, / for by them you have preserved my life" (v. 93). In fact, the Torah contains a built-in promise to preserve the faithful:

I have suffered much;
preserve my life, O LORD, according to your word.
(v. 107)

Hear my voice in accordance with
your love;
preserve my life, O LORD, according to your laws.
(v. 149)

Defend my cause and redeem me;
preserve my life according to
your promise. (v. 154)

Thus the purpose of the Torah was to build a life lived in accordance with the will of God revealed in his laws, and to build a secure and safe community in which the Torah can be joyfully kept. Yahweh has, therefore, provided a context of love (*khesed*) in which he gave his Torah, and those who keep it find that its benevolent purposes meet life's aspirations and produce human happiness.

Key Terms

piety
Torah
Torah psalms

14 "May They Be Blotted Out of the Book of Life"

The Imprecatory Psalms

Outline

- **The Imprecatory Psalms Defined**
- **The Problem**
- **The Solutions**
  The Nature of Poetry Itself
  Effective Magic
  An Inferior Ethic
  Prediction over Pronouncement
  Messianic
  Human Vindictiveness over Divine
    Instruction
  Representative of Human Injustice
  The Words of Others
  National Rather than Personal
  Distinction between the Sin and the
    Sinner
- **Interpreting the Imprecatory Psalms as the Word of God**
  The Psalmist's Theological Perspective
  The "Curses"
  Principles of Judgment

Objectives

After reading this chapter, you should be able to

1. Define the imprecatory psalms.
2. Discuss the moral problem these psalms raise.
3. Suggest solutions to the moral problem.
4. Understand the theological context of the imprecatory psalms.

enemies

curses

imprecatory
psalms

The Imprecatory Psalms Defined

As the name implies, some of the Psalms contain extremely harsh judgments upon the **enemies** of the psalmists. The term "imprecations" means **"curses"** and suggests that the psalmists prayed that evil would befall their persecutors. It is a rather strong term and perhaps not the most accurate one. "Psalms of anger" or "psalms of wrath" would be a better phrase, but the term **imprecatory psalms** is a standard one, and for the sake of genre classification and tradition, we will use it when referring to this group of poems. There are at least seven psalms that fall into this category, in a greater or lesser degree: Psalms 35, 55, 59, 69, 79, 109, and 137. Of these seven, Psalms 35, 69, and 109 are the most intense, although the others by their content and tone help to define the category.

The Problem

Anyone who reads the Psalms with even a superficial eye will discover some pretty caustic statements about the psalmists' enemies. Metaphorically the psalmists capture the vicious nature of these people, both foreign and indigenous, in their images as "lions" (35:17) or "snarling . . . dogs" who prowl about the city (59:6, 14–15). Their beastly temperament manifests itself in the phrase "bloodthirsty men" (59:2), while their militant disposition can be heard in their words that are like "drawn swords" (55:21). The psalmist rivals this language about his enemies with numerous expressions of ill will against them, which take the form of prayers that God will bring the worst imaginable fate upon them. The question the reader of the Psalms may ask, indeed should ask, is, Where is the love of God in these deprecations? Jesus' teaching that one should love one's enemies mandates the question: "You have heard that it was said, 'Love your neighbor and hate your enemy.' But I tell you: Love your enemies and pray for those who persecute you, that you may be sons of your Father in heaven" (Mt 5:43–45a). Thus the problem of the imprecatory psalms takes the form of an ethical question. How can one love one's enemies and pray at the same time that tragedy will suddenly strike them?

To put this issue in another perspective, the imprecatory psalms put both the psalmist and God in the context of anger and vengeance. Who is this religious poet who wishes, even prays, for such terrible things to happen to his enemies? Who is this God who, the psalmist assumes, would side with him and do such terrible things?

Lions were both feared for their ferocious strength and admired for their appearance, much like the enemies in the Psalms who were wicked, yet had influence and enjoyed success (Ps 73:2–12).

The Solutions

The Nature of Poetry Itself

Some scholars find a solution, or at least a partial solution, to the ethical problem of these psalms in the nature of poetry itself. Since poetry tends to utilize hyperbole and by its nature engages in strong images to make the point sharp and succinct, the patrons of this explanation propose that the problem is resolved in the nature of poetry itself. Erich Zenger finds this to be a partial solution, insisting that the poetic nature of the imprecatory psalms implies that they overrate the situation.[1] Subsumed under this position is the view that the imprecations contained in these psalms are only spiritual or figurative. Yet we must admit that however poetic these expressions of anger are, they wish others harm, shame, and even death.[2]

Effective Magic

Sigmund Mowinckel proposed that these psalms were cut out of the fabric of a world where black magic was part of religious belief and practice. He thought that the imprecatory psalms were examples of an "effective" magic by which the psalmist "cursed" his enemies and expected those evils to befall them.[3] The Old Testament, however, tends to shy away from that kind of pagan practice. Keel comments that "magic is forbidden to the Israelite in his strife against his enemies. He consequently turns to Yahweh with the entire burden of his need."[4] Further, such prominence in the Psalter, if indeed the editor of the Psalms knew about it, would seem rather blatant.

An Inferior Ethic

Interpreters of the Psalter sometimes resort to an explanation that puts the imprecatory psalms under the heading of the Old Testament ethic and draws a line of contrast to the New Testament ethic of Jesus that we should love our enemies (Mt 5:43–45). This view is sometimes represented as the Old Covenant/New Covenant explanation.

It is true that the Old Testament ethic pinnacles in the ethic of love (Dt 6:4) and bottoms out in the ethic of vengeance (Dt 19:21). One finds the pinnacle of the Old Testament ethic in the command to love God (Dt 6:4) and to love one's neighbor as one's self (Lv 19:18). In fact, there is no higher ethic than the love of God with all one's being and the love of neighbor as one's self. Jesus took these two commandments as the two greatest (Mt 22:36–40). Even though

the Old Testament never formulates the law of love as Jesus did, the law of love nevertheless required the Israelites to treat their enemies with the same kind of fairness and consideration they would want for themselves: "If you come across your enemy's ox or donkey wandering off, be sure to take it back to him. If you see the donkey of someone who hates you fallen down under its load, do not leave it there; be sure to help him with it" (Ex 23:4–5).

The lower end of the Old Testament ethic is the application of the law of retaliation in equal kind. While it is not entirely unworthy of an ethic framed in the law of love, it does not rise to the level of the ethic that Jesus taught in the Sermon on the Mount. The Book of Deuteronomy outlines this position in the case of one who brings false witness against one's fellow Israelite:

> If a malicious witness takes the stand to accuse a man of a crime, the two men involved in the dispute must stand in the presence of the LORD before the priests and the judges who are in office at the time. The judges must make a thorough investigation, and if the witness proves to be a liar, giving false testimony against his brother, then do to him as he intended to do to his brother. You must purge the evil from among you. The rest of the people will hear of this and be afraid, and never again will such an evil thing be done among you. Show no pity: life for life, eye for eye, tooth for tooth, hand for hand, foot for foot. (Dt 19:16–21)

While in its Old Testament context this law assures that one is responsible for one's actions, and that he or she might be repaid in kind, in the ethics of Jesus we might very likely expect that person to turn the other cheek. It is not hard to see then why this principle of behavior violates the spirit of Jesus. John L. McKenzie, however, rightly cautions that we must be careful not to read two opposing ethical systems from the two testaments.[5] In fact, Jesus taught that the law of divorce was an accommodation to human frailty and that the higher ethic had been the norm from creation (Mt 19:8).

The test case, of course, is the Israelite annihilation of the Canaanites, a direct command of God, even though it was never carried out absolutely. The writer of Judges himself was a bit uneasy with this position, as is obvious from the explanation:

> "Because this nation has violated the covenant that I laid down for their forefathers and has not listened to me, I will no longer drive out before them any of the nations Joshua left when he died. I will use them to test Israel and see whether they will keep the way of the LORD and walk in it as their forefathers did." The LORD had allowed those nations to remain; he did not drive them out at once by giving them into the hands of Joshua. (Jgs 2:20b–23)

The rationale behind the extermination of the Canaanites was that they would morally corrupt the Israelites and cause them to worship the Canaanite gods. That explanation, adequate enough for Old Testament Israel, still poses a problem for us who live within the New Testament context. But before we condemn it too quickly, we have to wonder what this world would be like if the Israelites had exchanged their religious faith for the faith of the Canaanites. But then, does the end justify the means? It is a difficult question in this case. We have to deal with the realities of the situation as we know them. In any event, the explanation of the higher ethic versus the lower ethic exaggerates the ethical differences between the Old Testament and the New Testament and produces a superior and an inferior testament. The ethical differences are indeed obvious, and the church has recognized that, but they are more differences of degree than kind.

Prediction over Pronouncement

Because of our discomfort with the imprecatory psalms, it is a temptation to lift them above their historical and personal circumstances and make them speak in typical rather than specific terms. One form this temptation has taken is the interpretation of these psalms as predictions of future judgment on the wicked rather than personal prayers for and pronouncements of doom upon them. It is certainly true that some of these psalms are applied to Jesus in the New Testament, but their personal nature and the historical circumstances that the whole of the Psalter validates are reasons to resist this temptation. In fact, if we lift them out of their historical context, it takes away from their powerful application to Jesus' suffering and death, and deprives us of a strong point of identification with him and he with us.

It cannot be denied that the imprecatory psalms describe the typical outcome of evil actions, and that is instructive. Yet, the personal nature of these prayers cannot be ignored. If by connecting wicked behavior to tragic consequences the psalmists instruct us on the results of individual actions, that is a welcome by-product, but it can hardly be the basic intention of the original writers.

Messianic

The fact that the New Testament writers quoted from these psalms on several occasions has contributed to the view that the imprecatory psalms should be seen as *messianic*. Jesus quoted from Psalm 35:19/69:4 to explain the world's hatred of him (John 15:25), and the disciples remembered Psalm 69:9 to put the cleansing of the temple into its biblical context (John 2:17). Paul also heard Psalm 69:9 speaking of Christ and his suffering (Rom 15:3), while Psalm 69:22–23 predicted the blindness of the Jews toward Christ's messianic mission (Rom 11:9–10). Further, upon the occasion of Judas's death and the question of succession, Peter found instruction for Matthias's assumption of Judas's office in Psalms 69:25 and 109:8 (Acts 1:20). Yet, these quotations are selective, and there seems to be no reason to think that the apostles looked at these psalms as exclusively messianic.[6]

Human Vindictiveness over Divine Instruction

Some have simply written the imprecatory psalms off the ledger of divine inspiration. They insist that the psalmists are literally expressing their own vindictiveness toward their enemies, and God had nothing to do with inspiring their words. While it is quite correct that the Bible contains hateful words that do not directly convey divine truth (for example, Job's strong accusations against God), it is the context of those words that gives them the perspective that makes them the Word of God. While God did not inspire some of Job's words in the sense that they reveal the will of God, he set him up in such a way that, knowing as he did the kind of character and personality Job had, he would react in a certain way and would likely say certain things about God, some true, some untrue. Thus the totality of the story and the dialogue, capstoned by the God speeches, produces a message of God's will and the human dilemma. So it is still quite appropriate, indeed imperative, that when we read Job 16:11–14, for example, we introduce it by "Hear the Word of the Lord."

Perhaps we can acknowledge that some of the words of these psalms are not appropriate on the lips of a believer (e.g., Ps 137:8), but the message of divine justice, which is an expression of his character, is nevertheless clear and quite in order. Personally, we should never say such things, even though we can confidently and justifiably commit the matter to God's justice. God, however, spoke through the psalmist, providing a perspective that highlighted the human need for justice and divine commitment to it. In our discussion of the imprecatory psalms we shall try to explain this perspective.

Representative of Human Injustice

This position takes the historical situation quite seriously, understanding these psalms to be written by individuals who have suffered injurious wrongs. But it does not stop there. These individuals are representatives of humanity in all times and places who have suffered injustice. The representative element of this interpretation is intended to qualify the imprecatory psalms for inclusion in Holy Scripture. The fact that these ancient voices speak on behalf of violated individuals everywhere and at all times, it is assumed, lifts them above the ethical question. While there is something to be said in favor of such a view, it still does not quite allay the concerns about the "curses" the psalmists pray would befall their enemies; and it certainly does not obviate the problem the imprecatory psalms pose in view of the ethics of Jesus. When one has been mistreated, the teaching of Jesus instructs one to love and pray for the wrongdoer.

The Words of Others

This view of these poems, though well intended, in effect bypasses the issue. In an artificial manner these interpreters try to assign the most vicious words to other individuals rather than to the psalmists themselves. While they are obviously interested in "protecting" the theological integrity of the Psalms, they ignore the historical reality of these particular poems. As unrealistic as some of these interpretive views are, this one is as impractical as any of them, and, to their credit, few scholars have espoused it.

National Rather than Personal

Others, in an attempt to keep Holy Scripture above any ethical suspicions, have applied these "curses" to the nations rather than individuals. At first this sounds like a pretty good idea. At least it avoids the personal hatred the imprecatory psalms express toward individuals, and raises it rather to a national level. It is true that in some cases, like Psalms 79 and 83, the psalmist speaks of national enemies, but this cannot be said of all the imprecatory psalms, in fact, of most of them. Psalms 69 and 109 definitely speak about personal enemies. Further, as McKenzie rightly contends, a personal ethic that operates by radically different principles from the national ethic would be inconsistent.[7]

Distinction between the Sin and the Sinner

This rather common and quite justifiable method of dealing with sin and the person of the sinner is also among the ways interpreters have dealt with these psalms. McKenzie espouses this position and says: "Now the hatred of the Psalmist is certainly directed against a hateful quality: sin."[8] He outlines certain limits to protect the person of the sinner against the psalmist's hatred of sin:

1. Hatred must not be directed at the sinner's person, but only at the quality of sin.
2. The psalmist, or any other believer, may desire that divine justice be accomplished against the sinner, but it must be *divine* justice, not the psalmist's revenge.
3. There must be allowance for repentance, and when that occurs the desire for divine justice must be relinquished.
4. It must be accompanied by love for the sinner: "In a word, the sinner may lawfully be hated only when he is loved."[9]

This view has much to commend it. The problem is that it is so difficult to separate one's hatred for sin from hatred for the sinner. And we always have to ask ourselves, "What is it that I really hate?" Most of us are such sinners ourselves that we confuse the two hatreds and cannot be sure where one breaks off and the other begins. It is only the true saints who can manage this delicate balance, even though all of us should aspire in that lofty direction.

Interpreting the Imprecatory Psalms as the Word of God

In this section I want to further discuss some aspects of the imprecatory psalms to try to understand their theological positives and negatives.

The Psalmist's Theological Perspective

We should notice right off the psalmist's perspective on the ill-treatment he has received from his persecutors. They have paid back his goodwill toward them with evil: "They repay me evil for good / and leave my soul forlorn" (35:12). His hurt had been compounded by the fact that the perpetrators of evil were his friends:

If an enemy were insulting me,
    I could endure it;
if a foe were raising himself against
        me,
    I could hide from him.
But it is you, a man like myself,
    my companion, my close friend,
with whom I once enjoyed sweet
        fellowship
    as we walked with the throng at
        the house of God. (55:12–
        14)

In return for my friendship they accuse me,
    but I am a man of prayer.
They repay me evil for good,
    and hatred for my friendship.
        (109:4–5)

This fact certainly puts these prayers in an interesting light, much like that of Job and his friends.

A second observation is that the psalmist contends that his persecutors have no reason for perpetrating their evil upon him:

For wicked and deceitful men
    have opened their mouths
        against me;
    they have spoken against me
        with lying tongues.

The Rancor of the Desert

George Adam Smith explains that the rancor of the desert breaks out in the cursing of the Psalms:

Under national or personal persecution the passion for justice grew awful in the heart of the Hebrew and he did not mitigate his anger before the Lord. *Let his children be fatherless, and his wife a widow, . . . neither let there be any to have pity on her fatherless children. Let them be as chaff before the wind, and the angel of the Lord driving them on. Break their teeth, O God, in their mouth; let them melt as water that runneth apace. Daughter of Babylon, happy be he that dasheth thy little ones against the rocks.* This is the delirium of the conscience produced by a famine of justice. Such outbursts are pathological, of course, but authentic proofs that the Psalms are the utterances of real men and not of tame creatures performing a part.[1]

1. George Adam Smith, "The Legacy of Israel," 22. Quoted by Jane T. Stoddart in *The Psalms for Every Day* (London: Hodder and Stoughton, 1939), 265–66.

With words of hatred they surround me;
they attack me without cause.
(109:2–3; also 35:7, 19; 59:3–5; 69:4)

Third, a key to understanding the feelings and the attitude of the psalmist, indeed, his theology, is that, at least in one passage, he recognizes that his suffering is for the Lord's sake:

For I endure scorn for your sake,
and shame covers my face.
I am a stranger to my brothers,
an alien to my own mother's sons;
for zeal for your house consumes me,
and the insults of those who insult you fall on me. (69:7–9)

That certainly puts the problem in a larger theological setting, and very likely strengthened the psalmist to endure his persecution.

Fourth, while the psalmist's confidence in men and women has been shattered, his faith in God and his goodness remain intact:

But you, O Sovereign LORD,
deal well with me for your name's sake;
out of the goodness of your love, deliver me. (109:21)

Help me, O LORD my God;
save me in accordance with your love. (109:26)

Fifth, the psalmist has a sense of community that undergirds his spiritual well-being. There were those who hoped for his vindication (35:27), and those who might be affected negatively by what was happening to him:

May those who hope in you
not be disgraced because of me,
O Lord, the LORD Almighty;
may those who seek you
not be put to shame because of me,
O God of Israel. (69:6)

While these observations may not have solved the problem of the imprecatory psalms, they provide a theological context within which to view the problem. The psalmist's relationship to God is in good order, and his gracious actions toward his enemies reflect that. Whatever has happened to him, it arises out of the character of his persecutors rather than from his own character and actions. Further, he understands his suffering broadly and is concerned about how it might affect the community of which he is a part.

The "Curses"

The terms the psalmist uses against his enemies range from prayers that they may be dismayed in their efforts to prayers that they and their offspring may be destroyed. He prays a long list of "curses" against them, seeming not to have forgotten any potential perils.

When one looks at the nature and scope of the "curses," the intent of the psalmist is quite clear, even though his inner motive may not be entirely apparent. Yet, in light of the totality of these prayers of judgment, the

233

judgment

Technically Israel has no desert in the sense of a Sahara Desert. "Wilderness" is a more appropriate term, even though "desert" is frequently used as a synonym. George Adam Smith's connection between the "desert" and the "curses" of the Psalms is descriptive. Regions of the Negev and the Judean wilderness presented a special challenge to human life. Nevertheless, humans overcame this challenge to produce a life of relative prosperity. Could this triumph of the human spirit over the wilderness be a code for the psalmist's victory, and ours, over the hatred of his enemies?

psalmist was not so self-focused as he was God-focused, not so personally offended that his self-image obstructed his vision of God and his kingdom, and not so introspective that he could not see the impact of his personal suffering on the community to which he belonged.

Principles of Judgment

The psalmist sees certain principles governing the way justice is meted out. First, he expects the Lord to contend with those who have done him harm: "Contend, O LORD, with those who contend with me; / fight against those who fight against me" (35:1). If we can expect to identify a consistent theology in this group of psalms—and I believe we can—we can say that his cause, as we have already observed, was the Lord's cause (69:7–9). Therefore, the Lord, being a God of justice, could hardly do anything less than deal with those enemies who had violated the psalmist and thus in essence violated the Lord himself.

Second, the psalmist believes, at least prays, that the devices of the

wicked will be self-destructive: "May the net they hid entangle them, / may they fall into the pit, to their ruin" (35:8b, c; see also 5:10; 7:15–16; 9:15). This principle of **judgment** sounds proverbial (Prv 26:27; 28:10), and incorporated in it is the moral law that an evil motive will cause the reverse of the intended effect. That is, God has so designed the universe and so superintends human actions that everything and every action become instruments of his will, however depraved the intention of the actor. This principle, found in the canonical wisdom literature in its raw form, is articulated in a classic phrase of the apocryphal Wisdom of Solomon. As the writer described how the Lord used fire to destroy the Egyptians in hot pursuit of the Israelites, even though the waters of the sea engulfed them (Ex 14:21–31), he formulated this classical statement of the principle: "For—most incredible of all—in the water, which quenches all things, / the fire had still greater effect, / *for the universe defends the righteous*" (Wisdom of Solomon 16:17 NRSV, also v. 24; 5:20).

Curses

—be disgraced and put to shame (35:4a; also v. 26)

—be turned back in dismay (35:4b)

—be like chaff before the wind with the angel of the LORD driving them away (35:5)

—their path be dark and slippery, with the angel of the LORD pursuing them (35:6)

—may ruin overtake them by surprise (35:8)

—may the net they hid entangle them (35:8)

—may they fall into the pit, to their ruin (35:8)

—confuse the wicked (55:9)

—confound their speech (55:9)

—let death take enemies by surprise (55:15)

—let them go down alive to the grave (55:15)

—may the table set before them become a snare; may it become retribution and a trap (69:22)

—may their eyes be darkened so they cannot see (69:23)

—may their backs be bent forever (69:23)

—pour out your wrath on them (69:24)

—let your fierce anger overtake them (69:24)

—may their place be deserted; let there be no one to dwell in their tents (69:25)

—charge them with crime upon crime (69:27)

—do not let them share in your salvation (69:27)

—may they be blotted out of the book of life and not be listed with the righteous (69:28)

—appoint an evil man to oppose him; let an accuser stand at his right hand (109:6)

—let him be found guilty (109:7)

—may his prayers condemn him (109:7)

—may his days be few (109:8)

—may another take his place of leadership (109:9)

—may his children be wandering beggars; may they be driven from their ruined homes (109:10)

—may a creditor seize all he has; may strangers plunder the fruits of his labor (109:11)

—may no one extend kindness to him or take pity on his fatherless children (109:12)

—may his descendants be cut off, their names blotted out from the next generation (109:13)

—may the iniquity of his fathers be remembered before the LORD;

—may the sin of his mother never be blotted out (109:14)

—may their sins always remain before the LORD, that he may cut off the memory of them from the earth (109:15)

—O Daughter of Babylon, doomed to destruction, happy is he who repays you for what you have done to us—he who seizes your infants and dashes them against the rocks (137:8–9)

Third, the psalmist prays that God will repay the wicked measure for measure for their evil, if not seven times over:

> He loved to pronounce a curse—
>   may it come on him;
> he found no pleasure in blessing—
>   may it be far from him. (109:17)

The evils the enemy had committed against the psalmist were as natural to him as the garment he wore. They had become the essence of his soul, and the wronged psalmist prays that this ugly garment might cling to him forever as a scourge:

> He wore cursing as his garment;
>   it entered into his body like water,
>   into his bones like oil.
> May it be like a cloak wrapped
>   about him,
>   like a belt tied forever around
>   him.
> May this be the LORD's payment to
>   my accusers,
>   to those who speak evil of me.
>   (vv. 18–19)

The shocking prayer of Psalm 137 belongs under this rubric too, for the Babylonians had dashed the Israelite infants against the rocks, and the psalmist prays that they will be repaid measure for measure:

> O Daughter of Babylon, doomed to
> destruction,
> happy is he who repays you
> for what you have done to us—
> he who seizes your infants
> and dashes them against the
> rocks. (vv. 8–9)

This eye-for-an-eye and tooth-for-a-tooth ethic, as much as it may trouble the Christian soul, belongs to one level of the Old Testament ethic. It is not the whole thing, only part of the whole, and we cannot really appreciate the part until we have seen the whole. In this case, we need to see the upper level of the Old Testament ethic where love of God and love of neighbor regulate and determine human behavior. And we must acknowledge that both biblically and historically there is also a place for judgment in the Christian ethic, a judgment that is not based on the law of retaliation of course, but on the justice of God.

Fourth, the reproach of the psalmist's enemies did not stand on its own but was rooted in a deep defiance of God himself. In that conviction the psalmist prays that God will punish them seven times over: "Pay back into the laps of our neighbors seven times / the reproach they have hurled at you, O Lord" (79:12).

The important thing about these principles of judgment is that the psalmist was not praying out of sheer malice toward his persecutors. Keel observes that the enemies are depicted in such a way that it is clear that they live and act as if there is no God. Therefore, it is on this basis that the psalmists plead with God to punish them, for "their conduct arouses the suspicion that there is no God to judge them."[10] He believed he was praying within the will of God. This is, in fact, the reason that Johannes Vos says these prayers may still be used in Christian worship:

> because the act of God which was
> prayed for conflicted with no actual rights of men, and because the
> prayers themselves were uttered
> by the inspiration of the Holy
> Spirit and therefore must have

been right prayers and could not have been immoral. The total destruction of evil, including the judicial destruction of evil men, is the prerogative of the sovereign God, and it is right not only to pray for the accomplishment of this destruction, but even to assist in effecting it when commanded to do so by God himself.[11]

The above considerations of the imprecatory psalms will not satisfy some readers. They will still feel uncomfortable with these "angry" prayers, and perhaps there ought to be some uneasiness in all of us that such prayers were prayed or had to be prayed, however one looks at it. Consequently some have been impelled to look for benefits that these psalms may provide to us. Erich Zenger reminds us that they give us a realistic view of the world.[12] That is, they will not permit us to ignore the violence and evil of the world we live in. Even though he cannot accept fully the worldview that produced them, he lists four aspects that make these psalms "serviceable" to the modern world:

1. The enemies of these psalms are never mythicized or demonized. Rather they are taken quite seriously and quite literally.
2. To the degree that these psalms reveal that violence is "a structural distortion of the earth as the abode of life, something that is offensive to God, they demystify every ideology that presents itself all too enthusiastically as promising happiness and liberation."
3. They bring to our attention the "web of violence" that attacks our world and inflicts pain on human beings, "especially for the weak, the sick, the suffering, and those under attack by a hostile environment (or one that is felt to be hostile)."
4. Although these psalms point to *others* as the perpetrators of evil, they at the same time call us to face our own complicity in the web of violence.

Study Questions

1. The imprecatory psalms introduce us to certain harsh judgments upon the psalmists' enemies. The term "imprecation" suggests "curses." What might be a title better suited to the content? And yet, why may we maintain the "imprecatory" title for these psalms?

2. The imprecatory psalms "put both the psalmist and God in the context of anger and vengeance." What moral problems does this raise for us today?

3. What ten solutions are offered to resolve the moral dilemma posed by these psalms? What solution(s) do you feel may offer a satisfying answer? Or do you think there is no good solution? Explain.

4. The chapter outlines a theological context for dealing with the imprecatory psalms as the Word of God. In your own words, describe this contextual paradigm. Does it make you more comfortable interpreting these psalms?

5. After examining the totality of the psalmist's imprecation/anger, is there any way one could claim the psalmist is more God-focused and community-focused than self-focused? Explain.

6. C. S. Lewis recognizes in these imprecatory psalms a reminder that the absence of indignation "may be an alarming symptom of the decline of righteousness and moral conviction," the modern relativism that gives "niceness" a higher value than goodness. In this sense, how does the psalmists' sense of justice differ from ours? Who is more correct, the psalmists or we?

7. How can the psalmists' strong understanding of the justice side of God's character instruct us today?

C. S. Lewis takes a different tack and observes that, on the side of Christian piety, the imprecatory psalms remind us that *the absence of indignation* may be an alarming symptom of the decline of righteousness and moral conviction.[13] To lose this sense of conviction is to lose our moral moorings.

Although this is certainly a by-product of these psalms, they may also teach us something about prayer, that in prayer we can "say everything, literally everything, if only we say it to GOD."[14] While our sense of piety may resist the kind of language we find in these psalms, as it does the kind of words Job spoke against the Almighty, does God not already know what we are thinking? And would it not be more honest if we laid it all out before him and dealt with our feelings in the presence of God and through the power of prayer? Of course, there is such a thing as restraint, and in the presence of God restraint and honesty can go hand in hand. We can confess our negative feelings while at the same time acknowledging how inappropriate and how much a part of our sinfulness they are.

Finally, the psalmist did not take matters into his own hands but committed them to God. Underlying his theodicy is the dictum " 'Vengeance is mine, I will repay,' says the Lord." Zenger remarks that they "affirm God by surrendering the last word *to God*. They give *to God* not only their lament about their desperate situation, but also the right to judge the originators of that situation. They leave *everything* in God's hands, even feelings of hatred and aggression."[15]

Whether or not the imprecatory psalms can ever become a core of prayers that we feel comfortable praying, they can, as our souls experience the resistance of the thoughts and words contained in them, remind us that the world is full of injustice and God is just, so we can leave the wrongs that others have delivered to us in his gracious hands. As C. H. Spurgeon comments, "Let us not fail to leave our case in the Lord's hand. Vain is the help of man, but ever effectual is the interposition of heaven."[16] This will move us a long way in the direction of the ethic of Jesus who calls us to love our enemies and pray for them.

Key Terms

enemies
curses
imprecatory psalms
judgment

Notes

Author's Preface

1. John Calvin, *Commentary on the Book of Psalms*, trans. Henry Beveridge (Grand Rapids: Baker, 1979), xxxv.

Chapter 1

1. C. Hassell Bullock, *An Introduction to the Old Testament Poetic Books*, rev. ed. (Chicago: Moody, 1988), 112.

2. See chapter 4.

3. John Calvin, *Commentary on the Book of Psalms*, trans. Henry Beveridge (Grand Rapids: Baker, 1979), xliv.

4. Ibid., xxxvii.

5. Ibid.

6. Brevard S. Childs, *Introduction to Scripture as Canon* (Philadelphia: Fortress, 1979), 517.

7. Ibid., 518.

8. *Pesahim* 117a.

9. S. H. Russell, "Calvin and the Messianic Interpretation of the Psalms," *Scottish Journal of Theology* 21 (1968): 41.

10. John F. A. Sawyer, "An Analysis of the Context and Meaning of the Psalm-Headings," *Transactions of the Glasgow University Oriental Society*, vol. 22 (1967): 31.

11. Tremper Longman III, *How to Read the Psalms* (Downers Grove: InterVarsity, 1988), 39.

12. Leslie McFall, "The Evidence for a Logical Arrangement of the Psalter," an unpublished work on the Psalms.

13. Derek Kidner, *Psalms 1–72* (London: Tyndale, 1973), 44.

14. Hans-Joachim Kraus, *Psalms 1–59: A Continental Commentary*, trans. Hilton C. Oswald (Minneapolis: Fortress, 1993), 22.

15. Ibid.

16. Sigmund Mowinckel, *The Psalms in Israel's Worship* (Nashville: Abingdon, 1962).

17. Kraus, *Psalms 1–59*, 25.

18. B. D. Eerdmans, *The Hebrew Book of Psalms* (Leiden: E. J. Brill, 1947), 77.

19. Kraus, *Psalms 1–59*, 25.

20. A. F. Kirkpatrick, *The Book of Psalms* (Cambridge: Cambridge University Press, 1951), xx and 29.

21. Kraus, *Psalms 1–59*, 26.

22. Ibid.

23. Ibid., 29.

24. John Alexander Lamb, *The Psalms in Christian Worship* (London: Faith, 1962), 35–36.

25. Kraus, *Psalms 1–59*, 29.

26. Ibid., 26.

27. Ibid., 31.

28. Lamb, *The Psalms in Christian Worship*, 5.

29. A. S. Gordon, *The Poets of the Old Testament* (London: Hodder and Stoughton, 1912), 65.

30. Lamb, *The Psalms in Christian Worship*, 5–6.

31. Ibid., 6.

32. L. Delekat, "Probleme der Psalmenüberschriften," *Zeitschrift für die Alttestamentliche Wissenschaft* 76 (1964): 280–97.

33. Kidner, *Psalms 1–72*, 42.

34. Lamb, *The Psalms in Christian Worship*, 6.

35. Also Ex 15:20–21; Jgs 11:34; 1 Sm 18:6–7; and Ps 68:25.

36. Othmar Keel, *The Symbolism of the Biblical World: Ancient Near Eastern Iconography and the Book of Psalms* (New York: Seabury, 1978), 326.

37. Cymbals are mentioned thirteen times in the Book of Chronicles, but elsewhere in the Old Testament the word occurs only in Ps 150 and 2 Sam 6:5. See Keel, *Symbolism*, 340.

38. Ibid.

39. Ibid., 342.

40. Ibid., 344.

41. Ibid., 345.

42. Ibid., 348.

43. Ibid., 348–49.

Chapter 2

1. Dietrich Bonhoeffer, *Psalms: The Prayer Book of the Bible*, trans. James H. Burtness (Minneapolis: Augsburg, 1970), 24.

2. Ibid., 24.

3. Robert Alter, *The Art of Biblical Poetry* (New York: Basic Books, 1985), 3–26, 62–84.

4. This follows Peter Craigie, *Psalms 1–50*, Word Biblical Commentary (Waco: Word, 1983), 228–29.

5. The Hebrew syntax is the reverse of the lines in NIV:

For he will keep me	safe	in his dwelling
in the day	of trouble.	

Thus the rhythmic pattern continues as 3:2.

6. Note the departure from the 3:2 pattern.

7. This *tristich* is found among mostly distichs. See also vv. 8, 9, 11, 12, 13, 14.

8. E.g., Leopold Sabourin, *The Psalms, Their Origin and Meaning* (New York: Alba House, 1974), 27.

9. Wilfred G. E. Watson, *Classical Hebrew Poetry: A Guide to Its Techniques* (Sheffield: JSOT Press, 1984), 13.

10. C. Hassell Bullock, *An Introduction to the Old Testament Prophetic Books* (Chicago: Moody, 1986), 264–69.

11. Robert L. Alden, "Chiastic Psalms: A Study in the Mechanics of Semitic Poetry in Psalms 1–50," *Journal of the Evangelical Theological Society* 17 (1974): 12.

12. Ibid., 13.

13. Franz Delitzsch, *Psalms* (Grand Rapids: Eerdmans, 1980), 1:306.

14. John Calvin, *Commentary on the Book of Psalms* (Edinburgh, 1845), 1:357.

15. James L. Mays, "Prayer and Christology: Psalm 22 as Perspective on the Passion," *Theology Today* 42 (1985): 323.

16. See the discussion on the structure of the book in chapter 3.

17. See William L. Holladay's discussion in *The Psalms through Three Thousand Years: Prayerbook of a Cloud of Witnesses* (Minneapolis: Fortress, 1993), 330–43.

18. Ibid., 162–63.

19. John Calvin, *Commentary on the Book of Psalms*, trans. James Anderson (Grand Rapids: Eerdmans, 1949), 1:xxxvii.

20. Ibid., 1:xliv.

21. Ibid., 1:181–82.

22. S. B. Frost, "The Christian Interpretation of the Psalms," *Canadian Journal of Theology* 5 (1959): 32.

23. Calvin, *Commentary on the Book of Psalms*, 2:173.

24. S. H. Russell, "Calvin and the Messianic Interpretation of the Psalms," *Scottish Journal of Theology* 21 (1968): 38.

25. Tremper Longman III, *How to Read the Psalms* (Downers Grove: InterVarsity, 1988), 67.

26. Ibid., 69–70.

27. Sigmund Mowinckel's summary of Gunkel's hypothesis, *The Psalms in Israel's Worship*, trans. D. R. Ap-Thomas (Oxford: Basil Blackwell, 1962), 1:14.

28. Hermann Gunkel, *The Psalms: A Form-Critical Approach* (Philadelphia: Fortress, 1967), 16–24.

29. The word "cult" is used in the scholarly literature to designate the worship system of ancient Israel, including temple and sacrifice.

30. Mowinckel, *The Psalms in Israel's Worship*, 1:22.

31. Ibid., 1:1.

32. Claus Westermann, *Praise and Lament in the Psalms*, trans. Keith R. Crim and Richard N. Soulen (Edinburgh: T. & T. Clark, 1965), 18.

33. Claus Westermann, *The Living Psalms*, trans. J. R. Porter (Grand Rapids: Eerdmans, 1989), 10.

34. Westermann, *Praise and Lament in the Psalms*, 21.

35. Ibid., 33–35.

36. Erhard S. Gerstenberger, *Psalms*, part 1 (Grand Rapids: Eerdmans, 1988), 33.

37. Ibid., 9–21.

38. See the discussion of the Asaph psalms in chapter 3.

39. See the discussion of the imprecatory psalms in chapter 14.

40. See the discussion of the imprecatory psalms in chapter 14.

41. Claus Westermann, *The Praise of God in the Psalms*, trans. Keith Crim (Richmond: John Knox, 1965), 64.

Chapter 3

1. William G. Braude, trans., *The Midrash on Psalms* (New Haven: Yale University Press, 1959), 1:5.

2. See James L. Mays, "The Place of the Torah-Psalms in the Psalter," *Journal of Biblical Literature* 106 (1987): 3–12.

3. R. Dean Anderson Jr., "The Division and Order of the Psalms," *Westminster Theological Journal* 56 (1994): 225.

4. See, for example, Gerald H. Wilson, "Understanding the Purposeful Arrangement of Psalms in the Psalter: Pitfalls and Promise," in *The Shape and Shaping of the Psalter*, ed. J. Clinton McCann (Sheffield: Sheffield Academic, 1993), 42.

5. See C. Hassell Bullock, *An Introduction to the Old Testament Prophets* (Chicago: Moody, 1986), 243–44.

6. James L. Mays, "The Question of Context in Psalm Interpretation," in *The Shape and Shaping of the Psalter*, ed. J. Clinton McCann (Sheffield: Sheffield Academic, 1993), 16–17.

7. For example, Peter C. Craigie, *Psalms 1–50*, Word Biblical Commentary, vol. 19 (Waco: Word, 1983), 64.

8. See N. Whybray, *Reading the Psalms as a Book*, JSOT Supplement Series 222 (Sheffield: Sheffield Academic, 1996), 89–90, for an interesting messianic interpretation of Ps 2.

9. Anderson dates the compilation of the early stages of the Psalter in the time of Hezekiah or earlier, and the final stage in the time of Nehemiah. He connects this editorial activity to the temple reforms of Hezekiah (2 Chr 29:30). See "The Division and Order of the Psalms," 24.

10. Leopold Sabourin, *The Psalms: Their Origin and Meaning*, new ed. (New York: Alba House, 1974), 161.

11. Derek Kidner, *Psalms 73–150*, Tyndale Old Testament Commentaries (Downers Grove: InterVarsity, 1975), 323.

12. J. Clinton McCann Jr., "Books I–III and the Editorial Purpose of the Hebrew Psalter," in *The Shape and Shaping of the Psalter* (Sheffield: Sheffield Academic, 1993), 103.

13. Ibid.

14. Cf. Marvin E. Tate, *Psalms 51–100* (Waco: Word, 1990), 222–23.

15. Gerald H. Wilson, *The Editing of the Hebrew Psalter*, SBL Dissertation Series 76 (Chico, Calif.: Scholars, 1985), 211.

16. Ibid.

17. Tate, *Psalms 51–100*, 232.

18. Ibid., 231.

19. McCann, "Books I–III and the Editorial Purpose of the Hebrew Psalter," 100.

20. Wilson, *The Editing of the Hebrew Psalter*, 220.

21. Erich Zenger, "The Composition and Theology of the Fifth Book of Psalms: Psalms 107–145," *Journal for the Study of the Old Testament* 80 (1998): 81.

22. Pss 138:7; 139:19–21; 140:1–5, 8–11; 141:4, 5b–10; 142:6; 143:3, 9, 12; 144:6–8, 11; 145:20

23. See chapter 4 sidebar: "Noncanonical Texts from Cave 11."

24. Alan M. Cooper, "The Life and Times of King David according to the Book of Psalms," in *The Poet and the Historian: Essays in Literary and Historical Biblical Criticism*, ed. Richard Elliott Friedman (Chico, Calif.: Scholars, 1983), 121.

25. Ibid., 122. See Braude, *The Midrash on Psalms*, 1:343–44.

26. Derek Kidner, *Psalms 1–72* (London: Tyndale, 1973), 33.

27. Sigmund Mowinckel, *The Psalms in Israel's Worship*, trans. D. R. Ap-Thomas (Oxford: Basil Blackwell, 1962), 1:77.

28. Franz Delitzsch, *Biblical Commentary on the Psalms*, trans. David Eaton (London: Hodder and Stoughton, 1902), 1:22.

29. Michael D. Goulder, *The Prayers of David (Psalms 51–72)*. Studies in the Psalter, II, Journal for the Study of the Old Testament Supplement Series 102 (Sheffield: Sheffield Academic Press, 1990): 24.

30. A. F. Kirkpatrick, *The Book of Psalms* (Cambridge: Cambridge University Press, 1898), 514–18. The quotations are as follows: Ps 86:1 "answer me"/55:2 "and answer me"; 86:1 "for I am poor and needy"/40:17 "for I am poor and needy"; 86:2 "Guard my life"/25:20 "Guard my life"; 86:4 "for to you, O Lord, I lift up my soul"/25:1 "To you, O LORD, I lift up my soul"; 86:6 "Hear my prayer, O LORD"/55:1 "Listen to my prayer, O God"; 86:7 "In the day of my trouble"/77:2 "in the day of my trouble"; 86:11 "Teach me your way, O LORD"/27:11 "Teach me your way, O LORD"; 86:11 "I will walk in your truth"/27:3 "and I will walk in your truth"; 86:13 "you have delivered me from the depths of the grave"/56:13 "for you have delivered me from death"; 86:14 "The arrogant are attacking me, O God; a band of ruthless men seeks my life—men without regard for you"/54:3 "Strangers are attacking me; ruthless men seek my life—men without regard for God"; 86:16 "Turn to me and have mercy on me"/25:16 "Turn to me and have mercy on me."

31. Michael D. Goulder, *The Psalms of the Sons of Korah* (Sheffield: Sheffield Academic, 1982), 3.

32. These are Goulder's figures, ibid., 4–5.

33. Ibid., 7.

34. J. P. Peters, *The Psalms as Liturgies* (New York: Macmillan, 1922).

35. Goulder, *The Psalms of the Sons of Korah*, 17.

36. Leslie McFall, "The Evidence for a Logical Arrangement of the Psalter," unpublished paper. McFall has put forward the intriguing proposal that Books 1–3 were compiled according to four criteria: (1) author, (2) divine names, (3) genre terms, and (4) thematic or word links. By this theory McFall is able to explain several baffling questions of arrangement. For example, the compiler's attempt to keep genres together (such as *maskil, miktam, mizmor, shir*) explains why he does not combine Psalm 16 with Pss 56–60 (all Davidic *miktam* psalms) and Psalm 32 with Pss 52–55. If he had, he would have violated the divine name criterion, which evidently took precedence over the other sorting criteria. Both Pss 16 and 32 are *Yahweh* psalms, while Pss 52–55 and 56–60 are *'elohim* psalms.

37. Ibid., 29.

38. Delitzsch, *Biblical Commentary on the Psalms*, trans. David Eaton, 3 vols. (New York: Funk and Wagnalls, n.d.), 3:140–43.

39. This feature is one that I have added to Delitzsch's list.

40. Walter Houston, "David, Asaph and the Mighty Works of God: Theme and Genre in the Psalm Collections," *Journal for the Study of the Old Testament* 68 (1995): 104.

41. Ibid., 103.

42. Michael D. Goulder, *The Psalms of Asaph and the Pentateuch: Studies in the Psalter III*, Journal for the Study of the Old Testament Supplement Series 233 (Sheffield: Sheffield Academic, 1996), 35.

43. Ps 129:8 contains a blessing that is very close to the blessing of the harvesters in Ru 2:4.

44. *Sukkah* 5.4, Herbert Danby's translation (London: Oxford University Press, 1933).

45. *Tosefta Sukkah* 4.7–9, Jacob Neusner's translation (New York: KTAV, 1977).

46. Zenger, "The Composition and Theology of the Fifth Book of Psalms," 92.

47. E. W. Hengstenberg, *Commentary on the Psalms*, 3 vols., trans. John Thomson and Patrick Fairbairn (Edinburgh: T. & T. Clark, 1854), 3:409.

48. The occurrence of the shortened form of the divine name in the third psalm of each heptad was not one of Hengstenberg's observations but that of J. Forbes, *Studies on the Book of Psalms* (Edinburgh: T. & T. Clark, 1888), 190.

49. Michael D. Goulder, "The Songs of Ascents and Nehemiah," *Journal for the Study of the Old Testament* 75 (1997): 43–58.

50. Wilson, *The Editing of the Hebrew Psalter*, 215.

51. Zenger, "The Composition and Theology of the Fifth Book of Psalms," 98.

52. Wilson, "Understanding the Purposeful Arrangement of Psalms in the Psalter," 42.

Chapter 4

1. John Calvin, *Commentary on the Book of Psalms*, trans. Henry Beveridge (Grand Rapids: Baker, 1979), xxxvii.

2. Ibid., xliv.

3. Dietrich Bonhoeffer, *Psalms: The Prayer Book of the Bible*, trans. James H. Burtness (Minneapolis: Augsburg, 1970), 85–86 (a letter of Feb. 21, 1944).

4. Ibid., 20–21.

5. William L. Holladay, *The Psalms through Three Thousand Years: Prayerbook of a Cloud of Witnesses* (Minneapolis: Fortress, 1993), 100. I am deeply indebted to Holladay's excellent discussion of the Psalms in worship.

6. Perhaps written between A.D. 30 and 51.

7. Cited by J. A. Sanders, *The Dead Sea Psalms Scroll* (Ithaca, N.Y.: Cornell University Press, 1967), 13.

8. Holladay, *The Psalms through Three Thousand Years*, 100–102.

9. In addition to Holladay, see J. A. Sanders, *The Psalms Scroll of Qumran Cave II*, Discoveries in the Judaean Desert of Jordan, vol. 4 (Oxford: Clarendon, 1965).

10. For a translation of these hymns, see Theodor Gaster, *The Dead Sea Scriptures* (Garden City, N.Y.: Doubleday, 1956).

11. Holladay, *The Psalms through Three Thousand Years*, 106.

12. Barbara Aland et al., eds., *The Greek New Testament* 4th ed. (New York: United Bible Societies, 1983), 887–90.

13. Holladay, *The Psalms through Three Thousand Years*, 115.

14. Aland et al., *The Greek New Testament*, 887–90.

15. Holladay, *The Psalms through Three Thousand Years*, 125–26.

16. For a detailed study of the use of the Psalms in Hebrews, see Simon Kistemaker, *The Psalm Citations in the Epistle to the Hebrews* (Amsterdam: Van Soest N.V., 1961).

17. Holladay, *The Psalms through Three Thousand Years*, 126–30.

18. Mishnah *Tamid* vii, 4.

19. Mishnah *Sukkah* iv, 9, 10.

20. Abraham Millgram, *Jewish Worship* (Philadelphia: Jewish Publication Society, 1971), 63.

21. John Alexander Lamb, *The Psalms in Christian Worship* (London: Faith, 1962), 12–17.

22. Holladay, *The Psalms through Three Thousand Years*, 162–64.

23. Augustine, *Confessions*, 9.6.14; 9.7.15.

24. Holladay, *The Psalms through Three Thousand Years*, 167.

25. Ibid., 182–83; see appendix 2 of Holladay's book for the order of the Psalms in the Eastern Orthodox Divine Office.

26. Ibid., 176; see appendix 1 of Holladay's book for the order of the Psalms in the Divine Office of the Roman Catholic Church.

27. Roland Bainton, *Here I Stand: A Life of Martin Luther* (New York and Nashville: Abingdon, 1950), 335.

28. Ibid.

29. Quoted by Lamb, *The Psalms in Christian Worship*, 140, from Calvin's *Opera, Corpus Reformatorum*, 6, 171.

30. Lamb, *The Psalms in Christian Worship*, 142.

31. Holladay, *The Psalms through Three Thousand Years*, 199.

32. Ibid., 200.

33. Lamb, *The Psalms in Christian Worship*, 145–46.

34. Ibid., 152–53.

35. Emily R. Brink, "Metrical Psalmody in North America: A Story of Survival and Revival," *Hymn* 44 (1993): 21.

36. Ibid.

37. Ibid., 21–22.

38. Ibid., 22.

39. Ibid., 23. She gives a helpful analysis of the occurrence of the Psalms in these hymnals.

40. Ibid., 24.

41. Bonhoeffer, *Psalms*, 64.

Chapter 5

1. S. Du Toit, "The Psalms and History," in *Studies on the Psalms*, (Potchefstroom: Pro Rege-Pers Beperk, 1963), 28.

2. Erik Haglund, *Historical Motifs in the Psalms* (Uppsala: CWK Gleerup, 1984), 102–3.

3. Clark Hyde, "The Remembrance of the Exodus in the Psalms," *Worship* 62 (1988): 405–6.

4. Ibid., 406.

Chapter 6

1. Westminster Shorter Catechism, Question and Answer No. 1.

2. The LXX reads, "But you dwell in a sanctuary, the praise of Israel."

3. See chapter 11.

4. J. Clinton McCann, *A Theological Introduction to the Book of Psalms: The Psalms as Torah* (Nashville: Abingdon, 1993), 53.

5. C. S. Lewis, *Reflections on the Psalms* (London: Geoffrey Bles, 1958), 94–95.

6. Ibid., 96.

7. Claus Westermann, *Praise and Lament in the Psalms*, trans. Keith R. Crim and Richard N. Soulen (Edinburgh: T. & T. Clark, 1965), 160–61.

8. Westermann gives the following form of the lament of the people:
   1. Address
   2. Lament
   3. Confession of Trust
   4. Petition
   5. Vow of Praise or Oracle of Salvation

   The lament of the individual takes the following form:
   1. Address
   2. Lament
   3. Confession of Trust
   4. Petition
   5. Assurance of Being Heard
   6. Petition/Wish that God Will Intervene

7. Vow of Praise

8. Praise of God

See Westermann, *Praise and Lament in the Psalms*, 52–90.

9. Ibid., 88–89.

10. F. Crüsemann, *Studien zur Formgeschichte von Hymnus und Danklied in Israel*, Wissenschaftliche Monographien zum Alten und Neuen Testament 32 (Neukirchen-Vlyn: Neukirchener Verlag, 1969).

11. Hans-Joachim Kraus, *Psalms 1–59: A Continental Commentary*, trans. Hilton C. Oswald (Minneapolis: Fortress, 1993), 43–46.

12. See chapter 11.

13. John Goldingay, *Praying the Psalms* (Nottingham: Grove Books, 1993), 8.

14. See also Ps 95:5.

15. See chapter 5.

Chapter 7

1. Gunkel's list of "Individual Complaint Songs" is Pss 3; 5; 6; 7; 13; 17; 22; 25; 26; 27:7–14; 28; 31; 35; 38; 39; 42; 43; 51; 54; 55; 56; 57; 59; 61; 63; 64; 69; 70; 71; 86; 88; 102; 109; 120; 130; 140; 141; 142; 143 (Hermann Gunkel, *Introduction to the Psalms: The Genres of the Religious Lyric of Israel*, completed by Joachim Begrich, trans. James D. Nogalski [Macon, Ga.: Mercer University Press, 1998], 121).

2. Claus Westermann, *Praise and Lament in the Psalms*, trans. Keith R. Crim and Richard N. Soulen (Edinburgh: T. & T. Clark, 1965), 55–61.

3. Ibid., 59.

4. Ibid., 73–80.

5. Ibid., 267. See also Claus Westermann, "The Role of the Lament in the Theology of the Old Testament," *Interpretation* 38:20–38.

6. John Goldingay, *Praying the Psalms* (Nottingham: Grove Books, 1993), 12.

7. Hans-Joachim Kraus, *Psalms 1–59: A Continental Commentary*, trans. Hilton C. Oswald (Minneapolis: Fortress, 1993), 47–52.

8. Ibid., 48–49. Kraus gives a form-critical analysis of this genre.

9. Ibid., 53–55.

10. Ibid., 51.

11. Alfred Rahlfs, *'ani und 'anav in den Psalmen* (Göttingen: Dieterich, 1892).

12. Hermann Gunkel and J. Begrich, *Einleitung in die Psalmen* (Göttingen, 1933).

13. Hans Schmidt, *Das Gebet des Angeklagten im Alten Testament* (Giessen: A. Töpelmann, 1928). See also his *Old Testament Essays* (London, 1927), 143–55.

14. Sigmund Mowinckel, *Psalmenstudien* (Amsterdam: Verlag P. Schippers, 1961), 1. Mowinckel interpreted the Hebrew word *'awen* in the phrase *po'ale 'awen* to mean magical power.

15. Harris Birkeland, *The Evildoers in the Book of Psalms* (Oslo: Jacob Dybwad, 1955). Mowinckel later adapted his theory to that of Birkeland, his student.

16. Patrick D. Miller Jr., "Trouble and Woe: Interpreting the Biblical Laments," *Interpretation* 37 (1983): 32–45. Udobata Onunwa presents a similar view by which he declares it appropriate to interpret Psalm 51 in the spirit of David, whether or not it was written by him—"Individual Laments in Hebrew Poetry: a Positive Response to the Problem of Suffering," *Jeevadhara* 18 (1988): 101–11.

17. Gunkel, *Introduction*, 149.

18. Miller, "Trouble and Woe," 36.

Chapter 8

1. Hans-Joachim Kraus, *Psalms 1–59: A Continental Commentary*, trans. Hilton C. Oswald (Minneapolis: Fortress, 1993), 51.

2. Kraus and Westermann list Ps 52 among the psalms of thanksgiving of the individual, but Gunkel and Mowinckel do not.

3. Sigmund Mowinckel, *The Psalms in Israel's Worship*, trans. D. R. Ap-Thomas (Nashville: Abingdon, 1962), 2:38–39.

4. This is an adaptation of Kraus's list, which is Pss 18; 30; 31; 32; 40A; 52; 66B; 92; 116; 118; 120. I have chosen to take Pss 40 and 66 in their totality, since I do not see the logic of extracting a psalm of thanksgiving from another psalm. I also have eliminated Ps 52 because the report is only an implied report and thus the psalm lacks one of the two essential elements.

5. Jacob Milgrom, *Leviticus 1–16*, Anchor Bible (New York: Doubleday, 1991), 219.

6. Claus Westermann, *Praise and Lament in the Psalms*, trans. Keith R. Crim and Richard N. Soulen (Edinburgh: T. & T. Clark, 1965), 121.

7. I have not listed Ps 107 among the psalms of thanksgiving of the individual because it cites four typical situations that should call forth thanksgiving rather than reflecting the reality of the psalmist's own experience. But it certainly belongs to the genre in the sense that it sets forth the pattern by which the psalms of thanksgiving came into being. Those psalms that are listed in table 8.1 reflect an individual experience that the writer had undergone.

8. Herman Gunkel, *Introduction to Psalms*, trans. James D. Nogalski (Macon, Ga.: Mercer University Press, 1998), 213.

9. Leopold Sabourin, *The Psalms, Their Origin and Meaning* (New York: Alba House, 1974), 277.

10. J. David Pleins, *The Psalms: Songs of Tragedy, Hope, and Justice*, (Maryknoll, N.Y.: Orbis, 1993), 46.

11. Westermann, *Praise and Lament in the Psalms*, 81–82.

12. James Luther Mays, *Psalms*, Interpretation (Louisville: John Knox, 1994), 24.

13. Ibid. Mays suggests this topic of importance.

Chapter 9

1. Leopold Sabourin, *The Psalms, Their Origin and Meaning*, 2nd ed. (New York: Alba House, 1974), 320.

2. A. H. van Zyl, "Psalm 23" in *Studies on the Psalms* (Pro Rege-Pers Bewperk, 1963), 68.

3. Patrick Miller, *Interpreting the Psalms* (Philadelphia: Fortress, 1986), 113.

4. Hans-Joachim Kraus, *Psalms 1–59: A Continental Commentary*, trans. Hilton C. Oswald (Minneapolis: Fortress, 1993), 305.

5. For example, van Zyl, "Psalm 23," 75–76; William Allen Knight, *The Song of Our Syrian Guest* (Boston: Pilgrim, 1904).

6. Leslie D. Weatherhead, *A Shepherd Remembers* (London: Hodder and Stoughton, 1937), 25.

7. For example, Claus Westermann, *The Living Psalms*, trans. J. R. Porter (Grand Rapids: Eerdmans, 1989), 146.

8. See chapter 12.

9. See chapter 3 for a discussion of the strategic place of Psalm 90 as the first psalm of Book 4.

10. Leslie C. Allen, *Psalms 101–150* (Waco: Word, 1983), 108.

11. Ibid., 163.

Chapter 10

1. Hermann Gunkel, *Introduction to Psalms: The Genres of the Religious Lyrics of Israel*, completed by Joachim Begrich, trans. James D. Nogalski (Macon, Ga.: Mercer University Press, 1998), 103.

2. Sigmund Mowinckel, *The Psalms in Israel's Worship*, trans. D. R. Ap-Thomas (Nashville: Abingdon, 1962), 1:119.

3. Derek Kidner mentions both of these methods in his discussion of the "enthronement psalms," *Psalms 1–72*, (London: Tyndale, 1973), 14–15.

4. Ibid., 15.

Chapter 11

1. Sigmund Mowinckel, *The Psalms in Israel's Worship*, trans. D. R. Ap-Thomas (Nashville: Abingdon, 1962), 1:115.

2. Derek Kidner, *Psalms 1–72* (London: Tyndale, 1973), 13.

3. Some include Ps 29.

4. J. D. W. Watts, "Yahweh Malak Psalms," *Theologische Zeitschrift* 21 (1965): 341–48, esp. 343.

5. David M. Howard Jr., *The Structure of Psalms 93–100* (Winona Lake, Ind.: Eisenbrauns, 1997), 119–31.

6. Ibid., 119.

7. Ibid., 122.

8. Pss 29, 44, 78, 68, 74, 84, 95, 98, 145, 149. Some scholars do include Ps 29.

9. The "rivers" may refer to the hostile nations who opposed Israel and thus Yahweh. Together the "rivers" and the sea combine the idea of hostile nations and the threatening "waters" of Gn 1 that raise their protest against the sovereign God. See Marvin E. Tate, *Psalms 51–100* (Dallas: Word, 1990), 479–80.

10. The Hebrew imperfect may be translated as a present (so NIV) or a future tense. The prophetic perfect speaks of the future as if it has already happened, for example, "The people walking in darkness *have seen* a great light" (Is 9:2).

11. John Calvin, *Commentary on the Book of Psalms*, trans. James Anderson (Grand Rapids: Eerdmans, 1949), 4:47.

12. Franz Delitzsch, *Biblical Commentary on the Psalms*, trans. David Eaton (London: Hodder and Stoughton, 1902) 3:34.

13. Ibid., 3:53–54.

14. I am indebted to Howard's helpful summary of the dating considerations in his *The Structure of Psalms 93–100*, 184–92.

15. Ibid., 190.

16. Ibid.

17. See Delitzsch, *Biblical Commentary on the Psalms*, 3:53, 58, 62.

18. Mitchell Dahood, *Psalms II: 51–100* (Garden City, N.Y.: Doubleday, 1968), 357.

19. Howard, *The Structure of Psalms 93–100*, 190–92.

Chapter 12

1. Sigmund Mowinckel, "Psalms and Wisdom," in *Wisdom in Israel and the Ancient Near East*, ed. M. Noth and D. Winton Thomas, Supplements to Vetus Testamentum 3 (Leiden: Brill, 1955), 205–24.

2. Roland E. Murphy, "A Consideration of the Classification, 'Wisdom Psalms,'" in *Congress Volume: Bonn, 1962*, Supplements to Vetus Testamentum 9 (Leiden: Brill, 1963), 156–67.

3. Leopold Sabourin, *The Psalms, Their Origin and Meaning*, 2nd ed. (Alba House, 1974), 371.

4. Murphy, "A Consideration of the Classification," 161.

5. J. Kenneth Kuntz, "The Canonical Wisdom Psalms of Ancient Israel—Their Rhetorical, Thematic, and Formal Dimensions," in *Rhetorical Criticism: Essays in Honor of James Muilenberg*, ed. Jared J. Jackson and Martin Kessler (Pittsburg: Pickwick, 1974), 208–11.

6. R. B. Y. Scott, *The Way of Wisdom* (New York: Macmillan, 1971), 201.

7. These criteria are for the most part those of Murphy.

8. Scott, *The Way of Wisdom*, 121–22.

9. Peter C. Craigie, *Psalms 1–50*, Word Biblical Commentary, vol. 19 (Waco: Word, 1983), 265.

10. C. Hassell Bullock, *An Introduction to the Old Testament Poetic Books* (Chicago: Moody, 1988), 136.

Chapter 13

1. See chapter 3.

2. James Luther Mays, *The Lord Reigns: A Theological Handbook to the Psalms* (Louisville: Westminster John Knox, 1994), 134.

3. James Luther Mays, "The Place of the Torah-Psalms in the Psalter," *Journal of Biblical Literature* 106 (1987): 11.

4. word(s) [*davar, 'omer, 'imrah*], at least 53 times combined; decrees/statutes [*khoqim*], at least 26 times; precepts [*piqqudhim*], at least 23; testimonies ['*eduth*], at least 26; commandments [*mitsvoth*], at least 23; covenant [*berith*], only 3; and law or Torah [*torah*], 27.

5. Mays, "The Place of the Torah-Psalms in the Psalter," 12.

6. See chapter 3.

7. J. Clinton McCann Jr., *Theological Introduction to the Book of Psalms* (Nashville: Abingdon, 1993), 35.

8. C. S. Lewis, *Reflections on the Psalms* (San Diego: Harcourt Brace Jovanovich, 1959), 63.

9. Peter C. Craigie, *Psalms 1–50* (Waco: Word, 1983), 183.

10. Lewis, *Reflections on the Psalms*, 64.

11. Craigie, *Psalms 1–50*, 183.

12. John Ker, *The Psalms in History and Biography* (Edinburgh: Andrew Elliot, 1888), 143.

13. Lewis, *Reflections on the Psalms*, 58–59.

14. Hans-Joachim Kraus, *Psalms 60–150: A Continental Commentary*,

trans. Hilton C. Oswald (Minneapolis: Fortress, 1993), 412. Artur Weiser, *The Psalms, A Commentary*, trans. Herbert Hartwell (Philadelphia: Westminster, 1962), gives a list of these genres with other examples on 740.

15. Harvey H. Guthrie Jr., *Israel's Sacred Songs: A Study of Dominant Themes* (New York: Seabury, 1966), 191.

16. Jane T. Stoddart, *The Psalms for Every Day* (London: Hodder and Stoughton, 1939), 286.

17. Weiser, *The Psalms, A Commentary*, 740–41.

18. The word "faithfulness" (or "truth") applies to the Torah also in Ps 119:30, 75, 86, and 138.

19. The word "truth" or "true" (*'emeth*) occurs in 119:43, 142, 151, and 160.

Chapter 14

1. Erich Zenger, *A God of Vengeance? Understanding the Psalms of Divine Wrath*, trans. Linda M. Maloney (Louisville: Westminster John Knox, 1996), 79.

2. John L. McKenzie, "The Imprecations of the Psalter," *American Ecclesiastical Review* 111 (1994): 84.

3. Sigmund Mowinckel, *The Psalms in Israel's Worship*, trans. D. R. Ap-Thomas (Nashville: Abingdon, 1962), 2:49.

4. Othmar Keel, *The Symbolism of the Biblical World: Ancient Near Eastern Iconography and the Book of Psalms* (New York: Seabury, 1978), 85.

5. McKenzie, "The Imprecations of the Psalter," 83.

6. C. Hassell Bullock, *An Introduction to the Old Testament Poetic Books*, rev. ed. (Chicago: Moody, 1988), 140–41.

7. McKenzie, "The Imprecations of the Psalter," 85.

8. Ibid., 90.

9. Ibid., 92–93.

10. Keel, *The Symbolism of the Biblical World*, 85.

11. Johannes G. Vos, "The Ethical Problem of the Imprecating Psalms," *Westminster Theological Journal* 4 (1992): 134–35.

12. Zenger, *A God of Vengeance?*, 74–76.

13. C. S. Lewis, *Reflections on the Psalms* (San Diego: Harcourt Brace Jovanovich, 1959), 30.

14. Zenger, *A God of Vengeance?*, 79.

15. Ibid.

16. Charles H. Spurgeon, *Psalms*, vol. 1, ed., Alister McGrath and J. I. Packer (Wheaton: Crossway, 1993), 136.

Select Bibliography of the Psalms

Afterlife

Alexander, T. D. "The Psalms and the Afterlife." *Irish Biblical Studies* 9 (1987): 2–17.

Asaph Psalms

Goulder, Michael. *The Psalms of Asaph and the Pentateuch: Studies in the Psalter, III.* Journal for the Study of the Old Testament Supplement Series 233. Sheffield: Sheffield Academic, 1996.

Houston, Walter. "David, Asaph and the Mighty Works of God: Theme and Genre in the Psalm Collections." *Journal for the Study of the Old Testament* 68 (1995): 93–111.

Ascents (Songs of Ascents)

Goulder, Michael D. "The Songs of Ascents and Nehemiah." *Journal for the Study of the Old Testament* 75 (1997): 43–58.

Keet, Cuthbert C. *A Study of the Psalms of Ascents.* London: Mitre, 1969.

Commentaries

Allen, Leslie C. *Psalms 101–150.* Word Biblical Commentary. Waco, Tex.: Word, 1983.

Augustine. *Expositions on the Book of Psalms.* Library of the Fathers. 6 vols. Oxford: Parker, 1847–1970.

Calvin, John. *Commentary on the Book of Psalms.* Translated by James Anderson, 5 vols. Grand Rapids: Eerdmans, 1949.

Craigie, Peter C. *Psalms 1–50,* Word Biblical Commentary, vol. 19. Waco: Word, 1983.

Dahood, Mitchell. *Psalms.* 3 vols. Anchor Bible. Garden City, N.Y.: Doubleday, 1966, 1968, 1970.

Delitzsch, Franz. *Biblical Commentary on the Psalms.* Translated by David Eaton. London: Hodder and Stoughton, 1902.

Gerstenberger, Erhard S. *Psalms,* Part 1. Grand Rapids: Eerdmans, 1988.

Kidner, Derek. *Psalms 1–72.* London: Tyndale, 1973.

———. *Psalms 73–150.* Downers Grove: InterVarsity, 1975.

Kirkpatrick, A. F. *The Book of Psalms.* Cambridge: Cambridge University Press, 1898.

Kraus, Hans-Joachim. *Psalms 1–59: A Continental Commentary.* Translated by Hilton C. Oswald. Minneapolis: Fortress, 1993.

———. *Psalms 60–150: A Continental Commentary.* Translated by Hilton C. Oswald. Minneapolis: Fortress, 1993.

Luther, Martin. *Luther's Works.* Vols. 10–11, edited by H. C. Oswalt. Vols. 12–14, edited by J. Pelikan. St. Louis: Concordia, 1974–76 and 1955–58.

Tate, Marvin E. *Psalms 51–100.* Waco: Word, 1990.

Weiser, Artur. *The Psalms, A Commentary.* Translated by Herbert Hartwell. Philadelphia: Westminster, 1962.

Creation

Clifford, Richard J. "Creation in the Psalms." In *Creation in the Biblical Traditions,* edited by Richard J. Clifford and John J. Collins, 57–69. Catholic Biblical Quarterly Monograph Series 24. Washington, D.C.: Catholic Biblical Association of America, 1992.

Critical Studies

Beckwith, Roger T. "The Early History of the Psalter." *Tyndale Bulletin* 46 (1995): 1–27.

Childs, Brevard S. "Reflections on the Modern Study of the Psalms." In *Magnalia Dei: The Mighty Acts of God,* edited by Frank Moore Cross, Werner E. Lemke, and Patrick D. Miller Jr., 377–88. Garden City, New York: Doubleday, 1976.

Collins, Terrence. "Decoding the Psalms: A Structural Approach to the Psalter." *Journal for the Study of the Old Testament* 37 (1987): 41–60.

Feininger, Bernd. "A Decade of German Psalm-Criticism." *Journal for the Study of the Old Testament* 20 (1981): 91–103.

Gunkel, Hermann. *Introduction to Psalms: The Genres of the Religious Lyric of Israel.* Completed by Joachim Begrich and translated by James D. Nogalski. Macon, Ga.: Mercer University Press, 1998.

Howard, David M., Jr. "Editorial Activity in the Psalter: A State-of-the-Field Survey." *Word and World* 9 (1989): 274–85.

Kuntz, J. Kenneth. "Engaging the Psalms: Gains and Trends in Recent Research." *Currents in Research: Biblical Studies* 2 (1994): 77–106.

Mays, James Luther. "Past, Present, and Prospect in Psalm Study." In *Old Testament Interpretation: Past, Present, and Future: Essays in Honor of Gene M. Tucker,* edited by James Luther Mays, David L. Petersen, and Kent Harold Richards, 147–56. Nashville: Abingdon, 1995.

Waltke, Bruce K. "A Canonical Process Approach to the Psalms." In *Tradition and Testament: Essays in Honor of Charles Lee Feinberg,* edited by John S. Feinberg and Paul D. Feinberg, 3–18. Chicago: Moody, 1981.

Westermann, Claus. *The Praise of God in the Psalms.* Translated by Keith Crim. Richmond: John Knox, 1965.

Whybray, Norman. *Reading the Psalms as a Book.* Journal for the Study of the Old Testament Supplement Series 222. Sheffield: Sheffield Academic, 1996.

Zenger, Erich. "New Approaches to the Study of the Psalms." *P.O.B.A.* 17 (1994): 37–55.

David

Cooper, Alan M. "The Life and Times of King David according to the Book of Psalms." In *The Poet and the Historian: Essays in Literary and Historical Biblical Criticism,* 117–31. Chico, Calif.: Scholars, 1983.

Mays, James Luther. "The David of the Psalms." *Interpretation* 40 (1986): 143–55.

Enemies

Anderson, George W. "Enemies and Evildoers in the Book of Psalms." *Bulletin of the John Rylands Library* 48 (1965–66): 18–29.

Birkeland, Harris. *The Evildoers in the Book of Psalms.* Oslo: Jacob Dybwad, 1955.

Croft, Steven J. L. "The Antagonists in the Psalms." In *The Identity of the Individual in the Psalms,* 15–48. Journal for the Study of the Old Testament Supplement Series 44. Sheffield: JSOT Press, 1987.

Gerstenberger, Erhard S. "Enemies and Evildoers in the Psalms: A Challenge to Christian Preaching." *Horizons in Biblical Theology* 5 (1983): 61–77.

Hobbs, T. R., and P. K. Jackson. "The Enemy in the Psalms." *Biblical Theology Bulletin* 21 (1991): 22–29.

Sheppard, Gerald T. "'Enemies' and the Politics of Prayer in the Book of Psalms." In *The Bible and the Politics of Exegesis: Essays in Honor of Norman K. Gottwald on His Sixty-fifth Birthday*, edited by David Jobling, Peggy L. Day, and Gerald T. Sheppard, 61–82. Cleveland: Pilgrim, 1991.

Hebrew Text

Sanders, J. A. *The Dead Sea Psalms Scroll*. Ithaca, N.Y.: Cornell University Press, 1967.

———. "Pre-Masoretic Psalter Texts." *Catholic Biblical Quarterly* 27 (1965): 114–23.

———. *The Psalms Scroll of Qumran Cave II*. Discoveries in the Judaean Desert of Jordan, vol. 4. Oxford: Clarendon, 1965.

History

du Toit, S. "The Psalms and History." *Studies on the Psalms*, 18–29. Potchefstroom: Pro Rege-Pers Beperk, 1963.

Haglund, Erik. *Historical Motifs in the Psalms*. Stockholm: CWK Gleerup, 1984.

Hyde, Clark. "The Remembrance of the Exodus in the Psalms." *Worship* 62 (1988): 404–14.

Imagery

Keel, Othmar. *The Symbolism of the Biblical World: Ancient Near Eastern Iconography and the Book of Psalms*. New York: Seabury, 1978.

Imprecatory Psalms

Martin, Chalmers. "The Imprecations in the Psalms." *PTR* 1 (1903): 537–53.

McKenzie, John L. "The Imprecations of the Psalter." *American Ecclesiastical Review* 111 (1944): 81–96.

Vos, Johannes G. "The Ethical Problem of the Imprecating Psalms." *Westminster Theological Journal* 4 (1992): 123–38.

Zenger, Erich. *A God of Vengeance? Understanding the Psalms of Divine Wrath*. Translated by Linda M. Maloney. Louisville: Westminster John Knox, 1996.

Interpretation (Hermeneutics)

Childs, Brevard S. "Reflections on the Modern Study of the Psalms." In *Magnalia Dei: The Mighty Acts of God*, edited by Frank Moore Cross, Werner E. Lemke, and Patrick D. Miller Jr., 377–88. Garden City, New York: Doubleday, 1976.

Day, J. "The Theology of the Psalms and the History of Their Interpretation by the Jews and in the Christian Church," in *Psalms*, 123–41. Sheffield: JSOT Press, 1990.

Mays, James Luther. "A Question of Identity: The Threefold Hermeneutic of Psalmody." *Asbury Theological Journal* 46 (1991): 87–94.

Tate, Marvin E. "The Interpretation of the Psalms." *Review and Expositor* 81 (1984): 363–75.

Introductions

Anderson, Bernard W. *Out of the Depths*. Rev. ed. Philadelphia: Westminster, 1983.

Bonhoeffer, Dietrich. *Psalms: The Prayer Book of the Bible*. Translated by James H. Burtness. Minneapolis: Augsburg, 1970.

Brueggemann, Walter. *Praying the Psalms*. Winona, Minn.: Saint Mary's Press, 1982.

Crenshaw, James L. *The Psalms: An Introduction*. Grand Rapids: Eerdmans, 2001.

Goldingay, John. *Praying the Psalms*. Nottingham: Grove Books, 1993.

Guthrie, Harvey H. *Israel's Sacred Songs: A Study of Dominant Themes*. New York: Seabury, 1966.

Holladay, William L. *The Psalms through Three Thousand Years: Prayerbook of a Cloud of Witnesses*. Minneapolis: Fortress, 1993.

Lewis, C. S. *Reflections on the Psalms*. San Diego: Harcourt Brace Jovanovich, 1959.

Longman, Tremper III. *How to Read the Psalms*. Downers Grove: InterVarsity, 1988.

Mays, James Luther. *The Lord Reigns: A Theological Handbook to the Psalms*. Louisville: Westminster John Knox, 1994.

McCann, J. Clinton, Jr. *A Theological Introduction to the Book of Psalms: The Psalms as Torah*. Nashville: Abingdon, 1993.

Mowinckel, Sigmund. *The Psalms in Israel's Worship*. 2 vols. Translated by D. R. Ap-Thomas. Nashville: Abingdon, 1962.

Sabourin, Leopold. *The Psalms, Their Origin and Meaning*. New Edition. New York: Alba House, 1974.

Seybold, Klaus. *Introducing the Psalms*. Translated by Graeme Dunphy. Edinburgh: T. & T. Clark, 1990.

Kingship of Yahweh Psalms

Eaton, John H. *Kingship and the Psalms*. 2nd ed. Sheffield: JSOT Press, 1986.

Gray, John. "The Kingship of God in the Prophets and Psalms," *Vetus Testamentum* 11 (1961): 1–29.

Howard, David M., Jr. *The Structure of Psalms 93–100*. Winona Lake, Ind.: Eisenbrauns, 1997.

Johnson, A. R. "Living Issues in Biblical Scholarship: Divine Kingship and the Old Testament." *Expository Times* 62 (1950–51): 36–42.

Watts, J. D. W. "Yahweh Malak Psalms." *Theologische Zeitschrift* 21 (1965): 341–48.

Korah Psalms

Goulder, Michael. *The Psalms of the Sons of Korah*. Journal for the Study of the Old Testament Supplement Series 20. Sheffield: JSOT Press, 1983.

Laments

Dillon, Richard J. "The Psalms of the Suffering Just." *Worship* 61 (1987): 430–40.

McConville, J. G. "Statement of Assurance in Psalms of Lament." *Irish Biblical Studies* 8 (1986): 64–75.

Miller, Patrick D. "Trouble and Woe: Interpreting the Biblical Laments." *Interpretation* 37 (1983): 32–45.

Language

Smick, Elmer B. "Mythopoetic Language in the Psalms." *Westminster Theological Journal* 44 (1982): 88–98.

Snaith, Norman H. "Selah." *Vetus Testamentum* 2 (1952): 43–56.

Tsevat, Matitiahu. *A Study of the Language of the Biblical Psalms*. Journal of

Biblical Literature Monograph, vol. 9. Philadelphia: Society of Biblical Literature, 1955.

Messiah

Durham, John I. "The King as 'Messiah' in the Psalms." *Review and Expositor* 81 (1984): 425–35.

Mays, James Luther. "'In a Vision': The Portrayal of the Messiah in the Psalms." *Ex Auditu* 7 (1991): 1–8.

Russell, S. H. "Calvin and the Messianic Interpretation of the Psalms." *Scottish Journal of Theology* 21 (1968): 37–47.

Metrical Psalms

Brink, Emily R. "Metrical Psalmody in North America: A Story of Survival and Revival." *Hymn* 44 (1993): 21.

Witvliet, John D. "The Spirituality of the Psalter: Metrical Psalms in Liturgy and Life in Calvin's Geneva." *Calvin Theological Journal* 32 (1997): 273–97.

Midrash

Braude, William G., trans. *The Midrash on Psalms*. New Haven: Yale University Press, 1959.

New Testament Use

Frost, S. B. "The Christian Interpretation of the Psalms." *Canadian Journal of Theology* 5 (1959): 25–34.

Harmon, Allan M. "Aspects of Paul's Use of the Psalms." *Westminster Theological Journal* 32 (1969): 1–23.

Harrisville, Roy A. "Paul and the Psalms." *Word and World* 5 (1985): 168–79.

Mays, James Luther. "Prayer and Christology: Psalm 22 as Perspective on the Passion." *Theology Today* 42 (1985): 322–31.

Piety

Anderson, Bernard W. "'Sicut Cervus': Evidence in the Psalter of Private Devotion in Ancient Israel." *Vetus Testamentum* 30 (1980): 388–97.

Brueggemann, Walter. "Psalms and the Life of Faith: A Suggested Typology of Function." *Journal for the Study of the Old Testament* 17 (1980): 3–32.

Butler, Trent C. "Piety in the Psalms." *Review and Expositor* 81 (1984): 385–94.

Harmon, Allan M. "The Psalms and Reformed Spirituality." *Reformed Theological Review* 53 (1994): 53–63.

Hasler, Richard A. "The Influence of David and the Psalms upon John Calvin's Life and Thought." *Hartford Quarterly* 5 (1965): 7–18.

Poetry

Alden, Robert L. "Chiastic Psalms: A Study in the Mechanics of Semitic Poetry in Psalms 1–50." *Journal of the Evangelical Theological Society* 17 (1974): 12–13.

Alter, Robert. *The Art of Biblical Poetry*. New York: Basic Books, 1985.

Cripps, R. S. "Two British Interpreters of the Old Testament: Robert Lowth (1710–1787) and Samuel Lee (1783–1852)." *Bulletin of the John Rylands Library* 35 (1952–53): 385–402.

Freedman, David Noel. "Acrostic Poems in the Hebrew Bible: Alphabetic and Otherwise." *Catholic Biblical Quarterly* 48 (1986): 408–31.

Kugel, James L. *The Idea of Biblical Poetry*. New Haven, Conn.: Yale University Press, 1981.

————. *In Potiphar's House*. San Francisco: Harper San Francisco, 1990.

————, ed. *Poetry and Prophecy: The Beginnings of a Literary Tradition*. Ithaca, N.Y.: Cornell University Press, 1990.

Kuntz, J. Kenneth. "Biblical Hebrew Poetry in Recent Research, Part I." *Currents in Research: Biblical Studies* 6 (1998): 31–64.

Miller, Patrick D. "Synonymous-Sequential Parallelism in the Psalms." *Biblica* 61 (1980): 256–60.

Praise Psalms (Psalms of Praise)

Fretheim, Terrence E. "Nature's Praise of God in the Psalms." *Ex Auditu* 3 (1987): 16–30.

Goldingay, John. "The Dynamic Cycle of Prayer and Praise in the Psalms." *Journal for the Study of the Old Testament* 20 (1981): 85–90.

Preaching from the Psalms

Sedgwick, Colin J. "Preaching from the Psalms." *Expository Times* 103 (Oct 1991-Sept 1992): 361–64.

Structure of the Book

Anderson, R. Dean. "The Division and Order of the Psalms." *Westminster Theological Journal* 56 (1994): 219–41.

Bliese, Loren F. "Structurally Marked Peak in Psalms 1–24." *Occasional Papers on Translation and Text Linguistics* 4 (1990): 265–321.

Brueggemann, Walter. "Bounded by Obedience and Praise: The Psalms as Canon." *Journal for the Study of the Old Testament* 50 (1991): 63–92.

———— and Patrick D. Miller. "Psalm 73 as a Canonical Marker." *Journal for the Study of the Old Testament* 72 (1996): 45–56.

Day, J. "The Composition of the Psalter," in *Psalms*, 109–22. Sheffield: JSOT Press, 1990.

Goulder, Michael D. "The Fourth Book of the Psalms." *Journal of Theological Sudies* 26 (1975) 269–89.

Walton, John H. "Psalms: A Cantata about the Davidic Covenant." *Journal of the Evangelical Theological Society* 34 (1991): 21–31.

Wilson, Gerald H. "Evidence of Editorial Divisions in the Hebrew Psalter." *Vetus Testamentum* 34 (1984): 337–52.

————. *The Shape and Shaping of the Psalter*. Edited by J. Clinton McCann. Sheffield: Sheffield Academic, 1993.

————. "The Use of Royal Psalms at the 'Seams' of the Hebrew Psalter." *Journal for the Study of the Old Testament* 35 (1986): 85–94.

————. "The Use of 'Untitled' Psalms in the Hebrew Psalter." *Zeitschrift für die alttestamentliche Wissenschaft* 97 (1985): 404–13.

Zenger, Erich. "The Composition and Theology of the Fifth Book of Psalms: Psalms 107–45." *Journal for the Study of the Old Testament* 80 (1988): 81.

Theology

Alexander, T. D. "The Psalms and the Afterlife." *Irish Biblical Studies* 9 (1987): 2–17.

Clifford, Richard J. "Creation in the Psalms." In *Creation in the Biblical Traditions*, edited by Richard J. Clifford and John J. Collins, 57–69. Catholic Biblical Quarterly Monograph Series 24. Washington, D.C.: Catholic Biblical Association of America, 1992.

Kraus, Hans-Joachim. *Theology of the Psalms*. Translated by Keith Crim. Minneapolis: Augsburg, 1986.

Titles

Childs, Brevard S. "Psalm Titles and Midrashic Exegesis." *Journal of Semitic Studies* 16 (1971): 137–50.

Delekat, L. "Probleme der Psalmenüberschriften." *Zeitschrift für die alttestamentliche Wissenschaft* 76 (1964): 281f.

Sawyer, John F. A. "An Analysis of the Context and Meaning of the Psalm-Headings." In *Transactions of the Glasgow University Oriental Society* 22 (1967–68): 26–38.

Slomovic, Elieser. "Toward an Understanding of the Formation of the Historical Titles in the Book of Psalms." *Zeitschrift für die alttestamentliche Wissenschaft* 91 (1979): 350–80.

Torah Psalms

De Pinto, Basil. "The Torah and the Psalms." *Journal of Biblical Literature* 86 (1967): 154–74.

Mays, James Luther. "The Place of the Torah-Psalms in the Psalter."
Journal of Biblical Literature 106 (1987): 3–12.

McCann, J. Clinton, Jr. "The Psalms as Torah, Then and Now," in *A Theological Introduction to the Book of Psalms: The Psalms as Torah,* 25–40. Nashville: Abingdon, 1993.

Sarna, N. M. "The Psalm Superscriptions and the Guilds." In *Studies in Jewish Religious and Intellectual History: Presented to Alexander Altmann on the Occasion of His Seventieth Birthday,* edited by Siegfried Stein and Raphael Loewe, 281–300. London: Institute for Jewish Studies, 1979.

Types

Anderson, Bernard W. "Index of Psalms According to Type." In *Out of the Depths,* 239–42. Philadelphia: Westminster, 1974.

Wisdom Psalms

Hurvitz, Avi. "Wisdom Vocabulary in the Hebrew Psalter: A Contribution to the Study of 'Wisdom Psalms.'" *Vetus Testamentum* 38 (1988): 41–51.

Kugel, James L. "The Canonical Wisdom Psalms of Ancient Israel—Their Rhetorical, Thematic, and Formal Dimensions." In *Rhetorical Criticism: Essays in Honor of James*
Muilenburg, edited by Jared J. Jackson and Martin Kessler, 186–223. Pittsburgh: Pickwick, 1974.

———. "The Retribution Motif in Psalmic Wisdom." *Zeitschrift für die alttestamentliche Wissenschaft* 89 (1977): 223–33.

Murphy, Roland E. "A Consideration of the Classification, 'Wisdom Psalms.'" In *Congress Volume: Bonn, 1962,* 156–67. Supplements to Vetus Testamentum 9. Leiden: Brill, 1963.

Worship

Hawn, C. Michael. "Current Trends in Hymnody: Psalm Singing." *Hymn* 43 (1992): 32–42.

Lamb, John Alexander. *The Psalms in Christian Worship.* London: Faith, 1962.

Maher, Michael. *The Psalms in Jewish Worship.* Proceedings of the Irish Biblical Association 17 (1994), 9–36.

Murphy, Roland E. "The Psalms and Worship." *Ex Auditu* 8 (1992): 23–31.

Shepard, Massey H., Jr. *The Psalms in Christian Worship.* Minneapolis: Augsburg, 1976.

Glossary

actualization
A mystical celebration of mythical history attributed to Israel. Although this was somewhat common among ancient peoples, its idea was alien to the Israelites, who celebrated their history as real through analogy and telescoping.

analogy
A Hebraic celebration of Israel's history by viewing a present or future event as equal to or even surpassing a past analogous event of evident glory. For instance, Jeremiah viewed the return from Babylon as an exodus of far greater proportions than the Egyptian one (Jer 16:14–15).

Anointed One
Hebrew *Mashiakh* or English "Messiah," with which the Psalms express a special relationship between God and the king, or Father and Son, that would bless the people with peace.

Asaph psalms
Eleven psalms (73–83) that form the lead collection in Book 3 of the Psalter, and one psalm in Book 2 (50). These psalms exhibit a concern with Israel's enemies and how God will deal with the wicked.

Baal of Peor
The infamous god worshiped on the Moabite plain where Israel fell into idolatry. Psalm 106 records this spiritual harlotry, along with the heroism of Phinehas, who intervened in faith and stayed the resultant plague.

chiasm
A feature of Hebrew poetry that structures thought in a mirror pattern, restating themes inversely. The name comes from the Greek verb *chiazein*, meaning "to place crosswise," and the pattern follows the shape of the Greek letter *chi* (χ). This device can either mark entire psalms or merely highlight certain segments.

colon *See* stich.

community psalms of thanksgiving
These psalms incorporate the essential criteria of thanksgiving (report of crisis and acknowledgment that it has passed) within communal terms. This community aspect is demonstrated by either plural pronouns or by clear signposts that the first person singular pronouns refer to Israel.

community psalms of trust
Psalms that articulate a deep sense of trust in God, in which the tone of trust is dominant. They are spoken on behalf of Israel. These psalms consistently have a *declaration of trust* and an *interior lament*. They are Psalms 90, 115, 123, 124, 125, and 126.

conquest
The time of Israel's history in which it was destined to conquer the Promised Land. Next to the exodus, this is the most frequently mentioned historical period in the Psalms. The psalmists paint this period in terms of Yahweh's power, promise, and provision.

creation
The formation of all things by the word of the Lord. To the psalmist, this was far more than a statement of beginnings, it was a key doctrine proving God's ownership of the earth and perfect control, both physical and moral. To affirm God as Creator was also to affirm the perfect justice and judgment inherent in his works.

curses
Caustic maledictions or imprecations directed toward the enemies of the psalmists. These strong words present an ethical problem for the interpreter: How can one love one's enemies and still pray for vengeance upon them? Resolution can only come as the interpreter commits him/herself to the psalmists' larger theological context of community, justice, and judgment within the kingdom of God.

Davidic psalms
The largest clusters of psalms in the Psalter, and traditionally attributed to King David, these psalms are represented in every division: Book 1 (3–41), Book 2 (51–65), Book 3 (86), Book 4 (101 and 103), and Book 5 (108–10, 122, 124, 131, and 138–45). Significantly, collections of these psalms bookend the Psalter at the beginning and the conclusion.

declarative praise
A form of psalmic praise where God is praised, or believers are commanded to praise him, in generic terms without narration. For example, saying, "Praise the LORD" (Hebrew *hallelujah*—"praise" [imperative] + jah, [shortened form of Yahweh or LORD]) without attendant details.

descriptive praise
This form of psalmic praise includes the details that evoke the praise. Here the psalmist praises God and then adds specifics: praise for creation, presence, salvation, etc.

enemies
The persons or peoples toward whom the imprecations of the Psalms are directed.

exodus
The freeing of Israel from Egyptian slavery which formed, in all its elements, a national paradigm of sinful bondage and divine deliverance. The psalmists repeatedly apply this lesson in order to evoke praise and spiritual introspection.

hallelujah psalms
Psalms 146–50, the concluding psalms of the Psalter. Each of the psalms begins and ends with the imperative *hallelujah*, "Praise the LORD." Separated from this group are two other psalms that have this characteristic, Psalms 113 and 117. Also, Psalms 111 and 112 begin with *hallelujah* but do not end that way. This category is not a formal genre, although Psalms 146–50 do clearly belong to the genre of praise.

Hillel
Born about 50 B.C., Hillel, a Pharisee, was the president of the Sanhedrin during the reign of Herod the Great, sharing the leadership with Shammai, his more conservative colleague. Hillel was known for his kind and accepting manner as well as his erudite scholarship.

imprecatory psalms
A group of psalms containing harsh judgments upon the enemies of the psalmists. At least seven psalms fit into this category to some degree: 35, 55, 59, 69, 79, 109, and 137. Because the term "imprecation" inordinately emphasizes the

249

"curses" called down upon the psalmist's persecutors, perhaps "psalms of anger" or "psalms of wrath" would better describe the scope of these psalms.

individual psalms of thanksgiving
These psalms appropriate the components of thanksgiving in personal terms, and often use the verb "to thank" (Hebrew *yadhah*) or the noun "thanks" (*todhah*).

individual psalms of trust
Psalms that articulate a deep sense of trust in God, in which the tone of trust is dominant. They are spoken by individuals, but they also frequently summon the community to trust in God. These psalms consistently have a *declaration of trust* and an *interior lament*. They are Psalms 4, 16, 23, 27, 62, and 73.

interior lament
In the psalms of trust the psalmist refers to some problem he has had or observed, which has shaped his faith and elicited his expression of trust in God. Given other circumstances, this problem would have been expressed as a lament. However, the psalmist has learned to trust despite the problem, and that is the point of the reference to the circumstances.

judgment
The inevitable result of breaching God's standard of justice. The psalmists understood this as inherent in the created order of the LORD and undertaken in order to bring the offender back into just harmony with God and humanity; it was not mere capricious whim or vengeful spite (as in the pagan paradigm).

justice
The divine standard by which all actions and attitudes are measured. The psalmists found this centered in the character of God, affirmed in his creation, and spoken in his Law.

kingship of Yahweh psalms
The group of psalms tied together by their assertion of the present reign of Yahweh and often containing the declaration, "*yhwh malak*," or, "The LORD reigns!" These psalms filled the silent void of a lost Davidic dynasty with the awesome affirmation that the LORD himself now sat upon the throne in regal power.

Korah psalms
Two major series of psalms attributed to the "sons of Korah," whom David had given responsibility for keeping the temple gates. The first series introduces Book 2 (42–49) of the Psalter while the second concludes Book 3 (84–85, 87–88).

lamenatstseakh
An expression derived from two terms, the preposition "to, for, by," and a form of the verb "to excel." It is probably a dedicatory note to the leader of the musical program in the temple or tabernacle.

laments of the individual
A personal lamentation, in which there are eight component parts: address and introductory cry to God for help, lament, confession of trust, petition, assurance of being heard, wish for God's intervention, vow of praise, and praise of God when petition has been heard. This personal cry often arises from illness or loneliness.

laments of the people
A community lamentation, in which there are five component parts: address and introductory petition, lament, confession of trust, petition, and vow of praise. This community cry often arises as a result of maltreatment from enemies or national defeat and despair.

maskil
A title of literary or musical genre alternately understood as an artistic or didactic song. Although the term titles thirteen psalms, its exact meaning is lost; perhaps understanding it as a "well-crafted Levitical song" is the closest we can come.

metrical psalms
The adaptation of the Psalms into the Latin meter and rhyme, primarily for singing in worship.

midrash
A method of interpreting the Bible that ranges from the literal meaning to the hidden meaning of a text, with emphasis on the hidden. Stylistically, many of the midrashim (pl.) seem to have been sermons on the biblical text. The term refers both to the method and the various collections of these interpretations, the latter of which range from the second to the twelfth century. One of the major collections is the *Midrash on the Psalms*, most likely

edited during the Talmudic Period of Judaism.

miktam
A title of literary or musical genre variously understood as golden, atonement, pillar, indelible, or silent. With a meaning obscure to modern scholarship, it prefaces only certain Davidic psalms that reflect situations of peril.

mizmor
A title of literary or musical genre meaning "psalm." It suggests a poetic form intended for musical accompaniment. In the LXX this word is normally rendered *psalmos*, from which we get our word "psalm."

monarchy
The rule of Israel by human kings, which the psalmists focus upon as the golden era of David, the sweet singer of Israel, and the perfect poet-warrior-king.

parallelism
A Hebraic literary pattern that states an idea in one line and then develops the idea more fully in the next line, either by restating it in somewhat synonymous terms, or by contrasting it antithetically.

pesher
The hermeneutic of "this is that," which sees a past biblical prophecy as being presently fulfilled before the very eyes of the interpreter. The apostles often used this method ("this is that which was spoken") in light of Jesus' person and work, and specifically applied it to prophetic aspects of the Psalms.

piety
The deep devotion and moral obedience that characterized Hebrew religion from its very beginning. Inspired by examples of Enoch, Noah, Abraham, and Joseph, the Torah and prophets called the nation of Israel into a humble and pure relation with Yahweh. However, with the onset of national instability and dissolution, the Psalms began to direct this call to devotion toward the individual.

prophecy
Hebraic literature that built upon the covenantal aspects of the Torah by highlighting the relational aspect between God and Israel, somewhat deemphasizing the legal aspects while calling for national moral

obedience to the spirit of the law. The Psalms not only exhibit this prophetic distillation of Torah into national obedience, but also, like wisdom, often take it one step further by making moral obedience a personal issue.

proverbial wisdom
An expression of life and truth that is concentrated in a wise saying or proverb, and is often called "lower wisdom."

psalms of lament
The psalms that are characterized by a stated lament or complaint to God along with the reasons for lamenting. Converse to the psalms of praise, which find their bulk in Books 4 and 5 of the Psalter, so these psalms find their bulk in Books 1 through 3.

psalms of praise
These psalms bring a word of praise to God and the reasons for praising him. Although they are represented in Books 1 and 2, they dominate Books 4 and 5 of the Psalter, and seem to be the goal toward which the collection moves. Four themes have a high profile in these praises: creation, the universality of Yahweh's presence and sovereignty, Israel's history, and God's awesome deeds.

psalms of thanksgiving
These psalms exhibit two essential components: (1) the psalmist's report about his crisis, and (2) the statement or declaration that the crisis has passed and deliverance is an accomplished fact. They share with the psalms of lament the common ground of crisis, the difference being, of course, that here the crisis is past and the prayer is answered.

qal vahomer
Literally, "light and heavy," the first hermeneutical rule of Hillel, which argued that if one thing of less importance was true, then, by analogy, another thing of weightier importance must also be true. Jesus used this method in the Sermon on the Mount: "If the Father concerns himself with the flowers of the field, then how much more does he care about you?"

reflective wisdom
A relating of life and truth that presents real problems without pat answers or precise summations. It is pondering rather than pithy, and explores life's desperate places with brutal honesty. This is often referred to as "higher wisdom."

royal psalms
A group of psalms united by their subject of kingship and generally characterized by three criteria: (1) they refer to the king, (2) they mention the anointed one as a noun or make use of the verb "to anoint," and (3) they refer to David by name. These are not ironclad rules, in view of the fact that some other psalms within the group clearly describe the power, paraphernalia, and exploits of the king without naming him. These psalms also describe a unique Father/son relationship between God and the king.

Selah
An enigmatic word occuring seventy-one times in the Psalms and three times in Hb 3. Traditionally associated with "always, everlasting" (Norman H. Snaith, "Selah," *Vetus Testamentum* 2 [1952]: 55), it may be more a liturgical term than a theological one. Snaith has proposed, based on 1 Chr 16:41, that *selah* marked the end of the strophe or stanza, identifying the spot where the Levites responded, "Give thanks to the LORD for he is good, for his mercy endures forever" (Snaith, 43). While the Levites made that response, the congregation of Israel would prostrate themselves before the Lord (Snaith, 56).

shir
A title of literary or musical genre meaning "song." It seems to suggest a vocal rather than instrumental rendering, and is connected with the Songs of Ascents or Songs of the Steps (Pss 120–34), the former referring perhaps to a pilgrimage to the temple, and the latter to a singing of these psalms on the steps of the temple.

Sinai
The mountain in the wilderness from which God revealed his person and law to Moses and the people of Israel. The psalmists broadly apply this as the saving presence of the Lord, before which each generation of the faithful should bow, keeping the Lord's commandments.

Songs of Ascents
The psalms included in Book 5 of the Psalter as Psalms 120–34 and titled *shir hamma'aloth*. One theory is that these were likely sung by Israelites as they journeyed to Jerusalem for a festival. Later the Levites sang these songs as they stood on the fifteen steps of the temple.

songs of prayer
A term used by Hans-Joachim Kraus to designate those psalms that fall into the category of prayer (*tefillah*)—the largest category of psalms in the Psalter. They are comprised of three groups: prayer songs of the individual, prayer songs of the community, and thanksgiving songs of the individual.

sovereignty
The absolute rule of God over space and time and human history. The psalmists understood this reign of God as complete in every aspect of life and universally affirmed at all times by his creation, righteousness, justice, judgment, and mercy.

stich or *colon*
Common Greek and Latin designations for the completed thought segment (or line) of Hebrew poetry. This line is composed of several units. A two-line compound thought is called a *distich* or *bicolon*, while a three-line compound thought is called a *tristich* or *tricolon*, and so forth.

strophe
A larger thought unit in Hebrew poetry composed of multiple stichs.

tefilla
A psalm title meaning "prayer." As a term for literary genre, it probably refers to "prayer of lament" or "bidding prayer."

Tehillim
The Hebrew title for the Book of Psalms, which means "Praises."

telescoping
The Hebraic understanding of the present as merely a continuation of divine activity in the past and the future as also participatory of blessings past. In this manner Israel hopefully celebrated the past by viewing the past, present, and future within one faithful lens. For example, Moses preached that the covenant of God was made with the second-generation Hebrews standing before him, even though it was spoken to their forefathers (Dt 5:2–3).

thank offering
A pledge of gratefulness given by the worshiper after he or she has passed some crisis of life. On the basis of Psalm 107 the rabbis spoke of four occasions for thank offerings: a safe return from a voyage, a safe return from a desert journey, a recovery from illness, and a release from prison.

Torah
God's revelation of his character and covenant as recorded in the first five books of the Bible. At its heart is the law, which God gave to Israel on Mount Sinai, a law already written on the heart of ancestor Abraham (Gn 26:5). In the Psalms, this concept takes on many companion terms, the sum being that God's will for human life is divinely revealed and historically implemented in the story of Israel and mankind. Here in the Psalms, discussion of law or Torah takes on at least three forms: God's ways, God's works, and God's Words.

Torah psalms
The psalms that focus on the multiple theological facets of the Torah. While only three psalms (1, 19, 119) make Torah their primary focus, sixteen others focus on Torah enough to be categorized thus (18, 25, 33, 68, 78, 81, 89, 93, 94, 99, 103, 105, 111, 112, 147, 148). In many ways, these psalms provide the skeletal structure that supports the body of the Psalter: they give a solid interpretive framework for its personal, moral wisdom and national identity.

typology
An interpretive method that notes the historical and textual rela-tionship between two matters of revelation and then more fully understands the separate parts on the basis of the whole. In this manner the preceding texts presage those to come, and the latter texts cast their hue back onto those that came before. For example, we can understand Jesus' forsaken cry from the cross by placing it in context of Psalm 22; we also can understand Psalm 22 in light of Jesus' cross.

unit
The basic words or phrases that make up the larger thought segment of a poetic line or *stich*.

universal reign
God's rule whereby he sits enthroned over all kings of the earth from all times. It is not simply a reign in power, but a reign that draws the world into salvation: he puts his claim on all peoples, drawing them to himself as "the people of God in Abraham" (Ps 47:7–9). His is a saving sovereignty.

wilderness
Israel's forty years of "wandering" before entering the Promised Land. The psalmists paint this segment of history in negative light, calling God's children away from rebellion and toward repentance.

wisdom motifs
The thematic exploration of the two contrasting ways of life, the problem of retribution of good and evil deeds, practical advice on living, and the all-encompassing doctrine of the fear of the Lord. These themes find expression in Job, Proverbs, Ecclesiastes, and also in wisdom psalms.

wisdom psalms
The psalms that examine the world within the style and motif of wisdom, both reflective and proverbial. As a literary style, several characteristics can be noted: proverb, wisdom admonitions, similes, the "blessed" (*'ashre*) formula, address to "sons" or "children," and the use of "better" sayings. The wisdom motif is demonstrated in four thematic attributes: the "two ways," contrasting the life of the wicked and righteous; the problem of retribution; practical advice; and finally, the fear of the Lord. These psalms represent a way of conceptualizing the Hebrew faith, which, along with priesthood and prophecy, composed the expanse of Old Testament theology.

Writings
The third division of the Hebrew canon in which the Book of Psalms is contained. Separate from Torah and Prophets, this division is sometimes referred to by its Greek name, the Hagiographa.

yhwh malak
The Hebrew declaration meaning "The LORD [*yhwh*] reigns," or "The LORD [*yhwh*] has become King." This clause functions within the kingship of Yahweh psalms as a clear proclamation of the kingdom of God, comforting Israel with the fact of Yahweh's present reign.

Subject Index

Scripture Index